PHOTOGRAPHED BY TRONE, SHERIDAN, WYO.

Yours Truly

Frank Grouard

THE LIFE AND ADVENTURES OF

FRANK GROUARD

Chief of Scouts, U.S.A

JOE De BARTHE

Skyhorse Publishing

Skyhorse Publishing books may be purchased in bulk at special discounts for sales promotion, corporate gifts, fund-raising, or educational purposes. Special editions can also be created to specifications. For details, contact the Special Sales Department, Skyhorse Publishing, 307 West 36th Street, 11th Floor, New York, NY 10018 or info@skyhorsepublishing.com.

Skyhorse® and Skyhorse Publishing® are registered trademarks of Skyhorse Publishing, Inc.®, a Delaware corporation.

Visit our website at www.skyhorsepublishing.com.

10 9 8 7 6 5 4 3 2

Library of Congress Cataloging-in-Publication Data is available on file.

ISBN: 978-1-62636-553-7

Printed in the United States of America

TO THE
JOURNALISTS OF AMERICA
THIS VOLUME
IS AFFECTIONATELY
SUBSCRIBED

CONTENTS.

PART FIRST.

CONTENTS

CHAPTER LIV.

CHAPTER LV.

CHAPTER LVI.

PART SECOND.

CHAPTER I.

CHAPTER II.

CHAPTER III.

CHAPTER IV.

CHAPTER V.

CHAPTER VI.

PREFACE.

I first met Frank Grouard at Fort Washakie, Wyoming, in 1887, being introduced to him by Nelson (Charlie) Yarnell, then a scout in the government service. I remember that meeting very distinctly. I was prepared to meet a man who, at one period of his life, had been forced through capricious circumstances to not only abandon but partly forget his native tongue; but I imagined that he would not be loth to speak of his life among the Indians; that, having been freed from the bonds of captivity, and dwelt among his own people for the past thirteen years, ample time had been given him to acquire familiarity with his native tongue. In short, I supposed that he would be glad of an opportunity to open his lips, sealed for so long a time, and recount some of the experiences and adventures which had made his life of so much interest to people generally.

As a newspaper correspondent I was more than anxious to get from Grouard the story of his life, snatches of which had come to me from various sources and divers places; and I did not imagine, successful as

I had been on many occasions in securing interviews from men who bore the reputation of being impregnable to "pen pushers," that I would have any great difficulty in securing the data I wanted from this noted scout.

How delusive were my imaginings as a matter of fact. I found the man a veritable sphynx. He made a few signs, which I did not understand, but which Mr. Yarnell kindly interpreted (on the side) as indicating that Grouard did not care to talk for publication. I discovered later that I had been more successful than any of my newspaper brethren in an attempt to interview this man, inasmuch as he had made signs to me, while the others had utterly failed to get this much from him.

I spent the next three years in an almost constant endeavor to make this man's acquaintance, and I am free to confess that I was as much astonished as gratified when, in the spring of 1891, at Fort McKinney, Wyoming, he informed me that if I would wait until he returned from a duck-hunting trip which he was then preparing to take with some of the officers of the Post, accompanied by a party of gentlemen from Chicago (among them Mr. Charles E. Nixon, musical critic of the Chicago Inter-Ocean), and which would occupy some three weeks' time, he would meet me at his home and listen to what I had to say to him.

In conversation in 1890 with Gen. James S. Brisbin (since deceased), an officer in the service whose writings cover many volumes and have interested thousands of readers, that gentleman told me, when I broached the subject of procuring in detail the life and adventures of Grouard for publication, that it was time thrown away to attempt to get anything of the kind. He stated that he himself had made an offer to Grouard several years previous of quite a sum of money for papers and information which the scout had in his possession, and which he (Gen. Brisbin) desired to get for use in a history he contemplated writing of the Sioux nation. He stated to me that Grouard had flatly told him that he was not ready at that time, and did not know that he ever would be ready, to give the facts concerning his life and adventures to any man, under any circumstances, for any consideration, for publication. The General also informed me that although he had learned enough concerning Grouard to write a thousand-page volume of his adventures while with the Indians and of the services he had rendered the government since his escape from the Sioux, it would not, when completed, be such a history as would bear the stamp of authenticity without the aid and assistance of Grouard himself in compiling it.

General Brisbin said he knew from personal knowledge that Grouard had in his possession at the time he attempted to secure the facts relating to the scout's life, a complete, unbroken record or history of the Sioux nation, covering a period of over eight hundred years; but that since that time, Grouard's house at Fort McKinney had been consumed by fire, and that all this documentary evidence had been destroyed by the hungry flames, the scout saving nothing but his dog and revolver. With the assistance of this record the general had hoped, could he have secured Grouard's individual assistance, to have written such a history of the redmen as would have at once and forever set at rest the constantly recurring controversies touching the origin of the aborigine. These records were kept in hieroglyphics which Grouard could readily have interpreted; but his want of disposition to talk, coupled with his total indifference to acquiring a competency through the medium of the Sioux records which chance had made him the possessor of, stood as a bar to the laudible ambition of Gen. Brisbin, and lost to the reading world one of the most unique chapters in the history of the universe.

I must confess that, from my previous endeavors and inability to in any way secure Grouard's friendly attention, this conversation with Gen. Brisbin gave to my hopes a terrible backset, but it in nowise dampened my ardor. Having started in to win, I proposed to overcome every obstacle.

Suffice it to say Grouard went upon the duck hunting expedition previously referred to, and was gone nearly three weeks. Upon his return I met him in the trail between the Post and his house, whereupon, without the formality of a hand shake, a nod of the head or a "How", he asked me what I wanted with him. I told him that I was anxious to secure a history of his life for publication in book form. He wanted to know what good that would do anybody. He said a dozen other men had told him they wanted the same thing, but that he could not see what use the story of his life would be to anybody, except to make a pauper of the man who attempted to have it published. It probably took half an hour to get this much out of him, when he informed me that if I would come to the Post on the following day he would have had time to think the matter over and would give me an answer then. It is almost needless to say that I was at the Post on the following day. We met in the old commissary building (since destroyed) and his first words to me were, "I will give you the story of my life."

Thereupon we entered into a written agreement and appointed a day to begin the work. From that time to the present day I have labored as steadily as I could to write the history and adventures of this strange, taciturn, wonderful man—a man whose life began 'neath the tropical sun on the island of Tihiti in 1850; whose childhood was passed in the home of those who were strangers to his blood and curious disposition; whose youth was spent, mid those frontier scenes which the epoch of the '50's record as strangely grotesque and terribly realistic, and the dawn of whose manhood was darkened by the bonds of captivity.

Without memoranda of any kind to guide him, relying wholly upon, what everyone must concede to be, his wonderful memory, Grouard has given, as detailed in the pages of this book, the most minute history of his adventurous career.

The object of the author of these pages has been and is, first, last and always to "nothing extenuate nor set down aught in malice." The hero of this volume has been permitted to recall his adventures in his own

way; to employ his own method in detailing his army
service.

Nothing has been shaded to suit a purpose, establish
a truth or raise a doubt. Grouard has told a plain, un-
varnished tale, and his words have been preserved in
shorthand as they fell from his lips.

In my relations with him, he has never given me
occasion to doubt a single statement he has ever made,
and I can thoroughly appreciate the confidence reposed
in him by Gen. Crook, who, in 1876, referring to
Grouard in his official correspondence with the War
Department, said:

"I would sooner lose a third of my command than
Frank Grouard!"

No greater compliment, no higher tribute, could be
paid any man, and Gen. Crook has never been accused of flattery. Above all the scouts in his command,
Crook held Grouard highest in his esteem. He had
weighed him in the balance, and found him not wanting.

The jealousies of other scouts, the outcome, in part,
of the General's preference, counted naught with Crook.
When Grouard first joined the command he had but recently escaped from captivity among the Sioux, and advantage was taken of this latter fact by some of the
scouts to poison the General's mind against Grouard. It
was even told Crook that Grouard had come among the
troops to carry out a well laid plan to lead them into
the hands of the Indians for the purpose of destroying
them. But Crook looked beyond these scandalous
stories. He was a good character reader, and he knew

JOE DeBARTHE.

"the silent man" (as he was fond of calling Grouard)
possessed a wise head and a brave heart. His confidence in Grouard was never shaken nor betrayed, and,
up to the day of his death, Gen. George Crook was a
firm and steadfast friend to the hero of this volume.
Nor was this friendship unreciprocated. Grouard would
have dared any danger, faced any contingency, in the
performance of a service for the man who had won his
affection by confidence and kindness.

In giving to the world this volume of adventure, I
may be permitted to say that no effort has been spared
to reach truthful ends. The years of labor I have devoted to the work have, indeed, to me been a labor of
love; and no reader of these pages will be more fasci-
nated by Grouard's recitals—more interested in the stirring events narrated by him—than I have been.

Enjoying as I have, and do, the confidence and
friendship of Frank Grouard, I can pay him no higher
tribute than to say I have never known him to prove
faithless to a promise, recreant to duty or false to a
friendship.

True to himself, how could he be anything but true
to other men!

B. F. GROUARD. (FATHER OF FRANK.)

PART FIRST.

CHAPTER I.

Early in the Seventeenth Century Francis Grouard, a French Huguenot refugee, the great grandfather of Frank Grouard, came from France and settled in New Hampshire, near Portsmouth, where Frank's grandfather and father were born. They were named respectively Francis and Benjamin F. Grouard. The great grandfather of the hero of these pages, served on board a privateer during the war between the American colonies and Great Britain in 1812, while the grandfather of Frank, touched with the same fire that burned within the breast of his ancestors, took early to the sea, and did service on the frigate Brandywine, under Commodore Wodsworth, on the coast of Peru, during the second term of General Jackson's presidency.

In the year 1843 Frank's father, then a young man of twenty years, went to the Paumoto Islands in the

South Pacific Ocean as a missionary.   These islands lie
about two hundred and fifty miles east of the Tahiti, of
the Friendly Group.

Becoming very much attached to the natives of
these islands, and looking forward to a life work among
them, in 1846 Mr. Grouard married the daughter of a
high chief of the island of Ana—the principal one of
the group.   The issue of that marriage was three sons—
Frank, born on September 20th, 1850, being the
second.

The French in the meantime having taken possession of this group of Islands, and making it so unpleasant for foreigners, in the year 1852 the elder Grouard
brought his family to California and settled in San Bernardino.   But the rigors of the climate proving to severe for the mother, she, in 1853, with her oldest and
youngest children, returned to the islands.

The elder Grouard finding it impossible to accompany his wife and children to their home in the South
Pacific, took charge of his second son and remained in
San Bernardino for some years.   He finally placed the
boy in the family of Addison Pratt, shortly after which
event the Pratt family moved to Beaver, Utah.   Frank
was then five years of age, and never looked again upon
his father's face until the month of April, 1893.   The
elder Grouard, who had long mourned his son as dead,
during the winter of 1893 read an item in. a California
paper about the compilation of "The Life and Adventures of Frank Grouard, Chief of Scouts, U. S. A", and
at once set about getting into communication with the

MRS. LOUISA B. PRATT. (GROUARD'S FOSTER MOTHER.)

man who bore his son's name. To the author Mr. Grouard, Sr., told the story about as follows:

"I had heard of Frank as being in the employ of the Government, but was unable to locate him. It must have been at the time he was carrying the pony express from Musselshell to Fort Hall that rumors concerning him reached me. Then followed news of his capture by the Indians. Long years came and went before I again heard of my son. The Sioux campaign of 1876 was on, and it was immediately after the published account of the Custer Massacre that I read of the 'Sibley Scout,' the paper giving details of the capture and death by torture of Frand Grouard. I never learned the untruthfulness of that report for many years, and had about given up the last hope, when I read an item in my home paper about a book that was soon to be issued, the title being the "Life and Adventures of Frank Grouard."

"I immediately put myself in communication with the war department, and was in turn referred to the department of the Platte, the officials at Omaha giving me my son's address at Fort McKinney, Wyoming. Imagine my surprise and joy upon receiving an answer to my last letter from Frank himself. I took no time in coming to Wyoming, and am anxiously awaiting my son's arrival here."

This conversation occurred in the City of Sheridan in the spring of 1893, and in the evening of that same day the writer witnessed the reunion of father and son—one tottering on the threshold of eternity, the other in the prime of magnificent manhood.

Thirty-seven years had come and gone since these two beings had looked upon each other's faces. All the love the human heart is capable of feeling for its own flesh and blood beamed in the eyes of the gray-haired man who held his long-lost son to his throbbing breast. The picture—the memory of that meeting—is ineffaceable. Not a word was spoken—silence was more eloquent than words—while these two men remained in each other's embrace. And when they drew apart, the father held his son at arm's length, and through his tears, smiled and said:

"I would know you among ten thousand."

Mr. Grouard remained in Wyoming with his son for something over a month. On his way into the state he was seriously affected by the high altitude, and while at his son's home at Fort McKinney suffered a stroke of paralysis, from which he never fully recovered. Upon his return to his California home his health failed rapidly, and on the 28th day of March, 1894, while passing from his garden to his house, the messenger of death met and overcame him.

Some years after the death of his first wife, Mr. Grouard married again, five children being born to him. He was engaged for a number of years in mercantile pursuits in Illinois and California, and left a fine estate. He was very highly esteemed by the people of Santa Ana, where he spent the last years of his life, and the following tribute to his memory was paid by one of the local papers of his adopted city:

"On last Sunday morning, about 8 o'clock, B. F.

CHARLES E. GROUARD. (BROTHER OF FRANK.)

Grouard, an old and well-known resident of this city, dropped dead from heart disease while returning to the house from a short walk in his door-yard. His sudden death was not unexpected, as his family had been warned by several physicians that such an end might occur at any moment. In April, 1893, Mr. Grouard made a trip to Wyoming, and while there was stricken with paralysis of the left side, which naturally aggravated the disease of the heart with which he had been afflicted in some degree for several years. The Deceased was aged 75 years, 2 months and 15 days. The funeral services were held Tuesday morning, at 10 o'clock, from the home place, Rev. Edw. T. Fleming officiating. The Congregational choir furnished several beautiful and appropriate selections for the occasion, and with the eloquent and well-chosen words of the pastor, formed a ceremony well fitted to close the long and eventful life.

"In the death of Mr. Grouard, Santa Ana loses one of the most picturesque figures in its history. Born of Puritan parents in New Hampshire, he grew tired of the rigid exactions then in vogue and ran away to Boston when fourteen years of age, from whence he embarked on a whaler and left the old home for good. Many voyages, embracing nearly all lines of ocean service, followed this one, and the world lost some of its mystery to him when he had circumnavigated it several times. His adventurous spirit finally landed him on the Society Islands, where, with the assistance of the natives and their crude implements, he constructed a vessel of

comfortable size and traded among the natives of the
fertile islands of that region for six or seven years.
His ship met the fate of many a good craft, and was
totally wrecked in a terrible storm in which the sturdy
navigator narrowly escaped with his life.

"Mr. Grouard first came to California in 1852, and
joined the great ranks of the gold miners, but with poor
success. He settled in Los Angeles a few years later,
and often told of the first orange trees that were
planted in Southern California, and of the curiosity they
excited. From the Golden State he removed to Illinois,
but the recollections of this good land were so tempting
that he again came to California fourteen years ago,
when he settled at Santa Ana, which has since been his
home.

"A complete history of his life would fade most of
the fictitious stories of adventure. He was always a
great reader, and possessing a most retentive memory,
his mind was stored with a knowledge, the vastness and
variety of which was scarcely realized except by his
most intimate acquaintances. For many years Mr. Grouard had conducted a successful business as brickmaker,
contractor and builder, with his son Charles. Being
naturally of an impulsive disposition, he did many things
which were heartily regretted; but inside the gruff and
hearty exterior of thé man there beat a heart always
warm for those in poverty and distress, and dwelt a nature which was sympathetic to the highest degree, as
many a recipient of his generosity can testify."

CHAPTER II.

Grouard has been well named "The silent man of the western plains." It must be borne in mind by the reader that his term of captivity among the Sioux Indians covered a period of nearly six years, and sixteen months of that time were spent under the strictest surveillance. Unacquainted with the language of the Sioux, and not knowing for a long time what disposition would eventually be made of him, he had no incentive to learn the red man's manner of speech, and satisfied himself by closely watching the signs made by the Indians in communicating with each other, for Indians will rarely be found conversing audibly, even among themselves, when they can so conveniently make themselves understood through the language of signs.

Numerous writers have claimed to have had long talks with Grouard, and have printed at various times a great deal of fiction regarding the noted scout. But the author wishes to emphatically enter his protest against the mode adopted by the aforesaid writers in fashioning history to their own liking, without any tangible facts upon which to build a truthful structure.

An amusing instance of the manner in which Grouard's name has been mixed up with matters he was never connected with came to the writer's attention during the past summer. A correspondent of an eastern paper visited Wyoming, and was introduced to the scout. He attempted to "interview" Grouard, and, finding he would not talk if he could make himself understood by a sign, the correspondent gave up the job and fell back upon his imagination for a long-winded special to his paper on Grouard's nativity, age, captivity and adventures.

The correspondent informed his readers that the scout was "part Sioux and part something else," he could not exactly tell what, as Grouard had been "captured by the Indians when only three years old." It was pretty generally conceded, however, explained the correspondent, that Grouard was some "kin to Sitting Bull," and that "his mother was a Cheyenne or Shoshone squaw." When the battle of the Big Horn was fought, this writer went on to explain, Grouard was one of the party making the attack upon the Custer force, "his object being to work the destruction of the Sioux." He had purposely drawn the attacking party "away from Reno in order to rush it against Custer, believing the latter had numerical strength enough to wipe the entire Sioux and Cheyenne nations off the face of the earth." "But he made a miscalculation," observes this astute writer. Reno, contrary to Grouard's expectations, "never left the entrenched position he had occupied when the first attack had been made upon him," and all the Indians, some five thousand in number, drew off down the Little Big Horn to meet the charge made by the Custer force, and one of the greatest of massacres was the result. Immediately after the battle, goes on the history maker, Grouard fled the Indian village, and stole his way to Gen. Crook's command, then located at the mouth of Little Goose creek canyon, where he informed that officer of the fate of the gallant Custer and his brave followers, and "from that day on became an invaluable scout to the government."

Thus, is history made! But the space writer must earn his daily bread, and the "truthful chronicler" must be permitted to sing his song for the plaudits of the same public that Barnum said would rather be humbugged than not.

Even so good an authority as Captain John G. Bourke — a writer than whom there is none more fascinating and whose graphic pen-pictures are preserved so faithfully in his latest book, "On the Border with Crook,"— who had a more intimate knowledge of Frank Grouard than any man outside of General Crook himself (and perhaps John F. Finerty, the Chicago Times correspondent who campaigned with the scout during the year 1876,) remembers Grouard as "a native of the Sandwich Islands, who for some years was a mail rider in northern Montana, and was there captured by the forces of Crazy Horse; his dark skin and general appearance gave his captors the impression that Frank was a native Indian whom they had recaptured from the whites; consequently, they did not kill him, but kept him a prisoner until he could recover what they believed to be his native tongue — the Sioux. Frank remained several years in the household of the great chief Crazy Horse, whom he knew very well, as well as his medicine man — the since renowned Sitting Bull.

That Grouard was a mail rider goes without question; but, as to his place of birth, his capture and the reason of his life having been spared by the Sioux, the line is drawn altogether to carelessly, as is explained further on. Captain Bourke, however, gives ample evidence of his appreciation of Grouard in the following glowing words:

"Grouard was one · of the most remarkable woodmen I ever met; no Indian could surpass him in his acquaintance with all that pertained to the topography, animal life and other particulars of the great region between the head of the Piney, the first affluent of the Powder on the west, up to and beyond the Yellowstone on the north; no question could be asked him that he could not answer at once and correctly. His bravery and fidelity were never questioned; he never flinched under fire, and never growled at privation."

From his appearance Grouard is often mistaken for a full blooded Sioux Indian. He stands six feet in height and weighs two hundred and thirty pounds. His massive head and neck rest upon broad, square shoulders, the head being surmounted by a heavy growth of black hair, now slightly tinged with gray. His forehead is broad and high, and his eyes, which are very large and expressive, have that peculiar appearance so noticeable and distinctive in persons born in the tropics. The

cheek bones are very prominent. The nose is large,
though none too large for his full, round face. He has
a very kindly mouth. The chin is broad and firm, and
evinces one of the man's most striking characteristics—
determination.

Many are the stories told of Grouard's origin, none
of which, so far as the writer has been able to discover,
bear any resemblance to the real facts. Nor is there any
truth in the stories that parties bearing the name of
Grouard and living in the Dakotas are in any way related to him. His two brothers, born in the tropics,
were brought from the Friendly Islands to San Francisco
in 1852; but the climate not agreeing with his mother's
health and she falling into a decline, these children, with
their mother, were taken back to the land of their nativity, and neither Grouard nor his father have ever discovered what became of them. The elder Grouard made
many unsuccessful attempts to place himself in communication with the wife of his youth and the children she
had borne him. He received, through the medium of
sea-faring men, news that his wife had died shortly after
her return to the Island of Tihiti, and that her children
had been taken in charge by her people ; but neither
Grouard nor his father have ever been able to discover
their whereabouts.

Grouard was two years old when he arrived in San
Francisco in company with his father, mother and two
brothers. When the other children were sent back to
their island home, Frank was kept in San Francisco by
his father, whose business at that particular time did not

permit him to accompany his family to Tihiti. Frank was finally entrusted to the care of a family by the name of Pratt, and while he was still a very small child, this family removed from California to southwestern Utah, where the boy remained until his fifteenth year, when, tiring of the monotony of the wilderness, he ran away and began life for himself.

The elder Grouard visited his son off and on until the boy arrived at the age of five years, at which time the Pratt family moved to Utah. From that time, 1855, father and son never met again until April, 1893, when they were reunited at Sheridan, Wyoming.

Grouard was captured by the Sioux Indians when nineteen years of age and, to all intents and purposes, became a full-fledged Indian. When he knew for certain that his captors did not intend to destroy him (a discovery he did not make until he had been in the village of the hostiles sixteen months) he made the best of his situation, and entered into the spirit of savagery with a zest that astonished even those who had been friendly toward him — none more so than Sitting Bull, who was very proud of his adopted brother. The torture, the dances, the sweats, the hunts and ceremonials were partaken of by the captive as they presented themselves. Civilized dress gave place to the breech-clout and moccasin; the demands of society to the customs of the aborigine. Young, hardy and superbly built, he became an object of pride among his captors. He outplayed them in their games and outran them in their races. His marksmanship became phenomenal. No Indian in the nation could outride him; he bore the fatigue of travel better than the best; he gloried in the chase; was successful in the hunt. The summer's heat and the winter's cold he bore with stoical indifference. In the eyes of his savage brethren he was an ideal Indian.

But Grouard had "method in his madness." He knew, instinctively, that the redman's sway could not endure forever; that the halcyon days of savagery were passing. He looked beyond the present into the future; saw that the knowledge he was acquiring of the redman's customs and habits would be of use to others as well as himself. He learned that the Indian's cunning was but the study of tradition — handed down — taught and learned. A riper intelligence — the mind of the Caucasian which could grasp all the wealth from the fountain of savage knowledge—could better on the instruction from Indian tradition. So he become content to bide the time of his deliverance, feeling, believing, knowing there was no loss in his transitory transformation.

For nearly six years he watched, and studied and waited. And when the hour of departure from the tepi and the tribe was at hand, he stepped forth eagle-plumed to do his fellow-man service. From the village of the redman to the camp of the frontier army! And back again, with vengeance in his wake, over those old, familiar trails, into the mountain fastnesses, across the sun-scorched plains, driving his former captors from the lands of their fathers into the circumscribed sections set apart by government for their use, or into the great and fathomless Beyond! The Uncapapa, the Minneconjou, the Ogallalla, the Sisseton, the Yankton, the Sans Arcs, the Assiniboine, the Brule, the Blackfoot, the Cheyenne, the Arapahoe, the Shoshone, the Yanktonnais, the Bannock, the Crow and Nez Perces fled before the host he led against them, stopping in their course to give battle against the conquering army — the riper intelligence — now striking a blow, like on the Little Big Horn, that sent a shudder through civilization, then meeting almost total annihilation beneath the shadows of the Bear Paw.

Grouard had suffered everything but death at the hands of the savages during the term of his captivity. He was now the avenging sprite, and the Indians feared and hated him. Revenge was not his controlling motive, however. He was righting myriad wrongs.

BIG GOOSE CANYON, ABOVE SHERIDAN, WYO.

CHAPTER III.

The policy of the government toward the Indian, up to a very recent date, has been one of vacillation and uncertainty. There has always been manifested a desire to "handle the red men with gloves." To this steadily-pursued policy may safely be attributed all the perplexities and uncertainties that have existed in our relations with the Indians on the western frontier. Treaty after treaty was made by the government on one side and the Indians on the other only to be broken ere the seals were secure and the ink of the signatures dry.

This was notably the case with the agreements entered into at Fort Laramie by the United States Peace Commission and the Sioux and Cheyennes in the year 1866. In fact, it was well known at the time the conference was held that but few of the head chiefs of either the Sioux or Cheyenne nations were present at that conference, and history records the fact that when the Commission sent trusted agents out to treat with the head chiefs of these nations, several of those agents suffered great indignities at the hands of the savage lead-

ers, and were sent back to the Commission with answers
that never found their way into print as part of the
report made by the members of that august body.
Like most of its predecessors, the Commission of 1866
accomplished nothing that lent any additional security to
the emigrant or the settler. On the contrary, its labors
but tended to confirm a long-standing belief among the
savages that the Great Father was afraid to attempt a
conquest by arms.

In the very face of the work of the Peace Commission of 1866, the Phil Kearney massacre occurred, and,
as if to establish more firmly the belief among the red
men that the government was afraid to "carry the war
into Africa," the posts of defense in the heart of the
Indian country were abandoned by the government
through one of the most compromising treaties ever
made between the government and the aborigine, thus
closing the country from the Laramie river to the British line, and giving to the warlike Sioux and Cheyennes
complete possession of the vast domain from the Platte
to the Missouri river on the north, and from the Dakota Black Hills on the east to the Wind range of
mountains on the west (one of the richest mineral and
agricultural sections in the United States, if not in the
world).

In fact, while the government was assured that the
Indians had patched up a lasting peace through the efforts of the Commission of 1866, and was congratulating
itself upon the success of its latest overtures, the Sioux
were covertly making preparations to carry on a war of

extermination in the region they had secured by conquest from the Crows; and it was under just such conditions that Colonel Carrington and his brave little garrison faced the heavy task of building Forts Phil Kearney and C. F. Smith at points where savage assaults were of daily and deadly occurrence.

Two years after the butchery of the Fort Phil Kearney command, the posts that menaced the Indians and afforded some protection to the emigrant and settler were dismantled and abandoned.

The Indian, once more, held arrogant and undisputed sway over one of the finest scopes of country in the United States—what to-day is the great commercial gateway to and from the land of the setting sun. But savagery could not long withstand the encroaching footsteps of advancement and civilization. What the government would not concede to frontier settlement, was wrested from the Indian by the hardy pioneer and the fearless adventurer.

Some slight show was made in the Black Hills by the government to remove the gold-seekers; but the demand for the opening of that section to settlement was stronger than the language of the treaty with the Indians to keep it closed, and in the fall of 1875 the Hills echoed and re-echoed with the victorious shouts of a newer race.

Stories of fabulous wealth hidden beneath the surface of the Dakota hills and under the majestic Big Horn mountain peaks had reached the hungering adventurers of the east, and nothing could beat back the wave of advancing humanity. The promised harvest was golden, and many were the reapers.

In this unequal battle for gold all hazards were scoffed at ; all dangers were dared. Anticipation, like some beckoning angel, lighted up the dreary western wastes over which men must travel to the land of Realization. Strangers became brothers in their new-found acquaintanceships ; and brothers, alas, rushing madly forward to secure a promised prize, became strangers to each other's love.

The Sioux, the Cheyenne, the Arapahoe and the Blackfoot disputed possession with this horde of incoming humanity. Their rights, resting on the parchment given them by the Great Father, made sacred through the promises that were fashioned only to be broken, like dicer's oaths, were suffering annulment, and the white man's government permitted it.

Right or wrong, the Indian stood his ground. Faith in treaties made with the Great Father was shattered. Sitting Bull and Crazy Horse, one a diplomat, the other a warrior, were yet fashioned in the same mould. Both hated the white race with a hatred born of savage blood. The overtures of government fell like funeral dirges upon their unwilling ears. The agency to them was a prison. Like Macbeth (with physic), they'd "none of it." They knew no methods of conciliation, but studied all means to crush. There was no happy medium with these men. They steadily and persistently maintained that the hope of the Indian was in war. They realized that, little by little, the sceptre of savagery was being wrested from the hand of the redman. Annihilation, striding like a Colossus over the western empire they had called their home, had already planted its iron heel on the southwestern slope of the continental divide. The shadows of everlasting silence were gathering for the aborigine over the valleys where their fathers had held undisputed sway. Nothing was longer secure to them. A newer, riper, alien race was driving the buffalo from its wallow, the deer, the elk, the antelope from mountain and plain. The steamboat and iron horse had formed a magic link between the lands of the rising and setting sun. The savage had nothing to concede. His safety, the safety of his race, was to be found nowhere if not in pitiless, unrelenting, never-ending war. This was the creed of Sitting Bull, and Crazy Horse echoed the sentiment.

"There is, indeed, in the fate of these unfortunate beings," says a learned writer, "much to awaken our sympathies and much to disturb the sobriety of our judgment; much that may be urged to excuse their own atrocities. What can be more melancholy than their history? We see by the law of their nature they are destined to a slow but sure extinction. Everywhere at the approach of the white man they fade away. We hear the rustling of their footsteps like that of the withered leaves of autumn, and they are gone forever. They pass mournfully by us and return no more. Two centuries ago the smoke of their wigwams, the fires of their councils, rose in every valley from the Hudson Bay to the furthest Florida. From the ocean to the Missis-

sippi and the lakes, the shouts of victory and the war-
dance rang through the glades; the thick arrows and
the deadly tomahawk whizzed through the forest. The
warriors stood forth in their glory. The young listened
to the songs of other days. The aged sat down, but
they wept not. They would soon in the far region be
at rest where the Great Spirit dwelt in a home prepared
for the brave beyond the western skies. Braver men
never lived; truer men never drew the bow. They had
courage and fortitude and sagacity and perseverance beyond most of the human race. They shrank from no
danger; they feared no hardship. If they had the vices
of a savage life, they had the virtues, also. They were
true to their country, their friends and their homes. If
they forgave not injury, neither did they forget kindness.
If their vengeance was terrible, their fidelity and generosity was unconquerable, also. Their love like their
hate, stopped not this side of the grave.

"But where are they? Where are their villages,
their warriors and youth? The sachem and his tribe;
the hunters and their families? They have perished!
They are consumed! The wasting pestilence has not
alone done the mighty work; no, nor famine, nor war!
There has been a mightier power; a moral cancer which
has eaten into their heart core; the plague which the
hand of the white man communicated; a poison which
has betrayed them into a lingering ruin. Already the
winds of the Atlantic fan not a single region they may
now call their own."

"I saw the last feeble remnant of the race prepare for their long journey beyond the Mississippi. I saw them leave their miserable homes; the aged, the helpless, the women and the warriors. Few and faint, yet fearless still. The ashes have grown cold on their native hearth; the smoke no longer curls around their lonely cabins; they move on with a slow, unsteady step. The white man is upon their heels, but they heed him not. They turn to take a last look at their deserted villages; they cast a last glance over the graves of their fathers; they shed no tears; they utter no cries; they heave no groans. There is something in their looks, not of vengeance nor submission, but hard necessity, which stifles both and has no method; it is courage absorbed in despair. They linger but for a moment. Their look is onward. They have passed the fatal stream. It shall never be repassed by them, ah, never; yet there lies not between us and them an impassable gulf. They know and feel there is for them one removal further, not distant nor unseen! It is the general burying-ground of the race!"

"The policy of the American people has been to vagadondize the Indian, and throttle every ambition he may have for his own elevation; and we need not hug the delusion that the savage has been any too anxious for work, unless stimulated, encouraged and made to see that it meant his immediate benefit and advancement."— Capt. John G. Bourke's "On the Border with Crook."

After the Fort Phil Kearney massacre congress appointed a special commission to "investigate" the causes leading up to it. The report of this commission is known in history as Senate Document No. 13, and is dated 1867. It is as fair and impartial an account of the labors of the United States Peace Commission which met at Laramie in 1866 and the subsequent slaughter of Col. Fetterman and party as could possibly have been made; and as it is in itself a summarization of the tragic events following the attempt to open a highway through the heart of the Indian country—the particular section of country which became the field of operation during the Custer, Crook and Miles campaigns ten years later—it is given here to better illustrate the "kid-glove policy" of the government toward the Indians:

The main object sought to be secured by the treaty of Laramie of July, A. D. 1866, was the opening of a new route to Montana from Fort Laramie, via Bridger's Ferry and the head waters of the Powder, Tongue and Big Horn Rivers. This country was occupied by the Ogallalla and Minneconjou bands of Sioux Indians and the northern Cheyenne and Arapahoe tribes, and the mountain Crows.

The region through which the road was to pass and does pass is the most attractive and valuable to Indians. It abounds with game, flocks of mountain sheep, droves of elk and deer; and herds of buffalo range through and live in this country, and the Indians with propriety call it their last best hunting grounds. All these Indians were reluctant to allow the proposed road to pass through these hunting grounds, but all would reluctantly assent to this for so liberal an equivalent

RESERVATION CROWS.

as the government was ready to give. The Indians were required further to stipulate that the government should have the right to establish one or more military posts on this road in their country. All the Indians occupying it refused thus to stipulate, and through the chiefs, headmen and soldiers protested against the establishment of any military post on their hunting grounds along the road north of Fort Reno.

While negotiations were going on with Red Cloud and their leading chiefs to induce them to yield to the government the right to peaceably establish these military posts, which they persistently refused to yield, saying it was asking too much of their people — asking all they had — for it would drive away all the game, Col. H. B. Carrington, 18th United States Infantry, with about seven hundred officers and men, arrived at Laramie, en route to this country to establish and occupy military posts along the Montana road, pursuant to General Orders No. 33, Headquarters Department of the Missouri, March 10, 1866, Major-General Pope commanding. The destination and purpose of Col. Carrington and his command were communicated to their chiefs. They seemed to construe this as a determination on the part of the government to occupy their country by military posts, even without their consent or that of their people, and as soon as practicable withdrew from the council with their adherents, refusing to accept any presents from the commission, returned to their country, and with a strong force of warriors commenced a vigorous and relentless war against all whites who came into it, both citizens and soldiers.

Quite a large number of Indians, who did not occupy the country along this road, were anxious to make a treaty and remain at peace. Some of this class had for a long time resided near Fort Laramie. Others (Brules) occupied the White Earth River valley and the sand hills south of that river.

The commissioners created and appointed several of the leading warriors of these Indians, chiefs, viz., Big Mouth, Spotted Tail, Swift Bear and Two Strikes. A portion of these Indians have remained near Fort Laramie, and a portion of them on the Republican fork of the Kansas river, and have strictly complied with their treaty stipulations.

The number of Sioux Indians who considered themselves bound by the treaty and have remained at peace is about two thousand, while the Minneconjou and a portion of the Ogallalla and Brule bands, the northern Cheyennes and Arapahoes, with a few Sans Arcs, numbering in the aggregate about six hundred lodges, remained in their old country and went to war under the auspices of their old chiefs.

We therefore report that all the Sioux Indians occupying the country about Fort Phil Kearney have been in a state of war against the whites since the 20th day of June, A. D. 1866, and that they have waged and carried on this war for the purpose of defending their ancient possessions and the possessions acquired by them from the Crow Indians by conquest after bloody wars, from invasion and occupation by the whites.

This war had been carried on by the Indians with

the most extraordinary vigor and unwonted success.
During the time from July 26th, the day on which
Lieutenant Wand's train was attacked, to the 21st day
of December, on which Brevet Lieutenant-Colonel Fetterman, with his command of eighty officers and men,
was overpowered and massacred, they killed ninety-one
enlisted men and five officers of our army, and killed
fifty-eight citizens and wounded twenty more, and captured and drove away three hundred and six oxen and
cows, three hundred and four mules, and one hundred
and sixty-one horses. During this time they appeared
in front of Fort Phil Kearney, making hostile demonstrations and committing hostile acts, fifty-one different
times, and attacked nearly every train and person that
attempted to pass over the Montana road.

General Orders No. 33, Headquarters Department
of Missouri, dated March 10, 1866, directed that two
new military posts should be established on this new
route to Montana — one "near the base of the Big
Horn mountains," the other "on or near the Upper Yellowstone," and designated the 2d battalion of the 18th
Infantry to garrison the three posts on this route, and
created the Mountain District, Department of the Platte,
and directed the colonel of the regiment (Colonel H. B.
Carrington) to take post at Fort Reno and command
the district, which included all the troops and garrisons
on this route.

General Orders No. 7, Headquarters Department of
the Platte, June 23, 1866, directed that the 2d battalion, 18th Infantry, should take post as follows: Two

companies at Fort Reno, on Powder river, two companies about eighty miles nearly south of Reno, on the
waters of Powder or Tongue river, which Post should
be known as Fort Philip Kearney, and two companies
at the crossing of the Big Horn river on the same road,
and about seventy miles beyond Fort Phillip Kearney,
to be known as Fort C. F. Smith, and directed that the
colonel of the regiment should take post at Fort Philip
Kearney, and command the "Mountain District."

The orders above referred to were issued with the
express understanding, apparently, that this road to Montana was to be opened through the Indian country by
compact or treaty with the Indians occupying it, and
not by conquest and the exercise of arbitrary power on
the part of the government. Hence Col. Carrington's
instructions looked mainly to the duty of selecting and
building the two new forts, Philip Kearney and C. F.
Smith, and the command assigned was only sufficient
for this purpose and properly garrisoning the posts.
This command numbered in all about seven hundred
men, five hundred of whom were new recruits, and
twelve officers, including district commander and staff.
The commanding officer, Col. Carrington, could not and
did not fail to see at once that, although his command
was entirely sufficient to erect the new forts, build the
barracks, warehouses, and stables, and make preparations
for winter, and properly garrison his posts, and could
protect emigration from the small thieving parties of Indians, it was still entirely inadequate to carry on systematic and aggressive war against a most powerful

tribe of Indians, fighting to maintain possession and
control of their own country, in addition to those other
duties. This officer carried the orders above referred to
into effect with promptness and zeal, organizing the
mountain district June 28th, 1866, establishing Foit
Philip Kearney on the 15th of July, and Fort C. F.
Smith on the 3d day of August, and as early as the
31st day of July informed Gen. P. St. George Cooke,
the department commander, that the status of Indians
in that country was one of war, and requested reinforcements sent to him, and two days previously had telegraphed the adjutant-general of the army for Indian
auxiliaries and additional force for his own regiment.

On the 9th of August, General Cooke, commanding department of the Platte, informed Colonel Carrington that Lieutenant-General Sherman ordered the
posts in his, Colonel Carrington's district, supported as
much as possible, and announced a regiment coming
from St. Louis.

No auxiliaries were assigned, and no reinforcements came until November, when company C, 2d
United States cavalry, reached Fort Kearney, sixty
strong, armed with Springfield rifles and Star carbines.
In December, about ninety recruits joined the battalion
in the mountain district, a portion of whom were assigned to a company stationed at Fort Phil Kearney.
No other reinforcements were sent to the district. Ap-
proved requisitions for ammunition were not answered.
The command at Fort C. F. Smith was reduced to
ten rounds per man ; the command at Fort Phil Kear-

ney to forty-five rounds per man, and the command at Fort Reno to thirty rounds per man. Recruits could not practice any in firing. Little time could be allowed from fatigue duty or drill, and with but twelve officers and three posts little could have been done in drilling recruits, if time could have been allowed.

The result of all this was that the troops were in no condition to fight successful battles with Indians or other foes, and this from no fault of Colonel Carrington; and I am astonished at the zeal with which they fought, and the damage they inflicted, December 21st.

The numerous demonstrations and attacks made by Indians prior to the 6th of December seemed to have been made for the sole purpose of capturing stock, picket posts, and small parties of soldiers who might venture beyond the cover of the garrison, and of annoying and checking the wood train constantly drawing material for the new forts.

On the morning of December 6th the wood train was attacked, a common occurence, about two miles from the fort, and forced to corral and defend itself. Brevet Lieutenant-Colonel Fetterman, with a command of seventeen mounted infantry and thirty-five cavalry, moved out to relieve the wood train, and drive off the Indians, and Col. Carrington, with twenty-five mounted infantry, moved out for the purpose of cutting off the Indians from retreat, and destroying them. On this day, at a point on Peno Creek, about five miles from the fort, the Indians, the second time after the fort was established, made a stand and a strong resistance, and nearly surrounded Col. Fetterman's party. The infantry obeyed orders and behaved well. The cavalry, with the exception of ten enlisted men, disobeyed the orders of Col. Fetterman, and fled with great precipitancy from this portion of the field. As the cavalry retreated, the Indians made a great display and effort to create a panic with the infantry, but Col. Fetterman, Lieut. Wands, and Lieut. Brown succeeded in keeping this small body of infantry cool, and by reserving their fire for proper range, rescued it from annihilation, and made a junction with Col. Carrington's party, on the east side of Peno Creek. Lieut. Bingham, after leaving Col. Fetterman's party, with Lieut. Grummond, a sergeant from Col. Carrington's command, and two men from his own, without the knowledge or orders of any of his superiors, pursued into an ambuscade, more than two miles from the main party, a single Indian who was on foot in front of their horses, and Lieut. Bingham and the sergeant were there killed. The results of this day's fighting, although not of a decidedly successful character to the Indians, were such as naturally to induce the belief on their part that by proper management and effort they could overpower and destroy any force that could be sent out from the fort to fight them, and no doubt at this time resolved to make the effort the first auspicious day, and postponed their proceedings from the new to the full moon. In the meantime everything was quiet about the fort, although they often appeared on the surrounding hills.

On the morning of December 21st the picket at the

signal station signaled to the fort that the wood train was attacked by Indians, and coralled, and the escort fighting. This was not far from 11 o'clock a. m., and the train was about two miles from the fort, and moving toward the timber. Almost immediately a few Indian pickets appeared on one or two of the surrounding heights, and a party of about twenty near the Big Piney, where the Montana road crosses the same, within howitzer range of the fort. Shells were thrown among them from the artillery in the fort, and they fled.

The following detail, viz., fifty men and two officers from the four different infantry companies, and twenty-six cavalrymen and one officer, was made by Col. Carrington. The entire force formed in good order and was placed under command of Brevet Lieut. Col. Fetterman, who received the following orders from Col. Carrington: "Support the wood train, relieve it, and report to me. Do not engage or pursue Indians at its expense; under no circumstances pursue over Lodge Trail Ridge." These instructions were repeated by Col. Carrington, in a loud voice, to the command when in motion, and outside the fort, and again delivered in substance through Lieut. Wands, officer of the day, to Lieut. Grummond, commanding cavalry detachment, who was requested to communicate them again to Col. Fetterman.

Colonel Fetterman moved out rapidly to the right of the wood road, for the purpose no doubt of cutting off the retreat of the Indians, then attacking the train. As he advanced across the Piney a few Indians appeared in his front and on his flanks, and continued flitting about him, beyond rifle range, till they disappeared beyond Lodge Trail Ridge. When he was on Lodge Trail Ridge, the picket signaled the fort that the Indians had retreated from the train; the train had broken corral and moved on toward the timber.

The train made the round trip, and was not again disturbed that day.

At about fifteen minutes before 12 o'clock Colonel Fetterman's command had reached the crest of Lodge Trail Ridge, was deployed as skirmishers, and at a halt, without regard to orders, for reasons that the silence of Colonel Fetterman now prevents us from giving, he, with the command, in a few moments disappeared, having cleared the ridge, still moving north. Firing at once commenced, amd increased in rapidity till, in about fifteen minutes and about 12 o'clock M., it was a continuous and rapid fire of musketry, plainly audible at the fort. Assistant Surgeon Hines, having been ordered to join Fetterman, found Indians on a part of Lodge Trail Ridge not visible from the fort, and could not reach the force there struggling to preserve its existence. As soon as the firing became rapid Colonel Carrington ordered Captain Ten Eyck, with about seventy-six men, being all the men for duty in the fort, and two wagons with ammunition, to join Colonel Fetterman immediately. He moved out and advanced rapidly toward the point from which the sound of firing proceeded, but did not move by so short a route as he might have done. The sound of firing continued to be heard during his advance, diminishing in rapidity and number of shots till he reached a high summit overlooking the battle-field, at about a quarter before 1 o'clock, when one or two shots closed all sound of conflict.

Whether he could have reached the scene of action by marching over the shortest route as rapidly as possible in time to have relieved Col. Fetterman's command, I am unable to determine.

Immediately after Capt. Ten Eyck moved out, and by orders of Col. Carrington, issued at the same time as the orders detailing that officer to join Col. Fetterman, the quartermaster's employes, convalescents, and all others in garrison, were armed and provided with ammunition, and held in readiness to reinforce the troops fighting, or defend the garrison.

Capt. Ten Eyck reported, as soon as he reached a summit commanding a view of the battlefield, that the Peno valley was full of Indians; that he could see nothing of Col. Fetterman's party, and requested that a howitzer be sent to him. The howitzer was not sent. The Indians, who at first beckoned him to come down, now commenced retreating, and Capt. Ten Eyck, advancing to a point where the Indians had been standing in a circle, found the dead naked bodies of Brevet Lieut.-Col. Fetterman, Capt. Brown, and about sixty-five of the soldiers of their command. At this point there were no indications of a severe struggle. All the bodies lay in a space not exceeding thirty-five feet in diameter. No empty cartridge shells were about, and there were some full of cartridges. A few American

KIRKPATRICK'S RANCH, PRAIRIE DOG VALLEY, WITH MASSACRE HILL ON THE LEFT.

horses lay dead a short distance off, all with their heads toward the fort. This spot was by the roadside, and beyond the summit of a hill rising to the east of Peno Creek. The road, after rising the hill, follows this ridge along for about half or three-quarters of a mile, and then descends abruptly to Peno Creek. At about half the distance from where these bodies lay to the point where the road commences to descend to Peno Creek was the dead body of Lieut. Grummond; and still farther on, at the point where the road commences to descend to Peno Creek, were the bodies of the three citizens and four or five of the old, long-tried and experienced soldiers. A great number of empty cartridge shells were on the ground at this point, and more than fifty lying on the ground about one of the dead citizens, who used a Henry rifle. Within a few hundred yards in front of this position ten Indian ponies lay dead, and there were sixty-five pools of dark and clotted blood. No Indian ponies or pools of blood were found at any other point. Our conclusion, therefore, is that the Indians were massed to resist Col. Fetterman's advance along Peno creek on both sides of the road; that Col. Fetterman formed his advance lines on the summit of the hill overlooking the creek and valley, with a reserve near where the large number of the dead bodies lay; that the Indians, in force of from fifteen to eighteen hundred warriors, attacked him vigorously in this position, and were successfully resisted by him for half an hour or more; that the command then being short of ammunition, and seized with panic

at this event and the great numerical superiority of the
Indians, attempted to retreat toward the Fort; that the
mountaineers and old soldiers, who had learned that a
movement from Indians, in an engagement, was equivalent to death, remained in their first position, and were
killed there; that immediately upon the commencement
of the retreat the Indians charged upon and surrounded
the party, who could not now be formed by their officers, and were immediately killed. Only six men of the
whole command were killed by balls, and two of these,
Lieut.-Col. Fetterman and Capt. Brown, no doubt inflicted this death upon themselves, or each other, by
their own hands, for both were shot through the left
temple, and powder burnt into the skin and flesh about
the wound. These officers had also often-times asserted
that they would not be taken alive by the Indians.

In the critical examination we have given this painful and horrible affair, we do not find, of the immediate participants, any officer living deserving of censure; and even if evidence justifies it, it would ill become us to speak evil of or censure those dead who
sacrificed life, struggling to maintain the authority and
power of the government and add new lustre to our
arms and fame.

Of those who have been more remotely connected
with the events that led to the massacre, we have en-
deavored to report so specifically as to enable your-
self and the President, who have much official information that we cannot have, to determine where the
censure must fall. The difficulty, "in a nutshell," was

that the commanding officer of the district was furnished no more troops or supplies for this state of war than had been provided and furnished him for a state of profound peace.

In regions where all was peace, as at Laramie in November, twelve companies were stationed; while in regions where all was war, as at Phil Kearney, there were only five companies allowed.

Following the massacre of Col. Fetterman and his command, came the treaty of 1867, which gave to the Sioux as a hunting ground all the lands lying between the Yellowstone on the north and the Platte on the south, the Black Hills (included) on the east, and the Big Horn range of mountains on the west. Stipulations for Indian schools were also made, but never kept, and this, together with the excitement consequent upon the reported rich gold fields in the Black Hills and the invasion of the Hills by prospecters and adventurers, led the Indians to believe that the treaty of 1867 was nothing but an expedient and was never made to be kept. In 1874 the Sioux and Cheyennes began acting very badly, and it was found necessary to establish military camps at the Spotted Tail and Red Cloud agencies, while Col. Custer and Col. Guy V. Henry were sent to the Black Hills to drive out the miners who had gone thither; but nothing of moment was ever done. The following year the government decided to call into agencies for registration all the Indians occupying the land ceded by the treaty of 1867; but Sitting Bull and Crazy Horse, with their following, refused to comply with the demands of the government. To the request sent these chiefs in 1875 to report at Red Cloud agency to negotiate a treaty for the opening of the Black Hills country, they sent a flat refusal to come in, and this led to the heroic measures adopted in 1876, when a force sufficient to subdue the hostile bands was sent into the Indian country, Gen. Crook entering from the south to form a junction with the troops under Generals Terry and Gibbon, whose approach was from the Yellowstone and Rosebud on the north, Crook's operations beginning in the early spring, entailing marches over ground deeply covered with snow, and under the most trying conditions imaginable.

When the Indians had at last been driven to the reservations set aside for them and were kept under the watchful eye of the army, the renegade whites, — horse-thieves and hold-ups — began to prey upon the settlers. No line of travel was safe; no man's life or property secure, and these conditions maintained until the United States authorities took the "gentlemen of the road" in hand and, in the end, suppressed them.

To-day, where thirty years ago the savage held absolute sway, a thrifty, energetic people are cultivating the soil and adding to the material wealth of the nation; the tepi and wickiup have given place to palace and cottage; cities have sprung up on the very sites where the turbulent and bloodthirsty Sioux and Cheyennes temporarily located their villages; the hum of

WAH-KA-PAMANE (ANNUITY), OF SPIRIT LAKE MASSACRE FAME.

machinery has supplanted the savage song of victory
and the chant of death ; the children of the white
man are playing on the green where once the living
sacrifice was offered at the burning stake.   Civilization
has wrought these various changes, and the blood of
countless forgotten heroes sanctified the soil which now
the plowman turns as he sings.

CHAPTER IV.

GROUARD'S OWN STORY.

I left school and hired out to a freighter named McCartney, in the Big Square at old San Bernardino, in 1865. I hired out to him to drive team from there to Helena, Montana. I worked for him for three and one-half years as mule skinner. The train I first started with was loaded with choice liquors. They put me in charge of the third team. The drivers go by rotation as a general thing. You have to work from the bottom up. I had never driven anything, but had done a little riding and could handle horses first rate, and I don't recollect that anything of moment happened for some time after we left Bernardino. I know the wagonmaster rode alongside of me the first three or four days, teaching me to drive mules. There were twenty-four mule-teams in the train.

It took eleven months to make the trip to Helena. We started in the fall from San Bernardino. I don't remember anything distinctly until we got to the Los Vegas river. There is where I first came in contact with the Indians. We reached the lower part of Utah early in the spring, and passed through the scene of the mountain meadow massacre. The bones of the victims were still bleaching in the sun. The wagons and wrecks of the whole train were lying around the plain, and showed very distinctly.

From there we came to old John D. Lee's place, the leader of the massacre. We camped at his place some time. We got right into that part of the country in the rainy season, early in the spring. The roads became so soft that the wagons sunk deep in the mire and sand along the road. Some were in the mud so deep it was hard to get them out. When we got a wagon mired down there was always trouble. Each of the drivers had a bundle of straws and a gimlet. They would draw the whisky out through a gimlet hole, and it was a sure thing to have a big spree or drunk whenover the wagons got stuck in the mud. I saw so much of the mule skinner's drinking and fighting that I took a dislike to whisky, and made up my mind I would never drink any whisky if it had that effect on a person. I have never touched a drop of whisky from that on without some good and sufficient reason.

We went up through the settlements of Utah to Salt Lake City, and camped there a month or more, and learned a good deal while there from and about the Mormons. Met old Brigham Young there Was all through his house. It gave me a pretty good insight into the life of the Mormons — coming through the settlement. From Salt Lake City we went to Helena; we were about a month on the road. Nothing of mo-

ment occured. Freighted between Helena and Salt Lake
all that summer. It was at the former place I first met
Bill Bevins, the highwayman. Helena was nothing but
a mining camp, then. The biggest part of the mining
was done in the lower part of the town. - The town was
in a gulch and the placer mines were right in the town.
The place was like every mining camp, full of shacks,
tents and some very good buildings at that time—lots of
open saloons, brothels and gambling dens. I became
acquainted with the notorious Bill Bevins, who was then
in the height of his career at Helena. I was down
town with him the night of a big shooting scrape in
which he was one of the principals. Of course, in all
the places there was gambling, more or less; but he had
his certain place to gamble. He owned the best claim
in the gulch and was supposed to be worth a million
dollars. He says to me after we had been looking over
the city :

"I am going to play poker. You can come up and
watch, if you want to, or run around town."

I went with him and stayed until about 12 o'clock,
when I left him. I never heard of the shooting until
the next morning. They told me that Bevins had been
shot and cut up pretty bad, and had won a good deal of
money in the bargain. I went down to the hospital
where he was lying, and he told me the circumstances.
He had won $120,000 that night. Of course, as quick
as he won this he got on a spree, and a row with other
gamblers followed, naturally enough. He got shot and
cut eighteen times, and was pretty well used up when he

got through with it. I saw him more or less that whole summer, after he had recovered from his wounds. It was all card playing with him. He was a regular gambler, and one of the "leading men" of Helena at that time. This was before the vigilant committee was organized, and that was how he came to go away from there. He got broke at last; lost all his money. The next time I saw him was in 1876, at Red Cloud Agency, Nebraska. He was without a cent. He was driving a stage then, and in '76 he started for the Laramie plains with two other parties. Their names were Herman Leslie, who is now in the state prison, sentenced for ninety-nine years, and George Hastings, nephew of the then agent at Red Cloud.

He went over to the Laramie Plains and jumped an old man named Robert Foote, and I think he tried to kill him for the money he was supposed to have. He didn't succeed in killing him. He was taken up for it and sentenced for three years. Herman Leslie got two years, and the other man, this nephew of the agent, got clear. Bevins was taken to the Laramie jail, and when I got back to Red Cloud Agency in the fall, I received a telegram from the Sheriff saying that Bevins had broken jail and started over our way, and for me to be on the lookout for him. I was given an escort. I was up about six miles from Fort Laramie, and was stopping with Big Bat, (Baptiste Pourier). I directed the soldiers to come up to Bat's place, telling them I would go ahead and change horses and clothing. When I went into the house somebody was lying asleep just inside the door, and who should it be but Bevins, with a gun lying across his breast. I hallooed at him as soon as I saw who it was, and said:

"Bevins, you ought to wake up."

He got up ready for fighting; but as quick as he woke up and saw who it was, he lays his gun down and says:

"I thought it was somebody else."

I says: "What are you doing here?"

He answered: "Resting, sleeping. I have not had any sleep for three or four nights."

"Well," I says, "You ought to get out of here; you are in a pretty hard fix."

He says: "I know it."

"I just got a telegram about you," said I.

He says: "I want a horse, and a suit of clothes from Bat."

I said all right. I gave him a horse, and he got a suit of clothes from Bat. There was not enough money in the United States to induce me to take him. I would rather have gotten into trouble myself than to have taken him. I asked him which way he was going. He said on to Running Water. I told him that I was going up the river. He said all right, and started out. That was about all there was said at this time. Of course, I went up the river and stayed there the next day and then came back. When I returned a courier had got in and said the Running Water stage had been held up and some horses had been stolen. We were just on the point of going to Red Cloud. Gen. Crook

was along. The latter got into an ambulance. I was
on horseback, and two other men were with us. We
had to go past the scene of the robbery, and past the
ranch where the horses were stolen. We passed on,
and finally saw the parties who had stolen the horses,
and Bevins was with them. I took the two men and
started after them to overtake them, and Bevins, knowing it was me, pulled up his horse until I came close
to him, and said:

"What do you want?"

"I want those horses, and am after you fellows,"
I replied.

He says, pointing: "There are the horses; you
keep on after us, and I will drop the horses."

So I followed until I overtook the horses and
turned them back, and that was the last I saw of
Bevins for years. I heard a good deal about his work,
and finally learned he had been caught, tried, sentenced
and served his term out. The authorities could not
bring anything against him about this stage robbery.
He served out a sentence of three years, and I never
saw him again until 1886, when we met at Buffalo,
Wyoming. I came down to Buffalo from McKinney one
day and went up to John Fisher's place. I went to the
door and saw somebody sitting at a table, and I entered the place. The door was on a direct line with the
man at the table, and who should it be but Bevins. He
had his back to me, but I knew Bevins. I sat down and
ate my dinner, and I looked at him, but he never
turned to look at me. After I had finished my meal I

went out, and just as I passed through the door Bevins came after me. I walked slowly down the street and he caught up with me.

I said: "When did you come here?"

"I just came in," he replied.

"Where are you going?"

"To the Black Hills," he answered.

"How did you come?"

He said: "Afoot."

He told me he had served out his term, and was pretty near dead, and wanted to go to the Black Hills as soon as he could. He said he was going afoot. I told him I would give him a horse, but he said he did not want it. Then I told him to go by stage; but he said he was going to walk, though he had plenty of money.

"I don't want any one to know I am here," he said.

"Anything out of the road?" I asked.

"No, I just want to get through to the hills as quick as I can," he replied.

I walked a mile with him and offered him the horse I was leading, but he would not take it. He went on to Spearfish and that was the last I saw of him—on the hills the other side of Buffalo. He said if he was all right when he reached the Hills he would write to me. He died two weeks afterward at the Spearfish Hotel, and that ended his career. He was between forty-five and fifty years old at the time of his death. He was an odd man, any way you could take him. He would do anything in the world for a friend. He was a perfect type of the western hard man of his time.

CHAPTER V.

THE HELENA FLOUR FAMINE.

The flour famine in Helena was in '68, the last year I was with McCartney. We had been freighting from Benton to Helena. The steamboat was running up the Missouri to Helena. All the freighting was done that way that year. After the freighting season was over, McCartney sent us down to the forks of the Gallatin and Madison, at the head of the Missouri. Sent us over there to winter. I was in charge of the train at that time. It was a very hard winter. We did not know anything about the suffering for food, as we had plenty of it.

I had been to town several times during the early part of the winter, but as the snow lay very deep along about Christmas, I could not get to Helena. When I did get in, it was about the middle of February. There was a regular famine there. Flour would have sold at its own weight in gold. You could not get it for that. Everything was in proportion. There was nothing to eat in the town. Everybody was crazy for something to eat. A freighter, a Frenchman, went to work and brought a load of flour from Blackfoot City, Montana, into Helena. He hired thirty men and gave them five dollars a day to

tramp snow across the mountains.   There was one load
brought in.   He had a regular old prairie schooner, the
tires of which were eight inches wide.   He hired these
men to tramp and shovel snow, and got this flour to
Helena.   He was paying five dollars a day for the men,
but when he did get the flour in, it went as fast as he
could hand it out, and the people would pay any price
for it.   He never sold a sack of the entire load for less
than five hundred dollars.   How much over that amount
he got, we never knew.

We had several thousand sacks at camp, and I
brought them in and sold them for two hundred and fifty
dollars a sack.   Of course it was nothing in my pocket.
McCartney got the whole benefit of it.   I had charge of
the outfit.   There were four of us, I believe.   I cleared
quite a sum, and turned it over to the bank for him.

AN INDIAN RUNNER.

CHAPTER VI.

LIVER EATING JOHNSON.

In the spring of '69 I came down to Seven Mile creek, seven miles from Helena, and went to breaking horses for the Holliday Stage Company. I broke horses there all that fall, or close to fall, and it was during this time that the Blackfeet Indians commenced to get ugly. The people had to do something to protect the outside settlers. It was at this time that the Montana militia was organized. I came down with them into the camp about forty miles from Diamond City. Huntley had got the contract to run the pony express from Diamond City to Fort Hall on the Missouri river, and I hired out as carrier. The militia went into camp about forty miles from Diamond City on our right, on the head of the Mussellshell river. I came down while they were getting things ready, and they were to overtake us. I was there at the time the militia were in camp, and camped right there with them. I was waiting for C. C. Huntley to come down. He and his party were to come on into camp, and we were to start out from there, and some of the militia were to go there with us as an escort. I was there about a month with this militia before the Huntley party did come down. There was an escort of twenty men ordered to go with us.

There was one of these militiamen who afterwards became quite a notorious character, and is so at the present day, being known by the cognomen of "Liver Eating Johnson." At present he is marshal of Red Lodge, Montana. One day it was pretty hot, and an antelope came close to us. Johnson says:

"Wait a minute ; I will kill that antelope."

He shot at it four or five times and missed it, and the antelope still stood there. That made him kind of hot, for he was a pretty good shot, and he says :

"I will eat your liver out if I do kill you," and he kept his word.

After he killed it he ate its liver. He was blood from one end to the other. That is how he got his name. Everybody called him "Liver Eating Johnson" after that. Huntley, I think it was, gave him the name.

We went on then to Fort Hall on that trip and fixed everything up, and turned around and came back over the same road. When we got back the militia had disbanded, and we went through to Diamond City. It was about a week afterwards that I took the first mail through, leading one horse packed and riding another. The distance was about two hundred and eleven miles from Diamond City to Fort Hall. It took me four days and nights to make the trip. I made one trip down one week and the other week made the trip back.

Diamond City was a mining camp — not much of a place. I think it was in November the Blackfeet captured me. I had not made many trips. I was going from Diamond City to Fort Hall when the redskins got me.

———

[Grouard says that as he neared Judith Springs he had to pass along a ridge, with little points of rocks standing here and there. As he crossed the ridge his attention was attracted by an immense herd of Buffalo grazing to his left, and being intent on watching the animals, he had paid no attention to the trail before him. Suddenly, and without a moment's warning, he was surrounded by almost twenty Blackfeet Indians in full war costume, one of whom yelled to him in good English, " Hold up! "

Grouard says he was incapable just then of doing anything else. It was his first experience with Indians, and he was frightened nearly to death. In a scabbard on his horse he carried an eighty-dollar Henry rifle, and had two revolvers stuck in a belt about his waist ; but the possession of the weapons never crossed his mind. He had imagined he was armed well enough to kill all the Indians in the country; but matters assumed a different light when he sat on his horse in the midst of twenty of the worst looking cut-throats he had ever heard of or read about. The redskins seemed to enjoy poor Grouard's fright and discomfiture, but did not keep him long in doubt as to their intentions toward him.

They partly pushed and partly pulled him off his horse, and stripped him of every vestige of clothing.

Then they pointed in the direction he had come and told him to go. Emboldened by the fact that they were not going to take his life, Grouard asked them to give him one of the blankets they had taken from him. For an answer they mounted their horses, drew their quirts and lashed their defenseless victim until his body was filled with gaping gashes, from which the blood flowed in streams. Realizing that his only chance of escape lay in flight, Grouard struck out across the sandy plain, the Indians following for over two hundred yards, raining blow after blow upon his bleeding head and body.

Darkness was settling over the earth. The sun had sunk behind the western hills about the time the Indians captured Grouard. The night was warm, and scarcely a breath of air was stirring. It was nearly seventy miles by the nearest known route from Judith Springs to Fort Hall.

The country was covered with patches of cactus and prickly pears. Into these the fleeing man rushed, lost to all sense of pain in the haunting fear of death. His imagination peopled the semi-darkness with pursuing savages on horseback. He had no hope but the present chance of escape.

On he sped, and on, covering mile after mile of the distance he must travel to find safety at the fort. He realized nothing but fear of pursuit, and that fear lent wings to his feet.

If, during that awful flight, he stopped for breath, he does not remember it. He had tasted no food since the previous morning, yet he knew not a pang of hunger.

No liquid had passed his lips since the preceding noon, but he would not have slackened his pace to slake his thirst if the purest of springs had invited him.

Onward into the cruel cacti, over the prickly pear vines, fled Grouard, the phantom horsemen lashing their steeds into a foam in a vain endeavor to overtake him.

Suddenly he stops.

Like a flash through the heavens the black veil of night had been lifted.

He could not tell at first whether he were waking from a horrid dream or had lost his reason.

One hundred yards ahead of him stood Fort Hall, and as he gazed the heavy gates swung open and a man appeared.

"In that single moment," says Grouard, "I realized all."

At his side flowed the river; behind him were the familiar cottonwoods and willow groves.

A trembling sensation seized upon the muscles of his body.

His brain was in a whirl; it was getting dark again. He raised his arms high above his head and tried to shout.

He knew no more.

Four days later Grouard opened his eyes. The first face he recognized was that of "Liver Eating Johnson." His condition was pitiful. His body was covered with festering sores, and his feet were swollen twice their natural size. His limbs were so stiff and heavy that he could not raise them, and he had not the power to utter an audible sound.

For three long months he lay upon his bed of furs, suffering the tortures of hell itself. "Liver Eating Johnson" nursed him with all the care and solicitude of a mother. The needles from the cacti which had entered his flesh as he had rushed through them in his efforts to escape the Blackfeet, worked their way out of his limbs through the festering sores, some of them appearing at the surface of the flesh as high up as the knees. —Author.]

CHAPTER VII.

GROUARD'S FIRST INDIAN FIGHT.

After I had recovered from the sickness which followed my experience with the Indians, prickly pears and
cactus, there was a report that the redskins had attacked
a white camp three miles above Fort Hall.   They had
the camp surrounded and had the men corralled in a
cabin.   The men in the cabin had dug a cellar under
the structure and tunneled from there to the bank of the
river, and could pass out from the cabin to the river
without being seen.   The man who brought the news to
us had stolen out through this passageway and come
down the river three miles to the fort.   The Indians attacked the cabin at daylight the following morning.

Part of us went with the help-seeker and rowed up
the other side of the river, keeping under the bank all
the way so that the Indians could not see us.   Crossing
over we went through the tunnel and got into the cabin
before daybreak, and when the Indians attacked the
cabin the next morning there were over twenty of us in
there.   When they did attack us we were ready for
them.   We killed eleven of them.   There were not over
seventy or seventy-five in the attacking party.   They

stayed with us for about an hour. When it became known to them that there was a large number of us in the cabin, they began to try to fight. We tore down the bars from the door and charged on them. There was not a man of our party hurt. We ran them up the hills as far as we could, killing the eleven spoken of.

WILD HOG, HIGH CHIEF OF THE CHEYENNES.

CHAPTER VIII.

CAPTURED BY THE SIOUX.

A short time after this I was put on the mail line from Fort Hall to Fort Peck, at the mouth of Milk river. Fort Hall is one hundred and forty miles from Fort Peck, up the river. I had to take care of the mail. Over to Milk river it was forty miles, and down the river it was one hundred and forty-five miles. I carried mail up one week and down the next. They could not get anybody to carry this mail because the Sioux were committing depredations down at the mouth of Milk river; so I took the two routes. That was in the spring. I carried all that summer and next fall, till the first of January. It was about the second of January, and I was making my last trip. It took me two days to go from the bend of Milk River to the station, and generally two days down. This station was run by a Frenchman; a trapper and hunter. I don't remember his name.

I went from Fort Hall to the bend of Milk river. Between that point and Fort Peck there is a big open flat. Through the center of this flat there is a gulch. In the rainy season the water comes through there.

There are large trees in the center of it, and right straight down and up again, this gulch is twenty or twenty-five feet deep. Anyhow it could not be seen for any distance. It was about 3 o'clock in the afternoon when I reached this gulch. The snow was coming from the south right in my face. I had on a big buffalo overcoat, a handkerchief tied around my throat, and had big buffalo mitts on my hand that were tied on at the elbows, and had on buffalo leggins and moccasins. I was riding one horse and leading another. There had been no indication of Indians at all, and I was not looking for any. When I was in the gulch — just as my horse started up the other side — the animal I was on jumped, and the next thing I knew somebody hit me over the back. That was the first indication I had of Indians.

They had waited for me to come into the gulch and catch me when I was crossing. Before I realized what was going on, they had secured my horses and pulled me to the ground, and were trying to take my coat off. They already had my gun. I never thought of having a gun. I was rattled, or something. They were using me pretty hard. I had not come in contact with the Sioux before, and could not understand a word they said. One Indian was trying to get my coat off, and another one was trying to shoot me. I was keeping the Indian who was trying to get my coat off between me and the fellow who carried the gun. I don't know how long the struggle lasted. It was but a short time, when an Indian rode up to the top of the gulch on horseback. We were on top of the gulch by this time, and this Indian came up on horseback and said something to the Indian I was trying to keep out of the way of—the one with the gun. I couldn't understand what he said. The first thing I knew, the Indian who was on horseback dismounted, went up to the one who had the gun, and knocked him down with a heavy bow he carried in his hand. The Indian who had hold of me, as quick as the other Indian was knocked down, left me alone and went off to one side. There were fourteen Indians in the party, I think. I saw it was a change for the better with me. They talked among themselves for some time. The fellow who was knocked down seemed to give up. The Indian who had been on horseback was talking, but I couldn't understand what he said. The fellow who was doing the talking seemed to be the head man. The one with the gun went off towards the river. After he went away, the leader pulled out his pipe and sat down, and motioned for me to be seated. I obeyed, and after he had got through smoking, he made a motion to me that he was going. I could understand his signs first rate. He made a motion for me to get on a horse, and we started for the mouth of Milk river. On our way to the Indian village I learned his name was Sitting Bull. He told me by signs who he was. He also told me where his village was. It was on the head of Bark creek, which stream empties into the Missouri above the mouth of Poplar creek. We camped on Milk river the first night after my capture, and left the next morning. The Indians had taken everything away from me and cut the mail sack open and rifled it. We were traveling continuously for three days before we got into the hostile camp.

CHAPTER IX.

TAKEN TO THE HOSTILE CAMP.

Grouard's entrance into the Sioux village did not have a very soothing effect upon his nerves. From the moment of his capture he had been constantly looking forward to the end of his troubles in a death by torture. His knowledge of the Indians had been somewhat limited, it is true; but his former experience as a captive did not tend to lighten the terrible load that weighed down his young heart. He knew that he had no means of communication with his captors; he did not even understand their simplest signs, nor comprehend a word they said. His position was a terrible one, but his fate, whatever it might be, was only conjectural.

Several of his captors escorted him through the main portion of the village, and it appeared to Grouard that every tepi had been emptied of its inmates to witness his arrival. What seemed particularly perplexing to him was the silence maintained by the redmen. They crowded about the animal he rode, and impeded its progress in their anxiety to look into the captive's face; but they gave no sign of anger, and raised no shout of triumph.

READY FOR THE DANCE.

"It is the calm," thought Grouard, "that precedes the storm. They are reserving their shouts till the fires are lighted about the stake to which they intend to burn me."

After what seemed an age to the captive, his guards stopped in front of a large lodge, and he was dismounted and led inside. Once within the tepi, he glanced hastily about to view his surroundings. His eyes were sore and swollen from exposure, and he was nearly dead from the cold, but he immediately discovered that he was not the only occupant of the lodge. Almost within touching distance from him, his eyes riveted on Grouard's face, stood the savage who had struck to the earth the Indian who was making an attempt to kill him when his capture was effected. A bright fire burned on the ground in the middle of the lodge, and reflected itself upon the massive face of the tepi's owner. For the second time in his life Grouard stood face to face with the most redoubtable Sioux warrior of the age. He was the guest of no less a personage than Sitting Bull himself.

At that time the Sioux chief was thirty-six years old, and in the prime of a magnificent savage manhood. His head was crowned with a profusion of long, black hair, which he wore brushed from a low forehead. His face was massive and swarthy. His eyes were large and expressive, while the mouth was large and the lips thin, indicating cruelty. His shoulders were broad and heavy, and his body tapered symmetrically. His wearing apparel consisted of breech-clout and leggins, a buffalo robe doing service as an overcoat. Grouard states that in all the years of his enforced residence with the Sioux he never knew Sitting Bull to rise to the dignity of a boiled shirt, although photographs said to have been taken of the chief in later years show him to have grown somewhat æsthetic and particular in this regard.

The only bodily defect Grouard noticed about Sitting Bull was a well-defined limp. The cause of this, he afterward discovered, was a wound in the left foot. The story of his receiving it is short and not out of place here:

The Sioux and Crows were constantly at war, and the latter were ever on the watch for their merciless and raiding enemy. During one of these scalping excursions, two war parties became tangled up on the banks of the Porcupine. The Sioux chief, Sitting Bull, ever ready to set an example to the young braves of his tribe and keep aflame the terror the Crows associated with his name, challenged the Crow leader to single combat. While the braves on both sides watched the progress of the battle, the two chiefs struggled for the mastery. The Crow, at last convinced that he was over-matched, and fearing the stigma of being overcome by Sitting Bull, seized a rifle and deliberately shot at the latter. In his rage and excitement, the Crow warrior took the worst sort of aim and made the lowest possible score, as the ball caught the Sioux beneath the toes and furrowed its way on a straight line through the sole of the foot. The next instant Sitting Bull had plunged his knife to the hilt into his adversary's breast, and the

battle was ended. When the Sioux chief's wound healed
the bottom of the foot contracted, and Sitting Bull, although soon recovering his wonted health, never placed
his left foot on terra firma afterward without limping.
Sometime previous to the event just narrated, Sitting
Bull, while battling against the forces led by Gen.
Harney at Lookout Buttes, on the Little Missouri, received a terrible wound through the body, and although
the great medicine men of his tribe shook their heads
and twirled their thumbs and despaired of saving the
life of their patient, Sitting Bull pulled through and
lived to fight many battles afterwards.

These circumstances, although unknown to Grouard
at the time he found himself face to face with Sitting
Bull in the latter's lodge, could not have heightened the
captive's terror one iota. He had heard enough of Sitting Bull to know that he was the unrelenting foe of
the white race. The reputation of the wily savage for
cruelty was the theme at every camp fire. No wonder,
then, that Grouard expected nothing but a lingering
death by torture at the stake.

Great was his surprise, therefore, when Sitting Bull
motioned him to lie down upon a pile of buffalo robes
at one side of the lodge, an invitation Grouard was not
loath to accept. The glowing fire, the warmth within
the lodge, and the soft, warm robes — these influences
added to the exhaustion of bodily and mental forces —
broke the charm that had driven sleep from his excited
brain, and his senses were almost instantly steeped in
forgetfulness.

While he slept his fate was settled. At the council which was called that night, Sitting Bull's voice was the only one raised in behalf of the unconscious captive. While in his dreams Grouard was again passing through all the agonies that had come to him since his capture and speculating upon the terrible ordeal that awaited him, this man, this savage, he whom civilization denied every generous impulse, feeling of pity, quality of mercy, was disputing with the mighty counselors of the Sioux nation over the disposition to be made of the pale-faced stranger.

For some reason that will never be known, Sitting Bull had formed a sudden attachment for Grouard, and later developments prove, though the Sioux chief gave no earnest of his intention to anyone, that he had determined not only to spare his captive's life, but to throw his protecting influence around him forever after. So it happened, when the council, headed by Gall and No Neck (both able and beloved warriors), decided on the death of Grouard, that Sitting Bull at once arose and said:

"The coups of Sitting Bull are like the stars, shining and almost numberless. I look; I act; I talk afterwards. That which I will, is so. The captive in the Sioux lodge is resting on the robes that Sitting Bull has taken with his own hand from the buffalo, and it is my will that the captive shall not die. When Little Assiniboine was taken from his people, it was Sitting Bull who bore him to his lodge and made him his brother. So with the paleface within the lodge of Sitting Bull this night. He is Standing Bear, the brother of Sitting Bull. My will is spoken."

This speech was received in silence. Little Assiniboine, then grown to manhood, loved his foster brother better than his life. His word was law. When Sitting Bull had taken him from the lodge of his parents during a battle between the Assiniboines and the Sioux, the little fellow had become the special care and pride of the Sioux warrior. To the tender care of White Cow, Sitting Bull's sister, the little captive had been entrusted. She reared him as she afterward did her own, and in time Little Assiniboine became one of the most powerful warriors in the nation of his adoption.

The rise of Little Assiniboine had been a source of great pride to Sitting Bull, and his wisdom in sparing the child's life was a theme never forgotten by his relatives and friends. Sitting Bull was not a great orator, but what he lacked in this particular he made up in diplomacy. He was as shrewd as he was cunning. His speeches in council were always blunt, but convincing because he ever worked upon his hearers through those avenues by which they had reached success. Therefore, without drawing a parallel, he adroitly reminded the wise men of the council that the course he had pursued in Little Assiniboine's case had been fruitful of much good to the Sioux nation. He left them to infer his meaning, that the sparing of Grouard's life would furnish a similar cause for congratulation.

So far as the council was concerned, the determination of Sitting Bull to adopt Grouard, settled the matter.

What view individual members of the tribe took of it
was another consideration. But Sitting Bull had thought
of that also. As a result, poor Grouard was kept a close
guarded prisoner for sixteen months. At the end of two
years he was able to converse in the Sioux tongue like a
native, and had made himself proficient in the language
of signs.

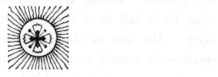

TWO INDIAN BEAUTIES.

CHAPTER X.

THE KINDNESS OF WHITE COW.

Grouard himself says that no human being will ever know the horrors that constantly surrounded him. Little by little he managed to pick up a word here and there of the strange gargon of his savage associates. Sitting Bull, in order to secure his captive's perfect safety, sent him to the lodge of his mother and sister, and to the latter, says the scout, more than to any earthly power, is he indebted for the preservation of his life.

The first fifteen years of his life had been passed under the influence of a loving foster mother. The next four years were spent amid scenes such as the American continent will never witness again. Inured to hardship and deprivation, with a stature of six feet and a constitution that mocked at the ills of flesh, he felt himself able to meet every trial that frontier life entailed. Yet, he found himself now, at nineteen years of age, in the center of a sea of savagery, cut off from every hope that had risen in his breast and debarred even of his liberty.

There was a practical side to this enforced existence, also. He had never attempted, and never imagined he would ever be compelled to attempt, to live on meat rations solely. The Sioux had no other wish than to live so. But Grouard found himself failing daily from this cause. Ravenously hungry, the meat diet, minus salt or pepper, did not supply the substitute or satisfy his cravings for bread, though he ate to satiety. What made matters worse, he knew nothing of the Sioux language, and therefore could not make his conditions or wants known. His waking hours were filled with a desire for bread. He thought of the crust he had thrown away, and lamented his extravagance. At night his sleep was disturbed by dreams in which he saw huge loaves of golden-hued bread floating through space almost within reach of his outstretched arms. And often he awoke with a start just as he was preparing to sit down to a feast of biscuit and coffee. He grew pale and emaciated. He was in a delirium of torment. He felt that his mind was getting enfeebled. He thought of escape, but his guards never left him. He contemplated self-destruction, but neither means nor opportunity presented themselves.

Then he was stricken down with a strange sickness. How long he was ill he did not know; but one day he awoke to the sudden consciousness that there was burning bread within the lodge. He sat up, weak as he was, to reassure himself that he was not dreaming. White Cow, the sister of Sitting Bull, was baking some dough in the ashes of the tepi fire. He stretched out his arms with an imploring gesture. The savage woman nodded her head and gave him a portion of the half-baked dough. He grasped it in both his thin hands and fell back upon his bed of robes. The knowledge that he had the bread overcame even his desire to eat it, and he clung to it with a joy that was childish. White Cow noticed it, and smiled, and soon she nearly frightened Grouard's wits out of him by placing some coffee in a cloth and pounding it preparatory to placing it in a can of water over the fire.

From that day on a new life opened to poor Grouard. He lived again, and hoped; and then it was he made a firm resolve to turn the term of his captivity to good account. His anxiety about bread, as well as the desire for it, grew less and less, until finally he ceased to care for it. It was many months before he knew how White Cow had secured the flour and coffee, but it came about in this wise:

In the spring and fall the Indians came out from the agencies and brought small quantities of coffee, flour, sugar, salt and pepper with them. For these articles they would charge and get fabulous prices; that is, they would trade the commodities off for ponies, furs and mules.

White Cow divined at once the cause of Grouard's decline, and some Indian traders very opportunely came to the Sioux village with provisions. Unknown to the others, this generous-hearted Indian woman traded off one mule that was worth $250 for less than a third of a bag of flour, and another animal, whose value was nearly as great, for small quantities of coffee, sugar, salt and pepper, and these articles she hid away and allowed no one to touch any part of except Grouard. The latter says the flour and coffee lasted a long time, and undoubtedly saved his life. When the flour was finally used up, White Cow would gather wild turnips and pound them into a pulp, and then make it into porridge.

In this manner Grouard managed to gradually wean himself from the use of breadstuffs, and toward the end of his captivity he had grown to look upon' the use of bread as entirely unnecessary. In fact, upon regaining his freedom, he had a hard time with his appetite and stomach over the bread problem, and was forced to acquire a liking for it as if it were some species of edible that nothing but custom and civilization demanded the consumption of.

CLOUD'S PEAK, HIGHEST POINT IN BIG HORN RANGE.

CHAPTER XI.

GROUARD MAKES A TEN-STRIKE.

For sixteen months Grouard was closely guarded in the Sioux village. With his better understanding of the Sioux tongue he found himself taking a lively interest in Indian traditions, manners and customs, and he also discovered that the Indians grew more and more friendly and confidential as they witnessed his eagerness to enter into all the minor details of their mode of living. Little Assiniboine and White Eagle, the latter a cousin of Sitting Bull, were Grouard's sole male companions. In reality they were his guard, and were as constant in their devotion to the orders of Sitting Bull regarding the captive as it were possible for human beings to be.

It was customary in the early spring to move the village toward the north to meet the vast herds of buffalo that came down, and from that time on to the last of September or first of October the village would be almost constantly on the move. In the fall the Sioux generally, if not always, made it a point to locate their village on the Belle Fourche or Little Missouri rivers, where small game was found in abundance. It was during one of these village-moving times that Grouard made a ten-strike and established his reputation as a marksman.

The Indian, as everybody knows, is nothing if not a gambler, and one day a large number of the Sioux were engaged in the enjoyment of their ruling passion, while the others went ahead to establish the village at a more favorable point for game. Grouard was with the loitering crowd. The Indians had begun to realize that the pale-face was really one of their own number, and Sitting Bull, in a burst of generosity, had given the scout an old flint-lock gun. Grouard says no one knows with what emotion he hugged this old muzzle-loading shooting iron to his breast. It was the first firearm he had been allowed to even grasp in his hands for nearly a year and a half, and he cleaned it up as well as possible, preparatory to taking a shot.

While the gambling was at its height, a big, fine deer came running over the brow of an adjacent hill, and made straight for the place where the Indians were squatted. Nearly all of them saw the animal at the same time, but having laid their arms aside, they were taken at a disadvantage for shooting. As soon as the deer got within what Grouard considered the range of his old flint-lock, and with the eyes of half the village upon him, he drew a quick bead and fired. The deer fell dead in its tracks.

At first there was an exclamation of surprise, then an outburst of admiration. The Indians, including Sitting Bull himself, had not believed the gun capable of killing a jack rabbit at a distance of ten paces, while Grouard had used it to great advantage at two hundred yards and made a remarkable running shot.

When Sitting Bull heard of the incident, he was very much pleased, and immediately presented his adopted brother Standing Bear with a powder-and-lead muzzle-loading Hawkins gun. All the bucks were thereafter anxious to have Grouard accompany them on their hunting trips, and in this way he developed into one of the best shots the country has ever produced.

Once the ice was broken, Grouard found no further bar to his outgoings and incomings. He roamed the wilds at will, and, being a natural plainsman, acquired a thorough and intimate knowledge of every mountain pass, crag, ravine and canyon in the great stretch of country now known as Wyoming, Dakota and Montana.

Having thus familiarized himself with the mountains and valleys, it is no wonder that his knowledge should be of incalculable value to the government. It can be stated without fear of contradiction that Frank Grouard's knowledge of western topography is more minute than that of any other man in the United States, a recommendation in itself that eagle plumes the possessor for the guidance of any force on the perilous undertakings that have marked the manouvres of every commanding officer who has campaigned in the mid-west against the natural foes to safety and settlement.

As a rule, the Indians place little dependence on appearances. Their reasoning is based upon experience rather than speculation. Their hatred can be overcome, but their prejudice never. This is especially true of the

Sioux. Against the whites they have waged war instinctively, because they know the Caucasian race establish a new order of things through their conquests. Civilization to them is synonymous with slavery. It is the present and not the future that concerns them most deeply. Like children, they cannot grasp the idea of a future except through mystification. In the burial of their dead they make ample provision for the self-protection of the departed by placing the implements of war upon the bier; but they also provide for the dead man's temporal necessities. They do not believe the dead warrior awakes to consciousness in the want of those things which are kept sacred to his memory. This spark of divinity in the soul of the savage is but the echo of immortality — the acknowledgment of Deity. In their prayers they address themselves not to a power they feel, but to an object they see. Pope expresses their condition exactly:

> "Lo, the poor Indian! whose untutored mind
> Sees God in clouds, or hears Him in the wind."

It is not strange, therefore, that Grouard was slow in overcoming the prejudice existing against him. His sixteen months' confinement had instilled into his mind two governing characteristics of the Sioux — silence and observation. By an almost strict observance of the former, natural, because of his lack of opportunity to acquire a language that was spoken about and not to him —he rapidly developed the latter quality. He therefore mastered the language of signs in an incredibly short time, and this served him as a key to the Sioux man-

OLD CROW, A "FRIENDLY."

OLD CROW, A NEZ PERCÉS.

ner of speech. And it must be borne in mind that the Sioux language contains six dialects, or rather, that the Sioux people give expression to a sentiment in six different modes of speech.

In their councils the orators confine themselves to a particular manner of speech that is little understood by any but the heriditary chiefs of the nation. Their most solemn deliberations are those heard but not comprehended by the braves who are not permitted to enter the charmed circle. In this particular they occupy the same plane as the white man who knows not a word or sign of Sioux—the deliberation's result must be interpreted to them. Grouard familiarized himself with every phase of the Sioux tongue, but it required years of study to accomplish so herculean a task, and had it not been for the friendship of Sitting Bull, Little Assiniboine, Black Kettle, Big Nose, No Neck, Gall, Four Horses and others of the head men of the nation, his labors would have ended in a confused comprehension of a language seemingly without beginning or end.

Grouard had gone by the name of Standing Bear for a year and a half before he discovered who had named him or what circumstance had suggested the curious title. It will be remembered that when Sitting Bull's party captured Grouard, he was wrapped in a huge fur overcoat, wore leggins of the same material, and had on a fur cap that completely hid his head, and wore a pair of gloves that extended half way to his elbows. In his struggles to throw off the Indian

who was attempting to pull the bear coat from his back
and at the same time hold him between himself and
the Indian who was trying to shoot him, Grouard was
at first mistaken by Sitting Bull for a huge bear, standing upright, fighting its would-be captors.

The Sioux chief was a great joker, and Grouard's
resemblance to a bear tickled him mightily. It was
probably this fact that saved the captive from a terrible
fate, also, although it did not have the effect of leaving
him in possession of his warm wraps.

Sitting Bull never explained to Grouard his reason
for preserving his life and adopting him as a brother;
but Little Assiniboine often recalled the Sioux chief's
notable speech in behalf of Grouard at the council fire
on the night the captive arrived in the village.
From the fact that a bear will reach out after its prey
and hug it close to its body, the Indians call it a
"grabber;" and so, while Sitting Bull had christened
Grouard "Standing Bear," he was as generally known
among the Indians by his nickname of the "Grabber."

CHAPTER XII.

INDIAN COURTSHIP.

There are people in this world who cannot appreciate the fact that a savage is capable of those finer sensibilities so much dwelt upon by sentimentalists and writers of fiction among the civilized nations.

They are perfectly willing to ascribe instinct and even knowledge to their favorite horse or dog; tell of the almost human actions and speech of a parrot; enlarge upon the understanding of a tame monkey and vouchsafe to the necessary, harmless house tabby an affection truly pathetic and surprising. But, somehow or other, these good people are loth to believe that the Indian youth or the aged savage has any conception of sentiment or any of the attributes of love.

To be able to appreciate this virtue in the aborigine, it is necessary to consider the fact that Indian tradition, like customs of some other nations, has so far circumscribed the life of woman that her sphere is narrowed down to one of servitude. Unmated, she occupies nothing but a negative position. From her infancy she is taught to resist any and all advances from her male companions, and even in the courtship that comes to her at an uncertain age (calculated by our "civilized" calendar), all her acquiescences are imperitive denials. No self-respecting lady of the Sioux pursuasion would be guilty of murmuring "yes" to the guttural appeal of the dusky swain who litterally lays siege to her father's lodge or follows her footsteps like the phantom is said to follow the guilty.

The Sioux women are, according to the traditional Sioux code of morals, moral. That is, they are given a standard of virtue and live up to it. It may not meet the approval of the orthodox whites, and it may be somewhat less rigid than the rule prescribed in Turkey, but it nevertheless serves its own purpose and obliterates among the savages one of the greatest scourges that afflicts our boasted civilization.

There is no "social evil" among the Sioux.

Inasmuch as the Indian maiden cannot consent, abduction pure and simple is the art generally employed by the amorous swain in search of a companion for his lodge.

Now, what would be considered the depth of degredation to our moral sensibilities, is applauded and countenanced by the redmen. For instance, White Hair, a rising young warrior, becomes enamored of Half Moon, the marriageable daughter of Big Storm. Tradition, as well as his inclination, tells him how to accomplish his purpose. She may be his by purchase, but in such a case all the heroism vanishes. Twenty other young men of the nation are as enamored of Half Moon as is White Hair. Possession means ownership, and tradition has woven the halo of glory over those who dare take that which the one taken denies.

White Hair, therefore, has but one mode of procedure. He arranges his lodge for the reception of Half Moon, and does not even take the maiden into his confidence about the matter. He speaks to her of his desire, but she says him nay. He is wrapped from toes to eyebrows in his blanket, and, in the darkness Half Moon knows him not from the other numerous suitors who look, act and talk just like him. He watches her exit from her father's lodge and importunes her; he follows her footsteps to the water course and pours his burning words into her ears. He is the sentimental sentinel always on the qui vive to trip her with a half consent. This once gained, he distorts it into a promise pure and and simple. Some night he lays in wait, and with just that show of force — no more — to quiet her struggles, bears her off in triumph to his lodge. She then becomes his particular property, and can be taken from him only in the same manner that he has taken her — not an uncommon occurrence.

Here again comes in a traditional arrangement that right reverends and wrong reverends will condemn to the top of their bent. White Hair, on the morn following his abduction of Half Moon, may see fit to divorce her, and there end the whole transaction. He simply sends her to her father's lodge, whither she wends her way in silence. No disgrace or stigma attaches to her from her enforced obedience to the young brave's will. He, according to his tradition, has won a victory — a

coup than which there is none greater, and the code of
Sioux morals permits him to boast of his conquest during the remainder of his days.

Do the numerous other young braves desist from
their courtship of the daughter of Big Storm? Nay,
gentle reader. In course of time she is again abducted,
and perhaps spends the remainder of her life in the
lodge of the brave whom she learns to love. Platonic?
Well, scarcely; but then we are looking at these matters
through the lens of civilization. The Sioux have practiced this mode of courtship for over eight hundred
years. Their chronicles record this fact. To them,
therefore, it is custom, not honored in the "breech" but
the observance.

To follow out this mode of procedure to its logical
conclusion it is necessary here to state that White Hair's
abduction of Half Moon did not necessarily end his
evening's conquest or night's revel. His wooings might
have been twofold or multifold. Had he been inclined
to lay siege to the hearts and persons of half a
dozen dusky maidens on the same night there was nothing to hinder his designs or thwart his purpose. The
appearance of other maidens in White Hair's lodge that
evening would have caused no surprise or jealously to
Half Moon. Trained in the manner of the young Sioux
brave, reared in the observance of might as the most
potent factor of right, the young squaw would merely
have viewed the additions to White Hair's lodge as a
matter of small moment to herself and one of supreme
satisfaction to the lord of her liberty. There is no limit

AN INDIAN SOCIETY BELLE.

to a Sioux warrior's household, so far as wives are concerned. He is supposed to be the best judge of that matter, and as long as the game is plentiful and his horse herd increases, he views the building up of a big family with feelings of pride. He is lord of the manor in all things. He plays no favorites with his squaws, and, being accustomed to nothing but obedience, the lives of the women are at least no worse in the lodge of their captor than when spent in the tepi of their parents.

There is "giving in marriage" also, among the Sioux.

When a young buck proves himself worthy of trust and has shown his ability to acquire property of his own ; when his rustling propensities increase the family larder, and his lady love's parents are satisfied that he is exceptionally above the rank and file, they do not force him to follow tradition and steal their daughter. The code prescribes another method of procedure :

At evening, when the camp is quiet and the supper has been discussed, a crier goes forth and proclaims the news that High Wind gives the young brave Fear Not, his daughter, Pale Dove. This proclamation is final. Fear Not and Pale Dove forever after share the same lodge.

"Now isn't that romantic, and proper, too?" some of my readers will ask. Proper, granted, but here is a dash to the romance : The taking of Pale Dove to his lodge does not deter Fear Not from abducting another dusky maiden before the honeymoon of Pale Dove is hardly begun, or if he feels inclined, from acquiring another wife by purchase, or if some love-lorn squaw so wills it, of accepting the latter's presence in his lodge because she sees fit to make his lodge her permanent abiding place.

Should he desire to purchase a wife, he selects the maiden, seals the bargain by the payment agreed upon — a horse and so many blankets, or whatever the father demands — and the crier is dispatched upon his errand about the camp to spread the news.

It will thus be seen that abduction, giving in marriage and purchase are the three popular ways among the Sioux of acquiring wives; but for fear that some of my "equal franchise" lady friends should still insist upon some "show of right" for their dusky sisters, I propose to give one short illustration of how some of the Sioux maidens set up an establishment for themselves and lay claim to the protection and affection of their victims.

It sometimes happens that a maiden falls desperately in love with a young warrior; but, with all her wild wiles, she is incapable of screwing him up to the abducting or purchasing point. She therefore is left the alternative of "giving herself away."

This is accomplished by her going direct to the lodge of the object of her unrequited love and taking possession of his blankets. The novelty of the situation tickles the buck's vanity, and he consequently puts up with what his savage sense of manhood will not permit him to put out.

Such marriages are not "made in heaven," however, and the novelty and buck's patience wear out about the same time. Then there is a room to let, but the squaw is soon consoled or soon consoles herself with some one else.

There is still one other method of acquiring a wife among the Sioux, although it smacks very much of the first method noted in this chapter. The same act in civilized communities is termed elopement, and the Indians pretty generally concede that the wife is always a "willing" party to the transaction. Sometimes this leads to murder among the redmen, though, according to the Sioux code, it is a matter that brave hearts will never notice.

When a squaw quits the lodge of her buck with some other buck, and the first buck seeks satisfaction at the muzzle of a gun, he falls outside the category of bravery and forever loses caste with the tribe. He is no better than a squaw, so the Sioux say, when he wishes to revenge himself on another for doing that which he himself had a perfect right to do. His proper plan would be to steal the squaw from her abductor, and keep her at all hazards. The Indians themselves have a way of turning a period on this wife-stealing business that is hard of interpretation. It is something after this fashion: "It is no easy matter to steal a maiden the first time; easy the second; heap easy afterwards."

Indian tradition and judicial reasoning may clash; but great minds will travel in the same groove.

What has been said of courtship in this chapter, I

desire to chronicle as maintaining in the villages of
the Sioux before civilization encroached upon their savage customs, and has no bearing upon the mode of life of
those who live within the agencies. The time may come
when the standard of virtue will be very high ‚among
the Indians at the latter places, but until that time arrives the veil of charity had best be drawn very tightly.
No man whose experience is worth recording can claim
anything but a state of uncertain transition for the Indian at the agency at present. Naturally quick to imi-
tate, the children of the forest, in their intercourse with
their white brethren, have acquired much of the evil and
little of the good from contact with our boasted civilization.

Reformation's footsteps are slow. Education has
accomplished something, but, in the light of the recent
outbreak in South Dakota, not much. Tribal relation
meant retrogression. Agency influence and control,
(O ! the mockery of appointment of civilians as Indian
agents) have resulted in much demoralization.

Cettewayo, the African potentate, remarked to his
English captors, on civilization :

"Yes, I know what it means: First came the mis-
sionaries ; then came the soldiers."

CHIEF GALL.

BY PERMISSION OF JOHN F. FINERTY.

CRITICAL-GALL.

CHAPTER XIII

SITTING BULL LEADS A DESPERATE CHARGE.

In the winter of 1870, Sitting Bull and a large party left the Indian village for a hunt. The village at that time was located north of the mouth of Powder river. It appears that the Crows, who were all the time creating disturbances with the Sioux when the Sioux were not creating disturbances with them, had learned that Sitting Bull and party had gone on this hunt, and concluded it would be a good time to get up a pony-stealing expedition against the Sioux. Accordingly a party numbering thirty-one left the Crow reservation and went to the Sioux camp with the intention of running off as many of the ponies of the enemy as they could. In some way or other Sitting Bull and his hunting party ran across the trail of the incoming Crows, and at once suspected what the mission of the enemy was. The Uncapapas concluded to return at once to their village and prevent the Crows from carrying out their design.

Arriving at their village the Sioux drove the Crows westward to the badlands and bottoms, the Crows finally seeking shelter in a basin, the edge of which was formed by a rocky eminence. In this naturally-fortified position the Crows stood their pursuers off for two nights and a day, at the end of which time Sitting Bull called a council of his warriors and urged upon them the necessity of charging the enemy's position and driving them out, or being killed in the attempt. Sitting Bull knew that to attack the Crows meant death to some of his party, and in the council which was called, told his followers that it would look very childish if they allowed this band of Crows to escape after they had them penned up among the rocks. He said that he did not want any of his party to join the attack unless they felt the same about it as he did; but he did not believe that any of his men were squaws. He did not ask them to take any risks that he was not willing to assume himself. He proposed to lead the attack, and he expected every one of his men to follow him. They would either drive the Crows out of the rocks, kill them where they were or be killed themselves in making the attempt.

The members of his party signified their willingness to follow their chief, and preparations for the attack were immediately made.

Little Assiniboine, who was of the party, told me afterwards that when the start of the Sioux was made for the Crow's position, Sitting Bull was far in advance of all his warriors; that upon reaching the rocks behind which the Crows were secreted, and notwithstanding the heavy fire of the enemy, the chief scaled the wall of rocks, jumped in among the imprisoned Crows and had killed several of them before the remainder of his party arrived to assist him. So far as numbers were concerned the two parties were about even, and the conflict was a hand to hand one. At the end of twenty minutes, however, all of the thirty-one Crows had been killed and scalped. The bodies of the slain were left where they fell, and Sitting Bull and party returned in triumph to the Sioux village where one of the greatest scalp dances I ever witnessed was indulged in. Two of the Sioux were killed during the fight.

Some men who have written of Sitting Bull, claiming that he was a medicine man and not a warrior, are unacquainted with the circumstances surrounding his life among the Indians themselves. No man in the Sioux nation was braver in battle than Sitting Bull, and he asked none of his warriors to take any chances that he was not willing at all times to share. I could recall a hundred different instances coming under my own observation to prove Sitting Bull's bravery, and in the first great sundance that I ever witnessed after my capture by the Sioux, I heard Sitting Bull recount his "coups in action". They numbered sixty-three, most of them being victories over Indian enemies.

CHAPTER XIV.

AN INDIAN JAMBOUREE.

In the fall of 1872 Sitting Bull formed the idea of entering into a treaty with the Red river half-breeds for the purpose of trading for ammunition and other necessaries. At this time Sitting Bull was not trading with anybody. He would not trade with the whites, and had no place to get his supplies from, so he formed the idea of making this treaty for the purpose of getting supplies. He went up into the half-breed camp to make this treaty, being gone pretty near a month, and he was very well pleased on his return with the treaty he had made. They had promised to bring him what articles he had mentioned, such as he would want to trade for, into camp that winter, and they came to the village about two months afterwards; but instead of bringing the articles the Indians were in need of, they brought liquor. They came in with five sleigh-loads of whisky. The appearance of these loads of whisky in camp caused a terrible disturbance. It was just nothing but drinking. The Indians were camped on the divide at the head of Dry Fork on the Missouri when they commenced drink-

ing. This Dry Fork has some time been the Missouri
proper. I forget what month it was, but it was in the
winter. The half-breeds came to the village in sleighs.

When they came I did not go into the council.
They held a kind of council, and what was said or done
in this council I don't know; but before the half-breeds'
visit was over you could hear the noise and singing
from the council lodge. The orgies continued for about
a week. It was the most horrible thing I ever saw.
I got on my horse as soon as they commenced drinking. When they were drunk they would cut down
lodges. The women were drunk as well as the men.
The majority in the village were drunk. Some places
it was kill on sight, either friend or foe. There were
two factions in the village—one for and one against
Sitting Bull. They were divided about half and half.

Those who opposed Sitting Bull turned on him. I
simply got on my horse and went to the hills, and stayed
there. There were several of us who did it. Sitting
Bull stayed in the camp and had his Indians protecting
him (some of his own faction), and he didn't get shot;
but there were several Indians killed, lodges cut up,
horses shot and tepis pulled down. It was a horrible
sight. I didn't come down to camp for three days.
The French half-breeds left after they saw what they
had started. They pulled stakes and quit in the night,
and took what whisky was left with them. An Indian
will pay anything for whisky, and there was a good
deal of money in camp; also mules and horses. It
was a large village, some two or three hundred lodges.

There were between four thousand and five thousand
Indians in the village.

All I could hear as I returned to the village was
the crying of the Indians for the ones that had been
killed. It was some four or five days after that before they could get everything gathered up. When
they did they split up in small bands, each party going in whichever direction it fancied. The immediate
relatives collected together in small bands ; and when
they had got together, these bands moved off in different directions to get away from the site of the village, so there would be no more trouble. After they
had sobered up they would have to take notice of those
Indians who had been killed ; their relations would have
to avenge them. Sooner than have this trouble on top
of the other, they moved in different directions. It
had the effect of scattering the whole village like a flock
of blackbirds.

BIRDSEYE VIEW OF THE CITY OF SHERIDAN, WYOMING.

CHAPTER XV.

SITTING BULL TRIES TO KILL GROUARD.

The next spring I got a chance to make a trip to the Fort Peck trading post. One of the Yankton Indians came into our camp from the Yankton tribe at Fort Peck — where their agency was. This trading post wanted to get the Sitting Bull camp trade. The agent had sent things over to Sitting Bull's camp by this Indian. They always sent a large amount of tobacco out for a treat to try and induce the Sitting Bull people to come in. But Sitting Bull had made a treaty with the half-breeds, and therefore, would not make any treaty with the trader at Fort Peck. Through this Indian I sent a note to the trader, telling him what these half-breeds had been doing, the amount of mischief they had done, and asking if it could not be stopped in some way.

The Yankton Indian returned to Fort Peck, and I think it was about two weeks before he came back again. When he did, some of the head men of the Yankton tribe came themselves to try and make a treaty with Sitting Bull. They brought me a letter from the agent, asking me to try and bring Sitting Bull in: if not, to come myself; that he wanted to see me. But in a council they had with these Yanktons, Sitting Bull had promised them he would go in. Sitting Bull always was hostile. He would not think of making a treaty with the whites. He was right on the war-path all the time, so far as the whites were concerned. A short time afterwards we started in — Sitting Bull, Little Assiniboine, Black Shield and his brother-in-law and myself. There were several of us. I can't think of all their names. Fort Peck was more of a trading post than an agency. We reached there the second day after we started. The second evening they rowed us over in boats and swam the horses over. There was nothing done that night between the whites and Indians, but I had an opportunity of having quite a long talk with the agent before going to bed, telling him everything that had occurred.

There was a plan on foot then to capture these half-breeds for trading whisky to the Indians. The agent asked me to go with the troops to identify these half-breeds. The next day a big council occurred. Sitting Bull flatly refused to treat or trade with the whites. We only stayed there a couple of nights and one day, and then started back to our camp.

In making my second visit to Fort Peck I had to get away from Sitting Bull without him knowing where I was going; so in order to fool him I told him I was going on the war-path to steal horses. He asked me if I was going by myself, and I told him I was. He wanted to know the direction I was going, and I told him up the Missouri some place, where I could find any thing that suited me to make a raid on.

I left camp after dark and rode all that night until the next day about noon, when I reached Fort Peck. I had to go there to get my letter to the commander of the troops that were to go with me. This Frenchman's creek, where these half-breeds were supposed to camp, was about ninety miles from Fort Peck. I had to go right up to Milk river, where Frenchman's creek empties into it. I met the troops at the mouth of Frenchman's creek, and we followed up Frenchman's creek to the forks of it, where the half-breeds were camped. There were just about one thousand of them. I went out with the troops through this camp, and picked out the men who had brought the whisky to Sitting Bull's camp. There were about one hundred of these half-breeds whom the troops arrested. They had a lot of others to arrest. They took their horses away from them and what whisky they could find. After everything was through with I told the commander that I would have to have three horses out of the captured animals to take back with me; that I didn't want to go empty-handed to Sitting Bull's camp. He told me to go and help myself; to pick out whatever I wanted.

I picked out three horses. Some Santee Indians were there, and they, of course, recognized me, telling the whole story later on to Sitting Bull. My trouble with Sitting Bull afterwards was through these Indians. I started back at daybreak. I rode pretty fast, for I was afraid some of the half-breeds would overtake and kill me. It took me three days to reach Sitting Bull's camp. When I got back to camp Sitting Bull saw

these horses and supposed that I had stolen them. I
told him I had. I told him to take his choice of any
of them he wanted, and I gave one to his sister and
one to his mother. He was tickled to death over it
—to think I had gone out and made this raid, and
told every Indian he met about it.

It was about ten days afterwards that two of the
Santee Indians came into camp along in the evening.
Of course, they went right to Sitting Bull's lodge and
told him the whole story about my being up there with
the troops. If you ever saw a mad Indian, he was
one. I never saw an Indian quite as mad as he was.
My being in his sister's lodge prevented me from being
killed right then and there. I don't think he would
have hesitated a minute in killing me if it had not
been for that. He asked me why I went; if I was
inclined towards the whites; what was my reason for
it, and told me that he should kill me.

As quick as this became known through the camp
the other faction that was not for killing me, came to
me and told me that they would stand by me. Of
course, there was only one thing for me to do; I had
either to kill Sitting Bull or be killed. That was the
way I looked at it. I had a gun and ammunition,
and I thought I would have as good a chance to kill
him as he to kill me; but his sister and mother prevented our coming together as much as they could while
I was at their lodge. The other faction wanted me to
go to their side of the village, but that I would not
do. Sitting Bull's mother wanted me to remain in

her lodge, saying her son would get over his anger. She was naturally a peacemaker, and told me not to pay any attention to the threats he made. She was a pretty good Indian woman. Every time the camp moved I would get on my horse and pull to one side, and Sitting Bull would go to the other side, and we never came together.

Indians are like average mortals. Some of them wanted to see the trouble between us urged on, and did everything they could to keep the fight going, while there were others who wanted to quiet it down.

CHAPTER XVI.

SEES CUSTER AND HEARS "GARRYOWEN."

Matters ran on that way until fall, when Custer's and Stanley's commands made a march through the Yellowstone followed by the Indians. I supposed the troops were after them, and the Indians were trying to flee from them. We went to the Yellowstone and crossed at the mouth of the Big Horn. While there we met the warriors of four other villages, that is — the Sans Arcs, Minneconjou, Ogallalas and Cheyennes.

We crossed the Yellowstone right in ahead of the soldiers, and could hear the military band playing. The soldiers expected to fight, and we were making preparations to protect the women and children if they should attack. I could distinctly hear the band playing. It was years since I had heard a band. They were playing Custer's favorite battle tune. That was "Garryowen." The other Indian village was camped on the Big Horn, about four miles up.

After we got all the children across, all the warriors of this other village came down to meet the troops for the purpose of fighting. That was the first fight I ever saw between the Indians and troops. The Indians were on one side of the river and the troops on the other. The troops could not get across, but the Indians could. The Indians swam across and fought the soldiers on the other side, on a kind of tableland there. It was just a running fight. I had a pretty fair scrap there myself. They were fighting on the other side, and I had got into the hills to look on. I didn't take any hand in the fight. I was back some distance from the river. There were lots of Indians there. The soldiers were throwing shells from there to the hill where we were. I got thirsty, standing on the hills watching them, and thought I would go down to the river and get a drink. It was across a big flat where I had to go. When I started they were fighting above on the other side of the river, and I thought I would not have any trouble in going down and getting a drink. Opposite me, about three hundred yards on the other side of the river, was a big bank, probably seventy-five feet high, where the river had washed into the bank and made a quarter circle around. I came right under this bank, got off my mule and went down to get a drink. While I was drinking I heard a kind of rattling noise, and, looking up, saw two companies of cavalry coming down to where I was drinking. I could not get down to my mule, as the soldiers commenced shooting as soon as they saw me. I ran for the trees. It was not over three hun-

dred yards, and I got behind one of those trees while
the two companies were shooting at me, and never got
touched. The mule, of course, stampeded and went back
into camp, so I just stayed there until the troops got
through fighting and went off. I didn't have any arms.
There was only one Indian killed during the fight, and
I heard there were a few soldiers killed.

CHAPTER XVII.

GROUARD MEETS CRAZY HORSE.

Shortly after we got back from this Custer fight, all the Indians in the four tribes found out about my trouble with Sitting Bull. There was an Indian in the Ogallala camp by the name of Little Hawk, an uncle to Crazy Horse, the latter one of the bravest of all the Sioux Indians. He sent for me and asked me how the trouble started, what I intended to do, and told me I had better come and stop in the Ogallala camp, which I did. I never went back to Sitting Bull's camp. I had never met Crazy Horse until this time. He was in the camp when I went in. There were several young bucks there, and he was among them. Crazy Horse had somewhat peculiar features. He had sandy hair, and was of a very light complexion. He didn't have the high cheek bones that the Indians generally have, and didn't talk much. He was a young looking Indian—appeared much younger than his age. There were a few powder marks on one side of his face. I stopped at the Ogallala village from that time on. The head men of the Ogallala village were Big Road, Little Hawk, He Dog and Crazy Horse, but the latter did not consider himself the chief. He generally attended the council or anything of that sort. The Black Twins were the most prominent Ogallalas. They were actually twins — were the most prominent among the older men in the village. I was there the rest of the time until 1875, close on to 1876. I never saw Sitting Bull again until 1875, when I went to him from Red Cloud to try to induce him to make a treaty with the whites about the Black Hills country. I had not left the Indians at that time, but had made up my mind to leave them. I was continually planning some scheme to get away after I had found out everything I wanted to know, and I was studying all spring how to get away without causing any trouble. I was with the Northern Indians, called the hostile Indians, and they never went into the agency, but the agency Indians would come to us. They were a kind of go-between. All our ammunition was supplied by these go-betweens.

CHAPTER XVIII.

From the time of my capture up to the year 1872 the Indians did not put me through any particularly painful ordeal. During the early part of that year, however, they constantly reminded me of the fact that I had never passed through any torture to prove my courage or fortitude. I did not know what to expect, and while I dreaded what I knew was inevitable, I found myself wishing they would make the test and free my mind of the suspense I suffered. I knew very well they would invent some means of making this test as excruciatingly painful as possible. It came soon enough. One day the whole village congregated around the sweat, and I was informed that I was to be put to the test. We were camped at that time on the Yellowstone, where Glendive, Montana, now stands. All the chiefs were present, and the ceremonies attending the sweat were gone through with. I was then laid on my back upon the ground, all the Indians gathering around and taking positions where they could watch the operations about to be performed. Sitting Bull sat near where I had been laid, smoking his pipe, and No Neck, Gall, Four Horns, Little Assiniboine and other head men were close to hand, anxious to see if I flinched under the ordeal.

I had no idea what torment and suffering I would be forced to undergo, but was not kept long in doubt. I made up my mind, however, that, if it were possible, no groans should escape my lips during the period of torture. The first thing done was to select four braves to operate upon me. They took positions upon each side of my body, and, with needles, raised up the flesh between the shoulder and elbow on each arm and cut out pieces about the size of a pea, taking four hundred and eighty pieces out of each arm. I did not mind it much at first; the cutting out, or off, of these pieces of flesh causing little pain. But the savages took the flesh off in five rows on each arm, and before they had finished the job I was suffering the agonies of the damned. The pain became so intense that it seemed to dart in streaks from the point where the small particles of flesh were cut off to every portion of my body, until at last a stream of untold agony was pouring back and forth from my arms to my heart. I managed to bear the pain, however, without a murmur, greatly to the delight of Sitting Bull and his faction.

The next operation consisted of pulling out, one at a time, my eyebrows, eyelashes and the hairs on my upper lip. After this, came the test of fire. They had prepared, by previous burning, several little cone-shaped blocks of peth from the stalk of a sunflower. These blocks were about half an inch in length, and very much resembled the pieces of punk the small boy uses on the fourth of July with which to light his firecracker. I know they hold fire a long while, at any rate. Well, they placed four of these blocks, half an inch apart, on my right wrist, and ignited them, and I lay there while the cruel fire burned down into my flesh, without giving any sign of the torture I was undergoing. When the fire had burned itself out—when the little blocks had been consumed—I was raised to my feet and shortly afterward put through the sweat, the Indians being satisfied that I was "good medicine," and would pass through any ordeal unflinchingly.

Five great ridges rose on my arm, and for a couple of months I could not bear the softest kind of fur to touch the half-raw spots. The ceremonies attending my tortures lasted four hours, but it seemed to me like a year. The Indians never again asked me to undergo further torture. Having put me through their severest ordeals, they were satisfied I could not be forced to weaken.

Late one fall we were camped near Pilot Butte, on the Missouri river, and our supply of food was very low; so low, in fact, that we were all very hungry. The slush ice was coming down the river, so that we were unable to cross the stream and get to where the buffalo fed, and it began to look as if we were in for a long stretch of starvation. The one great problem among the Indians was the securing of food. All other matters were of secondary consideration. One morning two fine buffaloes were seen to come down on the north side of the river opposite our camp. This sight was too much for us, and myself and two young bucks made up our minds that we would swim across the river and get the animals. We tied our ammunition pouches on top of our heads, fastened our guns to logs, and jumped into the angry stream, the entire village watching our movements.

We pushed the logs on which we had fastened our guns ahead of us while we swam, and at last reached the northern bank of the river. The current was very swift, and the sharp ice, rushing against our arms and breasts, cut great gashes in our flesh. We were covered with cuts and blood when we crawled out of the water; but we managed to keep our guns from being submerged, and they were ready for use as soon as loaded. We were not long in finding, killing, skinning and quartering the buffaloes, after which we made a raft, put the meat and our guns upon it, and once more trusted our lacerated bodies to the mercies of the ice-filled stream, arriving on the opposite bank after a terrible struggle.

The Indians were very thankful for the meat, and did everything in their power to alleviate our sufferings and make us comfortable; but it was many days before we were able to leave our tepis. The water in the river was as cold as the ice which floated in its current, and all three of us caught terrible colds; but the worst thing we had encountered was the ice itself, and its sharp, knife-like edges cut gashes in our bodies that were weeks in healing. It was a buffalo hunt under difficulties, and the Indians never tired of relating the story to their friends and acquaintances among the other tribes.

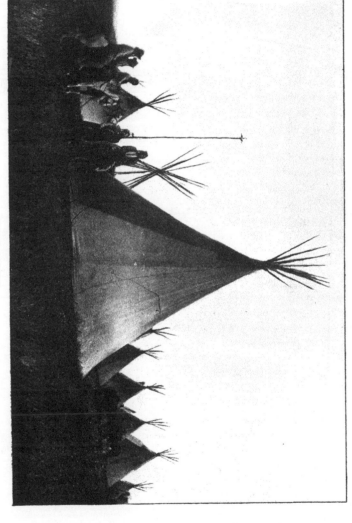

SIOUX LODGES.

During a trip I made that same year to the Big Wooded mountains in the British possessions in company with five Indians, we passed through the greatest herds of buffaloes I ever saw. We traveled over twelve hundred miles, and the country for four hundred miles of the distance was covered with thousands upon thousands of these animals. On this same trip I witnessed a big prairie fire and saw a stampede of wild horses. It was one of the most awe-inspiring sights I ever beheld, and it was a long time before the vividness of it died out of my mind. When we left the Indian village to take this trip our intention was to visit the country of the Blackfeet and run off a big band of their horses, but we became entangled in the swamps and were compelled to return.

CHAPTER XIX.

IN A RATTLESNAKE DEN.

During the year 1873 I did a great deal of hunting and running around. Early in the fall of that year our village was located between Beaver creek and the Yellowstone, and one day I had been out on a hunt and went up a divide over a game trail, and thought I would lie down and rest until the animals came down to water. A short distance from where I spread my blanket there was an immense ledge of rocks, rising some two or three hundred feet from the bottom of a deep gulch. I threw myself down on my blankets, and, being very tired, soon fell asleep. I don't know how long I had been asleep when I was aroused to partial consciousness by what I imagined was the whistling of the wind. I imagined that a big windstorm was in progress, and although I had nothing on but a gee-string, I was not conscious of any cold air blowing on my body, and soon fell asleep again. A second time I was partially awakened by this same sound. I remember that I pulled the end of the blanket over me and fell back into sleep. You see I had not opened my eyes at all, as I was not fully awake on either occasion when I thought I heard this wind blowing. But the third time that the noise aroused me I awoke with a terrible start, and, opening my eyes, glanced hastily around. I was completely surrounded by rattlesnakes, and, to my startled vision, there seemed to be fully a million of them. Some of them were nearly close enough to strike me, and all of them were coiled up as if ready to make an attack. To this day I do not know how I got out of that nest of writhing, rattling reptiles. I must have made jumps that would have put long distance champions to the blush. I do not think I ever was worse frightened in all my life. If I had not been awakened the snakes would undoubtedly have attacked me. As it was, I considered I had made a pretty lucky escape, and I waited around for about an hour, until the snakes disappeared, before I went back on the divide to get my blanket and gun.

When I returned to the village I told some of the Indians about my adventure, and described the place where it had occurred, and they informed me that in the high ledge of rocks was a famous rattlesnake den, and that thousands of the reptiles were secreted there. Quite a party of us visited the place afterwards and examined the ledge. I don't know how many snakes we killed, but the more we dispatched the more seemed to come out from between the crevices in the rocks, and as we did not care to waste all our ammunition on such game, we left the snakes in possession of their stronghold and returned to camp. I dreamed of rattlesnakes for three months afterwards, and never run across one of that specie but what I think of the time when I lay upon the divide surrounded by enough of them to start a full-fledged rattlesnake farm.

CHAPTER XX.

In his natural state the Indian was probably the most independent being on the face of the earth. His wants were few and easily satisfied. From his standpoint, the influences of civilization were detrimental and demoralizing. He recognized no temporal power superior to his own will, and breathed an air of freedom no other race on earth enjoyed. There was no landlord to torment him; no interest-hunting money shark to demand a pound of flesh or his soul. He measured the length of the day by the sun, the night by the moon. So many nights were so many sleeps; the months and years were moons and snows. Yesterday and today were time; tomorrow, eternity. He was the uncrowned monarch of the western hemisphere. He feasted when it pleased him, and fasted according to the traditions of his race. Bound in by no saucy doubts and fears, he paid no heed to the flight of time, and welcomed dissolution as the key to eternal happiness in the Hunting Grounds of the Great Spirit. He had no cares beyond the satisfying of his daily wants.

He knew that somewhere, and at some time, in the dim past, his people dwelt together in one mighty family;

but there had been a confusion of tongues—a great up-
heaval of some kind that had divided the nations into
seven tribes.   Tradition taught him of the future less
than the past—both were obscured.   Experience was his
school.   He had genius, because he was inventive ; reverence, because he worshiped a power superior to his own ;
affection, because he loved ; passion, because he was re-
vengeful.   He lived by the code of his nation, and within
that code there was no crime.   He might disobey a rule
or break a law, but he could not commit crime, because
crime was unknown to the council.   He worshiped God
in his dances, in his games, in his hunts, in his sweats,
in his feasts and in his wars.   He never lit the pipe or
bent the bow or sacrificed the victim but he did so in
accordance with religious tradition.   He lived, he loved,
he hated, and, with hope of immortality, he died.   Who
shall say that he did *not* fulfill the purposes for which
an all-wise Creator fashioned him — gave to his savage
soul the self-same spark of Divinity which He bestows
on all mankind !   There are problems of earth, and
problems of heaven.   The savage is the problem of
Deity.

The sweat is one of the greatest institutions known
to the Indian.   It is always built by the side of a
stream, and generally near a deep hole capable of permitting the submerging of the body.   The sweat is very
simple in construction.   A wickiup (or hut) made from
willows stuck in the ground and bent over in circular
form and fastened at the top, is first put together.   In
the center of this a shallow place is scooped out of the

ground. A fire is built on the outside of the sweat, and in it a number of large cobble stones are thoroughly heated, and are then rolled into the hut and put into the receptacle in the centre. Next the hut is covered with robes and blankets and made as perfectly air-tight as possible. Buckets of water are carried inside, blankets are drawn tight and the bather proceeds to pour the liquid on the hot stones. The result can be imagined. No Russian bath in the world can approach the Indian sweat. When the bather has steamed himself to his heart's content, he pulls aside the blankets, runs naked to the creek and jumps into the cool water — the "plunge" of the white man.

The Indians lay great store by this bath, and very correctly, too. Whenever sickness overtakes them they repair to the bath. It is the best of all nature's known remedies for rheumatism. Nobody ever saw a wild Indian afflicted with the gout, sciatica or rheumatism — the bath is as much a preventive as a cure. Before dancing, feasting, going upon the warpath or chase, in fact, before any and all ceremonials, the Indian takes the sweat. It is a part of his religious worship, and he prays and sweats at one and the same time. The Indian has three methods of treating disease — incantation, herb teas and poultices and the sweat, the latter taking precedence in nearly all cases. His knowledge of the medicinal properties of herbs is simply marvelous, and great prices are charged and paid (in horses) for certain curative leaves by the friends of sick savages. Nearly every Indian knows of some particular herb whose use is efficacious in some particular case, but here his knowledge generally ends. It sometimes happens (as it did once among the Sioux when Grouard was with them) that smallpox or cholera attacks some member of the tribe and spreads with alarming rapidity and disastrous results before the right herb can be secured to cure the patient and check the epidemic. In such times, any price demanded by the medicine men is freely given for the needed specific. In cases of burns, snake bites and other wounds, the savages have roots and grasses they apply at once, generally chewing the grass or weed before applying it, and oftentimes using nothing but the juice of the herb spat from the mouth upon the wound. Their mode of extracting bullets from the body or limbs is by massage treatment, in which they are eminently successful. They never use a probe, and never amputate a limb. Grouard says he never saw a one-legged or one-armed Indian during the whole time of his captivity.

It is but fair to state that no city in the world is more completely under the control of its chosen officers than were the villages of the Sioux tribes. In the first place there was a Supreme Council, composed of the hereditary chiefs of the nation. Their places were vacated by death only, and filled by succession alone. Upon all matters touching the good of the tribe or village, the decision of this body was final and binding. This was called the Circle of Silence, and its fires were lit and burned in secret. None but the elect were ever permitted to enter its presence, and in the entire Sioux nation its membership did not number above one hundred. This Circle represented the Masonry of the aborigine. It had its signs, its grips, its passwords and its unwritten law, and its influence was far-reaching and absolute.

The assertion has often been made, and never denied, that Masonic rites are practiced by the savages of every clime, and there is no good reason why this should not be so. Certain it is that the Circle of Silence was the one and only exclusive society known among the Sioux, notwithstanding the fact that several other secret societies flourished in the Sioux nation for over eight hundred years. These latter societies were three in number, and were known as the Strong Hearts, Badgers and Dog Soldiers. The duties of these latter societies, so far as their relation to the village was concerned, was to carry out any and all orders promulgated by the Supreme Council. Whenever the village was moved, a majority of those representing the Circle of Silence took precedence in the march, while the Brave Hearts and Badgers flanked the moving village, and the Dog Soldiers brought up the rear. In all the Indian ceremonials this order of priority and honor was observed. The buffalo hunt, preparations for which were attended by every traditional ceremony, invariably demanded the recognition of the rights of the societies.

Serious results followed the disobedience of the supreme council's propagandas. When it was suspected that an enemy was in close proximity to the village, an order would be issued by the council that no gun should be fired unless at the foe. This order was issued to the

Strong Hearts, who thereby became responsible to the council for its proper observance. The Strong Hearts in turn issued its orders to the Badgers that the village be warned of the danger. The Badgers then became responsible to the Strong Hearts for the faithful performance of the duty entrusted to it. The Badgers thereupon notified the Dog Soldiers of the decree, and the latter immediately sent out its trusted "criers" to carry out the order. Thus it will be seen that the order of the Council passed successively through three responsible organizations before it found its way to the people of the village, and each society was directly responsible to the one next higher in authority for the proper discharge of its duty. Governmental "red tape" could not be more exacting than this. Time was sacrificed to certainty. Should the order of the Circle of Silence not to fire a gun be disobeyed, the Dog Soldiers, who were the active agents of the Council, would seize the offender's gun and destroy it. If the order were for no brave to leave the village, and one stole out, he would be followed till captured, when his horses would be killed and his blankets cut up. For graver offenses, the culprit's lodge would be destroyed and sometimes his life taken. But it was seldom that any damage was done to the property of a brave that was not at once repaired. In case of death through carrying out an order of the Council, the dead brave's family were generally made wards of the nation.

Grouard states positively that members of the Circle of Silence could gain admission in safety to hostile camps at times when it was worth a man's life to go within shooting distance of the enemy's village. No matter if an hereditary chief were eligible to membership in the Circle, he could not gain admittance to it until he attained his thirtieth year. Visiting members were always received in a brotherly manner, and feted and otherwise royally entertained while they remained.

There is still another feature of village government worthy of attention. The inhabitants of the village were divided into clans, and these were in turn ruled by one or more chiefs. These clans comprised the relatives and adherents of certain chiefs, who shared all his misfortunes and conquests. In the Sioux village, when Grouard was still in captivity, these clans were two in number, being the Big Bellies, under immediate control of Big Nose, and the Sitting Bull, with Four Horns and Black Kettle as governors. The leaders of the different clans were always members of the Circle of Silence, so there was no danger of a clash of authority, besides which the scope of these leaders' authority extended only to the actual family life of its members.

This order of things has always been coexistent with the Sioux tribal relation, and it may be the key to solve the problem of Indian discontent and misunderstanding of government control of the redmen at the various agencies. We have too long viewed the Indian as being devoid of understanding and incapable of advancement. We have not paused to consider that the great lessons of civilization must be learned by the savage through the forgetting of those traditions which are a part of his natural self. In fact, he must first unlearn all he has acquired from savagery before he can be taught to appreciate (if he ever can) the manifold blessings and advantages of our riper civilization. There are two sides to the question: We consider only what civilization gains through the Indian's conversion; he realizes merely what he loses in his transformation.

The male aborigine is not so averse to clothing but what he will wear it; but it must be on state occasions and for ornament only. From his infancy he is accustomed to seeing the bucks about the camp in a condition bordering onto nudity and appearing at social gatherings and during religious festivals in the same condition. Nobody seems to know where the savage caught his first idea of a breech-clout, or as it is more commonly known, "gee-string." At best, it is but a slight improvement on the fig-leaf covering used by the man and woman who are said to have partaken of the forbidden fruit in the Garden of Eden; but inasmuch as it is satisfactory to the savage idea of a full-dress suit, and is custom more honored in the "breech" than the observance, the white man has no particular occasion to inquire too pertinently into its origin. It must not be inferred from this that the Indian has no love for dress, but he dresses more from a desire to ornament himself than to hide his nakedness. He considers the paint on his face, body and limbs just as essential to his proper appearance as the white man does his collar and cuffs and patent leather shoes.

The savage never seems so happy as when togged out in a costume composed of odds and ends and com-

AN INDIAN COURIER

AN INDIAN COURIER

prising a heterogeneous mixture of colors. He appears at some great society gathering of the tribe or participates in one of the dances arrayed like Solomon in all his glory. He struts about like a peacock—the observed of all observers—and is immensely proud of the attention he attracts. He would never think of going on the war-path with his best suit of clothes on, but lays it carefully in his lodge for use at his funeral if his medicine proves to be bad or if he falls beneath the tomahawk 'or is killed by the arrow or bullet of his enemy. At all times, summer and winter, the Indian believes in giving protection to his feet, and he is never found barefooted. In the winter season a buffalo robe 'or a heavy blanket forms sufficient body covering to exclude the winter's blasts.

He can not be induced to wear a hat or cap, and, unless he desires to hide his identity or conceal his face, his head knows no other covering than the one which nature provided—his hair—which, though course, is generally abundant and of luxuriant length. The Indian takes great pride in his hair, and spends no little time in plaiting it into braids and ornamenting it with shells and fancy-colored pieces of ribbon or cloth, and such other gewgaws as may please him. He is always fantastic in ornamentation, and dresses his hair with particular care for the council, the dance, the feast and the war-path.

The children are considered dressed when their hair is plaited, and they run about the camp at will with no other garments than "their happy looks." In their play they mingle with each other as do the children of the whites, intercourse between them being unrestricted until arriving at an age when precaution is made necessary, even among the savages. The women, as a rule, wear covering for their bodies, and some of their dresses are said by many æsthetic people to be "dreams." They are as vain in this regard as many of their white sisters. A favorite garment among the squaws is a waist, made of any material, but generally tanned buckskin, ornamented with the teeth of the elk, and the author has seen waists of this description having as many as three hundred and fifty elk teeth fastened upon it. They wear moccasins richly embroidered and elegantly worked, and wear skirts made from skins or blankets, which fall below the knee. Like the lords of their lives and liberty, they have no regulation head-gear except the end of a blanket. As they are totally unprotected from assault, or at least were while enjoying tribal relation, they had a custom of "roping" their bodies, but not to such an extent as would interfere with free locomotion. On all occasions of festivity or solemn deliberation, the bucks adorn their bodies and cover their heads with the most fantastic garments and bonnets imaginable, many of their war bonnets being both artistic and beautiful.

Thieving among the Indians is reduced to a science, and in recounting his coups it is a proud boast of the warrior that he has stolen horses and women and children from his enemy. With them theft is one of the highest accomplishments; yet, strange as it may seem, thieving is almost unknown among men and women belonging to the same tribe. In fact, Indians belonging to the same tribe seldom if ever steal from each other. Cases of this kind do happen occasionally, but the consequences are very serious, and summary punishment is visited upon the thief. If a buck steals from his neighbor the stolen property is taken from him and returned to its rightful owner, and the thief, after suffering all the indignities that can be heaped upon him, is, with his wife and children, cast out of the village and never permitted to return. His horses and dogs are killed, his tepi and blankets cut up, his cooking utensils destroyed and he is literally thrust out of the camp to find shelter where he can. Cases have occurred where the buck's life has been taken, but these are not plentiful. In case the thief is a squaw, she is soundly whipped and turned out of the camp, but her husband and children are left in possession of all the property which rightfully belongs to them. While, therefore, it will be seen that the Indian may steal the goods and chattels of his enemy and be applauded for the act, the theft of ever so small an article from a neighbor will call down upon his head the displeasure of his people and the direst punishment.

The religion of the aborigine is very peculiar. In the first place he believes in one Controlling Force, which he denominates the Great Spirit. He does not try to reason out the power of this spirit, but he places it above and beyond all other spirits. He believes in a Good Spirit and also in a Bad Spirit, but does not think they have any connection with each other. He recognizes the heavens as his father, the earth as mother.

If anything goes wrong with his plans, or if anything happens to thwart the accomplishment of his purposes, he attributes it to the Bad Spirit, and attempts in every possible way to propitiate it, oftentimes dedicating one or more ponies to it.   And as this act is made known to other members of the tribe, these ponies are forever after held sacred to the Bad Spirit, and no other Indian, no matter how much he might feel inclined to possess the animals, would dare touch them for fear of bringing down upon himself the displeasure of the Bad Spirit.   All his success he attributes to the Good Spirit.   In his prayers he appeals to the spirit of whatever he chooses, be the object animate or inanimate.   Each individual is left to his own choice of gods, and while the Indians can not be called idolators, they believe that the spirit of an ant has as much power to grant their requests as the spirit of anything else.   In this way they worship anything and everything they see.

The Indian's idea of the future state is, to the average mind, a very confusing one.   He believes implicitly in the existence of the Happy Hunting Grounds, but he does not seem to have any idea of any set order of things there.   He believes that the souls of those who enter that place appear there as they appeared here; that the young never grow old, that the aged never grow young.   And yet, all are happy.   He does not try to reason out how the decrepit man or woman, bent with age and suffering with disease, can be happy at any time or in any place.   Tradition has taught him that they are happy, and this is enough to satisfy him of its truth. He has a confused idea of a trip from his earthly home to the Happy Hunting Grounds, but does not seem to care to know how long the trip lasts, or whether he goes on horseback or on foot. He merely believes that when the breath leaves his body his soul at once starts for the Indian heaven and arrives there in some manner and at some time. He has been appealed to by several Christian denominations to throw aside this "unsatisfactory belief" for the more substantial doctrines of a higher faith, and in some instances has accepted the religion of the white man; but in nearly all cases, when sickness or misfortune comes upon him and he would seek consolation from a higher power than man's, he forsakes his new faith for the old. His reliance upon the Great Spirit of his fathers is thus shown to be perfect. So, as we have remarked elsewhere, civilization may have done something for the redman, but, in the light of all the facts, not much.

From his earliest years the Indian is taught that his success rests upon the kind of medicine he makes. Each individual, in making medicine, adds some ingredient that forever remains a secret between himself and his gods. This secret ingredient he carries in a little buckskin bag attached to his person, generally by a string about the neck, and, at his death, ingredient and bag are buried with him, nobody attempting to discover the dead man's secret. When he desires to discover his secret ingredient and make medicine, he goes to some lofty peak or lonely spot, and generally remains there from three to six days, tasting neither food nor drink. He repeats his prayers to the Good Spirit until he has worked himself into a delirium or falls asleep from sheer exhaustion. In his dreams the ingredient which shall forever remain his, is revealed to him. He then returns to his village, mixes his medicine and tries its efficacy. If the result is good, he is satisfied that his plans have not been interfered with by the Bad Spirit, and is contented. If, on the other hand, his plans miscarry and disaster overtakes him, he is fully persuaded that the Bad Spirit had a hand in making his medicine, and he forthwith proceeds to work himself into the good graces of the Good Spirit, has another dream, procures another ingredient, mixes his medicine, and so on ad libitum.

The Indian is taught early in life that he must never allow himself to be surprised at anything, as to be surprised is to be stampeded. Therefore if an Indian is actually surprised and thereby suffers defeat, he is cute enough to attribute it to some other cause foreign to the actual cause; otherwise he would lose caste with his people and be considered no better than a squaw.

The Indians were lavish in their love for their little children. Especially was this the case with the fathers. Wives were esteemed by their husbands in proportion to the number of children they bore them. The Indian father's greatest pride was in his sons. He was invariably kind to all his children. He allowed the mother full and absolute control over the girls until they arrived at a marriageable age, when custom gave him super-

THREE YOUNG SIOUX BRAVES.

THREE YOUNG SIOUX BRAVES.

vision. And as the girls were "marketable," the buck grew in wealth according to the esteem in which his daughter's suitors held her. It resolved itself into a matter of barter and trade; a sale outright wherein the daughter had no voice.

So much were little children thought of by the Indians, however, that the waif and foundling were unknown among them. In their tender age they probably received as much care as do the children of the whites, and very early in life entered into serious occupations. The boys were taught to handle bow and arrow as soon as they were big enough to walk. Some of the girls were adepts at fancy bead work. In their fifth or sixth year they began an apprenticeship to a life of drudgery and were never freed from its fetters. They were slaves to time-honored custom, however, and it is not to be presumed that they were unhappy with their lots. Marriage divorced them from the rigid rule of parents, and if they were not satisfied with their life partners they very easily induced some kind-hearted brave to elope with them.

Boys were never punished by the mother and seldom by the father. They had pretty much their own way in everything and ruled the lodge with an iron hand. As soon as they arrived at an age that fitted them for the war-path, they stole horses enough to purchase them a wife or in some other way managed to set up establishments of their own. Some of the most atrocious outrages ever committed on the frontier were perpetrated by the fledgling warriors, anxious to receive instant recognition for their bravery and daring at the hands of the council.

Indian boys were given what are called their family names by their fathers, but as the child grew to manhood he was permitted to re-name himself, if some member of the tribe had not given him a nickname that was distinctive and characteristic enough to stick to him. Thus the overcoming of a foe by a young brave, or the killing of some wild animal, or some other circumstance, might suggest a name which the young man adopted or was given, and which was liable to cling to him throughout his life, regardless of his family name. Indians often joined colors to the names of birds or animals and in this manner caught a combination that was striking and fitting. The mothers named the girls, and it must be admitted that they usually showed better judgment and taste in this regard than the fathers.

When the young buck has attained the age of ten or twelve, he turns his attention to the accomplishment of some feat that will rebound to his glory and give him a place among the braves and warriors. The stealing of a horse from an enemy is a great victory; the touching of an enemy's body with a coup stick reflects honor upon the victor, and the taking of a scalp brings to the brave the unstinted approbation of the entire tribe. The Indian believes that no soul can enter the Happy Hunting Grounds if the body has been mutilated, and scalping forever precludes the possibility of reaching happiness in the next world. It is also written in their faith, that those whom they slay here will become their slaves in the hereafter. Therefore they often refrain from scalping or otherwise mutilating a victim, in order to insure his safe entrance to the Happy Hunting Grounds, where he must forever remain the slave of the victor. The redmen did not believe a paleface ever reached the Indian heaven.

Chieftancy among the wild men formerly meant nothing more nor less than absolutism. The head chief was not chosen, but held his office by sublime right. The son succeeded the father. Nor was it always the eldest son, but the one whom the father chose in youth for qualities that fitted him to rule. The chief was a law unto himself, and his right to dispense or withhold favor or justice was never questioned. He, like the other members of his tribe, took unto himself as many wives as pleased his fancy or he wanted to support, and when one failed to suit him, or for any other reason became incongenial, he sold or disposed of her, sometimes killing her. He was subject to but one power or influence—the Circle of Science, or Supreme Council. He was not called upon, because of his chieftancy, to lead in battle, unless he was, by common consent, the acknowledged war chief of the tribe. Age, bodily infirmity or want of disposition to enter battle, were sufficient reasons for his remaining in camp during the progress of a fight. As a rule, however, the head (or hereditary) chief was a warrior, who scorned to shirk any responsibility or danger, and led his braves in all actions when circumstances permitted.

The war chief of the tribe, where the functions of that office were not monopolized by the hereditary chief, was elected by the tribe or appointed by the council.

He was generally the most ferocious warrior in the tribe ; one in ·whom everybody had great confidence. His medicine was always good and his valor unquestioned.

The "medicine man" or chief was a very dignified individual, and held in great awe and reverence. Sometimes he secured his office by election, sometimes by appointment, but more often by assumption. When by the latter method he was compelled to be ready to prove during battle the efficacy of his medicine, and was thus forced to rush head-long into dangers that he might otherwise have escaped. He was high priest and doctor at the same time, and if called in the latter capacity and declared against the chances for recovery of the patient, the sick man's friends immediately began preparations for the funeral.

The sub-chiefs owed their rise from the ranks to their own prowess and the kindly consideration of the council. They held sway, one over the other, by the estimation in which they were themselves held. While being recognized as head warriors they enjoyed no immunities that were not shared by every other male member of the tribe.

The pipe figured in each and every Indian ceremonial. When lit in council or during religious rites, or when used at dances or feasts, it passed from left to right, and never from right to left. It was usual for the chief or warrior lighting the pipe to offer to some particular spirit the first draught of smoke, and the stem of the pipe was then held toward the different points of the compass, the sun, moon, stars, or any object to which the holder of the pipe desired to offer homage. This little ceremony was never omitted. Before passing the pipe to the neighbor on his left, each Indian inhaled as much smoke as his lung cavity permitted, and the smoke was afterward expelled at the buck's pleasure. Indians invariably inhale the smoke, and are inordinately fond of tobacco. They used different pipes at the different ceremonials, and would scorn to sanction the use of the council pipe in any other place or on any other occasion.

The Indian found his greatest amusement in dancing, and during the winter months the village was a scene of constant jollity and excitement. The fall hunts being over, and plenty of game having been provided for the winter season, the long months were whiled away in terpsichorean and matrimonial pleasures. It has been said that the Sioux were a nation of dancers, a statement that will not admit of a doubt. They had no less than half a dozen different kinds of dances, none of which partook of the religious character of the sun dance. In these amusements the squaws were permitted to take part. No dance was complete unless accompanied with a feast. It is safe to say, therefore, that the Indian in his native state enjoyed life about as thoroughly as do his civilized brothers.

The sun dance, the scalp dance and the ceremony known as "striking the post" (which is often called the war dance by the whites) are the serious dances of the Sioux.

The sun dance is a purely religious ceremony, or a series of ceremonies, and was made in fulfillment of promises to the sun when danger was encountered or battles expected. In fact, if any wish were near to the Indian's heart, and its consummation was beset by extraordinary danger, he would make a vow to the sun to give a dance if he were successful in the accomplishment of his purpose. And inasmuch as the average Indian always had some wish to gratify, the sun dance was indulged in very frequently by the aborigine. This dance generally lasted three days, and sometimes resulted in the death of one or more of the participants, who underwent the most excruciating torture during the time the ordeal lasted. In case a death occurred during the dance, ceremonies were at once suspended, as it was believed that the Bad Spirit prevailed, and that some other time would have to be selected when the Good Spirit would be present and countenance the ceremonies.

At these dances the head medicine man directed everything, and was in absolute control. In former times, torture was a condition of manhood, and through it the buck obtained entrance into the ranks of the warriors. Some of these self-inflicted tortures were horrible to contemplate, but were born with that stoical indifference to pain so characteristic of the American savage. The temples in which the sun dances were held were built in circular form, the centre being reserved for the erection of a pole and the participants in the dance. From the top of this high centre pole horse-hair ropes were suspended, and one of the favorite methods of torture was

PREPARING FOR THE OMAHA DANCE.

for the warrior to have incisions made on both sides of his breast, the cuts averaging four inches in length by two inches in width. The flesh between this incision and the bone was then lifted, and underneath this was passed the horse-hair rope, on the end of which was fastened a stout piece of stick to hold it in its place. The warrior would then throw himself backward and forward for hours and sometimes days and nights in his endeavors to break lose from the fetters which bound him.

If dancing and his struggles did not effect his release, he would oftentimes be pulled into the air, and some of his friends would add the weight of their bodies to his own, in order to aid him in securing his release. When once free from the rope he would pass for treatment into the hands of the medicine chief, and from thence to his admirers. Sometimes incisions were made in the muscles of the back, ropes passed beneath the flesh, and heavy weights tied to the end of the ropes, and thus the weights were dragged about the enclosure by the warrior until the flesh had been torn out. During the period of torture the temple would be filled with excited people urging the braves on with all sorts of expressions and terms of endearment.

The favorite mode of burial among the Sioux was to build a platform high up in the stout limbs of a tree and deposit the dead thereon, placing on and beside the body the dead man's finery, guns, ammunition and accoutrements—in fact, all those articles which he used during life, that could not be fashioned by the Indian himself—the belief being that all these things were necessary for his well-being in the Happy Hunting Grounds. Food was hung about the body in the branches of the trees, fresh supplies being added from time to time. After being deposited upon the platform, the body was covered with furs, and over all was stretched a green buffalo hide, if it could be secured, and fastened with thongs made from the hide or intestines of some animal. Nearly all the head chiefs of the Sioux were buried in this manner, as were also many of the warriors and children; but where such burial was impracticable, four stakes were driven into the ground and a platform erected thereon and the body placed on it. Among some of the other tribes, bodies of the dead were laid away in gulches and crevices. The season of mourning among the Sioux was a matter left entirely at the option of the dead brave's wives and relatives, whose show of grief at the grave, and sometimes for months afterwards, would have been a revelation to the professional mourners among civilized people.

CHAPTER XXI.

SAVED BY A PONY.

Among the Indians no sport or excitement could equal a buffalo hunt. There was considerable danger in it, but nothing to compare with the excitement and joy. Every brave kept a trained pony for the buffalo chase — one that was used for nothing else — and the intelligence of some of those animals was wonderful. I really believe the ponies enjoyed a buffalo hunt as keenly as did their masters. When I became possessed of my first buffalo pony the Indian from whom I got it told me of all its good qualities, and laid particular stress upon the fact that the animal always gave warning of approaching danger. I paid little attention to the buck's talk at the time, but it was very distinctly recalled on an occasion I am about to speak of.

The Bark creek country, along the Yellowstone river, was a great feeding ground for the buffaloes, and one season we moved our camp down there. Our supply of meat had got very light, and we also wanted robes with which to make lodges. We killed a great many buffaloes during our stay in that locality, and were about ready to move. It was decided to have one more hunt before

leaving, and preparations were made accordingly.   The
buffaloes had drifted some distance from our camping
ground, and the Indians were in the habit of moving
camp from day to day as the chase progressed.   When
we started off in the last hunt the entire camp went
along, and as soon as the herd of buffaloes was sighted
the bucks jumped upon their ponies and began the
chase.

On this particular occasion I became so intent upon
running the buffaloes that I got a long way in advance
of the other hunters.   I killed a couple of buffaloes and
got off my horse to skin them, fastening my pony to
the carcass of one of the dead animals.   While I was
at work my pony began to act strangely.   It would
run around in a half circle, then back again, and
seemed to be trying to attract my attention.   I paid no
particular heed to the actions of the pony until I recalled what its former owner had told me about its
giving warning of danger, when I untied it, jumped
upon its back and rode up on a hill to see if anything
unusual was occurring.   Seeing nothing, I returned to
my work.   The pony began to caper about worse than
ever, and I finally became so nervous and frightened that
I left the two buffaloes and started back to where we had
left the pack animals.   I had not gone over two miles
before I heard shooting, and glancing over my shoulder
in the direction from which I had come, I saw a large
party of Crow warriors charging down onto our people.
I gave the alarm as quickly as I could, but before the
Sioux braves could get together the enemy had killed

nineteen of them and departed. My pony had sniffed the danger while I was skinning the buffaloes, but I failed to find the least sign of the attacking party, and supposed my animal was restless at being separated from the rest of the pony herd. If it had not been for the actions of the pony I would have been caught in a nice trap and lost my life. From that time on I always kept a sharp lookout, and if my pony gave any signs that there was danger in the air, I heeded him.

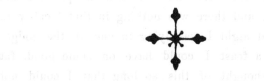

CHAPTER XXII.

ESTABLISHING A REPUTATION.

One winter we were camped on the Belle Fourche, and our supply of meat had run so low that starvation began staring us in the face. The snows had been so continuous and deep and the weather so cold that we were completely locked in. We had eaten up everything — even the dogs. Nothing was left but the ponies, and the Indians would not kill them. So we packed up and started off toward the buffalo grounds. Arriving at the Little Powder river we went into camp. We had nothing to eat, and there was nothing in that locality to hunt. Toward night I was lying in one of the lodges thinking what a feast I could have on some good, fat deer ribs. I thought of this so long that I could not get it out of my mind, and I went out and caught up my mule. The Indians asked me where I was bound for. I told them I was going to hunt something to eat, and was not coming back until I got it. I took my mule and started out, traveling the biggest part of the night to where I thought would be a good place to find game. I tied my mule up and started a fire and waited for daylight. As soon as it became light enough for me to see,

I got on my mule and started out on a search for game. I had not gone far before I ran onto a big elk trail that had been made the evening before, and I did not quit the trail until I reached the elk. It must have been nine or ten o'clock before I overtook them. As soon as I discovered them I tied my mule up and stripped myself, and taking nothing but my gun and ammunition pouches, started to get in the lead of the herd, which I finally did after running about three miles. Having accomplished this much, I fixed myself in such a way that I could watch them as they passed me, so that I could pick out the fattest one in the herd. Watching them for a few minutes as they passed by, and picking out one that I thought was the fellow I wanted, I shot it. But instead of the animals running after hearing the report of the gun, as they generally do, the elk gathered in a bunch, and this gave me a chance to kill thirty-one of them before they got away from me. After I had finished shooting them I went back to the place where I had left my mule and brought it down to the place where I had killed the elk, and cut up the slaughtered animals. Picking out the four best ones, I laid them to one side for my own use. After I got through, I loaded as much as I could onto my mule, and got up on top of the meat and started for camp. As soon as I came in sight of the village, some one gave the signal that I was coming in with a load of game, and before I reached the camp the squaws got every piece of meat there was on the mule; so by the time I reached my lodge I had nothing left. I told them that if they would get on their horses

early next morning and go over to where I had killed
the thirty-one elk, they could get all the meat they wanted.
The next morning every Indian in the camp was on hand
with his pony, and it was but a short while before we
had more meat than we knew what to do with. At any
rate, we had more than enough to last us until we arrived
at the feeding grounds of the buffaloes. From that day to
the time I left the Indians, they put great faith in me as
a hunter; and as I was passionately fond of hunting
game, and desirous of learning all I could of the country
at the same time, I not only gained a big reputation as
a nimrod, but acquired a thorough knowledge of all the
Indians' haunts, which was of great service to me in years
afterwards when I was on the plains with the soldiers.
I can say without boasting that there was not a canyon,
river, crag or creek in that great domain that I was not
more familiar with than with my own history; and as
many of the former game and Indian trails were afterwards utilized as highways, I needed nothing to guide me
when with the troops but the old familiar landmarks.

I went over the ground so many times that I fairly
carried a map of the country in my mind, and could
close my eyes and travel along and never miss a cut-off
or a trail. Night or day, light or dark, it made no difference to me; I always knew where I was and where I
was going. Gen. Crook once asked me if I knew every
rock in the country, and I don't think I misstated a fact
when I answered that I came pretty near it. From the
Platte river to the British possessions, and from the
Black Hills to the Big Wind range of mountains, the

country was an open book to me.   No Indian in the
Sioux or any other nation had a more intimate acquaintance with the mountains, rivers, trails and game grounds
in the country above mentioned than I possessed in
1876, or possess at the present time.

CHAPTER XXIII.

"THE WAY OF THE TRANSGRESSOR."

On one occasion two Indians and myself were selected by the council and sent out to locate a buffalo
herd. We were to follow up the Rosebud and cross
over the Little Big Horn to the divide between the Big
Horn and the Little Big Horn rivers. Whenever the
Indians send members of the tribe out preparatory to a
hunt, they are supposed only to locate and not kill the
game, and report results to the council. We went on
and reached the divide between the two rivers. On
reaching there we could hear the buffaloes very distinctly,
but could not see them. The latter part of July and
during August is the buffalo "running" season, and the
bulls make such a noise that you can hear them for
twenty miles. By putting your ear to the ground you
can hear them further than that. On reaching the divide
we could hear the buffaloes so plain that we thought there
was no use in going any further, as we could report on
our return that there were plenty of buffaloes in that
vicinity; but while we were sitting there resting ourselves, a buffalo bull and cow came across the flat. They
were right in below us, and we were so hungry for buf-

falo meat that we thought it would be a good idea to kill one of them and take what meat we could back to where we expected to camp that night.

I, being the best shot of the three, was asked to go down and shoot the buffalo. The animals being at some distance, I crawled down to the flat, and secreted myself in a place where I thought I was close enough to get a good shot at them as they passed. Shooting as they got opposite me, I hit the cow, breaking its back and killing it almost instantly. After awhile the bull began to sniff at the body of the dead cow, and as soon as it got a smell of the fresh blood seemed to go perfectly crazy. It ran around the cow's carcass, pawing the ground and giving vent to the most terrible sounds. I lay perfectly quiet and watched, knowing if I made a move the bull would see and attack me, and, if it did, nothing would prevent my being torn into ribbons or stamped and trampled into a jelly. For fully an hour the infuriated bull stood over the dead body of the cow. I thought that if I could load my gun and get one chance I could shoot the brute, and I did manage to pour a charge of powder from the flask into the palm of my hand; but the moment I tried to empty it into my gun the bull spied me, and with head almost dragging the ground and tail sticking straight up in the air, it came rushing madly toward me.

I had to think and act mighty quickly. Behind where I had been lying I noticed a washout, about three feet deep, and into this place I threw myself just as the snorting, bellowing beast reached the edge of it. The bull was so close that I actually felt its warm breath on my body as I fell into the washout. Being unable to reach me with its head, the animal stood over the place where I lay and pawed up the earth in its mad fury. Almost paralyzed with fear and unable to help myself, I could do nothing but remain perfectly quiet and wait until the bull became exhausted or left the spot.

After what seemed hours to me, the animal went back to the place where the dead cow lay, and I made a second attempt to load my gun. But the bull saw my movement and was back upon me in a twinkling. I had time, however, to crawl further into the washout than I had been in the first instance, and there I remained until darkness settled over the earth and the buffalo bull departed. I then crawled out of the hole and crept up over the hill where I left my two Indian companions. They were sitting on the brow of the hill awaiting an opportunity to go down on the flat and get my body. Having witnessed the antics of the bull and the attack it had made on me, they felt certain that I had been killed.

It is almost needless to say we got no buffalo meat that night. When we returned to the village we reported an immense herd of buffaloes, and the chase began on the second day thereafter, but we did not say anything about our adventure, as we had broken a very strict law of the council and subjected ourselves to heavy punishment. It was many months afterward before I told the story, and the Indians were much surprised that the bull did not overtake and kill me.

THE OLD WOMAN WHO LIVED IN A TEPI (NOT SHOE).

CHAPTER XXIV.

FACTIONAL DIFFERENCES.

Strange as it may seem, nearly every hostile Indian village was "divided against itself." That is to say, each village contained two parties, or factions. Grouard says this fact was very patent with the Uncapapas, where Sitting Bull and his immediate family following controlled on the one side, and No Neck and Gall on the other, the latter faction having a slight advantage; but Sitting Bull, being a first-class politician, could hold his own. The cause of these factions was hereditary, growing out of family differences generations back. Four Horns was the hereditary chief of the Uncapapas. His age in 1869 was seventy. His cousin, Black Kettle, was the same age. These two men had reigned since their youth, and were considered the head men of the tribe. Both had been warriors, very fierce. Black Kettle was the greater orator, and in the councils had more to say and carried greater weight than any other man in the tribe. When Grouard was led into the Uncapapa village a captive, the No Neck and Gall faction was the one that wanted to put him to death. The other side, with Sitting Ball at its back, of course opposed the scheme, and the fine Italian hand of the politician is again shown to advantage, for Grouard's life was spared. Three years later, when Sitting Bull and Grouard quarreled over the arrest of the half-breeds (who had sold the Uncapapas whisky, and been the cause of so much sorrow and trouble among the red men), nothing would satisfy the revenge of the politician but the blood of the man whose life he had preserved when the boy's capture was effected. It was then made a family affair, and No Neck and Gall (who three years previous had loudly demanded his death) were now foremost among his champions and protectors. Here is one instance, at least, where factional strife and jealousy saved a life.

Nearly all tribal trouble, says Grouard, among the Indians, is caused by the squaws. Even among the savages "there's a woman in the case," and these factional differences may smoulder for years before they lead to an open breach. But when the trouble comes, it is serious, and blood flows freely.

Grouard recalls an instance of this kind among the Minneconjoux. About a dozen lodges of Sitting Bull's camp were on a visit to the Minneconjou village at the mouth of Tongue river on the Yellowstone during the summer of 1872. A great feast was in progress — the Omaha dance was being celebrated. A young buck was beating the tom-tom and the best of feeling prevailed. The factions in the Minneconjou tribe had been created some years before, and a woman was at the bottom of it. When mirth was at its height one of the young braves of the tribe was noticed to mount his pony, stripped to his buff, and circle the camp several times, finally ending his pilgrimage in front of the tom-tom player, where he stood, enveloped in a blanket and holding a bow and arrow in his hand. Suddenly he threw the blanket aside and shot an arrow into the body of the brave beating the tom-tom.

The effect upon the camp was like magic. The dance immediately ceased, and pandemonium reigned. Each of the young braves — the one murdered and the murderer — were interested in the woman over whom the feud had originally been raised. Faction stood against faction, and murder was the order of the day. Grouard says the weaker side had finally to flee. They were pursued for a distance of forty miles, and eighty lifeless bodies were strewn along the length of that awful trail of vengeance.

Early in the fight Little Assiniboine had found Grouard among the warring factions, and the two, in company with Sitting Bull and others of the latter's village, moved down the river and awaited the result of the battle.

"We do not want to take sides in this matter," said Sitting Bull.

The trouble over, the Uncapapa chief, acting the part of peacemaker, took a dozen of his own ponies to the Minneconjou camp and presented them to the relatives of the tom-tom player who had been killed, and, by his persuasive eloquence, induced the warring factions to bury their differences and their dead. Grouard naively remarked that "of course Sitting Bull got these ponies back afterwards," but failed to inform the author whether they *followed* him, or reached the Uncapapa village *in advance* of the returning visitors. The scout doesn't say so, but the inference is irresistible that Sitting Bull being a great horse thief as well as a practical joker, stole his own ponies from the Minneconjou mourners in order to "keep his hand in."

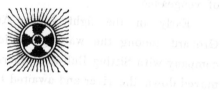

CHAPTER XXV.

FASTING FOR EIGHT DAYS.

In the spring of 1874 I had an experience in fasting that I am not likely to forget. The Indian village was located at that time at the head of the Rosebud river. Ammunition was so low that we scarcely had a round apiece left. We were expecting a party in from the agency with ammunition and other supplies, and had been on the lookout for them for some time. It was finally decided that a party should be sent out in search of our friends from the reservation. The day before the party started what we thought to be smoke signals were discovered near the mouth of Tongue river, distant some four days' travel. Myself and two Indians were selected to go to this latter place and escort our friends into camp. We had no doubt but that the smoke we saw was a signal from this party, who did not know the exact location of our camp and were waiting for some of us to come to them and bring them in. I was the only one in the party who had any ammunition, and my supply consisted of two cartridges. I took my bow and some arrows with me.

Well, to make a long story short, we left the village

with but one day's rations, as we did not expect to travel far and went afoot. The second day out, as luck would have it, I made two poor shots in an attempt to kill something to appease our hunger, and we were left at our wit's end to secure food to keep us from starvation. When we arrived at the mouth of Tongue river we discovered where a fire had been, but it had apparently been set by accident, and we had no other alternative but to retrace our steps. There was no evidence of a camp in the vicinity. On the way back to the village all three of us became nearly insane from hunger, having been eight days without a particle of food. We were very weak. When we were within twenty miles of the village I managed to kill three prairie chickens with my bow and arrow. I tried to induce my companions to eat as sparingly of the meat as possible, but they were so ravenously hungry that I could do nothing with them. I saved the necks of the chickens for myself, which I roasted, and thus got the benefit of the juice from the meat, which satisfied me until my arrival in camp. My two companions ate every particle of the bodies of the chickens raw. They were taken very sick shortly afterwards, and did not live long enough after reaching the village to enjoy another meal. We were ten days making the trip.

Our condition, when we arrived in camp, can be better imagined than described. We were literally skin and bones, the flesh being so drawn on our faces that we were almost unrecognizable by our most intimate acquaintances. It was a long while before I dared eat enough food to satisfy my hunger, my stomach being so weak that the least bit of anything I ate nauseated me. The distance we traveled was a little over three hundred miles. The sufferings of my companions were terrible, and the sight of their misery only added to my own, as they were like little children, and looked to me for assistance in everything. We became so weak that the flesh on our bodies was in a constant quiver, and at the end of the seventh day of our fast all three of us were on the verge of insanity. How we ever lived to reach camp is a great wonder, as, in our weakened condition, we could travel but a short distance before being compelled to lie down and rest. I had no way, of course, of telling how much flesh I lost on the trip, but it didn't seem to me that there was a particle of substance between the bones of my body and the skin which covered them. I didn't think I would pull through, even after I got back to camp, and I am certain that if I had permitted myself to eat heartily of what the Indians prepared I would have gone the way my two poor companions went.

A few days after we got back to camp our Indian allies came up from the agency, and we had no further complaint to make over lack of ammunition. I was in the hostile camp, but the friendly Indians who lived upon the reservation found it greatly to their benefit to hold the most friendly relations with us, and, as they received their ammunition from the agents of the Great Father, we had no need to give up our wild freedom for supplies and promises which were never kept. I in-

clude myself in the plural "we" because, being unable
to secure my freedom, and having made up my mind to
make a study of the character and habits of the Indian,
I was doomed to remain until Uncle Sam should force
the redmen to accept life on the reservations or I accomplished my purpose.

CHAPTER XXVI.

MASSACRE OF THE GROS VENTRES.

One of the biggest Indian clean-ups within my personal knowledge occurred in the fall of 1868. I was then carrying the mail from Fort Hall across the big bend of Milk river. Some four hundred Gros Ventres were camped on Beaver creek, about midway between Fort Hall and Milk river. The trail 1 traveled took me within about nine miles of this village, and as the country was very level I could see their tepis as I passed along. One afternoon in the year above mentioned I noticed a good deal of smoke and some fire in the vicinity of the Indian village, and could plainly see Indians riding around in that vicinity on horseback.

The next morning at Milk river I was informed that the Blackfeet had made a raid on the Gros Ventre's village and killed every man, woman and child they could lay hands on, about four hundred in number, some of whom were confined to their lodges with small-pox. Only two of the Gros Ventres managed to escape from the doomed village, and these had gone to the big bend of Milk river with the news of the massacre. The Blackfeet, after having killed all those found in the vil-

lage, rifled the lodges, drove off the ponies and set fire
to the tepis.

On one of my trips some time after the massacre,
I rode over to the scene of this killing and found the
half-decomposed remains of the dead scattered about in
every direction.   So far as I know, none of the bodies
ever received burial, but were left to be preyed upon by
the wolves and other wild animals.   In all my experience I do not know of another instance where so large
an Indian village was ever attacked by an enemy and
so completely wiped off the face of the earth.

CHAPTER XXVII.

ONE WAY OF COOKING MEAT.

After I became a privileged character in the Sioux village—that is, permitted to run around as I pleased—I went out with a scouting party that was going to Fort Buford, north of the Yellowstone. A rumor had reached the Indian village that a large body of soldiers was camped on one of the tributaries of the Yellowstone near Fort Buford. It was said to be the intention of these troops to move upon and attack Sitting Bull's camp. The Indian scouting party was sent out to discover whether or not there was any truth in these reports. Little Assiniboine, Sitting Bull's adopted brother, asked me to go along, and I accepted the invitation. I had never been away from the village before, and supposing that the Indians supplied themselves with food for a trip before starting out, I asked if I should take some meat with me (straight meat, minus seasoning, being the only food we had). I was told no; that we would kill plenty of buffaloes on the road.

The second day out we discovered a big herd of these animals some distance in advance of us. Some of the best hunters in our party were sent out to head the

buffaloes off, and we succeeded in killing eight or ten of
them.   After they had been dressed and quartered, the
Indians informed me they were going to cook the meat
and carry it along with them.   I did not understand how
they could do any cooking without some sort of utensils,
and asked Little Assiniboine to explain.   He told me if
I would wait and watch I could see better than he could
explain.   The Indians began making preparations to cook.
They were eating the raw buffalo meat while they did so,
one of the choice morsels being the kidneys.   It was my
first experience of that sort, and the sight sickened me ;
but I saw so much of it afterward, that I soon got over
feelings of qualmishness.   Some of the bucks took their
blankets and went off in search of buffalo chips, while
others gathered a number of rocks.

After making a big fire with the buffalo chips, the
Indians put the rocks in the fire.   Next they took the
paunch out of a buffalo, and, after emptying it of its
contents, turned it inside out and filled it about two-thirds
full of water—it must have held fifteen or twenty gallons.
Then they took four bows, stuck them in the ground and
fastened them together at the top, and suspended the
paunch filled with water between the bows.   As the stones
were heated they were put into the water-filled paunch,
and the same result was obtained as if the water had
been placed in a tea-kettle and the latter put on the top
of a stove or hung over the fire.   The stones were constantly changed, those coming direct from the fire being
put into the water as fast as the others were taken out.
The meat was put into this boiling water and cooked,

then taken out and packed up to make room for more. In this manner all the fresh meat was cooked, and I had taken my first lesson in Indian cookery. The redmen only cut off the choice parts of the animals killed, but we had enough meat to last us throughout our trip.

Another custom I learned on this trip was that of shooting life into the sun. There was a total eclipse of the sun one day, and as soon as the Indians observed the shadow on the face of Old Sol, they threw down their packs, drew their guns and kept up a continuous fire until the eclipse had passed away. They were under great excitement all this time, and I could not understand what they were doing. When it was over, I asked Little Assiniboine the cause of the shooting, and he told me they had been shooting the life and light back into the sun. They really believed their action had prevented the light of the sun from disappearing forever.

CHAPTER XXVIII.

GROUARD REGAINS HIS FREEDOM.

It was in 1874 that I studied about a plan to go to the agency at Robinson, called Red Cloud Agency, what is now Crawford,* Nebraska. I just made up my mind I would go in for a visit to see things in the fall. I went in with a party that was moving backwards and forwards. I didn't stop but a short time; came back and went down on Tongue river. The next spring I had to use some means of going in, so I went out with a war party going to Laramie river. The night they started to make a raid on the ranches I took a young Indian and started for the agency, and I stayed at the agency until the commissioners came out to make a treaty for the Black Hills. They got me to go, with others, some Indians and a couple of half-breeds, to make a treaty with the hostiles. I had not left the Indians at this time, but had got everything ready to do so. Louie Reshaw went with me. The rest were Indians — some one hundred agency Indians. I was instructed to induce the Indians to come in and hold a council and make a treaty. They sent out the necessary tobacco and everything to create a friendly feeling.

*Named for Lieutenant Emmet Crawford.

FRANK GROUARD, AT 26.
BY PERMISSION OF JOHN F. FINERTY.

We found the Indian camp on Tongue river, on the other side of where Dayton is now. They received us in a very hostile manner. They were just on the point of going on the war-path. I went out to Crazy Horse's lodge as soon as I got in, and told him what we had come for. His father went out and harangued the camp, and told them it was best to listen to what we had to say. Crazy Horse told me himself that all who wanted to go in and make this treaty could go; but, he said, "I don't want to go." He said that whatever the head men of the tribe concluded to do after hearing our plan, they could and would do. We had a council the next day after we got in. That was my first meeting with Sitting Bull after our trouble. He sent for me to come to his lodge. I went over there, but I took Crazy Horse with me. Sitting Bull asked me what I had come for. Of course, he did not say much of anything, but tried to make me talk. I told him just what I came for, and informed him that the best thing he could do was to go in and see what they wanted at Red Cloud Agency. He said:

"You will hear what I have got to say at the council."

The council was held next morning. All the buck Indians, about one thousand, made a big circle in the center of the camp. Big Breast was the first one to make a speech. He got up and refused flatly to come, and told me his reason why. He didn't want to sell the land, but he said:

"All those that are in favor of selling their land from their children, let them go."

He spoke for a long time, but to that effect.

Sitting Bull then got up and made a long speech. It had the same purport. He said he would not sell his land. He said he had never been to an agency, and was not going in. He was no agency Indian. He told me to go out and tell the white men at Red Cloud that he declared open war, and would fight them wherever he met them from that time on. His entire harangue was an open declaration of war.

Little Hawk got up and spoke for Crazy Horse, the latter refusing to talk. He said:

"My friends, the other tribes have concluded not to go in, and I will have to say the same thing."

Probably one hundred Indians got up and spoke. Our Indians that had come out with us got up and urged them to go back and see what was wanted and what would be gained by making this treaty. At the end of the council they asked us when we were going to start back. We told them, and said we would be there three days longer. They told us that all who wanted to go would probably move across to the other side of Tongue river, where Dayton is now; that we could take them and go back; but that the majority of them would stay there and fight it out. That night they came very near massacring the whole of our party. I know that Crazy Horse saved us. He told them there could be no bullet shot into our camp. He said that he supposed that when anybody came in amongst them they would feed him, water him and give him a smoke. He called the parties together who were the leaders of

the proposed massacre, called them by name, and told
them it would have to be stopped. He said :

" My friends, whoever attempts to murder these people
will have to fight me, too."

That cooled everything down and stopped it right
off, and there was no more said about it. We moved
away from there a day sooner than we expected. When
we got to the other side of Tongue river there was quite
a large camp there. These parties had pulled up and
intended to see us in to the agency. This was the beginning of negotiations for making the treaty for opening the Black Hills. That was the last time I went
back to the Indians. I got quite a little sum of money,
about $500, for making this treaty. That was the first
money I had received or handled since I had been captured by the Indians. It gave me the means to buy
what clothing I wanted, and I needed clothes badly. I
was dressed in regular Indian costume. I had long hair.
I stayed at the agency quite a little while. I was getting familiar with the English language again. It was
two or three months before I could talk English without
getting the Indian mixed up with it. I had been all
this time (since my capture — nearly six years) without
talking a bit of English.

I stayed around there about a month before I
changed my costume. It was one day after dark that I
changed my garb. I had my hair cut and put on a
suit of clothes. That same evening, right after dark, the
interpreter, Bill Rowland, killed a Cheyenne Indian. The
killing of this Indian caused a whole lot of trouble, and

nobody dared to go outside the agency. I was the only man who could go out — who dared to go out — as all of the Indians knew me. It took me two days to quiet this trouble down, and nobody dared go outside the agency while the trouble lasted. I stopped at the agency for a couple of months. I got $60 a month for stopping around for anything of that sort to happen.

B. F. GROUARD, AT 45.

CHAPTER XXIX.

GROUARD MEETS GEN. CROOK.

After I quit the agency I went to J. W. Deere's, out in Nebraska, on Snake river, on his ranch, and stopped. Deere and I were great friends before I was captured by the Indians. Got acquainted with him on the Missouri when I was carrying mail. I got acquainted with a great many officers, among them Capt. Egan of K company, Second regiment—"the White Horse Cavalry." Deere had told me about the expedition which was outfitting for the winter campaign, and through Deere and Capt. Egan my name was sent to headquarters as a scout—as a man who knew the country—and Deere told me that if there were any men hired he would send out and let me know.

So when they sent out orders to get men that were acquainted with the Indian country for scouts, Egan and Deere both thought that I would be just the man that they would want. They sent out for me to come in. I got in there along in the afternoon and was sent up to the Post to see the commanding officer, who told me I would have to go right over to Fort Laramie that night; that Gen. Crook was there and wanted to see me.

Fort Laramie was ninety miles distant. I went over
there on my horse that night, and reached there next
morning at eight o'clock. I met Gen. Crook there, and
also Louie Reshaw and Big Bat (Baptiste Pourier). That
was the first time I ever met Big Bat. I had an interview with Gen. Crook. He asked me if I was acquainted
with the country and I told him I was. Wanted to know
if there was any possible show of jumping Indians there
in the winter time. I told him if he worked it right
there might be. He said he would give me one hundred
and twenty-five dollars a month from the time I left the
ranch. He said if I would furnish my own horse he
would give me one hundred and fifty dollars; but I didn't
have a horse, and told him that he would have to furnish
the horse. So he said he would give me one hundred
and twenty-five dollars a month. He said that he expected
to start out the first of March. This conversation occurred
in February.

Gen. Crook gave orders to hire thirty men—men who
were supposed to know all about the country, and had
good judgment. I had nothing to do with that. These
men were to act as scouts, so by the time the expedition
was ready to start from Fort Laramie, there were thirty-
five of us. Col. Stanton was put in as chief of scouts.
Everything was organized by the time we got to Fort
Fetterman, forty miles up the Platte. It was the first of
March when we started from there.

The names of the scouting party I can't remember,
that is, all of them. Among them were Big Bat, Louie
Reshaw, Louis Shangreau and his brother John, Charlie

Jennesse, Charles Reshaw, Little Bat (Baptiste Gaunier), Ben. Clarke, Tom Reed (who afterwards became a noted road agent), Speed Stagner (who at that time was guide at Fort Fetterman), Joe Eldredge, and others whose names have escaped my memory.

Nothing occurred until we got to Powder river. On reaching Powder river, Gen. Crook wanted us to go out on Tongue river and see if there were any signs of Indians in that part of the country. Leaving camp at dark we went out about three miles. There were six of us— Louie Reshaw, Big Bat, Little Bat, John Shangreau, Charles Jennesse and myself. From where we stopped we could see the flash of guns at camp, so we knew that there was a fight of some kind going on. Turning around and going back to camp, we found that the Indians had jumped the camp just after we left, firing into the tents, but no casualties occurred. The Indians fired a few shots and left, but it set the camp in a terrible uproar.

The next day the command moved over to Crazy Woman. That evening the general called a council from amongst the scouts, asking if he could cross over with the command to the forks of Clear creek—if it were possible to go through the badlands. He wanted to cut loose from the wagons. But there were none of the scouts able to take him through. He wanted to make the trip after night had set in. He asked me if I could take him through. I told him that I could. He asked me what the distance was, but I could not tell him the distance, because I didn't know anything about miles. I told him I could tell him what time he could get there; that if he

would start after dark he could get there at daylight on
a good fast walk. That was about the first talk I had with
Gen. Crook after he hired me. Of course I didn't know
anything about the soldiers' way of traveling, mode of
living, or much of anything else pertaining to the army.
It puzzled me. He gave orders for the pack train to be
ready at six o'clock that evening to cut loose from the
wagon train, leaving the latter to go back to Powder
river to wait there for the command.

Everything being ready, we left there at six o'clock
at night. The weather when we started was fair, but
after we had set out sometime it commenced snowing,
and snowed from that time on until about nine o'clock
next morning. We traveled without any accident all night
at a good fast walk. Along towards daylight it commenced snowing fast and hard. I suppose the General
was getting anxious, for just at daylight he rode up to
me and said, "It is daylight." You could not see fifty
yards ahead of you on account of the snow. I told him
then that we had almost reached the forks of Clear creek.
I could not see anything, and he asked me how I could
tell, and I said I could tell by the lay of the ground.
He asked me how far away Clear creek was, and I said
it was not more than two or three hundred yards. He
laughed and said, "I don't see how you can tell it."

We didn't go over one hundred yards from where we
were talking till we got to the bank of the river, at the
spot where Kramer's ranch is at present, about four miles
from the forks. Gen. Crook did not express his satisfaction in words. His mode of expressing pleasure was by

a rapid twinkling of his eyes, and my recollection is that the General's eyes twinkled very merrily when the command reached Clear creek.   A big snowstorm was in progress.   We moved on the creek almost to the forks before going into camp, and stayed there the rest of that day.

CHAPTER XXX.

LOOKING FOR INDIANS.

While in camp the General came over amongst the scouts and tried to find out the different opinions held by them as to where the Indians were most likely to be found. The off-hand opinion amongst the scouts was that the Indians were camped on Tongue river or the Little Big Horn; but I knew better than that from my intimate knowledge of the Indians, but didn't care to express an opinion different from the majority, so I kept my mouth shut.

When we left Powder river the General asked me where I thought the Indians were, and I said on Powder river, and he asked me what made me think so, and I told him from my knowledge of the Indians and their mode of living in the winter time. I knew where they ranged during the winter months. They had a certain range where they went, just like animals. The next morning the General wanted us scouts to go ahead of the command and find whether there were any Indians camped on Tongue river. It was the same scouting party that started from Powder river—the same men with two additions.

MAJOR E. G. FECHET, CAPTURER OF SITTING BULL.

MAJOR J. G. FECHET, CAPTURER OF SITTING BULL.

We crossed along the forks where the Big Red is at present, and went on to the head of Dutch creek, following it down to its mouth ; from there down to the mouth of Prairie Dog, down to Tongue river. We found a spot there where the Indians had been camped about a month before. We waited there until the command came down and overtook us. It was to follow up our trail. It took the command two days to reach that point from Clear creek over to Upper Prairie Dog. From there all the scouts except Stagner (there were thirty-four of us started out) followed Tongue river down and scouted in the vicinity of Tongue river to its mouth on the Yellowstone, where we rested. The command was to go as far as Otter creek and wait there until our return. Gen. Crook asked me how he would know the creek when he got to it. I told him there were three pine trees in a row, tight in the forks, all by themselves, and were standing right on the bank of Tongue river just above where Otter creek empties in, and I said "when you see those pine trees, you go into camp there." He asked me if I knew every rock and tree in the country, and I told him I came pretty near it. He was surprised at my knowledge of the country. The other scouts could travel along the road, but after they got a little distance from the highway they didn't know a thing about the country.

We got back to the command two days afterwards. There is where we found another old camp ground of the Indians. We found where they had killed a Crow Indian, quartered him and hung him up. It was on

Tongue river just below the mouth of Hanging Woman. His arms, legs, head and everything were hung up in different places on the trees down where the village had been, and it had occurred before the command started. I heard the Indians had killed a man there in camp. He was stealing horses. It must have been done a month before. There is nothing left of a horse thief after the Indians catch him.

The General came over to the camp and called another council of the scouts. He asked their advice as to which way he would have to go to find the Indians. That is where I got the enmity of Reshaw. He claimed the Indians were on the Little Big Horn. I was positive that I knew where they were, and asked the General if he wanted to find the Indians. He told me it was either a fight with the Indians or starvation, and he says :

"We can't starve; we have too many mules, but only two or three days' rations left."

I said if that was the case and they did as I told them, I would take them to the Indian village inside of three days.

"That is what we want," remarked the General.

I said, "I will start out at 12 o'clock, and want the best horses there are in the command, or as good."

"All right, you shall have them," said he, and he asked how many men I wanted.

I said I would go by myself.

"All right," he said, "I will give the orders. Do you know of any horses with the command you would like to have ?"

"I said there were two good animals in the command. I would like one or the other of them. He told me to name them and he would have them fed for me. One was his lead horse — a French-Canadian horse. I told him, and he said :

"All right; I will have him fed."

I told him to follow my trail. The snow was very deep, so the command could follow my tracks, but, said I, "I want you to keep these scouts all with the command, and don't let them go away from you."

He said he would do as requested. Of course, there were several instructions that I gave him : To keep as close on my trail as he could, and I told him also that I should, probably, when I struck Otter Creek, follow up the creek ; that he wanted to watch my trail very close from there on. There were only three trails going to Powder river, and I didn't know which I would take. They were all Indian trails. They were the only ones we could travel on very well. I left the command at about 12 o'clock that night, and traveled until about 7 o'clock the next morning, when I reached Otter creek.

Just as I came on to the hills leading to Otter creek, or just before, I got off my horse and crept up to the hills to look up and down the creek with my glass. Up the creek about five miles from where I was I saw two Indians trailing a buffalo, or some animal track. They were tracking down the creek towards where I was. I watched them very close, all their movements, and was sure just as quick as I watched them awhile that they were out hunting, and that they had come from their

village. It was quite a ride to the command, and I
didn't suppose it would come to where I. was until
between 1 and 2 o'clock. I thought the Indians would
have plenty of time to get out of sight of the command
before it reached there. Well, I must have been watching them for about three hours. I did not dare to
move or show myself, but I was looking at the Indians
through my glass at this time, watching every move.
When they had got almost opposite me, they stopped
their horses all of a sudden and looked towards me. I
was not over a mile and a half from them, and could
almost see their features through the glass. All of a
sudden they commenced whipping their horses. There
were some pines right ahead of them, and they ran in
behind them and got off their horses, crept up on to
the brow of the hill and looked towards me. I could
just see the top of their heads. I thought to myself,
"What if they should see me?"

Well, I soon found out what it was that attracted
their attention. Pretty soon here comes all those scouts,
running their horses across the hills. They were scattered
for two miles along the hill in plain view of the Indians,
who stopped, and pretty soon started for the timber;
but instead of going back the way they came they went
in a northeasterly direction towards Powder river, and I
knew they were going on to the main trail to Powder
river. In fact, when I saw that the scouts had scared
the Indians, I waited until they had got up to me. Then
I took four of them and started after the Indians to
keep them out of sight of the command. The Indians

didn't wait for us, but just kept going. But they were out of the way of the command. They didn't see it. I was satisfied that they couldn't recognize whether we were Indians or whites. Probably they would think we were a war party of Crows, and go for camp as fast as they could. We went across Otter creek for convenience. The command had got there, and I told the General about it. It made me mad, because the scouts had got away from the command. I told him, that if he had kept the scouts away the Indians would not have known of our coming, and it would have been no trouble getting into their camp.

The General said he gave them orders but they escaped the command. He said he didn't think the command so close to me as it was. I explained that they were getting close to the Indians, and I could not tell how near we were, and that was the reason I had asked him to keep the scouts with the command. He asked me what I intended to do. I replied that I intended to jump the village tomorrow morning if he would give me four companies of cavalry. There were ten companies in the command. The General asked:

"Do you think you can find a village?"

I said, "I don't think anything about it; I know it."

"All right," he says; "I will give you six companies, and will keep four with the pack train. When do you want to start?"

"I want to start about an hour by sun, so I can reach the forks of Otter creek, before dark," I replied.

I was going to follow the back tracks of the In-

dians, or that was my intention. The General said he
would have the horses fed what grain there was left —
there was only one day's forage left — and that the cavalry would be ready to start by the time I wanted
them, with Col. Reynolds in command.

Reynolds was Colonel of the Third cavalry. Gen.
Crook gave the necessary orders, and then called the
Colonel over to headquarters and gave him his orders
in my presence, no other person being present. His
orders were very strict — that we should jump the village and capture the horses, take all the dried meat
we could get, and keep the Indian saddles and burn
the village, and to hold the village until we could
get a courier back to him. We were to capture the
Indians if possible. That was the purport of Gen.
Crook's verbal orders to Col. Reynolds.

Everything being ready, we started and reached the
forks of Otter creek about sundown. Finding that the
Indians we had seen had come down the left hand
fork, I was almost satisfied where the village lay.

CHAPTER XXXI.

THE BATTLE WITH CRAZY HORSE.

That night was the coldest one I ever experienced in the northern country. It was the night of the 16th of March. Just as quick as it became dark I got off of my horse and gave him to one of the scouts to lead. I had to go afoot in order to follow the Indian tracks. I footed it all night long. It was warm work for me. I came to the Powder river divide some six miles from Powder river, about 3 o'clock in the morning, and went on to locate the village, leaving the command six miles to the rear to await my return. One of the men with me was Buckskin Jack, a notorious scout (who is now traveling with Buffalo Bill), then a young man. He might be called the "Midget of the Plains." The other man's name was Phoenix. He was hanged afterwards down on the Yellowstone for horse stealing.

When I started out it was sixty degrees below zero; I think they said it was sixty-three. We had a couple of doctors with us. Dr. Hartsoff, now ranking colonel, was one of them. Just at daylight we came up a hill above Powder river. There was an immense fog, so thick I could not see anything. It had raised out of the river, but I could hear the bells on the Indian ponies. Of course that satisfied me that there was a village there. I sent Buckskin Jack back after the command, telling him to bring them up as soon as possible, while I went down and located the village. I could not tell where it was, on account of the fog. I was up about one thousand feet, and it was straight down to the village. I got about half way down the hill when the fog raised, so that I could look in under it and see the village down below me, about a mile off. I could see the tops of the lodges, and the horses, and could hear the Indians talk. An Indian was haranguing the camp, and it was from this one that I learned that a party of the Indians had gone back the trail to find out who we were, for they had seen us on Otter creek; but instead of going the upper trail, they had gone the lower one, so that we had missed them. I found this out through the crier. I could hear it as plain as could be. I could not tell how large a village it was from where I stood. They had camped in a low bed of a river, or where a river had been perhaps a hundred years ago, right under a big bank. The Indians had camped in the circle of this old river bed. There was timber scattered all through the bottom, and they were camped amongst this timber. I supposed there were some one hundred lodges, and from seven hundred to one thousand Indians. I came back up on the hill. Just as I reached there, Col. Reynolds and his company came up close to me. Said I:

"Colonel, here are the Indians. Now, that I have found them, all you have got to do is to fight them."

He says, "What am I going to do?"

"Fight them Indians," I replied. "I suppose that is what you want."

He says, "What can I do?"

He seemed lost. I says:

"Fight them Indians; that is all you have to do."

"How will I place my command?" he asked.

If I had known as much then as I do now, I would have told him terrible quick. I said:

"You wanted me to find the Indians. Now, there they are. Do what you want to with them."

He asked: "Can you place the command? Tell me how to place it?"

I said: "Yes, I can do that. Send some down this way, and some down the other way, and keep the Indians from going into the hills."

"Will you place them?" he asked.

I replied: "Yes, I will place one party, and send another man with the other."

He gave the orders. Captain Egan of the Second Cavalry was to make the charge down the river into the village. Captain Mills of the Third Cavalry was to support him. Captain Moore of the Third was to keep the Indians from going into the hills. Captain Noyes of the Third Cavalry, with the scouts, was to help run the ponies off. I sent Buckskin Jack with Captain Noyes, Little Bat and Charlie Jennesse with Captain Egan's company. I went with Captain Moore's battalion to put it into position. It was 7 o'clock when we started to take our positions. It was 9 o'clock before we got into position. It was 10:30 when Captain Egan charged the village.

After I put Moore's battalion into position I started down across the flat towards the village. I suppose it was about half a mile from there right down across the flat. The horses and everything were right in sight, and we had been in sight ourselves ever since seven o'clock, and the Indians had not seen us. We had been just where, if they had looked up the hill, they would have seen us, and they had not caught sight of us. I went right down across this flat and walked up to within twenty yards of the village and commenced talking to the Indians before they knew there was anybody around. By this time Capt. Egan had come up in sight.

This was the 17th of March, 1876, fight. When I got within twenty yards of the camp I yelled to Crazy Horse. I recalled what he had told me during my endeavors to secure the Black Hills treaty — that he would rather fight than make a treaty — and told him that now was the time to come out and get all the fighting he wanted, as the troops were all around his camp!

He did not have time to answer. The charge had begun. Egan's command came right up by the side of them. The battalion that I had stationed to keep the Indians from going into the hills, instead of going to the position assigned it, commenced firing from the position it held. I don't know whether they thought they were firing at the Indians or not, but they were firing into Egan's company. I suppose they imagined they were fighting the Indians. I had to go in with Egan's troops to keep from being shot. We charged right down into the center of the village. As Capt. Egan entered the village, Hospital Steward Will Bryant was riding alongside of him. As he dashed in among the lodges an Indian came from one of the tepis aiming to kill the Captain. Bryant, seeing that Egan was in danger, ran in front of him, his horse receiving the bullet in its head, killing it instantly. Bryant took in after the Indian on foot. He was a foot-racer, but he didn't catch him, though he ran the Indian in amongst the lodges.

The horses and soldiers charged right through the village. They fought, I guess, for thirty minutes, when Capt. Mills' command came to their relief. When Mills came to their relief the Indians went right into the hills, as there was nobody to stop them or head them off. They went right into the rocks. We had no chance to kill or capture many of them, but secured the village and horses and one Indian. I forget how many soldiers there were killed. Everything belonging to the village was destroyed by fire, even the saddles and meat. The Indians escaped to the hills with the loss of but one buck and one old squaw, and she was not lost, as she was captured after being shot; and as nobody in the command wanted her, she was left there.

She told me that Sitting Bull's village was situated down the river about sixty miles. The village we had destroyed was Crazy Horse's village. I knew this village by the horses. Knew every horse there was there. The old squaw told me Sitting Bull's village was at the mouth of Beaver creek, but I had suspected this all the time.

It was about an hour after the fight commenced that Col. Reynolds sent for me, and told me to be ready to

move at one o'clock, as he wanted to go to the mouth of
Clear creek that night. That was the first I knew of the
orders he had given. I asked him if he was going to
keep the dried meat and saddles, and he said he had
given orders for everything to be burned; that he would
not let any of the soldiers take anything; they had positive orders for everything to be burned up. We captured between twelve and fifteen hundred head of ponies.
I asked the Colonel then to give me some soldiers to drive
the ponies up with, as I only had twelve men to drive
the herd. He said:

"No; the scouts will have to drive them."

I said, "There are too many for them to drive."

"If they can't drive them," he replied, "shoot them."

I said, "They have not got ammunition enough to
shoot them."

And he answered, "What they can't kill, let go."

Captain Egan then came up and said, "I am the
rear guard, and I will see that the ponies get into camp
tonight."

Soon after this we left there. I put a scout with
each battalion. I put two men in two battalions, and I
took a battalion myself, so as to guide them during our
night's travel and keep them from getting lost. I was
not very long going that twenty miles with one battalion.
We got there just at dusk; was expecting to meet Gen.
Crook there. Not finding him in camp at that point, we
went into camp there ourselves. It was about nine o'clock
before the other battalions came in. It was about twelve
o'clock before the ponies came in with Captain Egan as
rear guard.

I asked the Colonel then if he would give me a guard for the ponies during the night; but he said the men were too tired and he didn't think the ponies were in any danger; that they would be perfectly safe turned loose, or that the scouts could guard them until morning. I caught up my horse and mule, tied them up and told the scouts to do the same with theirs, together with the horses they wanted to ride, and turn the rest loose; made down a bed and went to sleep. I didn't think I had been asleep ten minutes before somebody came and woke me up, and told me the Indians were driving off the ponies. I jumped up, and it was just break of day. Off about one half mile from camp were the Indians driving off the ponies. I went to the Colonel and woke him up, asking him for a company of soldiers to go out and capture the ponies. He told me the men not having anything to eat, were both hungry and tired, and he could not send them out. He told me I had better take the scouts and go out and see what I could do with them. There were probably twenty-five or thirty Indians driving off the ponies.

I didn't send the scouts out. I just asked if there was anybody wanted to go, but there were only four men volunteered — Little Bat, John Shangreau, Buckskin Jack and another scout. We saddled our horses and started after the Indians. They were going in the way that Gen. Crook was coming from, and I thought most probably that I could meet him; and as the General had four companies of soldiers it would have been a sure thing that we could have taken the horses away from the Indians. I overtook the Indians about two miles from camp, and had a kind of running fight with them until about 1 o'clock. We recaptured the horses and they got them back again. They did this two or three times. There were too many of them for us, and the last time we tried to recapture the ponies we charged in on them, and they shot Little Bat's horse out from under him, and left him afoot, and he had to get on behind me.

It was not very pleasant, fighting the Indians in that fashion. They saw that one of us was afoot and came right down for us. I kept them at bay as much as I could, and finally they left us alone. We were about twenty miles from the river on the head of Otter creek when this occurred, and not meeting the General I turned around and started back. It was dark when we reached where the camp had been in the morning, but it had moved. We followed the trail right up Powder river. We went up about ten miles and saw the camp seven or eight miles above us. We could see the reflection from the camp fires.

On our way we ran into another lot of Indians. It was perfectly dark and cloudy and I heard something coming along the trail and waited for them to come up, and who should it be but some Indians driving horses. I sent one of the boys ahead of the horses the Indians were driving, and one of the scouts and myself went to head the horses off, and the other two scouts fired into the Indians. Not knowing how many there were of us, the Indians just dropped everything and ran. We captured the horses, and Little Bat got an animal to ride .from there to camp, and we drove the other animals in with us.

There were eleven head of horses. The horses had been stolen from George Harris, who lived on the Platte river. The Indians had been to Harris' place, driven off the horses, and were taking them down to Crazy Horse's camp, not knowing of the battle that had been fought there. So from there we were fixed comfortably until we got into camp. We got within about half a mile of camp, when who should we meet but Gen. Crook, who had been watching for us. He came down and met us, saying he had been watching there ever since dark, about one-half mile from the command. The first thing I knew he asked me if that was me, and I said it was, and he came up and shook hands with me. He told me he had just caught up with the ranks, and had got into camp a little before sundown. I was plumb played out. I had been three nights without any sleep to amount to anything. The General didn't say much to me that night. When I got to camp, Captain Egan came over to where I was, and says:

"Frank, I have something warm for you."

He took me over to his quarters and gave me a cup of coffee and some hot biscuits and butter, and I think that was the finest meal I ever ate in my life. After I got through eating, the General told me to go to bed, and I don't believe it was over five seconds before I was asleep. The Indians and soldiers were fighting all night, but I never heard it. The General woke me the next

morning, and the camp was about ready to move. I
never knew anything about the fight. He asked me about
everything that had occurred at the Crazy Horse battle,
and why the orders were not obeyed. I didn't spare them
a bit in the world. I told him just how the whole thing
had been run. He didn't say anything to them, but said
that as Col. Reynolds was in charge of the command, he
didn't want to take the charge away from him. He never
said he was going to put him under arrest. He just simply went to work and put him under arrest, and never
told anybody. Reynolds was not relieved of his command until we got to Cheyenne.

_____

[Grouard, when the battle with Crazy Horse occurred, knew nothing of the stories concerning himself
that were being circulated in the command, nor did he
find out anything about them until Gen. Crook explained
matters on the way to Fort Fetterman at the close of
the campaign.

He says the indecision of Reynolds nonplussed and
worried him. He did not then even dream that Reynolds
and some other officers of the command suspected or
doubted his loyalty; but after his talk with Gen. Crook
everything was made plain. Fear of an ambush — a
vision hatched in the jealous brain of some "carpet
warrior"— prompted, so Grouard says, Reynolds in ordering a retreat, when every principle of war and manhood
demanded the exact reverse. It was, as Captain Bourke
so tersely expresses it, "one of those things that no man
can explain." General Crook divined the motive, how-

ever, and in his soldierly way placed the responsibility where it belonged. The facts related by Grouard are admirably borne out by the narrative of Captain Bourke, who, in speaking of the battle says, that "both Mills and Egan were doing excellent work in the village (destroying it), while the pony herd was held by Noyes." He does not try to find any excuse for the failure of Reynolds to fortify his position and send word to Crook (who was at no great distance with four companies) to come at once to the assistance of the rest of the command. He must have known that the captured pony herd consisted of over one thousand head; that the number of saddles run up to nearly two hundred; that a thousand robes and furs were in the captured tepis; that a great amount of ammunition had fallen into the hands of his soldiers, and that "tons upon tons of meat" had been left by the fleeing savages; yet, in the face of all this, Reynolds not only abandoned the camp of Crazy Horse, but did it so precipitately that the dead and wounded were left for mutilation and butchery. And Captain Bourke says, with considerable feeling, that it was whispered among the men "that one of our poor soldiers fell alive into the enemies hands and was cut limb from limb." The captain does not make this statement from his "own knowledge," but adds, "I can only say I believe it to be true."

Referring to the bivouac at the mouth of Lodge Pole creek on the night succeeding the battle with Crazy Horse, Captain Bourke says there was neither feed for the animals nor rations for the men —"not even for the

wounded men, of whom we had six." The men, after
two days' hard riding, marching and fighting, were completely tired out, and no attempt was made to place a
guard over the captured pony herd; and "even when the
loss was discovered"—when the report was carried to
Reynolds the following morning, as detailed by Grouard,
that the Indians were driving off the ponies —"no at·
tention was paid and no attempt made," concludes
Bourke, "to pursue and regain the mainstay of Indian
hostility."

When Crook reached camp about noon on the day
after the battle, says this same authority, he was very
much gratified to learn that the attempt to find the village
of Crazy Horse had been successful ; but he could not
hide his chagrin and disappointment upon discovering
that the dead and wounded had been left in the hostile
camp, and that his soldiers were suffering from cold and
hunger when a great abundance of furs and provisions
had been lost to the command through the hasty withdrawal from the Indian village of the victorious troopers.
There was no other alternative for General Crook but
to abandon the campaign and return to Fetterman, which
meant a long, suffering journey of over one hundred and
eighty miles, with the thermometer thirty degrees below
zero. From Fetterman the troops were distributed to
various forts pending the organizing of the spring campaign.

"We had no beef," says Bourke, "as our herd had
been run off on account of the failure to guard it; we
were out of supplies, although we had destroyed enough

FRED NEWCOMER'S RANCH, PRAIRIE DOG VALLEY, SHERIDAN COUNTY, WYOMING.

to last a regiment for a couple of months; we were en-
cumbered with sick, wounded, and cripples with frozen
limbs, because we had not had sense enough to save the
furs and robes in the village."

There is the story from the standpoint of as brave
a soldier as ever carried weapon in defense of country;
and yet there has been a monstrous waste of sentiment
over the fact that the battle with Crazy Horse led to a
court martial and other unpleasant recollections for General Reynolds.

Grouard maintains that the key to the immediate
settlement of all the Indian's troubles was lost in failing
to follow up the advantage gained through the capture
of the Crazy Horse village. The village of Sitting Bull,
situated but sixty miles below where Crazy Horse was
found, would have fallen into the hands of the troops
also had proper precaution been taken to capture the fleeing savages under Crazy Horse. But somebody blun-
dered, and the year 1876 was destined to bear awful
fruit from this terrible error. With Crazy Horse and
Sitting Bull conquered, the world would never have received the shocks it felt successively when news of the
battle of the Rosebud, the Little Big Horn, the War Bon-
nett and Slim Buttes electrified and horrified the people.
—Author.]

CHAPTER XXXII.

CLOSE OF THE SPRING CAMPAIGN.

The third day after the Crazy Horse battle, General Crook asked me how long it would take me to go up to the wagon train camp at old Fort Reno on Powder river. I told him three days or so. On the morning of the third day after we had started for the wagon train, Gen. Crook wanted me to take a message to Fort Reno, and asked me how far it was. I said about thirty miles. He said :

"I want you to get ready so as to start right away."

I said, "All right."

"What time can you get there?" he asked.

I said about twelve o'clock.

He said, "If you can make it by twelve, we can by three."

I started on the trip. It was just about fifty miles from there up to the wagon train. I got there at twelve o'clock. The wagonmen were eating their dinners when I arrived. The General and soldiers got there at dark.

"I would like to buy land by your measurement of miles," Gen. Crook remarked, when we met.

I told him I didn't know anything about a mile, and

I guess he believed it, for he never again asked me about a mile as long as I knew him. I was guided solely by the time I could get there. This is the Indian way of telling distances. We laid over at Reno the next day, and the following morning started out. Gen. Crook told me to go in his ambulance, and said he was going right through to Fort Fetterman. I got in and went with him. On the trip to Fetterman he spoke of the stories that had been told against me by the scouts; the bad reputation they had been giving me. He said that he had not paid any attention to what they had reported, and that he had as much confidence in me as if he had not heard any such stories. This March campaign in 1876 was the opening of what is known and called the Sioux war. After the Crazy Horse fight the troops were withdrawn from active service until May.

Reshaw had been trying to put up a job on me from the time I had started out by myself on Tongue river. He had circulated stories around amongst the officers, and told the General that I was in communication with the Indians every night; that I was fixing up a plot with them to have the command massacred. That was the story he tried to make them believe, and Gen. Crook told me that all the officers believed it except himself. Reshaw tried to make them believe that I was working against the command; that my object in leaving the Indians was to run the command into the hostile country far enough to give the Sioux a chance to kill off the last one of them — Crook, and his officers as well. Of course, I didn't know anything about it, so it didn't affect me the least bit.

You see, Reshaw was jealous of my knowledge of the country and the Indians. I had not met any of the officers very much. Deere was the only man I was acquainted with ; and the officers, not knowing me or anything about me, were suspicious after hearing these stories about me. Louie Reshaw was a brother of John Reshaw. The latter killed a soldier at Fort Fetterman in 1866, and fled, going among the hostile Indians to live. He was supposed to have been one of the instigators of the war waged by the redmen afterwards, which led to the massacre of Col. Fetterman and his command at Fort Phil Kearney that same year. This war continued until the treaty was made with the government at Fort Laramie in 1868. John Reshaw was pardoned by the president in 1868, the pardon being one of the treaty stipulations, but was killed shortly afterwards by his brother-in-law, an Indian. Louie had been interpreter for the different treaties and councils they had with the Indians, and acquired quite a reputation, and made two or three trips to Washington. He was a half-breed.

CHAPTER XXXIII.

WORKING OFF "BILE."

Shortly after the command reached Fort Fetterman, all of the scouts were discharged except Louie Reshaw, Big Bat and myself. Reshaw was sent over to the Red Cloud Agency, Bat was sent to Fort Laramie and I was stationed at Fetterman. Speed Stagner was also recommended as guide at Fort Fetterman. I was ordered to Cheyenne from there on the court martial of Col. Reynolds. Court had been convened to try him for disobeying orders at the Powder river fight with Crazy Horse. I didn't stop in Cheyenne but a few days, and then took a stage down to Sydney, and went from there to Fort Robinson. I was ordered down there. That is where I first found out that Louie Reshaw was trying to get me killed.

Shortly after I reached there I went down to a dance one night, just below the Agency. Of course, Reshaw and his relatives were there, five or six of them. After I got through dancing I went to the door. It was very dark outside, and I stood there cooling myself. The door was near the corner of the house, just about a foot and a half from the corner. While I stood there some-

body tried to fire a revolver in my face. The only
thing that kept me from being killed was that the cap
flashed. I think it was an old-fashioned Colt's revolver,
for there was no report — nothing but the flash of the
cap. The pistol was held right in my face. I took
right after the party, but I could not catch him. I
had no idea who it was, and didn't find out for some
time. About two weeks later I was at another dance.
This was a half-breed dance. Big Bat came in and said:

"You had better be on the watch. They are going
to try and kill you to-night, and have fixed a plan to
shoot you. I will watch while you dance."

He didn't dance any. In the room—it was small
—we could only dance one set. There was an up-stair
room in the house, and steps leading up to it. Bat
was sitting on the third or fourth step. He had told
me that whenever he gave me the signal I wanted to
be ready. I was to watch every move that was going
on. I was dancing so that I could face Bat, when he
gave me the signal. I saw that there were four half-
breeds standing against the wall, and Bat nodded his
head as much as to say:

"Watch out for that party."

After he had given me the signal, I heard him calling to me to watch out. As I looked around, he had
got after these men, having seen them make some
kind of a move; and before I could get my partner
out of the room, Bat had all four of the half-breeds
piled up in the corner, going after them right and left.
He never used a revolver—only his fist; but he was a
powerful man, anyway.

Of course, after that we didn't think any more of dancing. The dance broke up. I had to keep on the watch all the time. Bat told me who was trying to take my life. Two of these men were his brothers-in-law. He married a sister of Reshaw. Two of them were Reshaw's boys. He told me then that Louie was the instigator of it, and was trying to down me; for me to be on the watch for him. I never told the General about this. but Captain Egan got to hear about it, and asked me to tell him the story, and I told him as far as I knew what had happened. He told the General about this trouble. The General asked me about it, but I never told him anything about it. Shortly after this Reshaw was discharged from the service.

When the expedition was getting ready to go on its summer campaign, the General gave me orders to hire some more scouts. Not knowing why he had discharged Reshaw, I hired him over again, with other parties. After we had started on the expedition, Crook asked me the reason why I had hired Reshaw. I told him he was one of the best men I knew of—men not being very plenty—the kind of men we wanted. That was all that was said about it. After the summer's campaign we went back to the agency, and Reshaw was discharged again. In the winter campaign I got orders to hire some more men, and I hired Reshaw. After I gave the list to the General, he told me why he discharged this man; told me if I hired him again, he would discharge me. So that ended the Reshaw trouble, for after the fall (1876) campaign, Reshaw was never hired again by the government.

CHAPTER XXXIV.

IN A TIGHT PLACE.

It was in May of 1876 that the summer expedition was fitted out at Fort Laramie; that is, it congregated there. Fetterman was the starting point. While the expedition had moved to Fetterman and was getting ready and waiting for other troops and some Indians to join the command, I was sent out to look after the crossing of Powder river with ten picked men. The Platte being high, we took our things over in a boat, swam the horses across and started for Powder river. I had not gone more than five miles from the Platte before I found that the Indians were watching on both sides of us. Paying no attention to them, but watching very close, I kept on my way to the crossing of the Cheyenne river, and halted about fifty yards above the road where it crosses the creek, where I made preparations to camp for the night. It was along about three o'clock in the afternoon when we went into camp. The Indians had followed me and were watching all my movements. But I was watching theirs, also.

Not saying anything to the men about the Indians, I ordered them to get their supper ready, as we would

COL. W. F. DRUM, COMMANDER OF FORT YATES IN 1890-91.

pull out after dark, and I told them to get a big pile of wood up so that we could make a great fire on leaving camp. I had two pack mules loaded with provisions picketed near the camp, and seeing that it would be impossible to keep the animals with us, ordered the men to take the rations on their saddles, hide the pack saddles and let the mules run loose. After the sun had gone down and darkness began to settle, we built a big fire, put dummies up all around the fire and made our beds down. Of course, we had to leave our blankets, in order to fool those Indians. I was certain they were watching pretty close every movement we were making.

Taking our horses down into the bed of the creek and smuggling our saddles off to them, we saddled up where we could not be seen. I had the men show themselves around the fire with the dummies, and then we quietly slipped off to the bed of the creek where the animals were. Mounting our horses we went up the river in a westerly direction, almost the opposite direction we had originally been traveling. We moved very carefully until I thought we had got out of reach and hearing of the Indians. Then we gradually turned and made a circle in the direction that I wanted to travel. Making a very wide circuit, we traveled until almost daylight, and went into camp in a deep ravine and waited there for daylight. In the meantime, shortly after leaving our first camp, I heard the firing of the Indians. I supposed they were shooting at the dummies, which I found out afterwards to have been the case. They had crept up to the place where the camp was and fired in on the dummies, supposing we were there. Not finding us, they had started off in the direction they supposed we were traveling, that is, toward Powder river. The next morning I could see them riding over the country looking for our tracks.

Keeping our horses in the ravine, and a close watch-out, I camped there the balance of the day, leaving there after dark and traveling most of the night until I reached the head of Dry Fork of Powder river. From there on I had to travel in the daytime. I was expecting to meet the crow Indians who were to join the command, and had to be on the watch for them and could not travel after night. The next morning after starting out I kept the men traveling in a ravine every chance that I could, or out of sight, so that they could not be seen from a distance, and kept on ahead of them myself. After traveling that way for about ten miles I found out that the Indians had discovered us, and had laid a very nice trap for us to fall into. The men were some distance behind me when I discovered this. I got off of my horse, crept up on the highest point I could reach and watched the redskins' movements.

The trail which I was traveling ran right down into the forks of the creek. The Indians were stationed on each side of this trail, so that as we passed through they would have a cross fire, and this would not have left us much chance to get out if we should have happened to get in there; but I could see their plans so well that as soon as the men came up to where my horse was, I sent them right back the way they had come. After they got some distance away and were out of sight, I again got on my horse, rode up on the hill where the Indians could see me, and waited there a little while. Then I carelessly rode down, as if I was in no hurry to leave the locality.

As quick as I got out of their sight, however, I started back the way the men had gone as fast as my horse could carry me. Overtaking them, I gave orders to travel rapidly in the direction they were going until I overtook them — not to stop until then. I then went back to watch the movements of the hostiles. I saw there was no show for me to reach Powder river, so had made up my mind to go back to Fetterman. As soon as the Indians found out that I had discovered them, they turned back and gave us a very close chase. I remained behind long enough to discover the intentions of the Indians, when I made quick time in rejoining the party I had sent on ahead, and pushed them toward Fetterman as rapidly as the horses would travel. We arrived at the fort after dark, but the Indians did not give up the chase until we were so close to the command that they were afraid to follow any further. I have always considered that trip as close a call as I ever had, and I have been in positions where the chances of escape were so slight that I would have played the Indians for favorites if I had been buying pools on the outcome.

CHAPTER XXXV.

THROUGH THE HOSTILE COUNTRY.

When our scouting party reached Fetterman the command was camped on the other side of the river, and I left the men on this side and went over myself and told the General what had happened. The General told me that he was ready to move the command across the next day, which he did. They were two or three days getting everything across — the beef cattle, rations and ammunition.

It was the third day after crossing that the command started. The same scouts we had on the spring campaign were with us. Of course the command didn't move very far the first day, being late in starting, and the next night they camped near the place where I had camped a few nights before. This was the second night out. The Indians were around watching all our movements. I had seen them that day. They were watching around the command very close. I had the beef herd in charge, and was given two men to herd the cattle at night.

Along about 11 o'clock a shot was fired, and I heard an awful yell. The yelling continued for several minutes, indicating that the person was in great misery. I jumped on my horse and went out to the herd, and found one of the herders in the throes of death. An Indian had rode up to him and shot him, and then stampeded the beef herd. We overtook the beef herd, and got some of the animals back, but some of them we never did get back. We did not try to follow the Indians. Don't recollect whether the herder died in camp and was buried, or whether he was taken to Fort Fetterman and buried, as I left there the next morning at daylight.

I had orders to go to Powder river to find out if that stream was fordable. In going this time I took two companies, or one battalion. Leaving the road to our right, our first camp was on the head of the Seventeen Mile creek, a dry fork of Powder river. One of our men accidentally shot himself. I was sitting right opposite him when he did it. He let his gun fall suddenly, and it turned over and hit a rock, the bullet entering just about the calf of the leg. The wounded man was sent back to the command the next morning, but as he could not be sent to Fetterman then, he was kept in camp, and was afterwards brought to the north, where he died, and was buried on the banks of the Big Goose, near where the city of Sheridan now stands. [The body was taken up in 1892 and transferred to Custer, and buried in the military burying ground.] The next day we resumed our journey and reached Powder river that evening, but found no Crow Indians. The river was fordable. In the morning we started back and joined the command.

CHAPTER XXXVI.

A PERILOUS JOURNEY—"LEFT HAND."

Gen. Crook was much disappointed at not meeting his allies, the Crow Indians, at Powder river. He had telegraphed to the agent of the Crows, and sent an order up to have a lot of the friendlies enlisted as scouts. They were to join him at the crossing of Powder river. He was very anxious, because he had not heard from them. He asked me if it were possible for me to reach the Crow agency, knowing that the entire country was infested by Sioux—filling the whole country between Fort Fetterman and the Crow Agency. I told him I would make the attempt, but it might be possible that I could not get through. He asked me what way I wanted to go, and how many men I desired. I told him I would take two men with me. I would be back in fourteen days if I lived. Of course, there was a great deal of danger. I took Louie Reshaw and Big Bat with me.

Leaving camp that night, we started on our trip, reaching Crazy Woman creek next morning. We laid over in daylight and traveled by night. We killed some buffaloes on Crazy Woman, and cooked up what meat we wanted for the trip, so as not to make any more fires, and left there at daylight the next morning. In crossing Clear creek a bear jumped us, and I had to kill it. I didn't want to fire off the gun, but there was no help for it. While riding up onto the hill after this, we discov- ered a big camp of Indians right down on the creek be- low us. Of course, I had to go up into the mountains to get out of their way. The Indians had not heard the shot when I killed the bear, which was lucky for us. Keeping in the mountains all day, we went down on the Piney creek after dark. I intended to stop there for the night, but I ran on to a camp of Indians, so that I had to keep on the move. I reached Little Goose creek some time after daylight, and stopped there until the next morning. The next night we camped on Twin creek, but seeing the Indians at all times of the day, it kept me all the time dodging out of their way, so that I could not travel very fast.

The next morning we resumed our journey. We had not gone far when we came on to five Indians asleep in the brush; but not caring about any trouble, I left them alone. Crossing the Little Big Horn and going over on to Soap creek we camped there for the night. Early the next day, right after starting out, we discov- ered a large number of Indians trying to trail us up. They were on our tracks. Of course, I kept out of their way as much as I could. Reaching the mouth of the Black Canyon, on the other side of the Big Horn river, I saw three Indians horseback. That being the Crow country, I thought possibly they were Crows. I always carried a pocket looking glass. I used it for

signaling the Indians. Taking the looking glass out I
signaled to these three Indians. As quick as they saw
the signal they went down on the other side of the
hills. A short time afterward two more Indians came
in sight way below old Fort Smith, and I signaled to
them. As soon as they discovered us they went in
the same direction the others had taken.

After waiting awhile to see if I could discover any more Indians, I started for the river, intending to make a raft to cross on. That was the first
time after leaving Crazy Woman that I had to make
a fire. We left Louie Reshaw cooking some dinner,
while Big Bat and myself went down the river to
make a raft. Bat thought it was better to have a
smoke before we started, so we sat down on the river
bank and commenced smoking. Looking around while
enjoying my smoke, I saw that a large party of Indians had tracked us and were charging down on us.
I told Bat the Indians were charging, and told him to
yell to Louie to catch the horses, which he did. We
were quite a distance from them. At the same time
Bat was looking over on the other side of the river.
He says: "Yonder come a lot more Indians on the
other side." There were probably five or six hundred
Indians charging down on us from both sides of the
river. So we ran for our horses, got on to them bareback and came over on to the bank of the river. We
had nothing to do but fight it out. There was no
chance of our getting away, and I told Bat we would
get on to the flat and fight as long as our ammuni-

TONGUE RIVER CANYON, ABOVE DAYTON, WYOMING.

tion lasted. Reshaw wanted to run for the mouth of the canyon; but there was no use of our trying to run, and Bat told him so; that if he started to run he would shoot him himself.

It was hard to tell what Indians they were. I could not hear anything but the noise of their horses' hoofs, and I suspected that they might be Crows, for I had never known the Sioux to be on that side of the river; but I was certain that the other party were Sioux. Looking around for them I found they had turned, had got out of sight, so that we only had this other party to contend with, if they were Sioux. Of course, being such a distance we could not tell whether they were Sioux or Crows. The river being in between us I thought probably it would kind of check them for awhile, and we would have the advantage of them crossing the river, and the great trouble was they never hallooed or spoke a word or signaled until they got to the bank, and when they did reach it they plunged in and commenced swimming across as if there had been no river there.

All we could see were the heads of the horses and the Indians. The Indians that were on the bank commenced firing on us and began hallooing and giving their war-cry, to let us know what tribe it was. Bat was very well acquainted with the Crows, as he had lived with them for some time. They called him the "Left Handed." As soon as he found out that they were Crows he commenced yelling that he was "Left Hand," and as quick as they heard the name they stopped all hostilities. You could hear them hallooing "Left Hand" from mouth to mouth all over the line. The Indians were strung out for a mile, and you could hear nothing but "Left Hand."

The Indians swam right across to where we were, and shook hands with us, and I thought they would go wild with joy at meeting "Left Hand." They asked us where we were from, where we were going and what was our business. We told them we were from Gen. Crook's command (they called Gen. Crook Lone Star); that we were going to their village ; that we had come after them. They went to work and made a raft and put us and our trappings on it. Three or four of them got hold of our horses and swam them across. After we got across the river there was shaking of hands for two or three hours.

Indians are very demonstrative, and it don't make any difference how urgent the business is they are on, if they meet a friend or friends they drop everything else to renew old associations. The Crows were overjoyed at seeing Bat, and every one of them wanted to grasp his hand, after which Reshaw and myself were greeted in the same friendly manner, so that our meeting might be termed a great American hand-shaking tournament. This turn of affairs was very pleasant for us, as we had anticipated a fight, and it wouldn't have taken much of a guesser to name the victors if such a contingency had arisen.

Finally we got onto our horses and went to the Crow camp, which was about eight miles from the river. The Crows had seen my signals with the looking glass, but never thinking that anybody besides an Indian would know their signals, they had supposed we were the advance guard of a war party of Sioux. That night, after reaching their camp, they held a council, and I told them what we came for, and asked them if they would go with us; telling them that Lone Star (Gen. Crook) wanted them to be sure and come, and had telegraphed them before through their agent. But they didn't seem much in favor of going with us ; that is, they didn't say anything whether they would go or not. Black Foot and Crazy Head being there, the next day I got them together and talked to them alone. They gave me their promise ; said they would call another council of all the young men.

The next day they called another council. If they would not go I should start back the next day — so I told them at the council; that I was going the next morning, and that anybody who wanted to go with me should let me know. They told me if I would wait they would move down on to the river the next day, and a lot of young men would go with me. So I waited over. The next day the camp moved to the Big Horn. Then there was more delay. They were very changeable about the business. They were a little afraid of the Sioux, or something, I could not tell what. An Indian by the name of Old Crow, who seemed to be one of the head men, came to me and asked me when I intended to start, and I told him the next morning. He says, "All right, I will go with you." So he got onto his horse and went around haranguing the camp, telling his people that he was going to start, and asking what they were afraid of. Of course it made a great deal of talk. The next

morning he and three others came up to where we were
making a raft ready for the trip.

It didn't take long to make a raft, and we soon
crossed the river and went into camp on the other side.
Before night we had one hundred and fifty-nine Indians
ready to start back the next morning. Next day we
started back to the command, camping on the Little Big
Horn that night, sending scouts out down the river to
find out whether the Sioux were in the immediate vicinity. Next morning we were killing buffalo; could not
travel very far on account of airing the meat, and camped
at the head of Owl creek. The command was to be
camped at the mouth of Prairie dog, and was to wait
there for me until my return ; so I came through the
Wolf mountains. After going on top of the mountains
I could see the camp right at the forks of Big and Little
Goose creeks.

The Indians, on seeing the camp all in white tents,
thought it was a Sioux village, and it was all that I
could do to keep them from turning back. They began
to suspect that we were connected with the Sioux, and
were trying to bring them into camp to have them killed.
I told them that what they saw were the tents of the
troops and the soldiers of Lone Star's camp ; that if they
would wait there I would leave Bat and Louie with them
and would go into camp and send an officer out to meet
them. They consented to that, and promised to stay
there until the officer came. So I went on into camp,
rode up to the General's tent and told him to send Capt.
Burt (he being acquainted with the Crows) out to meet

them; that they refused to come until I sent some officer out. Capt. Burt immediately started out to meet the Crow Indians.

The General supposed that I had been killed. How they got the information that I had been shot I don't know, but they showed me a paper in which it was stated that I had had a terrible fight with the Indians and had been killed by them. I suppose some of the reporters wanted to write something, and put that down. The General was very glad to see me when I got back. I was three days over time. Along about three o'clock the Crow Indians arrived. About two hours afterwards the sentinel gave the alarm signal. Going out to learn the cause I found it was the Snake (Shoshone) Indians, with Tom Cosgrove as their interpreter, coming to join the command. I think he had one hundred and sixty-four or one hundred and eighty-two Indians—I am not quite certain which. Their chief, Washakie, was with them.

During my absence Gen. Crook had given an order to mount the infantry, and the only animals available were the mules belonging to the wagon train. On the day following the arrival in camp of our Indian allies (June 15) the work mules were turned over to the tender mercies of the infantrymen (or vice versa), and the first circus the Goose Creek valley ever beheld begun. Many of the infantry ("walk-a-heaps," as the Indians called them), had never been in a saddle in their lives, while none of the mules had ever had a saddle on their backs, and, under supervision of experienced riders, the officers proposed to give the infantry a lesson in equestrianism.

I never saw so much fun in all my life. The valley for a mile in every direction was filled with bucking mules, frightened infantrymen, broken saddles and applauding spectators. Having nothing else to do, the entire command took a half holiday to enjoy the sport, and some of the most ludicrous mishaps imaginable were witnessed. But the average soldier is as persevering as the mule is stubborn, and in the end the mule was forced to surrender. The city of Sheridan is now located on the immense flat where this incident occurred, and I never pass down the streets of the place but what the memories of those ludicrous scenes are brought vividly to mind, and I laugh as heartily as I did on that bright June day in the memorable year of 1876.

COLONEL GUY V. HENRY.
BY PERMISSION OF JOHN F. FINERTY.

COLONEL GEO. L. BEAL.

FROM A PHOTOGRAPH BY J. CORELL.

CHAPTER XXXVII.

BATTLE OF THE ROSEBUD.

The General asked me, upon my arrival in camp, from my trip to the village of the friendly Crows, if I had any idea where the Sioux camp was. From all signs I had seen I supposed they were on the Rosebud, and I so informed him. He told me that he wanted to start as soon as he could get ready. Two days afterward the infantry was mounted on mules, and the command started for the Rosebud, leaving the wagon train upon the Big Goose, about a mile from the forks. We traveled in light marching order, taking as little with us as possible — much less than we needed. The first night out we camped on Tongue river, near the mouth of Big Goose, the next morning starting off through the hills over to Badger creek, sending out two parties of scouts from there to try and discover the Sioux village.

There being plenty of buffaloes along the line of march, the Indians killed hundreds of them. Camping on the Rosebud, we ran onto a scouting party of Sioux just before reaching the river, but from the direction they took I was satisfied the camp was on the Rosebud, down the stream. The next morning we moved down toward the Big Bend of the Rosebud and went into temporary camp there to await the report of the scouts who had been sent out to discover the hostile village. We had not reached the Big Bend before we went into camp.

It was the morning after the scouts had been sent out that the Sioux were reported to be coming in large numbers. Then we moved down to the Big Bend. There we laid down our arms and rested without unsaddling. Our Indian allies had caught up their horses ready for anything that happened to turn up. The scouts commenced to come in then, telling us that the Indians were coming. Not having had much experience with the troops I could not tell whether they were ready to meet the enemy or not; but I supposed that they were always ready for a fight, and did not pay much attention to them. It was not long before an Indian they called Humpy, a little hunch-backed Sioux, came riding down over the hills as fast as his horse could carry him, hallooing "Sioux." As he came into camp he said the Sioux were charging on us, and almost at the same time you could hear the Sioux war-cry.

The Indians and the scouts jumped on their horses, and just then the Sioux came charging down over the hills. But the troops were not ready to meet the attack, so the Crows met the first charge of the Indians, and I believe if it had not been for the Crows, the Sioux would have killed half of our command before the soldiers were in a position to meet the attack. It was a

MRS. T. J. FOSTER, THE FIRST NORTHERN WYOMING LADY SETTLER.

hand-to-hand fight for quite a while between the Crows and Sioux. It was on a kind of plateau where they were fighting, and the troops were down under the hills. I charged up the hill when the Shoshones and Crows started out, so that I could see everything that occurred. It was all of twenty minutes, I think, before the soldiers appeared over the hill. As soon as the soldiers came up and commenced fighting, the Sioux fell back. The coming together of the Sioux, Crows and Shoshones I think was the prettiest sight in the way of a fight that I have ever seen. They were all mixed up and I could hardly distinguish our allies from the hostiles. After the fight became general with the troops, our Indians drew back. I passed where one Crow Indian was sitting on the ground, and he didn't act as if he was one bit hurt. He was watching the fight between the Indians, and every once in awhile he would yell like a madman. He was unable to get on his feet, having been shot just above the knee, and the bone was terribly shattered. His horse was lying dead by his side. He seemed to be so interested in the fight that he had entirely forgotten his wound. The soldiers could not tell one Indian from another, but the redskins knew each other all right, and if a man was familiar with them he would know ; but it was very hard to keep the soldiers from firing into our allies after the troops became engaged with the Sioux, mistaking the Crows and Shoshones for the enemy.

After the troops came up they formed into line and commenced driving the Sioux back. Then the Shoshones, Crows and Sioux commenced separating. The friendly

Indians came back, and the Sioux went on the hills. The soldiers kept driving the hostiles back until they got them on the big flat beyond the first line of hills. Col. Guy V. Henry, with his battalion, was stationed on the left, and he was ordered up the river. Mills' battalion was down below on the right, and the other battalions were in the centre of the fight. The Crow and Snake Indians got scattered out, but would keep in behind the troops out of harm's reach as much as possible. I was close to the position held by General Crook, and he was in about the centre of the field. The General ordered a battalion to charge the Indians and drive them back.

In the charge that followed, one poor fellow's horse ran away with him, and the animal went right for the Indians, just as the order had been given to retreat. The horse kept straight ahead after the command had driven the Indians away and turned back, and ran up to within forty or fifty yards of the hostiles before they turned. Of course, they began shooting at the horseman, and as his horse began to turn, both of his hands were shot off at the wrists. When he came past me both of his hands were dangling. The Indians had turned the horse by firing at it. I rode up on the hill, and the poor fellow was calling for some one to check his horse. I rode very rapidly and tried to get in ahead of the frightened animal, and then I could see his hands dangling from his wrists.

I tried to head off the horse, but the animal got in ahead of me, started down the divide and went right through the troops, never stopping for anything. The

Indians were on that side of the flat fighting, and he went through the line of troops towards them, and I went after him. I got up as close as I could to him. My horse was a fast one, but I could not reach the runaway animal's bridle, and, whip as much as I would, I was unable to grasp it. If he had been a man of any nerve or had not lost his head, he might have helped turn the horse by grasping the reins with his wrists. I hit the horse over the head as hard as I could in an effort to turn it, but the horse was stubborn and frightened and was not very easily turned. I told the wounded man to throw himself off when I hit the horse the second time. He gave me one look that I will never forget. I got up as close as I could to the horse and hit it on the side of the head. The blow turned the horse some, but not clear around, and the wounded man threw himself off. The horse went right in among the Indians and was lost to view. The wounded man picked himself up and ran down over the hill out of sight. The Indians were shooting at us all of this time.

When I got back to the command the Indians were going down below us, and the General had sent all of his aids out with orders to the different commanders. It was right after this runaway horse incident occurred that the Indians got Col. Henry's battalion in a tight place, and seriously wounded that gallant officer. The Indians were pressing down pretty close. Henry's battalion received an order to retreat, but I do not know who gave the order. I suppose while standing there Col. Henry was shot. As quick as they commenced to retreat the Indians rushed down. Yute John made a dash to the place where the Colonel fell, got off his horse and turned it loose just as the Indians got to Col. Henry. Single-handed he stood them off until the soldiers commenced shooting and drove the Indians away.

In the meantime, Yute John, as quick as the Indians were driven away, put Col. Henry on his back and carried him over to where Henry's battalion was. If it had not been for this Indian (Yute John) Col. Henry would have been killed and scalped where he fell. The battalion that was on the other side of Henry had retired at the same time that Henry's battalion retreated.

I saw an Indian run right in among the soldiers as they were retreating. I don't know whether it was done purposely, but I saw a soldier hold up a gun as though he were giving it to this Indian; but I think the gun was held up to protect his head from a blow aimed at it by the Sioux. There were several soldiers killed. It was right after Henry was shot that I went over to where Gen. Crook was. There were no aids there with him, so he told me to go down and tell Capt. Mills to drive the Indians out of the Rosebud canyon. I went down and carried the order to Mills. It was but a short time afterwards that one of the aids came to me and said the General wanted to see me. When I got to Crook, he said:

"I am going to move down the Rosebud canyon, and want you to go with two battalions as far as you can down the defile and find out whether the village is at the other end of the canyon or not."

I went down the canyon with the two battalions. After getting down into the rocky pass, and seeing what was going on amongst the Indians, I became convinced they would not attack us; would not pay any attention to a detachment when they wanted the entire command. I was aware of this as quick as I got in there. They wanted to draw the entire command down into this canyon and massacre every soul in it. I had not been in the canyon twenty minutes before I knew what was going on. The canyon rose to a height of one thousand feet on both sides of us. The Indians had all of this fortified. I had got almost through the canyon with the two companies when an aide-de-camp (Col. Nickerson) overtook us. The Indians had tried so hard to draw the command down into the canyon that the General thought it was a fresh attack made, and wanted the two battalions to come back to the field and take the Indians in the rear—wanted us to come up in behind them. So, going up into the right of the canyon on the north side, we attempted to come in behind the redskins. But the Indians were watching all our movements, and before we could get in behind them they had drawn off.

["Subsequent investigation shows what an awful fate we escaped by obeying Crook's order to file out of the trap by our left flank. Immense piles of felled trees in our path and on the sides of that savage ravine showed where the Sioux had lain in ambush for our approach. Half a mile further on, and not a man of our battalion would have come out alive. The five companies of the Second, following to support us (the Third Cavalry) would have been massacred without fail, for there was no room to deploy or rally. The Indians held the timber barricades in front and flank. They would have closed upon our unguarded rear, and another horror would have been added to the long and ghastly catalogue of Indian-American warfare. However, a miss is as good as a mile, and we felt duly thankful that we escaped being the awful example of that unfortunate campaign."—Finerty's Warpath and Bivouac.

"In one word," says Capt. Bourke in his "On the Border with Crook," "the battle of the Rosebud was a trap, and Crazy Horse, the leader in command here, as at the Custer massacre a week later, was satisfied he was going to have everything his own way. He stated afterwards, when he had surrendered to General Crook at the agency (Red Cloud) that he had no less than six thousand five hundred men in the fight, and that the first attack was made with fifteen hundred, the others being concealed behind the bluffs and hills. His plan of battle was either to lead detachments in pursuit of his people, and turning quickly cut them to pieces in detail, or draw the whole of Crook's forces down into the canyon of the Rosebud, whence escape would have been impossible, as it formed a veritable *cul de sac*, the vertical walls hemming in the sides, the front being closed by a dam and abatis of broken timber which gave a depth of ten feet of water and mud, the rear, of course, to be shut off by thousands of yelling, murderous Sioux and Cheyennes. That was the Sioux programme, as learned, that day, or afterwards at the agencies from the surrendered hostiles in the spring of the following year."

It will be seen from what both Finerty and Bourke say of the Rosebud canyon that Grouard had noted things very accurately, and divined the purpose of the Sioux to a nicety as he passed down the " *cul de sac* " in advance of Mill's courageous battalion. He knew, because his six years' experience with these same Indians had been a practical lesson to him, that death awaited the entire command at the lower end of the canyon. One of the great wonders now is why Crazy Horse, when it was discovered that Mills' battalion turned to leave the death trap, did not fall upon and annihilate it. The explanation seems to be found in the words of Crazy Horse himself. He wanted the entire command, and even then had hopes of getting it. Failing, he repeated the tactics then attempted at the Custer battle, and, with the same force he had thrown against Crook, caught the five troops of the Seventh Cavalry (rank and file) to the very last soul.—AUTHOR.]

I had seen all I wanted to see to convince me of what was going on, and when I got back the General was just ready to start down the canyon. In fact, the whole command had started when I met it. I asked Gen· Crook where they were going. He said :

"Down to take the village."

"You can't go through the canyon," I told him.

He asked why.

I said, "You can't go through. They will kill your whole command if you attempt to go through there."

He could not believe that ; laughed quietly about it. I did everything I could to dissuade him, and the only way I could prevail on him to abandon the undertaking was by telling him there was no ammunition in the command. The scouts didn't have any, and a great many of the companies didn't have any, and when the General gave orders to find out how much ammunition there was, it didn't average ten cartridges to the man; and that was the only thing that stopped him. In fact, it was the only thing that saved his command, because he would have made the attempt to go through the canyon under any other circumstances.

When Crook made up his mind to do anything, it was generally done. The only way I could convince him not to go was by satisfying him of there being no ammunition in the command. I had seen all day how the Indians and troops were firing, and especially the scouts, so I asked the General to find out the amount of ammunition each company had. He found he would have to wait until he got more ammunition from the wagons before taking the offensive. We went into camp at the lower end of the battle-field. As far as the fight was concerned, I don't think that either side could claim a complete victory, although the troops held the ground. The Indians had tried to lead the troops down through the canyon where they had fortified on each side; and if the troops had ever gone down through there, there would not have been one of them left to tell the tale, for the Indians were fixed in such a way that they could have cross-fired them without getting hurt themselves, or could even have rolled rocks down in amongst them and crushed them.

CAPTAIN JOHN G. BOURKE.
BY PERMISSION OF JOHN F. FINERTY.

CAPTAIN JOHN G. McGUIRE.

Seeing this while I was going down through the canyon is the reason I tried so hard to stop the command from going through. To sum up the whole battle, there were twenty-eight soldiers killed and fifty-six wounded. One of the Indian scouts was killed and three of them wounded. On the Indian side there were thirteen of them killed, that I know of, and I could not tell the number that were wounded, but there were a good many of them. The next morning we started back to the wagon train. Starting up the Rosebud, we camped at the head of it. After we had been in camp sometime the Crow allies got stampeded for some cause, drove in their ponies, saddled them up and left us, starting back for their village, taking their wounded along with them, and nothing we could say or do would stop them. Breaking camp next morning, we reached the wagon train the same evening, and the wagon train and a large escort of troops were sent back to Fetterman for supplies.

[Finerty, the Chicago Times war correspondent, who in common with the soldiers shared all the dangers of the campaign, entered into the battles with all the spirit of a free lance and had many narrow escapes from capture and death, still "kept one eye open" as a newspaper correspondent. He missed little of detail and lost nothing of the horrors or humor of battle. I here quote (with his permission) from his wonderful volume (Warpath and Bivouac) some portions of his account of the battle of the Rosebud:

Gen. Crook divined that the Indian force before him
was a strong body — not less perhaps than 2,500 warriors — sent out to make a rear guard fight, so as to
cover the retreat of their village, which was situated at
the other end of the canyon.   He detached Troop I of
the Third Cavalry, Capt. Andrews and Lieut. Foster, from
Mills to Henry, after the former had taken the first line
of heights.   He reinforced our line with the friendly Indians, who seemed to be partially stampeded, and brought
up the whole of the Second Cavalry within supporting distance.   The Sioux, having rallied on the second line of
heights, became bold and impudent again.   They rode
up and down rapidly, sometimes wheeling in circles,
slapping an indelicate portion of their persons at us, and
beckoning us to come on.

One chief, probably the late lamented Crazy Horse,
directed their movements by signals made with a pocket
mirror or some other reflector.   Under Crook's orders,
our whole line remounted, and, after another rapid charge,
we became masters of the second crest.   When we got
there, another just like it rose on the other side of the
valley.   There, too, were the savages, as fresh, apparently,
as ever.   We dismounted accordingly, and the firing began again.   It was evident that the weight of the firing
was shifted from our front, of which Maj. Evans had general command, to our left where Royall and Henry
cheered on their men.   Still the enemy were thick enough
on the third crest, and Colonel Mills, who had active
charge of our operations, wished to dislodge them.   The
volume of fire, rapid and ever increasing, came from our

left. The wind freshened from the west, and we could hear the uproar distinctly.

Soon, however, the restless foe came back upon us, apparently reinforced. He made a vigorous push down our center down some rocky ravines, which gave him good cover. Just then a tremendous yell arose behind us, and along through the intervals of our battalions, came the tumultuous array of the Crow and Shoshone Indians, rallied and led back to action by Maj. George M. Randall and Lieutenant John G. Bourke, of General Crook's staff. Orderly Sergeant John Van Moll, of Troop A, Mills' battalion, a brave and gigantic soldier, who was subsequently basely murdered by a drunken mutineer of his company, dashed forward on foot with them. The two bodies of savages, all stripped to the breech-clout, moccasins and war bonnet, came together in the trough of the valley, the Sioux having descended to meet our allies with right good will. All, except Sergeant Van Moll, were mounted. Then began a most exciting encounter. The wild foemen, covering themselves with their horses, while going at full speed, blazed away rapidly. Our regulars did not fire, because it would have been sure death to the friendly Indians, who were barely distinguishable by a red badge which they carried. Horses fell dead by the score — they were heaped there when the fight closed — but, strange to relate, the casualties among the warriors, including both sides, did not certainly exceed five and twenty.

The whooping was persistent, but the Indian voice is less hoarse than the Caucasian, and has a sort of wolfish bark to it, doubtless the result of heredity, because the Indians, for untold ages, have been imitators of the vocal characteristics of the prairie wolf. The absence of very heavy losses in this combat goes far to prove the wisdom of the Indian method of fighting.

Finally the Sioux on the right, hearing the yelping and firing of the rival tribes, came up in great numbers, and our Indians, carefully picking up their wounded, and making their unwounded horses carry double, began to draw off in good order. Sergeant Van Moll was left alone on foot. A dozen Sioux dashed at him. Major Randall and Lieutenant Bourke, who had probably not noticed him in the general melee, but who, in the crisis, recognized his stature and his danger, turned their horses to rush to his rescue. They called on the Indians to follow them. One small, misshapen Crow warrior, mounted on a fleet pony, outstripped all others. He dashed boldly in among the Sioux, against whom Van Moll was dauntlessly defending himself, seized the big Sergeant by the shoulder, and motioned him to jump up behind. The Sioux were too astonished to realize what had been done until they saw the long-legged Sergeant, mounted behind the little Crow, known as " Humpy," dash towards our lines like the wind. Then they opened fire but we opened also, and compelled them to seek higher ground. The whole line of our battalion cheered " Humpy" and Van Moll as they passed us on the home-stretch. There were no insects on them, either.

In order to check the insolence of the Sioux, we were compelled to drive them from the third ridge. Our ground was more favorable for quick movements than that occupied by Royall, who found much difficulty in forcing the savages in his front — mostly the flower of the brave Cheyenne tribe — to retire. One portion of his line, under Captain Vroom, pushed out beyond its supports, deceived by the rugged character of the ground, and suffered quite severely. In fact, the Indians got between it and the main body, and nothing but the coolness of its commander and the skillful management of Colonels Royall and Henry saved Troop L of the Third Cavalry from annihilation on that day. Lieutenant Morton, one of Colonel Royall's aids, Captain Andrews and Lieutenant Foster of Troop I, since dead, particularly distinguished themselves in extricating Vroom from his perilous position.

In repelling the audacious charge of the Cheyennes upon his battalion, the undaunted Col. Henry, one of the most accomplished officers in the army, was struck by a bullet, which passed through both cheek bones, broke the bridge of his nose and destroyed the optic nerve of one eye. His orderly, in attempting to assist him, was also wounded, but, temporarily blinded as he was, and throwing blood from his mouth by the handful, Henry sat his horse for several minutes in front of the enemy. He finally fell to the ground, and, as that portion of our line, discouraged by the fall of so brave a chief, gave ground a little, the Sioux charged over his prostrate body, but were speedily repelled, and he was happily rescued by some soldiers of his command.

Several hours later, when returning from the pursuit of the hostiles, I saw Col: Henry lying on a blanket, his face covered with a bloody cloth, around which the summer flies were buzzing fiercely, and a soldier keeping the wounded man's horse standing in such a position as to throw the animal's shadow upon the gallant sufferer. There was absolutely no other shadow in that neighborhood. When I ventured to condole with the Colonel he merely said, in a low but firm voice, "It is nothing. For this are we soldiers!" and forthwith he did me the honor of advising me to join the army. Col. Henry's sufferings, when our retrograde movement began, and, in fact, until—after a jolting journey of several hundred miles, by mule litter and wagon—he reached Fort Russell, were horrible, as were, indeed, those of all the wounded.

As the day advanced, Gen. Crook became tired of the indecisiveness of the action, and resolved to bring matters to a crisis. He rode up to where the officers of Mills' battalion were standing, or sitting, behind their men, who were prone on the skirmish line, and said, in effect, "It is time to stop this skirmishing, Colonel. You must take your battalions and go for their village way down the canyon." "All right, sir," replied Mills, and the order to retire and remount was given.

Troops A, E and M of Mills' battalion, having remounted, guided by the scout Grouard, plunged immediately into what is called, on what authority I know not, the Dead Canyon of Rosebud valley. It is a dark, narrow and winding defile, over a dozen miles in length, and the main Indian village was supposed to be situated in the north end of it. Lieut. Bourke, of Crook's staff, accompanied the column. A body of Sioux, posted on a bluff which commanded the west side of the canyon, was brilliantly dislodged by a bold charge of Troop E, under Capt. Sutorious and Lieut. Von Leuttewitz. After this our march began in earnest.

The bluffs, on both sides of the ravine, were thickly covered with rocks and fir trees, thus affording ample protection to an enemy, and making it impossible for our cavalry to act as flankers. Col. Mills ordered the section of the battalion moving on the east side of the canyon to cover their comrades on the west side, if fired upon, and *vice versa*. This was good advice, and good strategy in the position in which we were placed. We began to think our force rather weak for so venturesome an enterprise, but Lieut. Bourke informed the Colonel that the five troops of the Third Cavalry, under Maj. Noyes, were marching behind us. A slight rise in the valley enabled us to see the dust stirred up by the supporting column some distance in the rear.

The day had become absolutely perfect, and we all felt elated, exhilerated as we were by our morning's experience. Nevertheless, some of the more thoughtful officers had their misgivings, because the canyon was certainly a most dangerous defile, where all the advantage would be on the side of the savages. Gen. Custer, although not marching in a position so dangerous, and with a force nearly equal to ours, suffered annihilation at the hands of the same enemy, about eighteen miles further westward, only eight days afterward.

Noyes, marching his battalion rapidly, soon overtook our rear guard, and the whole column increased its pace. Fresh signs of Indians began to appear in all directions, and we began to feel that the sighting of their village must be only a question of a few miles further on. We came to a halt in a kind of cross canyon, which had an opening toward the west, and there tightened up our horses' girths, and got ready for what we believed must be a desperate fight. The keen-eared Grouard pointed toward the occident, and said to Col. Mills, "I hear firing in that direction, sir." Just then there was a sound of fierce galloping behind us, and a horseman, dressed in buckskin, and wearing a long beard, originally black, but turned temporarily gray by the dust, shot by the halted command, and dashed up where Col. Mills and the other officers were standing.

It was Maj. A. H. Nickerson, of the General's staff. He has been unfortunate since, but he showed himself a hero on that day at least. He had ridden, with a single orderly, through the canyon to overtake us, at the imminent peril of his life.

"Mills," he said, "Royall is hard pressed, and must be relieved. Henry is badly wounded, and Vroom's troop is all cut up. The General orders that you and Noyes defile by your left flank out of this canyon and fall on the rear of the Indians who are pressing Royall." This, then, was the firing that Grouard had heard.

Crook's order was instantly obeyed, and we were fortunate enough to find a comparatively easy way out of the elongated trap into which duty had led us. We defiled, as nearly as possible, by the heads of companies, in parallel columns, so as to carry out the order with greater celerity. We were soon clear of Dead Canyon, although we had to lead our horses over and among the boulders and fallen timber. The crest of the side of the ravine proved to be a sort of plateau, and there we could hear quite plainly the noise of the attack on Royall's front. We got out from among the loose rocks and scraggy trees that fringed the rim of the gulf, and found ourselves in quite an open country. "Prepare to mount — mount!" shouted the officers, and we were again in the saddle.

Then we urged our animals to their best pace, and speedily came in view of the contending parties. The Indians had their ponies, guarded mostly by mere boys, in the rear of the low, rocky crest which they occupied. The position held by Royall rose somewhat higher, and both lines could be seen at a glance. There was very heavy firing, and the Sioux were evidently preparing to make an attack in force, as they were riding in by the score, especially from the point abandoned by Mills' battalion in its movement down the canyon, and which was partially held thereafter by the friendly Indians, a few infantry and a body of sturdy mule packers, commanded by the brave Tom Moore, who fought on that day as if he had been a private soldier. Suddenly the Sioux lookouts observed our unexpected approach, and gave the alarm to their friends. We dashed forward at a wild gallop, cheering as we went, and I am sure we were all anxious at that moment to avenge our comrades of Henry's battalion.

But the cunning savages did not wait for us. They picked up their wounded, all but thirteen of their dead, and broke away to the northwest on their fleet ponies, leaving us only the thirteen "scalps," one hundred and fifty dead horses and ponies and a few old blankets and war bonnets as trophies of the fray. Our losses, including the friendly Indians, amounted to about fifty, most of the casualties being in the Third Cavalry, which bore the brunt of the fight on the Rosebud. Thus ended the engagement which was the prelude to the great tragedy that occurred eight days later in the neighboring valley of the Little Big Horn.

GENERAL GEORGE A. CUSTER.
FURNISHED BY CUSTER POST, G. A. R., ST. JOSEPH, MO.

GENERAL GEORGE A. CUSTER

CHAPTER XXXVIII

THE CUSTER MASSACRE.

A short time after the battle of the Rosebud, Gen. Crook got dispatches ordering him to await the arrival of reinforcements (the Fifth Cavalry). In the meantime the command moved up the Little Goose creek close to the Big Horn range. Our Snake or Shoshone Indians had left us, so that we were without any Indian allies whatever. There was not much going on for awhile. Gen. Crook spent most of his time in the mountains hunting. While the General was up in the mountains hunting, I was out riding around the country trying to find some traces of hostile Indians; and one day, happening to be up on the mountains, I saw some Indian signals down on the divide between the Rosebud and Little Big Horn. These signals were to the effect that the Indians and troops were fighting, and the Indians had the best of it. This was between 9 and 10 o'clock in the morning. Getting on my horse and going down into camp, I told the officers that the Indians were having a fight—I supposed with the troops—and had got way the best of them. The officers had never heard of Indian signals, and didn't suppose such things were in existence.

They laughed at the idea of Indians having smoke signals; hardly crediting my statement. It made me a little bit out of temper the way they talked about it, and I told them that I would prove to them I was right.

I saddled up my horse and started for where the signals had been given, reaching what at first seemed to be the trail of troops on the divide between the Rosebud and Little Big Horn just about dark on the night of June 25th, and soon found that troops had been along there. I started to follow up the trail, which led down a creek. In following up the trail, it led me almost to the mouth of the creek where it empties into the Little Big Horn, then turning off to the right, traveling along parallel to the creek and back into the bluffs. I found out afterwards that Custer and Reno had separated there where the trail left this creek, but not knowing this at the time, I could only follow the plainest trail I could find. I followed the trail out where the Custer command had tried to cross the Little Big Horn, out again, and went still further down the creek, but away from it. It was just 11 o'clock at night when I got to this place. I must have passed close to where Reno's command was entrenched, but did not know it. It was very dark and I could not see things plainly. It was cloudy and trying to rain; in fact, a few big drops of rain did fall.

The first intimation I had of getting onto the battlefield was when my horse got scared at something lying in the trail ahead of me, and I could not get him to pass it. I was riding an animal that did not usually scare at anything—a jet black beauty that Gen. Crook had given

me. Getting off the horse and stooping down, so that I
could feel along with my hands, I came in contact with
some object. I did not know what it was, so I commenced
examining it, when I found that I had my hand on the
head of a man who had been scalped. Well, of course,
I cannot exactly tell .the feelings I did have ; but I got
onto my horse pretty quickly after I found out what it
had frightened at. I was going on to a kind of divide
— on to the main divide. It seemed as though the
soldiers had tried to reach a main divide from there, and
I thought by taking down the ridge I would avoid any
more such horrible objects, such as I had found on the
lower ridge ; but instead of that I got right into the midst
of the dead, and was forced to follow the ridge all the
way down. It seemed to me for a long time — I could
not see them, but could tell by the way my horse acted
— that I was traveling amongst dead people all the way
down the ridge. I don't think I was over ten minutes
riding down the ridge, but it seemed quite awhile before
I could get away.

Finally I did get up through them, and went down
and crossed the Little Big Horn to the other side onto
the high lands, then turned and followed up the river,
but keeping away in order to find the Indian trail, if
possible. It was along toward morning before I found
the trail leading up the Little Big Horn towards the
mountains. Following that up and keeping off the main
trail, I could hear the Indians traveling backwards and
forwards, but could not see them. I heard no firing of
guns. Reaching the outskirts of the Indian camp on

Pass creek at the mouth of Twin creek on the Big Flat, I arrived at their main camp close to daybreak. Riding around from the lower end to the upper end, and keeping away from the lodges, I found an old Indian driving up his ponies, or herding them, rather.

I rode up to him for the purpose of finding out, if I could, what had been the result of the battle I knew had so recently occurred. I was dressed up as an Indian, and had a blanket over me, so the old fellow could not tell who or what I was. As soon as I commenced talking to him in the Sioux tongue, he asked me who I was. I told him that I was Sitting Bull's brother; that I was looking for my horse; that I had been out on a scout and had not seen the fight, as I had just got back that evening He suspicioned me of not being what I said I was, and tried to find out who I was by getting up close to me, and I saw I could not get any information out of him. It was then daybreak, and on his asking me again who I was, I told him that they had always called me the "Grabber." That was the nickname the Indians had for me when I was among them.

Quick as he heard who I was, the old man gave one yell and about two jumps, and was across on the other side of the creek hallooing that the troops were on them. Well, by this time the whole camp was in commotion. I had started back toward Tongue river on a pretty good gallop. I got quite a distance—five or six miles, I guess—before any of them came in sight, and by that time it was broad daylight. I had such a start of them that they could not catch me. They ran me

MAJOR–GENERAL A. H. TERRY.

MAJOR-GENERAL A. H. TERRY.
By permission of Scribner's Sons.

clear back to Tongue river—a distance of forty miles. Not being able to overtake me, they gave up the chase. After they left me I was so tired out that when I got over on Soldier creek I went into the brush, unsaddled my horse and went to sleep. I must have slept there all that night until the next morning between 10 and 11 o'clock.

When I woke up I could hear Indians talking. Crawling out so that I could see what was going on, I discovered that quite a large scouting party had camped right in below me—not over five hundred yards from where I was resting. For fear they might run across me or see me I led my horse into the brush, threw him down, tied his feet so that he could not get up and went off to the best hiding place I could find and stayed there until after dark. Then, everything being safe, I untied my horse, saddled him up and started to get out of there as quietly as I could. I reached the command about 4 o'clock the next day. The command had received rumors of the Custer massacre just before I got back.

———

[The Custer massacre will always be a prolific theme for speculative minds. The story today is an oft-told tale, and writers will never tire of relating it. The responsibility for the awful catastrophe will forever remain in doubt, and mayhap it is as well that it should. Custer had every confidence in himself, and his men shared that confidence. When the junction had been formed at the mouth of the Rosebud on the 15th of

June, 1876, between the different battalions of Gibbons' command, Indian scouts were sent out to discover the whereabouts of the hostiles, and secure, as near as possible, the numbers of the enemy. Upon the return of these scouts, who located the Indian village in the vicinity of the Little Big Horn, they reported the strength of the hostiles to be between three and five thousand fighting warriors. But the agents at the different agencies had previously given it as their opinion that the hostile force did not amount to over one thousand fighting men; and, strange as it may appear, both Gibbon and Terry seemed to have placed greater reliance on the estimates of the agents than in the actual observation of the friendly Indian scouts. Custer, from all accounts, shared the opinion of his superiors, and expressed himself as able to whip the allied forces of Sioux and Cheyennes with his own regiment if he were only permitted the apportunity.

Camp at the mouth of the Rosebud was broken on the morning of June 22d, Custer, with his regiment (the Seventh Cavalry) and pack train, moving up the Rosebud, and Terry and Gibbon with their forces, going up the Yellowstone. At the council of war held before the commands separated, what was determined upon as the line of action is now shrouded in doubt, some holding that Custer was not to attack the hostiles until the different commands were close enough together to form a junction, while others maintain that Custer himself said he was authorized to attack the enemy whenever and wherever he found him.

MAJOR-GENERAL JOHN GIBBON.
BY PERMISSION OF JOHN F. FINERTY.

MAJOR-GENERAL JOHN GIBBON.
BY PERMISSION OF JOHN L. GIBBON.

But there is documentary evidence in existence which goes far toward proving that Custer received "definite" instructions, and that he permitted his enthusiasm to take advantage of the loophole left in them. He was to have moved up the Rosebud in pursuit of the Indians whose trail Reno had discovered some days previous. "It is of course impossible to give any definite instructions," reads this interesting memento, "in regard to this movement, and, were it not impossible to do so, the department commander places too much confidence in your zeal, energy and ability to wish to impose upon you *precise orders which might hamper your action when nearly in contact with the enemy.* He will, however, indicate to you his own view of what your action should be, and he desires that you should conform to them, *unless you shall see sufficient reason for departing from them.*"

Here's a case of "close the door, please, unless you desire to leave it open."

If Custer found that the Indian trail (discovered previously by Reno) turned toward the Little Big Horn, he was to have kept to the left toward the headwaters of the Tongue river, in order that no band or bands of hostiles should be permitted to escape to the south or southeast by passing around his left flank. He was to feel his way cautiously from the Tongue river westward to the valley of the Little Big Horn, where he was to carefully examine Tullock creek (a tributary of the Big Horn) at its upper end, and report to Gen. Gibbon, whose command would be located at the forks of the Little and

Big Horn rivers. With Custer's command on the headwaters of the Little Big Horn (east), Crook's in the Goose
creek valley (south), and Gibbon's at the head of the Little Big Horn valley (north), the Indians (if located in the
latter valley, and it was almost impossible to suppose they
were anywhere else, as the trail led in that direction and
the scouts had located their village on or in the vicinity
of the Little Big Horn), would find it impossible to escape
the cordon of troops unless they penetrated the mountains and crossed the range to the west, a move which
was highly improbable because next to impossible.

But Custer did not allow instructions to "hamper his
actions" when he found himself upon the hot trail of the
Indians on the Rosebud. The headwaters of the Tongue
were permitted to take care of themselves. Custer saw
sufficient reason for departing from his orders, and pressed
on in pursuit of the savages. By the time the valley of
the Little Big Horn was reached, he had other plans than
the one mapped out by the commanding General to examine
the upper part of Tullock creek. His scouts had reported
the Indian village but a short distance ahead, but whether
they also reported on the strength of the hostiles will
never be known.

It is enough to know, however, that the hostiles' trail
was discovered when the Custer command reached a point
twenty miles up the Rosebud, after leaving the Gibbon
command. It lead up that stream for many miles, and
finally turned off to a tributary of the Little Big Horn.
When Custer reached a point eighteen miles from the Indian
village, he called Reno, Benteen, McDougal and his other

officers together and divided his command into three battalions, taking troops C, E, F, I and L himself. Troops A, M and G were assigned to Reno, while Benteen was given charge of troops H, D and K. B troop, under Captain McDougal, was made an escort to the pack train. From the scouts the exact location of the Indian village had been obtained. Some authorities claim that Benteen was to cross the Little Big Horn and attack the village at its upper end; Reno was to keep on the east side of the stream until he came to about the center of the village and then begin the attack, and Custer was to follow down stream to the extreme lower end of the camp and attack it there, so that the three forces would begin the fight at different points almost simultaneously. When the three battalions had reached a point five miles from the village, Benteen crossed the river and followed down under the shadows of the mountain, while the Custer and Reno commands marched side by side yet a little further. Then Custer bore off to the east, into the hills, while Reno passed down to the river and soon after engaged the Indians. He met a force that he could not drive—a host that he had not looked for. Demoralization took possession of his battalion, and in the retreat which ensued his men were mowed down like grass.

Benteen, in a statement made to Mr. Finerty, says there was to have been no connection between Reno, McDougal and himself in Custer's order. He was sent off to the left several miles from where Custer was killed to "actually hunt up more Indians." When he set off on his mission, he left the remainder of the regiment at a halt and dismounted. He soon saw, he says, after carrying out Custer's order, and two other orders which were sent to him by the General, that "the Indians had too much horse sense to travel over the kind of country I had been sent to explore, unless forced to," and concluding that his battalion would have plenty of work ahead with the others, obliqued to the right to strike the trail of the main column, and got into it just ahead of McDougal and his pack train. After watering the horses of his battalion at a morass near the side of the road, he went briskly on, "having a presentiment that I'd find hot work very soon." On the way he met two orderlies with messages—one for the commanding officer of the pack train and one for himself, written and signed by the regimental adjutant, Lieut. Cook. They read: "Come on. Be quick," and "Bring packs." Benteen did not return for the pack train, but pushed on at a trot, and (to use his own words) "Got there in time to save Reno's outfit." McDougal came up later, and a junction was then formed. From that time on until the morning of the 27th they were kept busy repelling the attacks of the hostiles.

From this statement of Benteen's it does not seem that he had received any orders from Custer to attack any portion of the Indian village, and this view is further borne out by the statement of Benteen that he carried out the orders that Custer had given him. But both he and Reno must have known that Custer was battling with the hostiles at some point not far distant; and yet no effort was made to reach the Custer command the day of the 25th of June.

There is little if any doubt but what Reno's command would have been annihilated had it not been for the timely arrival of Gibbon. The Indians claimed that they had Reno just where they wanted him, but were not given time enough to move their camp far enough from the scene of battle before making their final cleanup of the soldiers. Notwithstanding this claim of the Indians, and admitting that Reno would have taken desperate chances in attempting to go to the assistance of Custer, the people of the United States will always think he should have taken the chances, and believe and know Custer would not have hesitated a second in making such a move had matters been reversed. Custer would have fought his way to Reno, under such circumstances, or died on the bluffs in making the attempt.

Grouard, whose acquaintance with the Indians was more extended than that of any man who has ventured to speak on this subject, and who was on the battlefield at 11 o'clock on the night succeeding the day of the butchery, says the Indians told him Custer made an attempt to cross the Little Big Horn where the trail of the command was afterward discovered leading down to the edge of the river. But the Indians met him in great numbers at this point, and he found it impossible to cross. The water was high, and the bed of the river at all times is full of quicksand at this point, and the Indians told Grouard that one of the soldiers' pack mules, loaded with ammunition, was swallowed up in the sand when the attempt to ford the river was made.

Custer then seemed determined, after his first repulse, to cross the river at a point lower down. To do this he was forced to back out into the bluffs, and the Indians, divining his intention, crossed the river below his command in thousands, attacking it on all sides at once. Custer must have recognized the almost hopelessness of his position from the moment he found himself unable to cross the Little Big Horn where he first made the attempt; but that he did not lose his head is proved by the fact that he attempted to lead his command on to the bluffs overlooking the valley. As soon, however, as he left the river, the Indians got in between it and his command, so that, with the hostiles occupying the draws on the south, the high bluffs on the east and the river bottom on the west, the soldiers were forced to occupy a midway position between the higher points and the valley, and were driven along the slope east and north until the last one had been killed.

"The Indians congregated so rapidly and were in such positions," said one of Grouard's Indian informants, "that there was no earthly chance for the command to extricate itself. The troopers fought bravely and to the last, but the battle was over in less than one hour from the time Custer made his first attempt to cross the Little Big Horn."

One peculiar thing about the entire matter is found in the uncertainty expressed by all the officers concerning the time of day when the attack on the Sioux village (made by Reno's battalion) occurred. If, as the official reports claim, Custer was in the valley of the

CURLEY, THE ONLY SURVIVOR OF CUSTER'S COMMAND.

CURLEY, THE ONLY SURVIVOR OF CUSTER'S COMMAND.

Little Big Horn at eight o'clock in the morning of June 25th, it would seem highly probable that the attack occurred long before noon of that date. Some of Reno's soldiers claim that the two battalions (Custer's and Reno's) were still marching side by side when the indications of the Sioux village were so plain as to be unmistakable, and that the Colonel of the Seventh, elated at the prospect of an immediate engagement, cried, "Hurrah! Custer's luck!" Immediately after this the commands separated, Reno "charging down the valley a considerable distance, finally halting in the timber, where he was attacked by superior numbers."

Grouard says he first noticed the signals made by the Indians on June 25 between nine and ten o'clock in the morning. These signals indicated a big battle with the soldiers, the Indians having "way the best of it," as the scout expresses it. Grouard immediately repaired to Crook's camp on the Little Goose creek, and imparted his information to the officers he found there (Gen. Crook being up in the mountains on a hunt). Not having had any experience with Indian signals, the officers in camp ridiculed the idea advanced by Grouard that the troops and savages were engaged. The scout thereupon informed them he would prove he was right, and immediately jumped on one of the best horses in the command and started for the locality whence the signals had been given. The distance from Goose creek to the Custer battlefield is about seventy miles, and as it was close to noon when Grouard started, and the latter part of the trip was made after dark, he necessarily had to ride at the rate of seven miles an hour to reach the Custer bat-tlefield by eleven o'clock.

Horned Horse, who related the story of the battle many times after he arrived at the agency, maintained that "by noon all of one party were killed, and the oth-ers (Reno's) driven back into a bad place. The reason we did not kill all of this party was because while we were fighting his (Reno's) party, we heard that more sol-diers were coming up the river," whereupon the hostiles drew off. "The troops first charged from up the river," he said. Then all the young bucks charged the troops. "Then there was another party of troops on the other side of the river. One half of the Indians pursued the first body of troops; the other half went after the other body." Which shows that Custer's attack was made al-most simultaneously with that of Reno.

Custer did not proceed northward over three miles from the spot where Reno's fortifications were thrown up after his retreat across the river, so that he could not have been over two miles from Reno when the latter was holding the Sioux at bay in the timber. Knowing that Custer had intended to strike the village at its lower end as soon as he could make the distance from the point where he and Reno separated, and the latter having in-vested the woods on the southeast side of the camp, people can not but wonder why he failed to hold this point of vantage until he could satisfy himself that Cus-ter made his proposed attack below. Instead of doing this, however, Reno withdrew from the woods, retreated across the Little Big Horn, and took up a position infi-

nitely less desirable than the one he had first held on the
west of the stream, where he was protected by a heavy
growth of timber. This retreat is said to have been so
precipitous that many of the fleeing soldiers were actually
dragged from their horses by the pursuing savages and
hacked to death at leisure.

There must have been a respite given the Reno command to gain its second position, for it was then that
Benteen came upon the scene from the west, and he was
followed somewhat later by McDougal's troop and the
pack train. There is no account of the packs having
been attacked while on their way southeast over the main
trail to reach Reno's position, so it necessarily follows
that the Indians at that particular time had withdrawn
from Reno to repel the charge of the Custer battalion
three miles down the stream. "Indecision" on the part
of Reno may have led to the force under himself and
Benteen being kept at a standstill while Custer's command
was undergoing destruction; but military men used a very
mild term when they called it such.

On the afternoon of the massacre the soldiers of
Reno's command distinctly heard a "charge" sounded on
a bugle, and they arose with a cheer to welcome Custer,
only to be met with a yell of derision from the savages.
This circumstance could not have escaped the notice or
knowledge of Reno, and yet he claims he had no suspicion that annihilation had overtaken Custer's command.
A little later on in the day the white hats and blue
coats of soldiers were noticed in the possession of the
Indians who swarmed about Reno's entrenched position,

but this circumstance does not appear to have made any deep impression on Maj. Reno. His "indecision" may have saved his command, but it will never write the name of "hero" on his monument.

Grouard, as stated in his narrative, reached the Custer battlefield about 11 o'clock on the night of June 25th. He had struck the trail of the Custer command where the commands separated, and followed it down to the bluffs on which the bodies of the killed were strewn. On his way to this spot he must, as he says, have passed close to the entrenched position held by Reno, but he did not know it. When he crossed the Little Big Horn he heard (but did not see) the Indians passing backward and forward over the travoi trails, but the camp at that time had been moved to a point fully twenty miles southwest of the battlefield. The scout heard no shooting while in the vicinity of the Little Big Horn, and saw nothing which led him to suppose that Reno's command was besieged. He was in the Indian camp at sun-up on the morning of the 26th of June, and left that place with hundreds of the savages in hot pursuit, reaching the Crook command on Goose creek two days afterwards.

In their haste to get their families out of the way of danger, the Indians undoubtedly left many tepis and much rubbish, and which was, later on, destroyed by the savages themselves, as they had no means to convey it from the spot, the travois having been taken to a point twenty miles to the southwest. The only view Reno's command obtained of the Indian camp was at the

THE LITTLE BIG HORN, BELOW CROW AGENCY.

time that command was first thrown against the savages. Its subsequent retreat across the river cut off the view of the camp entirely, and Reno could not know when the hostile village was moved. Grouard states positively that it was moved on the night of the 25th, and as he visited it on the morning of the 26th when it was located twenty miles southwest of the battlefield, it could not have occupied its former site on the banks of the Little Big Horn on the morning of the 27th of June.

The Indians, whose numbers were constantly augmenting, were getting as rapidly as possible into a section of country where game was plentiful. They therefore had their families with them. They had runners out all over the country, north, east and south; knew that Crook's command was in the valley of the Goose creeks; that Gibbon and Terry were marching up the Yellowstone from the mouth of the Rosebud and that Custer's force was moving rapidly up the latter stream toward the Little Big Horn where their village was located. But they had no idea, as they afterwards said, that Custer would be rash enough to attack them when he discovered their force. They were greatly surprised that he did so.

Grouard had seen their village on two occasions — once before and once after the massacre; and he states that on the morning after the battle of the Little Big Horn there were no less than nine thousand fighting men in the hostile camp. He says there were fully six hundred wickiups in the village. These wickiups were used by the young bucks who had escaped from the different agencies; and the scout thinks there must have been over or quite five thousand of these young warriors, while the force of the village proper was not less than four thousand fighting men. Grouard further says that each wickiup would accommodate from six to ten persons, and all of them were crowded to their fullest capacity.

The Indians told Grouard that when Custer's attempt to cross the Little Big Horn had been frustrated, the command headed directly east for the high bluffs, behind which hundreds of Indians were secreted. These rose up to meet Custer as his men advanced. Not knowing that the savages were there, Custer was taken completely by surprise, and attempted, by a charge, to force his way through the enemy to the northeast. But he met with such a withering fire that he was compelled to seek lower ground, and in doing so he met the enemy's force that, by this time, had crossed the river and filled all the draws to the north, and was compelled to feel his way west and south, which accounts for the finding of the bodies of his command lying in almost a perfect circle.

When the charge up the bluff was made, the Indians stated (and they related the story many times to the scout), that an officer on a magnificent animal, unable to check the speed of his charger, rode directly through the enemy's line, escaping the hundreds of bullets that were fired at him. Some of the young braves gave chase, but as they were afoot when the charge was made and lost some little time in getting their ponies, the officer was soon far in advance of his pursuers. They followed him for several miles, however, and watched him as he crossed

Poplar creek (due east from the Custer battlefield). Beyond this creek is an immense flat, and while the Indians sat upon their ponies, having given up the chase, and watched the fleeing horseman as he reached the plain, they beheld a puff of smoke, and saw the officer fall from the saddle. They then rode over to where he fell, secured his horse and trappings, and left the body lying where it fell. The officer, for some unknown cause, had ended his life at the point of his own gun.

Grouard's explanation is that the officer, being convinced that the command would perish to a man, did not wish to survive his comrades in arms, so put an end to his life when escape was within his grasp; or, that being unable to rejoin the command, and fearing that his escape would be construed into desertion and forever remain a blot upon his honor, he ended his existence within sight of the spot where the five troops of the heroic Seventh met their Waterloo.

This story of the Indians is borne out by a fact: The body of one officer (Second Lieutenant H. M. Harrington of Troop C) was never recovered. It was supposed that he fell in the first charge, and was swallowed up by the treacherous quicksands in the bed of the Little Big Horn ; but it is just as possible that he escaped death by the river and found it on the plain east of Poplar creek, though it must be admitted that nothing but the fact that his body was not found on the field of battle lends any evidence to his identification as the officer referred to by the savages.

The Indians were sure that the officer was trying to check the speed of his horse when he passed through their line ; but the animal was crazed with fright and could neither be stopped nor overtaken. It went like the wind, and proved itself afterwards to be one of the fleetest-footed horses possessed by the savages.

As soon as possible after the battle begun, the camp, with the women and children, was moved, the mutilation of the Custer dead having been done by the bucks, Horned Horse, who viewed the scene from a distance, stating that the warriors only desisted in their horrible work from sheer exhaustion.

A great deal has been said and written about the manner in which Custer received his death wound, and to Rain-in-the-Face, whose picture will be found in these pages, has been attributed the killing of this gallant and daring spirit. It is already known that Custer's body was the only one escaping mutilation; also that the wound which caused death was in the head and made by a bullet. No other wound or mark was found upon the body, and it apparently lay where it had fallen. The reading world need not be shocked by the knowledge that no man has honor in Custer's death. "Nothing can be retentive to the strength of spirit." Rain-in-the-Face did not kill Gen. Custer. But Custer, brave to the last, surrounded by the dead bodies of his relatives and troopers, and realizing the horrors that awaited him as a captive — tortures a thousand times worse than death — turned his weapon against himself and escaped the terrible fate for which the Indians attempted to spare him.

RAIN-IN-THE-FACE, REPUTED SLAYER OF CUSTER.

RAIN-IN-THE-FACE, THE FLOWER OF CUSTER.

Custer was well known to and by the savage horde which encompassed him. There was a chance for his capture, and the only way the General had to defeat it was in anticipating his own end. The gallant Fetterman and Brown died by each other's hands at the Phil Kearney massacre in 1866, and a hundred other cases might be cited of a like nature. The friends and admirers of Custer have nothing to regret in the knowledge that the brave soldier opened the gateway to eternity with his own right hand.

Among the Sioux there exists a superstition concerning those who suicide. They will not touch the body of a man or woman who meets death at his or her own election. Custer's body was not disturbed. Had it not been for the fact that all the bodies of the Custer command lay in the scorching sun four days before they were recovered, the tell-tale powder marks on Custer's temple would have put at rest the question of Custer's taking off without recourse to the evidence of savages.

Curley, a Crow scout, who accompanied the Custer command, and is the only survivor of the battle of the Little Big Horn, claims to have saved himself by hiding in a gulch while the fight was going on, and afterwards escaping by drawing his blanket about him and passing through the ranks of the hostiles, being taken for one of their own number in the excitement which prevailed. Curley's account of the battle is meagre, as his time was pretty well occupied in looking to his own safety. His statement that the fight commenced at 2:30 or 3 o'clock in the afternoon (his calculation of time being based

upon the position of the sun) and continued until nearly
sunset, is entirely overcome by the statements of parties
in the Reno command that clothing and guidons belonging to the Custer battalion were seen and recognized in
possession of the Indians who besieged Reno's position
early in the afternoon of the 25th of June.

Scores of the Indians who were engaged in the
attack upon Custer have told Grouard that the fight with
the ill-fated command did not last over an hour, at the
end of which time every man in it had been killed.
"Officers in Reno's battalion," says Finerty, "who, late
in the afternoon, from high points surveyed the country
in anxious expectation of Custer's appearance, and who
commanded a view of the field where he had fought, say
that no fighting was going on at that time — between
five and six o'clock. It is evident, therefore, that the last
of Custer's command was destroyed at an hour earlier in
the day than Curley relates." Some of Curley's statements
are borne out by facts related by the Indians, while some
are not; therefore his story gives rise to many perplexing doubts.

The battle between Reno and the Indians may be
said to have been almost continuous from the time of
the attack on the morning of June 25th until the fore-
noon of the 27th, when, upon the approach of Gibbon's
column, the hostiles drew off. As positive proof that
the engagement between Custer and the Indians lasted
but a very short time may be mentioned the startling
fact that but seven of the hostiles were killed during the
three days' fighting on the Little Big Horn, and but few

THE CUSTER MONUMENT.

THE CRESTED MONKEYS

were wounded. This statement is made by Grouard after a full knowledge of all the facts, and demonstrates, without further argument, that Custer's battalion was literally swept from the face of the earth by the storm of bullets which savage hatred hurled against it.

On the side of the soldiers, some two hundred and seventy officers, privates, scouts and civilians were killed outright, and many received wounds from which they never entirely recovered. The dead belonging to the Reno command were collected and buried by Gibbon's battalion on the 27th of June, and on the following day the same office was performed by the same command for the Custer battalion. The bodies of the soldiers were, in most cases, horribly mutilated, accounts of which have been published many times. General Custer's remains were not disturbed by the Indians. They were eventually transferred to the military cemetery at West Point, where they rest.

On a knoll overlooking the valley of the Little Big Horn—not far from the spot where Custer fell—a monument has been erected to the memory of the heroes who perished in that unequal battle which has no counterpart in the history of our country. The sides of this mute remembrancer are tablets upon which are engraved the names of those who perished with Custer. Relic hunters have defaced this monument to a great extent, but its erection at best is but an incident in the wave of regret and sorrow that passed over the nation's heart when the fate of Custer and his gallant followers was learned—a slight token of the love the American nation cherishes for her heroic dead.—AUTHOR.]

CHAPTER XXXIX.

A MIRACULOUS ESCAPE.

Some days after my return from the Custer battle-field, I started out in company with Big Bat to find which way the Indians were moving. I found the Sioux village up the other side (north) of Tongue river. I returned to camp and made report of these facts. Gen. Crook expected some more Crows to join the command, and thought it was best for me to go on the north side of the Sioux village, intercept the Crows and return with them. When I spoke to Bat about going he asked me to take an escort along. I told him it would be better for us to go by ourselves than to take troops with us; that we would be perfectly safe. He thought not, and everybody else thought we had better take an escort; and finding the General thought it would be best to take soldiers along with me so that the Crows would recognize them and come in with us, I finally consented to take them; but it was against my judgment. The worst thing I could have done was to take those soldiers along.

There were twenty-five picked men and one officer (Lieut. F. W. Sibley) from the Second cavalry detailed to go with us. The names of the soldiers were Oscar

LIEUTENANT F. W. SIBLEY.
BY PERMISSION OF JOHN F. FINERTY.

LIEUTENANT L. W. SLADEN.
BY PERMISSION OF JOHN C. FRENCH.

Cornwall (sergeant), Henry Collins, W. J. Crolley, W. R.
Cooper (sergeant), Wm. Dougherty, James Dorr, Charles
W. Day (sergeant), Charles L. Edwards, Wm. P. Egan,
Hugh J. Green, Patrick Hasson, G. P. Harrington (ser-
geant), S. W. Hone, Wm. H. Hills, Martin Hahon, Daniel
Munger, Henry Oakey, Jacob Rhend, George Rhode,
George Robinson, Valentine Rufus, George A. Stone,
Thomas C. Warren (corporal), Joseph Ward, George Watts.
One packer volunteered to accompany the party. The
packer was called Trailer Jack. A reporter of the Chi-
cago Times, Mr. John F. Finerty, also volunteered to go.
He had been wanting to go with us on every scout that
I had been upon. He had asked me to go several times,
but it had never been so that I could take him before.
He accompanied us on this scout.

Everything being in readiness we left camp a little
before 8 o'clock in the evening on July 5, 1876, making
our way along the foot of the mountains toward Tongue
river. It was 8 o'clock when we reached Big Goose. We
left there about 4 o'clock in the morning. It was daylight on reaching Beaver creek, where I discovered an
Indian looking over the hills at us. Not seeing anything but this solitary sentinel, I got onto my horse and
rode up to where this Indian was in hiding; but he got
down Beaver creek into the brush before I could get to
his hiding place. It was through this Indian that all
the trouble came that we had afterwards. He went back
to the hostile village and reported that we were about to
make an attack. He must have rode back that night.

It was just 8 o'clock in the evening of the 6th when

we crossed Beaver creek; 1 o'clock when we reached Tongue river; but I was getting close to the Sioux village. After crossing the river we rode about three miles, got off our horses, picketed them out, left one man to wake us up at daylight and went to sleep. I gave the sentinel orders to wake me up as soon as day commenced to break. It seemed to me that I had no more than closed my eyes when he woke me up. Getting on my horse and telling him to wake the others up and tell them to follow me closely, I rode up half a mile to a little butte. Getting off my horse I went up on the butte. It had got light enough so I could see. With my glass I discovered that the whole country was covered with Indians on horseback moving toward Tongue river. I called to Bat that the Indians were all over the country and moving toward Tongue river. He got off his horse and came up to where I was. He was no more scared than I was, but the first words he said were:

"My God, we are gone!"

As quick as it became light enough, I could see they were a war party moving along with the expectation of fighting something from the way they acted. I told Bat to go down and get the party ready; to tell the men what was in store for them; that as soon as the Indians struck our tracks it was all day with us; but that I would watch them until then. So I watched their movements until they came onto our track. One of the Indians, who was in the lead, as soon as he saw our track, commenced circling his horse and waving his blanket,

and it was just about ten minutes before every Indian in
the country knew they had struck our trail. Then they
commenced moving onto this one place and to follow
our trail up. Watching them until they got close to us,
I gave Bat the signal to start for the mountains. My
only hope was to get into the mountains and so far
ahead of the Indians that they could not catch us, and I
thought that we would have a better chance of getting
away from them in the hills than we would down on the
flat, where it was almost impossible to fight them. My
idea was to keep out of the way. I thought it was our
only chance. If we could possibly keep away from them
we might save ourselves.

By the time that we reached the trail that leads up
onto the mountains from Dayton, the Indians were within
half a mile of us, watching us while we were climbing
the mountains, but not attempting to follow us up the
trail we were on, but, instead, going to the upper trail
on the head of Twin creek to try and cut us off. A
large number of them stopped at Tongue River, at the
mouth of the canyon, in case we might attempt to come
down off the mountains and escape that way. They had
us shut in from all sides, and our only chance was to go
further back into the mountains. I thought it possible
we might escape them by traveling very fast. As soon
as we reached the top of the mountain I gave orders to
Lieut. Sibley to follow up the trail on a fast trot, but on
no account to stop anywhere until he overtook me. I
went on to where the two trails met—Twin creek trail
and the trail that we were on. Riding very fast and

reaching this point, I kept on the watch for the Indians to make their appearance. I was watching the Twin creek trail to see whether the Indians would go there After being there quite a while, I thought enough time had elapsed for the troops to reach me; and by their not coming up, I began to think that probably the Indians had got across some way and headed them off. The Indians making their appearance on the other trail, I got on my horse and rode back to meet Sibley's party. I met them just pulling out of the north fork of Tongue river, where they had stopped to make coffee.

I asked them why they had stopped — what excuse they had. They said the men were hungry and wanted something to eat. I told them I did not imagine they would want anything to eat after this; that the Indians had got in ahead of us and cut us off from ever getting away from them—had cut us off from the only chance we had of making our escape. There was no use of making any trouble about it. I simply told them to keep close together and ride as fast as they could, and to keep up with me. I was well aware that the Indians were in ahead of us, and not seeing our trail they would be very apt to meet us between where we were and the forks of the trail. I warned every man to be ready, as the Indians would most probably charge on us unexpectedly. Instead of following the trail I kept as much to the right of it as I could.

But as short a time as the red devils had to work on, they had laid a trap to ambush us. The main trail ran between two high, tree-studded buttes, and if we had

GATEWAY CASTLE HOME.

H. F. PEIRSON & Co. DENVER, COLO.

SCENE NEAR THE SIBLEY BATTLEFIELD, BIG HORN RANGE.

passed through there they would have been most likely
to have killed every one of us before we could have
fired a shot; but my going to the right had saved us
from getting ambushed. As we passed these buttes about
one half of the advance Indian party got a chance to
fire on us. There were from one hundred and fifty to
two hundred of them that fired on us, and how they
missed us — why some of us were not killed — is more
than I can tell; but I suppose they were excited and so
sure of getting us they were more careless about their
aim than is their custom. There was only one horse
shot at the buttes, and that was the animal rode by the
Chicago Times correspondent, (Mr. Finerty), and that was
the only mishap. The first gun fired by the Indians
stampeded all the soldiers' horses. The first thing I saw
was Mr. Finerty lying flat on his back. Supposing him
to be shot, I asked him where he was hit. He said he
was not shot, but his horse had thrown him. I told him
to get into the edge of the timber right below us; that
I would get the men together, go down into the timber
and make a stand there, it being about four hundred
yards from there to the top of the hill where the Indians
had fired on us.

Collecting the men as well as I could, and pushing
them on to where we were going to make our stand,
keeping Mr. Finerty in ahead of me, I got him down
into this timber, the rest of the party reaching there soon
after. Dismounting and tying the horses all in a bunch
so that they could be seen by the Indians from the top
of the hill, I gave the men orders not to fire a shot. I

placed them in position from fifty to one hundred yards away from the horses. After instructing them not to waste their ammunition ; that we could expect no relief ; that we had to fight it out ourselves as long as our ammunition lasted, I told them to make every shot they fired kill, if possible. The Indians had recognized me when they fired the first volley, and had spoken to me in the Sioux language, telling me there was no chance for me to get away ; that I could not " go up into the air nor down into the ground," and that they would get me before sun-down.

After seeing the men placed and giving them the caution about the ammunition, I crept back to the edge of the timber so that I could see all the movements the Indians would make. I was asked by some of the soldiers if there was any possible chance of getting out of there, and I told them there was no more chance of our getting away alive than there was of our jumping into the moon ; that the only thing we could do was to fight as long as our ammunition would last, and *to save the last load for ourselves;* not to be taken alive if it could be helped ; that I didn't expect to get out of there, but I was certain I was going to save my last shot for myself ; that I knew the Indians were going to try to capture me if there was any possible show, for they had told me so.

Well, on some of the men this had a very queer effect. Three or four of them commenced to cry about it. Some of them didn't mind it at all. Finerty was the most jovial one of them all. Lieutenant Sibley took the situation very coolly and deliberately. As near as I could judge the Indians were increasing every minute. It looked to me as if they were thicker than the pine trees that sheltered us, and they had us almost completely surrounded. We could look through the timber and see them, and it did look as though there was no chance of getting away from there. It was about 10:30 o'clock in the morning, July 7th, 1876, that we took our stand in the timber, and from the time we got in there until 3 o'clock in the afternoon we had not fired a shot. The Indians were trying in every way to draw our fire. The trees were not big enough to protect our bodies, they all being small spruce and pines, and our poor horses were getting the full benefit of the Indian bullets. They were firing into them all the time. They could see them from the top of the hill, and at 3 o'clock there were only eight horses standing there alive; the rest had been shot and killed.

By that time the Indians got more daring and kept riding a little closer. There were two of them especially that were trying to outdo the others. One was White Antelope, a Cheyenne chief and warrior. I could see right away that these two Indians were the most daring, and my aim was to get one of them, if not both of them. After a good deal of waiting I got a chance to shoot them both at once. One was coming right towards me at a slow lope. I could almost see the color of his eyes, he was so close to me. The other was following in behind, very close to him. They were about five yards from each other, but it so happened that they both came in line,

and it was such a pretty shot that I could not help
taking it. After a good, careful aim, I pulled the trigger; but instead of the nearest one falling, the one behind him fell off his horse. The foremost one fell on his
horse's neck; but before he could fall to the ground two
Indians ran up and held him on his horse until they got
him over the hill out of sight. I found out afterwards
that I had killed them both at one shot.

This double shot raised such confusion amongst the
Indians, and they were so excited about it that a chance
of our getting away presented itself. This chance lasted
probably fifteen minutes. I told the Lieutenant to take the
ammunition, his and the soldiers, and instruct the men to
crawl on their hands and knees down to a kind of washout close by where we were, as the Indians were so confused and stampeded over White Antelope's death that
they would not notice our movements, and if we could
once get through the line we would be all right. The
Lieutenant objected a little to going off and leaving the
horses; but I told him there would be a lot of horses after
we were dead; that it was our only chance, and we had
better take it; that there were none of our party wounded,
but if one were wounded there would be no chance of
our escape. So, getting his men together and going
down on their hands and knees, the Lieutenant and party
crawled out. I stood there close by the horses and
watched them till they got clear through the Indians on
the outside of the circle.

Then I took the rope from my own saddle and
wound it about my body and followed the troops. It

didn't take me long to overtake them. They were running through the timber when I did overtake them, and some of them had pretty heavy falls, but they didn't mind it in the least. Much of the timber was blown down, and we had to step from log to log. Some of the men would slip and get awful falls, but none of them made complaint. It was just about a mile from where we had made our stand down to the main fork of Tongue river. The men never waited when they got to the river, to find a crossing, but just plunged into it. They never stopped until they got into the timber on the other side of the river. They had plunged into the water, and it was very deep there, and they were dripping wet. We could hear the Indians firing into the trees where we had been. They kept up a continual firing there until after dark. I learned afterward that they did not know we were gone until the next day about 10 o'clock. Our holding fire there all day long, and waiting until they got close to us and then firing at them and killing two of their leaders, scared them, and they did not dare to make a rush into the thicket for fear a lot more of them would be killed. They just kept firing in there in hopes of killing us all without any danger to themselves.

After I had caught up with the soldiers, I put Bat in the lead and cautioned them not to step on the ground, but from rock to rock, and keep away from the timber and avoid touching the limbs if possible. We traveled on until dark in that way. Along about dark it commenced blowing and raining, and I think one of the worst electrical storms I ever saw in the western

country overtook us that night. Timber was falling all
about us, so that it was dangerous to travel; but we
moved along pretty well until midnight, when the storm
became so bad that we could not travel any further.
Getting under a big rock, we stopped beneath its friendly
shelter until the wind and rain ceased.

Our only chance of getting entirely away from the
Indians was to keep on such ground that they could not
follow us on horseback. Keeping well up in the mountains we traveled all the rest of the night, stopping only
for a few minutes' rest at a time until we reached Wolf
creek. After crossing Wolf creek one of the men became unmanageable—went stark mad. The excitement
had turned his head. He imagined everything he saw
was an Indian, so that I had to keep him right along
by my side all the while. From time to time he would
commence to yell, and I would have to stop his mouth
until he became quiet. After we crossed Wolf creek I
had to crawl up the canyon in places and throw my
rope down to the rest ～of the party and pull them up
with it.

We came down off the mountains at the head of
Soldier creek. As we reached the foot of the mountains we
came onto a very large party of Indians that looked to
me as if they had been on the watch for us. It struck
me that way at first; but I found out afterwards that
they were going down to the command to make a fight
with Crook. I came up to within five hundred yards of
where they were sitting, smoking. Their horses were
feeding with their saddles on. They had apparently

just got there and wanted to take a rest. Of course, we thought they were watching for us. I think from the way the men in our party expressed themselves, they would have fought the entire Sioux nation then and there before they would have tried to run or get away. Some were anxious to fight this small body of Indians in front of us, especially Mr. Finerty.

Just at sundown the Indians mounted their horses and started toward the command. We sat there and watched them until they got within a short distance of the command, when it became so dark that we could not see any longer. By this time the men were thoroughly exhausted and hungry; but there was no help for it, we had to travel, and started out toward the command. We could not walk over a hundred yards at a time without sitting down and resting. Reaching Big Goose creek we found the stream had been swollen by the rain we had had the previous night, and the current being very swift it was hard to cross. Two of the men refused to cross it. These two had gone crazy and were like children. They begged to be allowed to lie down in the brush and sleep. We could not get them to cross, and there was nobody in the party strong enough to carry them across where the water would reach up to our necks. There was nothing in the world that would make them go with us. Finally we decided to leave them, the rest of the party crossing.

Of course, after getting wet it made it a great deal worse for us to travel, our clothes being soaked and the water cold. I don't think we went over two or two and one-half miles before daylight, and the men were so hungry that they would eat anything they could lay their hands on. They would catch little birds and eat them, feathers and all, and would not wait to kill them, even. There would be four or five young birds in a nest, and the men would get them and eat them right down. Finally I showed them some Indian turnips; gave each one a top so they would know what they were, and set them to digging. It was not long before they had plenty of these wild turnips, and their hunger was thus partially appeased.

About 10 o'clock we discovered a man on horseback riding along the hill ahead of us. Taking out my glass I saw it was a soldier. He waited until we got up to him, and we found he was out hunting. He told us about the Indians making a raid on the camp on the previous night. We sent him to bring horses out to us, for some of the men could not walk any further. We waited on the hill until the horses were brought to us. As soon as the horses arrived we got on to them, and it was but a short time before we were in camp. There were two companies of cavalry sent out with the horses. One company went out for the two men we had left on the other side of the Big Goose creek. The soldiers found them where we had left them, sound asleep, and brought them in. One of them strayed away from the command afterwards and was never heard of. I think the Indians must have captured and killed him. The other one was taken to Washington, but never got over being crazy. Of course after we got to camp, the first thing we did was to eat, and then we went to sleep.

I told the General as quick as we got in what had happened—reported it to him. They all told us we were pretty lucky in getting away, but we knew that ourselves.

"The 'Sibley Scout' is famous among Indian fighters as being one of the narrowest escapes from savages now on record. The hero (Lieutenant Sibley) of that hazardous encounter with the dreaded Sioux, passed the winter at this place in company with the writer," says a San Diego correspondent of the New York Tribune, " and favored him with a sketch of that memorable action of a handful of troopers away up in the Big Horn mountains, far from the main command. It was in 1876, at the time of Custer's massacre, when E. W. Sibley of General Crook's column, then a young lieutenant, was ordered out with twenty-five mounted men to look about the country and see what was going on. Frank Grouard, one of the best scouts living, accompanied Sibley. The young officer was fresh from West Point, and rather inexperienced in frontier warfare, so cautious General Crook bade him heed the scout's advice should emergency arise, and off the troopers started almost at the very hour when Custer, a hundred miles or so away, was being cut to pieces by the cut-throats of Sitting Bull.

"The scouting party was ignorant of this, however, and traveled for two days without incident. As they neared the mountains Grouard, who always traveled ahead, suddenly signaled to halt. Indian signs were

seen.   From an eminence commanding a vast area of
rolling country, little specks could be seen here and
there.   The glass proved that each speck was a squad
of Sioux in war costume.   The specks began to concen-
trate.   They moved toward the trail made by the troopers, but without discovering it for a long time.   The
Indians were ignorant of the presence of soldiers.   After
holding a pow-wow, one of the savages rode toward the
tell-tale trail.   By chance he discovered it and returned
to his comrades waving his blanket ·and gesticulating.   It
then seemed to the young cavalry officer as if Indians
sprang from the earth in all directions to see what had
been discovered.   There were swarms of them.   But,
happily, they were miles away.   Then began the race
for life.   The mountains offered the only refuge.

"Up and up scrambled the horses.   On came the Indians.   They were occasionally along canyons in the rear.
The band had divided and was trying to head off the
soldiers and surround them.   Suddenly, as the soldiers
ascended the side of a gulch and gained a small plateau,
a party of redskins sprang at them, firing their rifles and
yelling.

"The men scattered like sheep," says Captain Sibley, "and I confess for the moment my heart was in my
mouth.   My horse fell down an embankment, which added
to my discomfort.   I ordered the men to fire, even if
they didn't aim at the enemy, for a rifle made a noise
like a cannon amid those hills.   Finally the men got
together and we retreated up a slope to a bit of wooded
ground which protected us from the Indians' fire.   This

BAPTISTE GAUNIER. (LITTLE BAT.)

was about 9 o'clock in the morning. The Indians began
to gather about us rapidly. The situation was growing
more serious every minute. It pleased me to see one
man shoot a noted chief right through the heart. That
old sinner never twitched a muscle after the lead hit
him. We never knew how many we killed, because
when an Indian is shot his comrades keep him out of
sight. Well, we held them off for four hours, and they
were four hours of red-hot work, I can tell you. My
scout then told me that the Indians were on three sides
of us. We had one chance left to retreat, and this
chance was fast lessening, because fresh Indians were
coming.

"I did not like to abanbon our horses, but it was
that or die. So the retreat was ordered. I inspected
each man personally to see that his equipment was all
right, but owing to my inexperience and the excitement
of the moment, I forgot the rations. Only one man
in the command took his rations.

"It was an hour or so before the Indians discovered
we had fled. By that time we were up in the mountains
in places so steep that one man had to help the other up.
Horses could not follow us. So, for the time being, the
Sioux would not strike us. Grouard took a mountain
trail which we followed on foot for fifty hours without a
mouthful to eat. Such fearfully vigorous exercise without food nearly killed us. Toward the end of the perilous
march we all became so weakened that we marched for
ten minutes and then would lie down and rest. Several
of the most robust men became insane and one or two

never regained their wits. When we reached Crook's camp I slept for twenty-four hours without waking, and during that time the camp was sharply attacked by Indians. Even the roar of the musketry did not disturb my sleep in the least. Not a single man was lost on this trip."

———

[The escape from peril so imminent—the very jaws of death—is graphically told by Mr. John Finnerty in his highly interesting volume, "Warpath and Bivouac." Finnerty devotes many pages to the object and movement of the "Sibley Scout," as it has always been called, and by his kind permission we reproduce in this volume his realistic account of the escape of the Sibley party (himself included) from the horde of bloodthirsty savages which surrounded it.—AUTHOR.]

As the volume of the Indian fire seemed to increase, says Finnerty, "no surrender" was the word passed from man to man around the thin skirmish line. Each of us would, if necessary, have blown out his own brains rather than fall alive into the Indians' hands. Doubtless, if we had remained long enough, the Indians would have relieved us of all responsibility on that score. A disabling wound would have been worse than death. I have often wondered how a man felt when he thought he saw inevitable, sure death upon him. I know it now, for I had little or no idea that we could effect our escape, and, mentally at least, I could scarcely have felt my position more keenly if an Indian knife or bullet had wounded me in some vital spot. So, I think, it was with all the

command, but nobody seemed, therefore, to weaken. It
is one thing, however, to face death in the midst of the
excitement of a general battle. It is quite another thing
to face him in almost cold blood, with the certain prospect of your dishonored body being first mutilated in a
revolting manner, and then left to feed the wolf or the
vulture among the savage mountains. After a man once
sees the skull and cross bones as clearly as our party saw
them on the afternoon of Friday, July 7th, 1876, no subsequent glimpse of grim mortality can possibly impress
him in the same manner.

Well, the eternal shadows seemed to be fast closing
around us; the Indians' bullets were hitting nearer every
moment, and the Indian yell was growing stronger and
fiercer, when a hand was laid on my shoulder, and Rufus,
a soldier who was my neighbor on the skirmish line,
said, "the rest are retiring. Lieutenant Sibley tells us
to do the same." I quietly withdrew from the foot of
the friendly pine tree, which, with a fallen trunk that lay
almost across it, kept at least a dozen Indian bullets
from making havoc of my body, and prepared to obey.
As I passed by Sibley, who wanted to see every man
under his command in the line of retreat before he stirred
himself, the young officer said, "Go to your saddle bags,
with caution, and take all your ammunition. We are going
to abandon our remaining horses. The Indians are getting all around us, so we must take to the rocks and
thick timber on foot. It seems to be our only chance of
escape." I did as directed, but felt a pang at leaving
my noble animal, which was bleeding from a wound in

the right side. We dared not shoot our surviving horses, for that would have discovered our movement to the enemy.

Grouard advised this strategy, saying that as the Indians occupied the passes east, west and north of us — all of them being difficult at the best — we could not possibly effect a retreat on horseback, even if our animals had escaped unwounded. If the grass had happened to have been a little bit dryer, and it would not take long to dry, as there had been only a light thunder-shower during the afternoon, the Indians, in Grouard's opinion, would have tried to burn us out of the timber. He bluntly told the Lieutenant that the position was untenable, at such a distance from Crook's camp. And even if a man could succeed in getting through to the General, we could not expect timely relief, and all would be over with us long before an attempt at rescue could be made. Therefore, Grouard said, if Lieutenant Sibley did not choose to take his advice, upon the officer should rest the responsibility of whatever might happen.

There was no time to be lost if we meant to get away at all, and certainly there was nothing to gain, but everything to lose, by remaining where we were. Sibley, although very averse to retreating, finally yielded to the calm voice of the scout, whose great experience among the Sioux rendered him familiar with all the methods of Indian warfare. The arguments used by Grouard were warmly seconded by Baptiste Pourier, one of the most reliable scouts on the frontier, who was acquainted from childhood with the subtle tactics of the savages.

When the retreat was decided on, we acted with an alacrity which only men who have, at some time struggled for their lives, can understand. A couple of scattering volleys and some random shots were fired, to make the savages believe that we were still in position. As we had frequently reserved our fire during the fight, our silence would not be noticed immediately. We then retired in Indian file, through the trees, rocks and fallen timber in rear of us. Our horses were, evidently, plainly visible to the Indians—a circumstance that facilitated our escape. We retreated for, perhaps, a mile through the forest, which was filled with rugged boulders and trunks of fallen pine trees, through which no horse could penetrate, waded one of the branches of Tongue river up to our waists, and gained the slippery rocks of the great mountain ridge, where no mounted Indians, who are as lazy on foot as they are active on horseback, could pursue us. Then, as we paused to catch our breath, we heard, in the distance, five or six ringing volleys in succession. It was most likely the final fire delivered by the Indians before they charged our late position, with the hope of getting our scalps.

"That means we are safe for the present," said Grouard, "but let us lose no time in putting more rocks between us and the White Antelope." We followed his advice with a feeling of thankfulness that those only who have passed through such an ordeal can appreciate. How astonished and chagrined the reinforced savages must have been when they ran in upon the maimed horses and did not get a single scalp! Even under such circumstances as we were placed in, we could not help indulging in a laugh at their expense. But we had escaped one danger only to encounter another. Fully fifty miles of mountain, rock, forest, river and canyon lay between us and Crook's camp. We were unable to carry any food upon our persons. The weather was close, owing to the thunder-shower, and we threw away everything superfluous in the way of clothing. With ravening Indians behind us, and uncounted precipices before us, we found our rifles and what remained of our one hundred rounds of ammunition each, a sufficient load to carry. The brave and skillful Grouard, the ablest of scouts, seconded by the fearless Pourier, conducted our retreat through the mountain wilderness, and we marched, climbed and scrambled over impediments that at any other time might have been impossible to us, until about midnight, when absolute fatigue compelled us to make a halt. Then we bivouacked under the projections of an immense pile of rocks on the very summit of some unknown peak, and there witnessed one of the most terrible wind and hailstorms that can be imagined. The trees seemed to fall by the hundred, and their noise, as they broke off and fell, or were uptorn by the roots, resembled rapid discharges of field artillery. To add to our discomfort, the thermometer fell several degrees, and, being attired in summer campaign costume only, we suffered greatly from the cold.

Almost before dawn we were again stumbling through the rocks and fallen trees, and, about sunrise, reached the tremendous canyon, cut through the mountain by what is called the southern branch of Tongue river. Most of

the men were too much exhausted to make the descent
of the canyon, so Grouard, finding a fairly practicable
path, led us to an open valley down by the river, on the
left bank, hard as we could walk, for if discovered by any
considerable body of Indians, we could only halt, and
worn out as most of the little band were, die together.
Fortune favored us, and we made the right bank of the
stream unobserved, being then, according to the calcula-
tions of the scouts, about five and twenty miles from
Crook's encampment. In our front, toward the east, we
could see the plain through which Tongue river flowed,
where, no doubt, as it was then a fine game country, hostile Indians abounded, while our only safe avenue of escape was to cross the stream and climb the enormous
precipice that formed the right side of the canyon. But
the dauntless Grouard was equal to the emergency. He
scaled the gigantic wall diagonally, and led us along what
looked like a mere squirrel path, not more than a foot
wide, with an abyss of, perhaps, five hundred feet below,
and a sheer wall of rock two hundred feet high, above
us. After about an hour's herculean toil, we gained the
crest and saw the point of mountain, some twenty miles
distant, where lay our camp and comrades. This, as well
may be imagined, was a blissful vision, but we were half
dead from fatigue, and some of us were almost famine
stricken. Yet the indefatigable Grouard would not stop
until we reached the eastern foot-hills, where we made,
so to speak, a dive into a deep valley to obtain water—
our only refreshment on that hard, rugged road. The
leaves from the pine trees made the hillsides as slippery

as glass, and where there were neither grass nor trees, the broken stones and "shale" made walking absolutely painful. Scarcely had we slaked our thirst when Grouard led us up to the hills again, and we had barely entered the timber belt when the scout uttered a warning "hush," and threw himself upon the ground, motioning us to do the same. He pointed toward the north, and there, wheeling around the base of the point of the mountain we had doubled so shortly before, appeared another strong party of the Sioux in open order. The savages were riding along quite leisurely, and, although fairly numerous, were evidently only the advance or rear guard of some larger party. This sight made us desperate. Every man examined his carbine and looked to his ammunition. We all felt that life would be too dearly purchased by further flight, and, following the example of the brave young Sibley and the gallant scouts, we took up a position among the rocks on the knoll we had reached, determined, if called upon, to sell our lives as dearly as possible.

"We are in pretty hard luck, it would seem," said Sibley, addressing me; "but, d—— them, we'll show the red scoundrels how white men can fight and die, if necessary. Men," he said, addressing the soldiers, "we have a good position; let every shot dispose of an Indian."

At that moment not a man among us felt any inclination to get away. Desperation and a thirst for vengeance on the savages had usurped the place of the animal instinct to save our lives. In such moments mind rises superior to matter and soul to the nerves. But fortune spared us the ordeal of another fight in our weakened condition. Our position, as the Lieutenant had said, was a good one. On the left, or north of us, there was a difficult precipice, which hung above the stream of whose waters we had just drank to satiety. The woods grew thinly on our front, toward the east and the south of us was an almost open slope. Our rear was well secured by an irregular line of huge boulders, and rocks of good size afforded us fair shelter in nearly all directions. There was also some fallen timber, but not enough to make a serious blaze if the enemy should try their favorite maneuver of burning us out. The Sioux, fortunately for them, and, no doubt, for us, too, failed to observe our party, and did not advance high enough on the hills to find our trail. They kept eastward, following a branch of Tongue river.

The excitement over, we all again felt thoroughly worn out, and fell asleep, all except the tireless and ever vigilant scouts, and awoke at dark feeling somewhat refreshed, but painfully hungry. Not a man of us, whatever the risk, Sioux or no Sioux, could endure the mountain route longer, so we took our wearied, jaded lives into our hands, and struck out for Crook's camp across the plains, fording Big Goose creek up to our armpits at three o'clock in the morning, the water being as cold as the melting mountain snows could make it. Two of the men, Sergeant Cornwall and Private Collins, absolutely refused to ford the creek, as neither could swim, and the current was exceedingly rapid. Sibley threatened and coaxed them alternately in vain, but those men, who could face bullets and tomahawks without flinching, would not

be induced to cross that stream. They begged to be allowed to hide in the bushes on the north side of the
creek, until horses could be sent after them. Sibley, after
providentially escaping so many dangers, could not sacrifice the rest of his command for two obstinately foolish
men, and the scouts urged him to push on. This we did
reluctantly, but there was no alternative. We judged
that our main camp must still be some dozen miles away
on Little Goose creek, but every step, chiefly because of
the toil attending the previous mountain journey, became
laborious. My readers can judge for themselves how
badly we were used up, when it took us four hours to
accomplish six miles. The rocks had broken our boots
and skinned our feet, while starvation had weakened our
frames. Only a comparatively few were vigorous enough
to maintain a decently rapid pace. About five o'clock
we saw some more Indians toward the east, but at some
distance. We took no pains whatever to conceal ourselves, which, indeed, would have been a vain task on
the nearly naked plain ; and the savages, if they saw us,
which is highly probable, must have mistaken us for an
outlying picket, and being only, comparatively speaking,
a handful, kept away. At about 6:30 o'clock we saw
two horses grazing on a little knoll, and the carbines
glittering on their "boots" on the saddles proclaimed
the riders to be cavalrymen. Presently the men rose out
of the long grass and made for their guns, but we hailed
them and they recognized us. They were men of the
Second Cavalry, who had obtained permission to go hunting, and who were bound for Tongue river, where they

would have certainly fallen in with the Sioux. Lieut. Sibley sent them into camp to ask for an escort to proceed as far as Big Goose creek for the two men who had stopped there. Most of Sibley's men threw themselves on the ground, unable to move further, and awaited the arrival of the horses. Within an hour and a half Capts. Dewees and Rawolle, of the Second Cavalry, came out to us with led horses and some cooked provisions. They greeted us most warmly, and, having aided us most kindly, proceeded to pick up Sergeant Cornwell and Private Collins, who were found all safe, concealed in the thick undergrowth of Big Goose creek, and who reached camp a few hours after ourselves. It was ten o'clock Sunday morning, July 9, 1876, when we rode in among the tents, amid congratulations from officers and men alike.

Thus, after passing through scenes of great peril and privation, our little band found itself in Camp Cloud Peak, surrounded by devoted and hospitable comrades. After we had somewhat recovered from our great fatigue, and refreshed ourselves by a most welcome bath in the creek, we were obliged to relate our experience again and again for the benefit of the entire "outfit." All agreed that Frank Grouard, for the good judgment and skill with which he managed our retreat, deserved to take rank among the foremost of scouts and plainsmen. Nor did quiet, intrepid Baptiste Pourier (Big Bat) lack admirers around the camp-fires of Crook's brigade. The oldest among Indian fighters, including such officers as Colonel Royall and Lieutenant Lawson, concurred in saying that

escape from danger so imminent and so appalling, in a
manner so ingenious and successful, was without a parallel
in the history of Indian warfare. It was fortunate, they
said, for our party that an officer possessing the coolness
and good sense of Lieutenant Sibley had command of it.
A rash, bull-headed commander would have disregarded
the advice of Grouard and Pourier, and would have thus
brought ruin and death upon all of us. Colonel Royall, in
the absence of General Crook, who was in the mountain
on a hunt, was kind enough to say that while a spare horse
remained in his regiment, it would be at my disposal, in
lieu of the one I had lost in the Sibley Scout, as the
reconnoissance has ever since been called by the American army.

CHAPTER XL.

SOMETHING ABOUT SCOUTING.

Gen. Crook (who had become impatient at being in camp so long after getting orders to wait for reinforcements—the Fifth Cavalry) made up his mind he would jump the hostiles with what command he had. The Indians were watching us every day. We could see them around on the hills. Finally we broke camp, and moved from the Little Goose creek, where our camp then was, to the Big Goose canyon, where Beckton is at present, crossing the river there. That night the Indians fired on us and tried to stampede the horses and pack train. We were forced to make a corral every night for the mules. That night I had my horse tied right by the side of my bed, which I had made down in one end of the corral. When the mules stampeded I jumped on my horse, and when they broke through the corral, I went with them on horseback. They ran four or five miles before I could get them stopped. One of the packers had presence of mind enough to jump on one of the horses as the mules were going out of the corral, and with his help it was not long before I had the herd turned back towards camp. All this time the Indians were following and shooting on both sides of the herd. We finally got the animals back into camp.

The command then moved from there over to Tongue river, but we could find no trace of the Indian camp. The hostiles had left that locality, going in an easterly direction, and Gen. Crook brought the command back to Little Goose creek, Gen. Merritt, with the Fifth Cavalry, joining us on Soldier creek. Moving down to the forks of Big and Little Goose creeks, where Sheridan is now located, we went into permanent camp, and got ready to follow the Indians, wherever they had gone. Some of our scouts had to leave us while we were camped on Goose creek, so I got orders to hire all the scouts I could find. I hired Charlie Chapin, Bill Zimmers, Jim Phoenix, Black Hills Frank and Calamity Jane. When the Fifth cavalry joined us they had brought Buffalo Bill, Buffalo Chips (Charlie White), Jack Crawford (Captain Jack), Smalsey, Limber Jim and Little Bat. There were others whose names I do not remember.

Everything being ready and preparations made for a long march, we left the wagon train on the east side of Goose creek above the forks and started down Tongue river, through the canyon, and crossing over to the Rosebud. I was out in that locality one day with Gen. Crook trying to find a trail of the Indians — which way they had gone. On passing through the canyon of the Rosebud I took Gen. Crook up and showed him where the Indians had fortified themselves in order to draw the command down during the fight we had on June 17th with them on the head of the Rosebud. After the General had seen the ground and gone over it and comprehended how the Indians were fortified; how they could have killed us without our harming them, he turned around, but never said a word. Afterwards, shaking hands with me, he said he was glad he "didn't get bullheaded." That is the way he expressed it. Finding the Indian trail from where their village had been located, we started to follow them up; but they having such a long start of us—some three weeks, I think—there was not much chance of our catching them. They had gone into camp or scattered to the different agencies.

Following down the Rosebud until we met Gen. Terry's command, about forty miles from the mouth of the Rosebud, we followed the Indian trail where it left the stream, and crossed to Tongue river, following it down to the mouth of Mizpah (the Indian name was Four-Horn creek). Then we went up that creek, and crossed to Powder river. Both of the commands kept together until that time. Being short of supplies and not knowing how long we would have to follow the Indians, we went down to the mouth of Powder river to the cantonment, or supply camp. Bill Cody (Buffalo Bill) left us there, taking a steamer and going back east, so he was not with us but a very short time. That was the first scouting he ever did, I guess. We went down as far as Glendive to find out if the Indians had crossed. After getting all the supplies that were at hand, we started up the river to where the Indian trail left Powder river, leading toward the Little Missouri.

Taking the trail and leaving the command there to follow up the Indian trail, I took Capt. Jack Crawford with me. It was the first trip he had ever been out on as a scout. My idea was to find out which way the Indians had gone; whether they had separated or kept together. Striking the head of Beaver creek we kept right down for about forty miles, and then went across towards the Little Missouri on the north side of Lookout Butte, and from there down across to the Little Missouri. One Indian trail led down the Little Missouri and crossed over to the head of Heart river, giving every indication that the camp had divided just about half and half. From the appearance of the trail, however, I was satisfied that those going down the Missouri were Sitting Bull's band making for the British possesssions, and that the other party was going over into the Black Hills.

Turning back at that point to meet the command (it was pretty late when we turned back) and going away from the river, we stopped in a dry gulch and cooked something to eat. After we finished our meal it was just a little after sundown. I was sitting there smoking, and a party of Indians came down the trail that we had taken. It was just dark enough for me to see there were a lot of horsemen, and we were camped right on the trail. The fire had almost gone out at that time, and it was but the work of a minute to cover the fire over with dirt, but the Indians had seen it. They came riding down within about eighty yards of us, stopping and asking who we were. I an-

swered with a bullet, and continued shooting rapidly at
them. As soon as I began to shoot they turned and
ran. I killed one of their horses. There were only a
few of them, and they were as badly scared as we
were.

After I got through shooting I could not find anything of Capt. Jack Crawford. I looked all around for
him, but failed to discover him. The horses were in
the gulch feeding, and I commenced hallooing for Jack,
as there was no time to be lost. I had to get out of
there. Thinking he might have gone up the gulch, I
got on a horse and started up, yelling for him, and
finally found him up the gulch in a patch of brush.
He had run off and hid. I never said anything to
him, but told him we must hurry back, and would be
forced to ride as hard as we could. So we got on our
horses and rode all night, reaching the command at daylight. I reported to the General about the different Indian trails and the manner in which the band had split
up, and also explained that I thought it would be best
to follow the band that had gone toward the Hills. The
General thought it would be best, also, as we were
short of provisions. So sending a party of scouts across
over to the Little Missouri at the mouth of the Cannon
Ball to try and find out if their trail headed that way,
the command started on the main trail, following it
across the Little Missouri, up through the badlands and
on to the head of Heart river.

Just as we got out of the badlands we discovered
a large number of Indians and a great many horses go-

ing in a northerly direction. The animals appeared to be packed. Starting on to try and overtake them, and taking some of the scouts, I chased them about ten miles into the badlands. There they made a stand, and it was such a strong one we could not do anything with them.

Bill Hamilton, one of the scouts I had, who was very deaf and who could not hear ordinary speaking, went with us into the badlands. Just as quick as we got up to where the Indians were, they commenced shooting at us, and we had to come down over the hills to keep out of range of their bullets. Bill Hamilton came up and asked us where the Indians were. I pointed over the hill, and one of the boys told him not to go over there; that they would kill him. But Bill didn't hear it, and commenced whipping his horse, telling the rest of us to come on; that we would kill every last one of them. As soon as he raised the hill the Indians commenced firing at him, and being so deaf and not hearing the shooting, he got down over and went to the bottom of the hill, where one of the Indians shot a bullet through his hat.

That was the first intimation he had that they were firing at him. He yelled, "They are firing at me!" and pulled off his hat and looked at it. As quick as he saw the bullet had gone through his hat, he lost no time in getting back over the hill, and made some sarcastic remarks about it, and wanted to know why the boys did not tell him the Indians were firing at him. He looked up as surprised as could be, to think they were firing at him and he not know it. He was on a lazy horse, and was whipping it with all his might when he went over the hill, and paid so much attention to his animal that he did not see the Indians. It was very funny to see him coming back over the hill, though.

He had been deaf to onr warnings of danger, but the manner in which he returned to our party clearly proved that he at least possessed the faculty of making a lazy horse "take the wings of morning" when occasion required. And occasion required it right then.

CHAPTER XLI.

THE SLIM BUTTES FIGHT.

Finding our small party of scouts could not get the Indians, and that it was not worth while trying to dislodge them, we went back to the command, which had gone into camp. All the supplies had been used — all the rations. It was just about one hundred miles to Fort Lincoln and the same distance to Deadwood and the Black Hills. At Lincoln there were government supplies, and at Deadwood we would have to purchase them, or run our chances of buying enough to do us. Then, again, if we went to Lincoln, we would lose the object of our summer's march and the opportunity of overtaking the Indians. On the other hand, if we went to the Hills we had the chance of jumping the Indians and not having had all our summer's work for nothing. The rain — it had been raining then just about a week — was falling in a steady drizzle, and there was not a dry article of any kind in the whole command.

Between us and the Hills the entire country had this sticky, gumbo soil. In either case it would be a hard trip for the command, and would entail a good deal of suffering, whichever way we went. I thought it would

COLONEL ANSON MILLS.
BY PERMISSION OF JOHN F. FINERTY.

BRIGADIER-GENERAL ANSON MILLS
BY PERMISSION OF BRIG.-GEN.

be best to go towards the Hills; that we would be sure
to jump the Indians before they got into .the agency.
The General said there was no possibility of our starving, as we had plenty of horses and mules. He called
his field officers together, and gave orders to march to
the Black Hills, telling them that we would have to live
on horse and mule meat until rations could be procured.

The next morning we started towards the Hills. It
was a pretty hard struggle from there on. The horses
commenced to play out. As fast as the poor brutes fell
the quartermaster had them killed and issued as rations,
so the soldiers had nothing but played-out horses to eat
from there on into the Hills. It looked funny to see a
soldier ride his horse until it dropped exhausted, and
then get off and shoot it and cut its carcass up and issue
the meat to the soldiers of the different companies. The
command was out of everything. I suppose, from what
I saw and what they told me, that it was a pretty hard
struggle for the troops. I didn't get much of the hard
part of it, as I was out killing game; besides, we had
a mess of our own and our own pack mules, so that
we had plenty of provisions all through the whole trip.
Myself, Tom Moore, the packer, Dave Meers, his assistant,
and Big Bat, were all together. My being out so much,
I killed game and brought it in to the mess. Gen.
Crook fared just the same as the soldiers. Once and
awhile the staff would steal down to our mess and get a
square meal of beans, but the General had prohibited
them from going to our mess. That was one distinctive
characteristic of Gen. Crook's—he would not take any

advantage of his command. If they starved, he starved with them.

On the fourth night from Heart river it was thought best to send part of the command on to the Black Hills for supplies, and knowing the Indians to be between us and the Black Hills, the General thought I had better go with them, and said he would send sufficient force to jump any village we would come across. Picking out one hundred and fifty men, with six pack trains (Tom Moore in charge of the pack trains), we left camp at 9 o'clock in the evening, with Captain Mills in command, and Lieut. Crawford, Lieut. Schwatka and Lieut. Von Leuttewitz accompanying us. Crawford was killed by the Mexicans afterwards. Schwatka became famous as an Arctic explorer, and is now dead; Von Leuttewitz was shot in the Slim Butte fight, had his leg amputated, was pensioned off, and is now living in Washington. I took Captain Jack Crawford with me. We traveled all night, striking Big Plum the next morning, and making our breakfast off of plums. After resting up awhile we started again about 8 o'clock. We could not travel fast. It had stopped raining, but the fog had settled so that we could not see but a short distance ahead. Keeping the command about three hundred yards behind so they could watch all our movements, we traveled until about 1 o'clock. Once in a while the fog would rise so that I could see a mile or two ahead of me, and during one of these rises of the fog, I discovered a lot of Indian ponies on ahead of me about a mile.

Giving the signal for the command to stop, I rode

back to them and told them there was an Indian village in
front of us. Putting the soldiers into a deep ravine so
they could not be seen from a distance, I went on as far
as I could without being discovered. I could not see the
village, but knew it was down in the bed of the creek.
I wanted to find out how large a village it was, and
whether it would be practicable for our small command
to jump it. Cautioning the men not to show themselves,
and muffling the bells on the pack mules so they would
make no noise, I went forward again and kept watch the
rest of the day. As soon as darkness came on I rode
down to the village, and found it was only a small affair
— thirty-nine lodges and about two hundred people.
Disguised as an Indian, I went all through the village,
looking for the best point to attack it from. I finally
concluded we had sufficient force to capture the entire
village.

In front of one of the tepis in the village I saw two
very fine looking horses. Both animals were on picket
lines, and I made up my mind that they were a little too
rich for Indian blood, but not too rich for mine. So I
just waited around until everything was quiet, slipped up
to the tepi, untied the ropes and led the animals out of
the village as unconcernedly as if I were taking them to
water. They became famous horses afterwards. One was
a pinto and the other a black stallion. One of them I
gave to a young lady from the east — a Miss Collins —
and the other I gave to Big Bat. I heard afterwards
that the latter horse was sold back east for five hundred
dollars. Telling Captain Mills on my return how the

camp was situated, I informed him the best way to attack
it would be to jump it at the break of day. We placed
one man as sentry, and the rest of us laid down and slept
until 3 o'clock. At that hour the command was awakened.
We got everything ready, and Lieut. Crawford was detailed to take charge of one party of fifty men, Capt.
Mills in charge of another party, and Lieut. Schwatka,
with twenty mounted men, was to take charge of and drive
off the ponies. The rest of the command we dismounted,
with the pack train, to follow up with the horses.

Telling them to come on towards the village, I went
down to see if the Indians suspected our presence, or if
there was anything amiss in camp. I told Capt. Mills
to come up as close to the village as he could, until I
could go back to him. When I got down in the village,
the Indians had turned most all of their horses loose,
and had gone back into their lodges. In fact, one squaw
came out and turned her horses loose when I was in
plain sight. They were tied in front of the lodge. She
turned them loose while I was watching her. I was lying
down on my horse, so I don't think she could see me.
She supposed the animal I was on was one of the Indian horses that had been turned loose, and paid no further attention to it.

Just as I turned to go back to the command, the Indian horses came stampeding through the village, and
when I got up on the hill the command had arrived
there. Capt. Mills had reached within seventy yards of
the village. As the horses stampeded through the village
it woke the Indians up, and they commenced to run out

of their lodges to see what the matter was. Seeing there would be no time to place the other company of soldiers on the other side of the village, and that all our chance was to surprise them, we commenced firing on them from where we were. I told Capt. Mills he had lost all chance of capturing the village with the Indians in it; that he had better commence the fight at once. I then went to Schwatka and told him to charge and drive the horses off, and went with him myself.

When the troops first opened fire, I did not see what the result was; but going back a short time afterwards— when we had got the horses driven away—I saw there had been a mistake made, and the Indians were firing back and the fight was general. Capt. Mills had given the order to retreat, and Crawford had told him that it was impossible to retreat. The Indians had run out of the village and got on the other side of the creek, so that the village lay in between the Indians and the soldiers. It was a sure enough fight there for a little while across the village. Knowing the Indians would have reinforcements before a great while, I tried to send Capt. Jack back with dispatches to Gen. Crook, but he didn't want to go, and one of the packers volunteered and went back. Giving the courier a verbal message to Crook, telling the General how we were situated, and asking him to hurry up his command, or part of it, as quickly as possible, I went back to the fight, and found that Lieut. Von Leuttewitz had been shot through the knee. A corporal had also been wounded. The surgeon amputated their legs afterward.

We then moved around so as to drive the Indians from the other side of the creek, which we did; but a few of them got into a kind of cave, and they could not be driven out, and it was a long while afterward before we could get them out. They killed several of our men before we could dislodge or capture them. Up to that time nobody had ventured down into the village. Of course, we did not know about these Indians being in this cave until we got down into the village; not until the soldiers went down to plunder the village. Dried meat was the first thing the soldiers looked for. The troopers found a great many things that had belonged to Custer's command, such as a guidon, a great deal of clothing and money.

During the charge made on the village Private W. J. McClinton, of Troop C, Third cavalry, discovered one of the guidons belonging to the ill-fated Custer command. It was fastened to the lodge of American Horse, and McClinton lost no time in securing the trophy. The guidon was given by McClinton to Captain Mills, and finally found its way back to the Seventh cavalry. Mr. McClinton was very proud of the capture he had made at the Slim Buttes battle, and when he received his discharge papers he found the face of the document embellished, in red ink, with a statement of the fact of the guidon's capture by himself. Mr. McClinton is at present a resident of Sheridan, Wyoming, where he has lived for many years, and has been successful in business. He never tires of singing the praises of General Crook and the brave men who opened up the rich valleys of the Tongue and Goose creeks to settlement.

WM. J. McCLINTON, WHO RECAPTURED THE CUSTER GUIDON.

The lodges were full of furs and meat, and it seemed to be a very rich village. One man found eleven thousand dollars, I think it was, all in one roll, in one of the tepis. Of course, it had come from the Custer command. Then another article the soldiers found was tobacco, which they were very much in need of, as everybody was out of the weed. Some of the men went into a lodge and turned over the robes and blankets. A little Indian girl jumped out from under the robes. She commenced crying and screaming as quick as they found her, and she ran everybody out of the lodge. When she began to cry and yell the soldiers supposed there were more Indians in the lodge, and they got out in double quick time. The little girl was about eight or nine years old.

It was right at this time that we found that some of the Indians had got into a cave at one side of the village. One of the men started to go past that spot on the hill, and as he passed the place he and his horse were both shot. This cave or dugout was down in the bed of a dry creek. The Indian children had been playing there, and had dug quite a hole in the bank, so that it made more of a cave than anything else— large enough to hold quite a number of people. Quick as we located the Indians we commenced shooting in there without seeing anything. Not knowing how many Indians were in there, the soldiers surrounded them and continued shooting into the cave until they got tired. They commenced again afterward and kept up a rain of bullets until after General Crook got into camp.

I kept on the watchout, and was expecting the Indians to charge in on us most any time, being afraid they would renew the attack before Crook joined us, and I knew we would not have much of a chance with them in such an emergency, as the main village was not far from us. I kept a watchout for them, and also for Crook's appearance. It was 11 o'clock, I should think, before I saw General Crook coming over the hill with some of the cavalry—those who could keep up with him. I got on a horse and went out to meet the General and told him what had taken place. I informed him that I was expecting the Indians, reinforced, to charge on us every minute. I also told him of the Indians who were secreted in the cave in the gulch. It was after 1 o'clock when the last of the command came over the hill. They had just got into the village when the Indians (reinforced) made their charge on us.

The Indians had made their charge with the expectation of finding only a small body of troops, as had been reported to them by the Indians who had escaped from the village. I could tell pretty well from the way they charged down from all directions at once that they never expected to find such a large body of troops, and it gave them quite a surprise to find that we were ready for them. It was not more than ten minutes before the fight became general all around the camp. After the General had given orders for the disposition of the troops, he took what stragglers he could find and tried to get the Indians out of the cave. We had commenced shooting into them, and he asked me if I would not go and talk to them and try and persuade them to come out without any more fighting. On the south side of the village I could walk right over the place where the Indians were hiding. It was a very steep bank, probably eight to ten feet high. I could go right up to them without them seeing me or there being any danger of getting shot. Going up to that point and talking to them, I told them if they would come out they would not be molested, and said everything I could to induce them to come out. Not getting any answer from them, the soldiers surrounded the place and commenced firing into the cave, but the Indians would not fire back. They would not shoot unless they had a chance to kill somebody, either. Most every shot they did fire was sure to kill or wound somebody.

While the firing was going on Big Bat and Buffalo Chips (Charlie White) came up alongside where I was standing over the Indians. After the firing into the hole had been going on for about half an hour, the General gave orders to cease firing. He asked me to talk to the Indians again, which I did, asking them to come out. I talked to them some time, but I could get no answer from them, so I thought by that they would rather die than come out. Now Buffalo Chips was standing opposite me. He was one of those long-haired scouts, and claimed to be a partner of Buffalo Bill's. He thought it was a good place to make a name for himself, I suppose, for he told Big Bat that he was going to have one of the Indians' scalps. He had no more than got the words out of his mouth before he yelled, " My God, I am shot."

There was such confusion then that I was looking out for myself as best I could, but just as I heard this cry and looked around, Buffalo Chips was falling over into the hole where the Indians were hiding. Bat was looking into the cave where White fell, and must have seen something I could not see from where I was. Before I could say anything Bat had jumped into the cave where the Indians were, and about five seconds afterwards jumped out with an Indian's scalp in his hand, telling me he had scalped one of the redskins alive, which I found out to be true. He had seen the Indian that had killed Buffalo Chips, and he jumped down onto him as the Indian was reaching to get White's six-shooter. Bat had jumped right down on top of him and scalped him and got out of the cave before anybody knew what he was doing.

When matters had quieted down I asked the Indians again if they would come out of the hole before there were any more of them shot, telling them they would be safe if they would surrender. They told me they would come out if we would not kill them, and upon receiving this promise they came out. There were three bucks and five squaws. One of the Indians had been shot through the bowels and was holding his entrails in his hands as he came out. Two of the squaws were also wounded. Eleven were killed in the hole. As this wounded Indian came out I recognized him as American Horse, but you would not have thought he was shot from his appearance and his looks, except for the paleness of his face. He came marching out of that death trap as straight as an arrow. Holding out one of his blood-stained hands he shook hands with me. I took him and his people over to the General, who ordered them taken up to the pack train. One of our doctors attended the wounded. There was no chance for American Horse to live; he was wounded so badly. It was just a matter of a short time when he would die. I asked him why he didn't come out of the hole when I first spoke to them. His answer was that they were afraid they would be killed, and they thought it better to die than be captured.

The fight kept up all that day and night—until after the time the command pulled out of there. Gen. Carr of the Fifth Cavalry was in command of the rear guard as we pulled out the next morning. Our killed were Privates John Wenzel (Third Cavalry), Edward Kennedy (Fifth Cavalry) and the scout Charlie White. Over a score were wounded. We secured only seven captives—two bucks, four squaws and one little girl. American Horse died that night, and we left him on the field for the Indians to bury or dispose of as they thought best. We got the village, securing everything that was worth taking, meat, etc., and burned the rest of the village up. We took the horses along. They amounted to three or four hundred head. The country was so muddy that we only made a short march of about twelve miles that day, but the soldiers were glad to find rest on the damp ground after passing through the terrible scenes of the past day and night.

CHAPTER XLII.

A WONDERFUL RIDE.

After going into camp on the evening of September 10th, Gen. Crook gave orders for the same picked men (Capt. Mills in command), also the pack trains (Thos. Moore in charge), and quartermaster Bubb, who had been selected two days before, to proceed that evening on into the Hills for supplies. The General gave me the official dispatches concerning the Slim Buttes fight, and other matters, with strict orders to see that they got through to the nearest telegraph office before any other dispatches reached there of the fight. He wanted me to be on the close watchout and see that no other dispatches got in ahead of them, also giving me orders how to proceed in case I should need any help in forwarding the dispatches. When I was ready to leave, the correspondents of the different papers gave me their dispatches to take through with the official dispatches. I took Capt. Jack Crawford along with me, as he was acquainted in the Hills, and would be of great service to the quartermaster in buying the supplies. I was to go on with the dispatches, leaving the supply train at Whitewood City. We left the command about nine o'clock at night.

COLONEL T. H. STANTON.

COLONEL T. H. BLACTON.
BY PERMISSION OF JOHN KENNEDY.

Not being familiar with that part of the country, Capt. Mills thought it would be best to travel by the compass. That was my first and last experience with a compass. The night was so dark that we could see no object to travel by, and about twelve o'clock we crossed our own trail. I told the Captain we had come back to our own trail. Taking out his instrument he looked at it and said that we were going right according to the compass, and that the compass was right, and we were going in the right direction. But I was satisfied we had crossed our own trail. About an hour afterwards we came to our own trail again. There was so much mineral there that the compass pointed in a circle. Telling the Captain to stop, I got off my horse and lit a match so I could make sure it was our trail; and finding that it was, I asked him to let me look at his compass. Without even looking at it, I took the thing and threw it as far as I could throw it. He asked me what I was doing, and I said I was throwing the compass away.

"We are lost without the compass," he said.

"We were lost with it," said I; "but I don't think we will be lost from this on."

We then started in a southerly direction, as near as I could judge, for the mouth of Whitewood, where it empties into the Belle Fourche. I reached there just at daylight, a short distance from Whitewood City, going into camp there until about noon. Breaking camp, we reached Whitewood City a little before sundown. After we got into Whitewood and people found out that we had been starved so long, they were very liberal and

hospitable toward us, and gave us everything they could.
Before going to bed that night I had told Capt. Jack
that I wanted him to be on hand at daylight to go with
the quartermaster to buy supplies. He was to remain
with the command while I went on. Telling me that
he was going to sleep with a friend that night, he said
he would be on hand at break of day. So in the morning I got up and didn't pay any attention to Capt. Jack.
I wanted to go over to Deadwood, so that I could forward the official dispatches from there by courier. I
started over as soon as I got my breakfast.

On reaching Deadwood and going to the livery stable,
I found the mule that Capt. Jack had been riding hitched
in one of the stalls. I asked the stableman where the
mule had come from and who had brought it there.
From the way he hesitated about telling me I thought
there was some mystery about it. Asking him what time
the mule had got there that morning, he told me it had
come in at five o'clock. I asked him where the man
who rode it was. He said that he had left there soon
after arriving in town; that he had got a horse from
him and gone on to Custer City. That was the first I
knew that Capt. Jack had taken some of the private dispatches through, or at least I thought he had.

Having received strict orders from Gen. Crook to
have the official dispatches in as soon as, if not before,
other dispatches, and thinking I had all the dispatches of
the command, I now learned that Mr. Davenport, a reporter for the New York Herald, had only given me
duplicate dispatches, and had made a bargain with Capt.

Jack for a very large sum of money to take his (Davenport's) original dispatches through to the telegraph office and reach there twelve hours before any other dispatches.

There was only one thing for me to do, and that was to take the dispatches through myself. Thinking that if anybody could overtake Capt. Jack I could do it better than I could hire somebody to do the work, I asked the livery stable man to let me have the best horse he had, and going to an acquaintance of mine in Deadwood by the name of Mart Gibbens, and taking him to the bank with me, I got five hundred dollars in money, and, with the order I had from Gen. Crook, thought that I had a pretty good chance to beat Capt. Jack Crawford to Fort Laramie, as that was the closest telegraph office, it being something like two hundred miles distant.

Knowing there were troops at two different places along the route, I was sure that I could reach Capt. Egan's company (stationed at the mouth of Red Canyon), and that I could send some of his men on with the dispatches. Jumping in the saddle at 10:30 I started out, riding the first horse about twenty-five miles, but at such a gait he weakened on me, and I had to abandon him about five hundred yards from a road ranch. Packing my saddle to the ranch, I found three horses tied up in front of the place. I took the best animal that was standing there and put my saddle on it. The owner of the ranch came out and asked me what I was doing. I told him, asking him how much he wanted for the horse, or if he would prefer to hire him, showing my order from Gen. Crook. He told me to give him fifteen dollars for the use and return of the horse. It took me but a few minutes to saddle this horse up and get out of there. I rode that horse until it dropped dead under me just as I reached another ranch. I changed six times on the road, killing three of the horses and using three of them up so they never were any good afterwards.

Next to the last horse I got was almost played out, and not seeing any ranch ahead of me, I didn't know what in the world I was going to do, for the horse I was on could not travel much further. The first thing I saw come around the point of the hill towards me was a man on horseback. Just before he got to me I got off my horse and pulled the saddle off, and as he came up I caught his horse and told him I wanted it. He was a big-boned German, but I saw he had no gun with him, so I was not afraid of his shooting me. He told me I could not have the animal; but I was unsaddling his horse, and told him I had to have it, and he said: " You can't have him." In the meantime I got his saddle un-girthed.

I caught hold of the German and threw him off on one side and his saddle on the other, and put my saddle on his horse, he telling me all the time that I could not have the horse; that it belonged to him. After I got my saddle and bridle on I asked him how much he wanted for the horse, or, if he would rather hire it to me. He told me he would neither hire nor sell it. Being in a hurry to get away from him I told him I would go without paying him if he did not tell me the price of the horse. He saw there was no way to get around it; that I was going to take the horse anyway, so he told me I could have him for eighty dollars. I gave him the money and started off. After riding some distance I found that I had made the best bargain I think I ever did make.

About five miles beyond the place of the last changing of horses I caught up with Capt. Jack. The animal he was riding was completely winded. I asked him as soon as I caught up with him if he had not had orders to go with Lieut. Bubb to buy supplies. He made the reply that he was taking some dispatches through for the New York Herald. Telling him he was discharged from the time he quit the command, I went on and left him, reaching Custer City twenty minutes before 3 o'clock, making the ride in four hours and ten minutes, the distance being one hundred and one miles. I had to be taken off my horse when I reached there, as I did not have the strength to get off myself. Securing a good man to take the dispatches through to Capt. Egan at Red Canyon so they would be sent on by troops from that point to Fort Laramie, I wrote a note to Capt. Egan, telling him to have them forwarded without any delay, also sending Gen. Crook's order with the note. I wrote a note to Gen. Crook, telling him what I had done and then went to bed. I lay there for three days. I could not move around very lively, and it took me that time to recover from my trip.

When I got rested up somewhat from my one hundred and one miles' ride, I received a dispatch from Gen. Crook, telling me I might go on to Red Cloud and lay off until the fall campaign, but to keep my eyes open for

anything that I might see or hear while at the agency.
I learned afterwards that Capt. Jack Crawford reached
Fort Laramie three days after the official dispatches had
arrived. The New York Herald did not receive Davenport's dispatches for three days afterwards, and particulars
of the Slim Buttes fight were then known all over the
United States. Crawford was to have received several
thousand dollars if he had reached Fort Laramie twelve
hours ahead of any other dispatches. By getting there
two days late, I heard that he only received two hundred
dollars.

I stayed around the Red Cloud Agency till Gen.
Crook came in. Gen. Sheridan had come to Fort Laramie
and had sent for Crook to join him at that place. On
Gen. Crook's arrival at Robinson, I went over to Fort
Laramie with him. After the conference with Gen.
Sheridan he ordered me back to Robinson to find out all
I could about the Indians that had come in from the north ;
also the disposition of the Indians at Red Cloud Agency,
telling me to keep a strict lookout for them. Upon my
return to Fort Robinson, I went around through the
Indian camps and watched them as close as I could, and
kept track of the Indians that were coming in from the
north, trying to find out how the Indians felt in general
towards the northern (hostile) tribes. It was about the
hardest work I ever did. After the command reached
Robinson (the 1876 expedition), Gen. Merritt being in
command, Gen. Crook returned, and concluded to take
the horses, arms and ammunition away from the Indians.
After everything was ready the troops started out after

dark, marched down to the main camp (then located near where Chadron is at present), surrounded it, took all the ponies and arms away from the Indians and sent the horses over to Fort Laramie to be disposed of, keeping the confiscated arms at Robinson. After we had captured the ponies I got into an ambulance with Gen. Crook and started for Fort Laramie, as he made that his headquarters during the winter campaign.

CHAPTER XLIII.

THE "HEARTY LAUGH CURE."

It was while enroute to Fort Laramie with Gen. Crook that I was taken very sick. On reaching the Post I was sent to the hospital. I was in the hospital about a week, and the longer I stayed there the worse I seemed to get. I finally became so weak I could not speak or talk. The packers were in the habit of coming over to see me. It was "headquarters" for the pack train at Fort Laramie. The only way I could communicate with anyone was by writing. One evening I told the boys that if I stayed there any longer it would kill me; that I wanted to get out of there, or wanted them to take me out and send me over to Cheyenne. The stage left Cheyenne at 12 o'clock at night, and four of the packers came over, took me out of the hospital and put me on the stage. Two of them went with me. Reaching Cheyenne about sun-down the next day, I secured accommodations at the Inter-Ocean hotel. The officers discovered next morning where I had gone, and Gen. Crook telegraphed to the doctor at Fort Russell to find out where I was stopping, and to give me all the medical care he could. He also sent Lieut. Clark there to see that I was taken care of. But I saw that

BRIGADIER-GENERAL WESLEY MERRITT.
BY PERMISSION OF JOHN F. FINERTY.

BRIGADIER GENERAL WESLEY MERRITT

I had not bettered my condition by the change of locality, and thought it would be better for me to be traveling.

I recovered my health in a very curious way. I got on the train at Cheyenne and was intending to go to Ogden, Utah. Two packers and the doctors were with me, and I was pretty sick. They had to carry me on board the cars. I had not spoken a word since leaving Fort Laramie. I could not talk; had lost my voice. On the train were a lot of school girls just coming home from school. They had been to Denver, and were going to Laramie City, I think. Seeing what a fuss the packers made over me, bringing me into the cars, of course, their curiosity was aroused, and they began asking questions to find out who I was. At that time I was very popular. You could not pick up a paper without seeing my name in it. The conductor told them who I was. They wanted to see me and talk with me; wanted to be introduced to me. I could not talk with them at all; just had to lie there and look at them. It was at their talk and the questions they would ask that I was trying to laugh, I suppose. It was very funny to me, not being used to anything of that sort, the way they would ask questions; and all at once I burst out laughing. Just as soon as I got through that laugh, it cured me right up. I was weak, but that was all. I did not feel a bit of the old sickness—just weakness. As soon as I commenced laughing I could hear a ringing in my ears. It sounded as if bells were ringing in them, and I found that I could talk just as well as I ever could.

During my illness the expedition had been getting

ready for the winter campaign against Dull Knife and
his Cheyenne warriors, and it worried Gen. Crook to
think that I was not able to go with the command. But
getting over my illness before I reached Laramie City,
in the way I did, I telegraphed the General from
Laramie City that I would overtake him at Fort Fetterman. Stopping at Laramie City until I got rested up and
strength enough to travel, I took the stage at Medicine
Bow, reaching Fetterman two days after the expedition
had started northward.

BAPTISTE GAUNIER, (LITTLE BAT.)

CHAPTER XLIV.

BATTLE OF THE RED FORK.

[It was in November, 1876, that reports came into headquarters concerning the depredations of Dull Knife and his band of Cheyenne warriors in the Powder river country, and General Crook at once determined to give the bold chief a brush that would quiet him. The column thus formed was made up of troops from the Second, Third, Fourth and Fifth Cavalry, Fourth and Ninth Artillery, the Ninth and Twenty-third Infantry. Scouts were sent out in advance of the column to locate the Cheyenne village, and were successful. The trail they discovered led up the Crazy Woman and on to the Red Fork of Powder river, and General Mackenzie, with all the cavalry in the command, took this route to the village of Dull Knife on the night of November 23d, surprising and destroying the hostile camp on the following morning. The weather was terribly cold. Dull Knife and his people were reduced to the verge of starvation through this battle, losing everything they had, even to the pony herd, and it was not long (after an unsuccessful attempt had been made by them to get assistance from Crazy Horse) before Dull Knife surrendered at Red Cloud

Agency. The warriors of this band were afterwards transferred to the Indian Territory, whence they returned to
Red Cloud Agency, joined a revolt and suffered complete
annihilation at the hands of the Third Cavalry. The battle on the Red Fork of Powder river with Dull Knife
resulted in the loss of Lieut. McKinney, a dashing and
brave young officer (who was killed while charging a number of the Indians who had taken shelter in a coulie),
and six soldiers, besides a large number wounded. The
Indian loss was never definitely ascertained, but conserva-
tive estimates placed it at not less than forty. Grouard's
account of this engagement will be found in the subsequent pages.—AUTHOR.]

————

After we had taken the horses and guns away from
the Indians at Red Cloud Agency, Gen. Crook had formed
the idea of enlisting a lot of Sioux Indians. So he took
a great many of them—some as soldiers and some as
scouts—for a three months' term. It was a pretty dangerous experiment, but it worked first rate. The two
Indians we took as prisoners in the Slim Buttes fight—
the ones we captured in that cave—were the first to enlist. Billy Hunter was interpreter. It didn't take but a
short time to enlist one hundred and fifty-nine. Col.
North joined the command with one hundred Pawnee
scouts. The Pawnees had enlisted as scouts for one year.
The horses taken away from the Sioux had all been sold
with the exception of one hundred, and that number had
been saved to give to these Pawnees, in addition to their
pay. The Government paid the Sioux for these horses
afterwards.

When I reached Fetterman from Laramie City I secured my horse and overtook the command at Antelope
Springs. The General was glad to see me, too. Nothing
of note happened during our stop at the Springs, except
that a lot of Shoshone (Snake) Indians joined us at that
place. There were something over one hundred of them,
swelling the number of our Indian scouts to about five
hundred. The General concluded to establish a cantonment at this place. Capt. Pollock of the Ninth Infantry
was put in command, and the main body pulled over to
Crazy woman. We had been in camp but a short time
when two Indians came up in sight of the camp. They
held up a flag of truce. I went out to meet them, and
they told me they had been to Lame Deer's camp; that
he was camped down on the Rosebud, and that the Cheyennes were camped somewhere on the head of Powder
river. Indian scouts from the three tribes were detailed
to go in the direction of Powder river, for the purpose
of trying to locate the Cheyenne camp, the object in
picking a few from each tribe being to get one to watch
the other.

Everything being in readiness, we started out the
next morning from Antelope Springs, with Gen. Mackenzie
of the Fourth Cavalry in command. We marched up
the Crazy Woman on to Beaver creek, where it comes
out of the mountains. Soon after we got into camp
there, one of our Indians rode up the hill on the divide
south of us and gave the signal that the Cheyenne camp
had been discovered. On his reaching the command, we
found it to be one of the scouts we had sent out the

day before; that they had gone on to Powder River,
and followed the stream up to the Red Fork, there discovering a fresh sign of Indians leading towards the head
or into the canyon of the Red Fork. After following
the creek about six miles they had discovered the camp
located at a point where the creek leaves the mountains,
in a little open valley. Leaving some of the Indian
scouts to watch the village, two of them returned to inform us that they had found it. The locality being about
eighteen miles from where the command was camped, I
thought it would be better to make a night march in
order to get there by daylight. Gen. Mackenzie gave
orders for everything to be in readiness to leave our
Crazy Woman camp at sundown.

We accordingly left just as the sun went down, and
went over onto the North Fork of Powder river. From
there we passed over to Red Fork, striking it about eight
miles below the village, then following up the creek to
within two miles of the village and making a halt there.
Specific orders were given to the different troops. Our
Indians were to drive off the horses. I do not know
what the exact orders were. I did not pay any attention
to them. After the orders had been given and we moved
up onto the village, we could hear the Indian songs and
tom-toms. The Cheyennes were dancing the scalp dance.
It seems they had killed a Crow Indian, and had been
dancing all night. When we came up in sight of the
village there were a large number of Indians between us
and the lodges, dancing. They were so busy they did
not notice us until we got within one hundred yards of

them. As soon as the Indians saw us the squaws set up a horrible noise and ran. One of the Indian bucks ran right towards us with a gun in his hand. He was probably watching the dance, and must have had his gun lying beside him, as he was in fighting trim when he jumped to his feet. He ran towards Gen. Mackenzie. He waited until the General got up to within ten steps of him, and then he fired, but he did not make a good shot. At the same instant some of the orderlies who accompanied the General (of whom there were a good many) fired on the Indian, riddling him with bullets.

Just then the Indian scouts and the different troops that were to charge into the village, gave a whoop and yell and charged, driving the Indians to the other side of the village. The Indians ran into the ravines and hills. Of course, there were some hand to hand encounters that I did not see, but heard of afterwards; but the Indians, recovering from their fright, got into a position that it was hard to get them out of, and returned our fire with deadly effect. As the fight became general, one small party of Indians got into a gulch close to the main part of the troops, so close that it was very hard for them to miss us. They did a great deal of damage, and General Mackenzie thought the best thing to be done was to charge the Indians and drive them out of this gulch, and he ordered Lieut. McKinney to charge on them and drive them out, asking me if I would go with the troopers and show them where the Indians were. Riding up to within about two hundred yards of the gulch, Lieut. McKinney gave the order to his men to charge the gulch where the Indians were lodged. While the charge was being made I was riding alongside of the Lieutenant. The Indians waited until we got within about ten yards of them, when they fired, their bullets killing Lieut. McKinney, a sergeant and two men at the first volley.

Seeing there was no chance to drive them out, I wheeled my horse and got in behind some rocks on a hill. Then I turned my horse loose and watched for a chance to get a shot. I stopped there some time, and tried to get a chance to kill some of them, but I could not get a shot at them for a long while. The troops were firing into the gulch, and the Indians soon got out of there. We finally drove them all out. They didn't annoy us from that part of the field any more. I shot Chief Little Wolf myself. He had been jumping up on a small hill, and nearly every trooper in the command was shooting at him. Every time he dropped to the ground the soldiers supposed they had killed him. I could see by the way he dropped that he had not been shot; so telling Mr. Roache that I would kill him when he rose up again, I awaited an opportunity. It came in about ten minutes. As he jumped to his feet I took quick aim and pulled the trigger. With the report of my rifle Little Wolf fell to the ground and lay motionless, his limbs being spread out like a huge frog's. It was a dead certainty he had been shot, and I knew that my bullet had done its work. After we had driven the Indians from that part of the field, I rode over the ground where Little Wolf had fallen, and found the Cheyenne chief's body lying where it fell. I did not examine it to see where the ball had struck him, but I don't imagine he ever knew what hit him. At any rate, he never caused the troops any more trouble.

After the killing of Little Wolf the Cheyennes drew back into the hills, so that we were compelled to deploy our force into a skirmish line in following them. They had sent their squaws and children back from the scene of the battle when the village was first jumped, and the intense cold told awfully on the little children, no less than a dozen babies being frozen to death in the arms of their mothers. The Indians, by this time, had become desperate, and while the skirmish line held its place in front of the stronghold selected by the savages, two of the latter, in war-paint and unarmed, came out in full sight of the command and walked up and down within twenty paces of the troops, waving buffalo heads high in air and apparently tempting fate. Every man in the skirmish line was shooting at these two savages, including Big Bat and myself; but they seemed to bear charmed lives and left the field unharmed. Their intention was to draw the fire of the troops upon themselves until the Cheyennes could have time to get the women and children far enough up into the mountains to escape danger, which they finally did.

During the fighting toward the close of the day, the movements of our Sioux scouts were watched very closely, as it was believed by a great many that they would not stay with the troops when the emergency of battle arose. But no drilled soldiers ever stood the test better. In fact, some of the hardest fighting that was done these same Sioux scouts did, and the wisdom of Gen. Crook in enlisting them was established beyond question.

When it was at last determined that the troops could not dislodge the Indians, Gen. Mackenzie sent for me and asked me to go back to the wagon train on Crazy Woman and inform Gen. Crook of the situation and urge him to bring up the infantry at once. So taking one of the Sioux scouts with me, I started for Crazy Woman, reaching there about 2 o'clock in the morning. I had gone from the battlefield directly across country, and when I arrived at Crook's camp I found that he had left with the infantry the night before, following the trail previously taken by Gen. Mackenzie. As I had had no sleep for over fifty hours I turned in, and the next day the command arrived with the killed and wounded. The result of the battle was the death of Lieut. McKinney, as dashing and brave a young officer as there was in the service; the killing of six soldiers and the wounding of twenty-seven others, two of whom were Indian scouts. There was no way of finding out how many of the Indians had been killed, although something like thirty dead bodies fell into our hands. We killed a large number of the Indian ponies and drove over seven hundred others from the village after capturing it.

[In his book, "On the Border with Crook," Capt. John G. Bourke, speaking of the dismay and dissatisfaction among the Cheyennes, caused by the appearance of the Sioux scouts in the Crook command during this battle, says the Cheyennes told the Sioux to "Go home—you

have no business here; we can whip the white soldiers
alone, but can't fight you, too." Addressing themselves
to the soldiers, the warriors of Dull Knife cried, according to the authority given above, "You have killed and
hurt a heap of our people, and you may as well stay
now and kill the rest of us." It was undoubtedly the
action of Gen. Crook in enlisting the Sioux as scouts
that ultimately led the Cheyennes to enter the government service in the same capacity. After Dull Knife's
camp had been wiped out by Gen. Mackenzie, that noted
chief went to Crazy Horse for succor and assistance,
believing that Crazy Horse detested those of the Sioux
who had renounced savagery as heartily as he (Dull
Knife) did; but Crazy Horse received the Cheyenne chief's
advances in the coldest manner, refusing to have anything
to do with him.

The Cheyennes had a very high opinion of Crazy
Horse, knowing that he was an uncompromising foe of
the whites, and his treatment of Dull Knife (who had
gone to him in the hour of dire disaster—when his people were on the verge of starvation and were seeking an
asylum of safety) undoubtedly led to the ill-feeling which
arose between the Cheyenne and Sioux nations, and
prompted many of the members of the former tribe to
become government scouts that they might the better revenge themselves upon Crazy Horse when the soldiers
directed their maneuvers against that chief and his
people.

The opportunity came soon enough, and although
Crazy Horse's followers gave up their arms and submit-

ted tamely to the inevitable—accepted their lot as " agency Indians "—the fires of hatred which burned within the bosom of Crazy Horse were unquenchable, and he sought and found death (never once uttering a complaint or groan) in a battle where he stood alone and single-handed against an entire garrison.   Grouard says that a great many articles easily identified as belonging to the ill-fated Custer command were found in the lodges of Dull Knife's village, thereby proving that the Cheyennes were allied with the Sioux in the memorable battle on the Little Big Horn on that bright June morning when the gallant Colonel of the Seventh and five of his heroic troop met death.—AUTHOR.]

After burying the dead, the command went to Powder river, at which place two scouts who had been sent out from the Red Cloud agency three months previous to locate, if possible, the Indian villages, came in and reported that Lame Deer and war party were on their way in to the Little Powder river from the Belle Fourche, and Gen. Crook at once started for that section to head them off.

The snow was very deep and the cold intense.   The command, failing to find Lame Deer and his people, returned to Fort Fetterman, and so closed the winter campaign.

COLONEL GEORGE M. RANDALL.
BY PERMISSION OF JOHN F. FINERTY.

CHAPTER XLV.

CALIFORNIA JOE.

In the fall of 1876, after the battle of Slim Buttes, I received orders from Gen. Crook to hire some good man to drive a band of horses from Fort Laramie over to the northern part of the Black Hills. The animals had been purchased by the government and were to be sent to the Fifth Cavalry, then stationed in Dakota. California Joe was recommended to me as just the man I wanted. He was at Fort Laramie at that particular time, so I went to Joe and asked him if he would undertake the journey, and he said that he would. I told him to be ready to start the following morning. He knew the country thoroughly, and at the time designated started out with the horses and escort. Arriving at his destination he made arrangements to remain with the Fifth Cavalry until its return to the Red Cloud Agency. After reaching the latter place he was still retained, as he was found to be a good man, and it was thought plenty of work could be found to keep him busy.

Before I met him he had had some trouble with a man named Thomas Newcomb, but I knew nothing about it when I hired him. Sometime previous to the killing of Joe, old man Reshaw, father of Louie Reshaw, had been murdered on the Running Water. The day following the old man's murder, California Joe happened to go into Fort Robinson, and Newcomb had him arrested, charging him with old man Reshaw's murder. When Joe's preliminary examination came off, Newcomb swore that old man Reshaw had been killed by Joe; but he had no evidence to substantiate the statement. Nobody who knew Joe believed a word of it, and the actions of Newcomb made Joe awful mad; and I don't doubt but what he may have threatened to get even with his accuser. I don't believe, however, that Joe ever threatened to kill Newcomb, and never found a man who did believe it. Newcomb claimed, nevertheless, that he was constantly in fear that Joe would kill him. When Joe was employed at Red Cloud, Newcomb lived near there, spending most of his time with the Indians. One morning as Joe was coming from breakfast Newcomb hid behind the building where the former was messing, and just as the unsuspecting scout passed the corner of the building, Newcomb leveled a double-barreled shotgun at him and pulled the trigger. The entire contents of the gun entered Joe's body, killing him instantly. Newcomb escaped both trial and punishment for this crime. I believed at the time, and still think, this was as cold-blooded a murder as I ever heard of, and if I had been at Robinson when it was committed, I should have exerted every effort to have had Newcomb punished for the crime.

Joe was born in California, and was justly celebrated as a scout, having been with General Custer as Chief of

Scouts for some time. Custer says, when he first knew him (in 1868), "he was a man about forty years of age, some six feet in height, and possessed a well proportioned frame. His head was covered with a luxuriant crop of hair, almost jet black, strongly inclined to curl, and so long as to fall carelessly over his shoulders. His face, at least so much of it as was not concealed by the long, waving, brown beard and moustache, was full of intelligence and pleasant to look upon. His eye was handsome, black and lustrous, with an expression of kindness and mildness combined. On his head was generally to be seen, whether awake or asleep, a huge sombrero, or black slouch hat. A soldier's overcoat, with a large circular cape, a pair of trousers, with the legs tucked in the top of his long boots, usually constituted the make-up of the man whom I selected as my chief scout. He was known by the euphonious title of California Joe. No other name seemed ever to have been given him, and no other name appeared to be necessary."

Grouard states that Newcomb was a first-class bluffer, and was so anxious to acquire a reputation as a bad man that he never missed an opportunity of whipping a "kid" or doing up some poor, drunken fellow. When the spring campaign of 1876 opened, Newcomb went along with the troops, but not as a soldier. At old Fort Reno, on the night when the command was fired into by some marauding hostiles, Newcomb was regaling the men with a story of how he once jumped upon the back of a Texas buffalo and rode it several miles, spurring and quirting the beast unmercifully. Just as he got to the end of the

story and was posing as one of the bravest of all brave
men, the Indians fired into the tent where he had been
entertaining the boys, and Newcomb became the scarcest
commodity in camp.   From that day on the soldiers
called him "Texas Buffalo."

California Joe's body was laid to rest at Red Cloud
Agency.   His untimely end was universally regretted, for
he was as popular as he was brave.

FRANK GROUARD, AT 30.

CHAPTER XLVI.

SURRENDER AND DEATH OF CRAZY HORSE.

It was in the spring of '77 that Crazy Horse sent an Indian courier in from the Ogallala village, between Tongue and Powder rivers, with a message that he would allow his people to surrender if Lone Star (Gen. Crook) would let him come in peace. Lieut. William P. Clarke, who had the Indians in charge at Red Cloud Agency, sent word to Crazy Horse that if he would come in and give up his ponies and arms, he and his people would not be harmed in any way, but that there must be a clear understanding that he was to give up his horses and guns, which shortly afterwards he did, giving them all up without any trouble.

Shortly after his surrender, Crazy Horse, with his principal men, were enlisted as scouts, so that we had a great time in drilling them; but it soon caused dissatisfaction amongst them to such an extent that I thought it best to keep a close watch over them. At times I went amongst them dressed up as an Indian, so that I could keep a close watch on all their movements. Sometimes I would dress as an Indian and attend their councils. Oft' times I would have an Indian (in fact, I had an Indian and a squaw,) bring me all the news they could get from the camp. I heard of their plot to kill Lieut. Clarke and myself and afterwards massacre the people at the Post. Thinking that the report was exaggerated, I set about finding when the next Indian council would take place. I thought it would be best to attend it myself.

It was a very secret meeting, so the Indians supposed. It was held about midnight. Dressing myself up as an Indian I got on my horse bareback and went down amongst them, their camp being situated on the site where Chadron, Nebraska, now stands, thirty miles below Robinson. If I had made use of a saddle, they would have soon found out who I was. Tying my horse in front of one of the lodges, I went right through the village looking for the lodge where the meeting was to be held. After traveling through the camp for some time I found the tepi where they were to meet. Standing at the door watching the Indians go into the lodge, I drew the blanket over my head so that I could not be recognized by any of them, unless they should pull the blanket off of me; but they very seldom did anything like that.

I took a back seat when the council met and heard everything that was said; how Crazy Horse was to take a few of his best warriors and go up to the office of Lieut. Clarke and ask to have a friendly council with him, as they wanted to talk matters of the tribe over with him. Each one of these Indians was to have his gun concealed under his blanket, and at the given signal, while Crazy Horse was making a speech, he (Crazy Horse) was to shoot Lieut. Clarke, and the Indians were to kill all the whites in the room, myself included. They were to give secret warning to all the other Indians that wanted to join them, so that they would be ready to massacre all the whites at the Post as soon as the shooting began. After listening for some time and finding out all I cared to know, I took the first opportunity that presented itself and departed.

Reaching my house before daylight, I turned my horse out and went to bed, knowing that these Indians would be at my place about 9 o'clock. I knew how superstitious they were, and I thought the best thing I could do would be to work on their superstition, so I remained in bed until they came up, which was about 9 o'clock in the morning. They knocked at the door of my house, and the woman who was cooking for me came and told me the Indians wanted to see me. I told her to send them in, but to tell them I was sound asleep. They came stamping into my room. I heard them, but pretended to be asleep, and they thought I was asleep. As soon as they got in they began to talk, telling me to get up, as it was high sun. As soon as they squat down on the floor, I sat up and began to rub my eyes, as anyone would do who had been asleep, and commenced to tell them what I had dreamed, and how it had scared me, especially when I woke up and saw them in my room.

They asked me what I dreamed. It was only a dream, I said, but they wanted to know what it was, so I said I would tell them. I went on to describe their plot; the killing of Clarke and myself and the massacre of the whites at the Post afterwards. I described everything just as I had heard it the night before at the meeting, and then told them it was only a dream. I could see how their faces changed. They did not know what to make of it; they never ate the breakfast prepared for them, and it was the only time they ever did miss a meal with me. They said they had pressing business that morning and departed. I afterwards informed Lieut. Clarke of the plot, so he could be on the outlook if they tried to make this break. I thought what I had told them would perhaps stop them.

On the day set for the conference with Clarke at the Post, we were ready to give Crazy Horse and his men as warm a reception as they would want. About nine o'clock in the morning the Ogallala chief, accompanied by twenty young bucks, came into the office in the headquarters building. They all wore their blankets and had their weapons concealed beneath them. They were not aware that the room adjoining the office was full of armed soldiers, ready at a moment's notice to pounce upon them, nor that mounted men had been stationed all around the garrison. I think, however, that Crazy Horse suspected we had got an inkling of his intentions, for he could not help but notice that we had a large number of Indian scouts, armed to the teeth, in the office when he came in.

Some of the young men with Crazy Horse did considerable talking to Lieut. Clarke, and they were (according to the plot) to be followed by Crazy Horse; but before the latter could begin his speech, which was to end in the murder of the Lieutenant and myself, a young

chief named Three Bear from the Cut-Off tribe interfered. He was enlisted as a scout and was a warm friend
of Clarke's. He undoubtedly knew of the plot, as he
jumped up and told Crazy Horse if he wanted to kill
anybody to kill him, as he would not be permitted to kill
his (Three Bear's) friend; that not one of the conspirators
would get out of the building alive if they raised any
trouble; that the place was full of armed soldiers, ready
to do their share of the killing.

Considerable confusion followed the speech of Three
Bear, and Crazy Horse did not seem to know what to
do. I do not think Crazy Horse was afraid. He did
not care for himself, but hesitated about getting his companions into trouble; for Crazy Horse was the bravest
man I ever knew or met — white, red or black. The
meeting broke up immediately after this, and the Indians
went back to their camp.

When Gen. Crook heard of the plot to assassinate
the whites, he secretly ordered two more regiments into
the Post, and at once gave orders for the arrest of
Crazy Horse and the disarming of the Indians in his
village. On the morning of the 4th of September eight
companies with about four hundred Indian scouts started
down toward Crazy Horse's village, situated on the north
side of White Earth creek, six miles east of the agency,
so as to surround it by daylight; but as the troops were
reaching the village I found Crazy Horse had flown.
Hearing of the intended arrest of himself, he had started
out on horseback for the Spotted Tail agency. As soon
as we discovered that he had gone, Three Bear, accom-

panied by some of the Indian scouts, was sent after him
with orders to bring him back. If he would not come
peaceably they were to bring him back by force. As
soon as Crazy Horse reached Spotted Tail agency he
gave himself up to Capt. Jesse M. Lee of the Ninth Infantry, who was acting Indian agent there. The Captain
assured him, if he would go back peaceably, that he would
not be put in the guard house, so that he came back
with the full understanding that he would be treated
square.

Starting back for Robinson on the morning of the
5th, Crazy Horse riding in the ambulance and the Indian
scouts acting as an escort, he reached Robinson about
four o'clock in the afternoon. Before Capt. Lee had time
to explain to the commanding officer about the promises
he had made to Crazy Horse, Lieutenant Clarke had seen
the ambulance arrive at the Post, and ordered it driven
in front of the guard house, and had likewise given
orders for Crazy Horse to be locked up without knowing
anything about the promise of Captain Lee to the chief.
As soon as I found out that he had given these orders
for Crazy Horse to be put into the guard house, I knew
there would be trouble, as Crazy Horse would not submit to go in peaceably; that he would make a fight for
it. I think there was a big misunderstanding there by
Lieut. Clarke not going to see the commanding officer
before he gave these orders; also in not consulting Capt.
Lee about it.

When I learned what orders had been given by
Lieut. Clarke I got on my horse and reached the guard

house just as Crazy Horse had stepped out of the ambulance. By that time there were two or three hundred Indians congregated about the guard house, a great many of them friends of Crazy Horse. Crazy Horse's arms had not been taken from him ; that is, he had his six-shooter and knives which he always carried. I could tell by the way he walked into the guard house that he did not know that he was to be placed in confinement. After he had got inside the building, passed through the second door and the guard opened a cell for him, he realized what was up. Then it was he drew both his knives and started for the outside. An Indian by the name of Little Big Man was standing in the doorway as Crazy Horse rushed out. Little Big Man grasped both of Crazy Horse's wrists as the chief reached the door, but the now furious captive jerked one of his hands loose and dealt Little Big Man two terrible thrusts, both wounds being made in the latter's arm.

Crazy Horse came through the outside door as the sentinel was passing. I do not think that Crazy Horse intended to attack the sentinel, but rather to kill one or more of the Indians who were standing in front of the guard house, for he made a lunge at one of them. I did not see the death thrust given Crazy Horse, as it was given from behind the captive, and I do not know whether it was dealt by the sentinel with his bayonet, or by one of the officers with a sword. There was a great deal of confusion at the time. I could plainly hear the cartridges being thrown into the guns held in the hands of the Indians who stood about, and the click of gun hammers.

It looked very much as if we were about to have a general fight. The next instant I saw Crazy Horse turn completely around on his left foot and fall over backwards. I knew he had been stabbed, but could not see who did it.

I immediately rode over to General Bradley's quarters and reported the killing of Crazy Horse to that officer, telling him it were better to get the troops in quarters at once, as a big row seemed inevitable. As a matter of fact, none of the soldiers standing around had any firearms with them and were completely at the mercy of the Indians in case of an outbreak — half the garrison could have been killed in a twinkling had the Indians broken loose. But the counsel of the older heads among the redmen kept the young bucks quiet and averted a massacre.

A doctor was sent for and Crazy Horse was made as comfortable as possible. I asked the man of medicine if there was any chance for the chief to live, and he said there was not; that one of his kidneys had been pierced; that there was no chance of saving him. Just then Crazy Horse's father came up; everybody else had left him, and shortly afterwards the Indians all dispersed and went back to the village, where most of them camped. Crazy Horse died at 8 o'clock that evening.

Around the house where I was staying some five or six hundred Indians had gone into camp. They were camped so thick around my place I could hardly get out. The commanding officer sent for me right after dark, telling me I had better go down and stay amongst the Indians, and try and find out what they thought of the

CROOK'S OLD CAMPING GROUND—PRESENT SITE OF SHERIDAN, WYOMING.

Crazy Horse affair, and if there would be any outbreak, and for me to report the first thing I heard of their intentions. I went down to the village. I visited the lodges, first one and then another. The whole camp was talking about the killing of Crazy Horse, but I heard nothing which led me to suppose that there would be any trouble. Everything was very quiet around the village pretty much all the time I was there. I think the Indians were a little bit scared themselves. Along about 3 o'clock in the morning I thought all the trouble was over, so I went to bed.

I do not know how long I had been asleep, when I was awakened by a rapid discharge of firearms. My first thought was that the troops had jumped the village; but as soon as I got out of doors I heard some of the Indians laughing and talking, and found out there was an eclipse of the moon, and the entire village was shooting at the inconstant old girl, trying to "bring her back to life." As soon as I found out what the firing was about, I reported the matter to the commanding officer.

The killing of Crazy Horse ended most all of the trouble we had with these particulars Indians — the Sioux and Cheyennes, and a great many enlisted after that. There was no more trouble until '79. That was with the Sioux. It was in the fall of '77 that the Indians were moved from Red Cloud to the Missouri river. The Nez Perces trouble in 1877 was followed two years later by the Miles' campaign against Sitting Bull, and no further uprisings occured until the South Dakota outbreak in 1890.

[Captain Bourke, who was at the Red Cloud Agency when Crazy Horse surrendered, describes his meeting with the renowned Sioux warrior in his work " On the Border with Crook." He states that Crazy Horse took his first supper at the agency with Grouard, and the latter invited the Captain to go over to the former's tepi with him and meet the Sioux Chief. He states that as they appoached the tepi Crazy Horse remained seated on the ground, but that when Grouard spoke to him he "looked up, arose and gave me a hearty grasp of his hand." The Captain remembers the chief " as a man who looked quite young,, not over thirty years old, five feet eight inches high, lithe and sinewy, with a scar in the face. The expression of his face was one of quiet dignity, but morose, dogged, tenacious and melancholy. He behaved with stolidity, like a man who realized he had to give in to Fate, but would do so as sullenly as possible. While talking to Frank, his countenance lit up with genuine pleasure, but to all others he was, at least in the first days of his coming upon the reservation, gloomy and reserved. I never heard an Indian," concludes Captain Bourke, "mention his name save in terms of respect."

For generation after generation the name of Crazy Horse had been handed down among the Sioux from father to son. This particular family had always been held in high esteem by the redmen. The archives of the Sioux nation were entrusted to and preserved by it, and it was from the old father of Crazy Horse that Grouard secured the history (preserved on buckskin) of the Sioux nation. This history covered a period of over eight hundred years, and would have proved of incalculable value to future historians could it have been preserved. Grouard kept these precious documents after he regained his freedom. When first stationed at Fort McKinney the house in which he lived was destroyed by fire, and all its contents, except a dog and revolver, went up in smoke, these documents with the rest. There was also destroyed at this time, the scalp cape of Sitting Bull—a ghastly relic of huge dimensions made from the scalps of white victims who had fallen by the hand of that crafty old war chief.

Crazy Horse, like the other members of his family, was remarkably white for an Indian, and many who met him imagined he was not a full-blooded Sioux. His hair, which was a sandy brown, was unlike any other man's in the tribe. Grouard says the Ogallala chief was a fine-looking savage in 1873, when he first met him. A trifle less than six feet tall, he was straight as an arrow. He was naturally spare, and could stand any amount of hardship. He was proud of his people and their history, and, like Sitting Bull, was opposed to any and all intercourse with the whites.

Grouard says Crazy Horse was the bravest man he ever met. Reserved at all times, his counsel was greatly sought after, and even in the most solemn deliberations of the Ogallalas he spoke only through some chosen friend. In leadership he outranked every man in the tribe. In reality, he was an hereditary chief. His battles with the whites proved his prowess, and the honors which he brushed aside in savagery were thrust upon him

by the "advance guard of civilization." He possessed
nothing but his native intelligence and cunning. He gave
no thought to the acquisition of wealth, as that bauble is
understood by the savage. He was a warrior at all times
and in all places, and he left the counting of his coups
to those who were as familiar with them as himself.
Quick to act, he was first in battle and shrank from no
danger. It was to this man's tepi that Grouard went and
found shelter and protection when Sitting Bull sought to
destroy him, and the regard the two men had for each
other transcended the affection of brothers. Crazy Horse
was the Napoleon among the Sioux, and the death-knell
of savagery was sounded in his murder.

Grouard tells many interesting anecdotes concerning
Crazy Horse. From his boyhood he was greatly attached
to Lone Bear and Hump or the Spotted War Bonnet.
As children the three were always together; in youth
they were firm friends; in manhood they were insepara-
ble; in battle they fought side by side. Lone Bear was
always the unfortunate one of the trio. He was never
known to enter a battle but what he received a wound.
At the Phil Kearney massacre he was so desperately
wounded that he could not crawl from the place where
he lay, and through the awful storm and bitter cold
weather which succeeded the battle, Lone Bear was at the
mercy of the elements. When found by his trusty companions, he was given all the care they could shower upon
him; but the poor savage was beyond human aid, for
beside his wounds, his limbs and body were frozen terribly. He died in the arms of Crazy Horse while Hump

stood by, weeping. Thus the trinity of savage love was
shattered, and Lone Bear was laid away to rest. That
was in 1866.

During the year 1873 twelve Ogallala Sioux, among
whom were Crazy Horse and Hump, to revenge themselves upon the Shoshones for some injury inflicted, went
to the camp of the latter on the Wind River reservation,
and in the darkness fired into a tepi, killing several of
Chief Washakie's braves. A running battle resulted, the
Sioux making a determined stand and desperate fight on
Badwater creek, many miles from the scene of the reservation killing. Here Hump was killed, and the Sioux
said that Crazy Horse was beside himself with grief
and rage. He fought like an enraged bear, rescuing the
body of his friend and placing it on the back of his
own horse while he fought. He gave the bridle rein
to one of his own tribe and sent him toward the Ogallala
village with Hump's body, while he, in desperation, ran
in among the pursuing Shoshones, and with his quirt,
put them to flight. From that very hour, said his nearest
friends, Crazy Horse sought death.

He had a superstitious belief — an abiding faith —
that he would never be killed by a bullet, and this
encouraged him in all his conflicts, whether with oppos-
ing tribes or the whites. He had no desire to live, his
two friends having passed to the Great Beyond; and
he wooed death at all times. He avowed this on many
occasions to his intimate friends.

Grouard relates a touching instance of the Ogallala
chief's parental affection. Crazy Horse had but one child

—a little girl about four years of age—whom, in his savage way, he idolized. While the village was located between the Little Big Horn and the Rosebud, in 1873, the chief went out with a war party against the Crows. In his absence the little girl was taken sick and died. The camp was moved from the valley of the Little Big Horn toward the Little Missouri on Tongue river before the Ogallala warriors returned. When Crazy Horse learned of the death of his child his grief, Grouard says, was pathetic. The child's body was buried seventy miles from the place where the Sioux camp was then located, and large parties of warring Crows infested the intervening country. But Crazy Horse had determined to visit the grave of his loved little girl, and he asked Grouard to accompany him. It took them two days to reach the place of sepulchre. Crazy Horse asked Grouard to select a site for a camp while he visited the grave of his child. He went alone to the raised bier (or platform on which the body had been placed), crawled up beside the little girl's remains, and there stayed for three days and nights mourning for the departed one. On the morning of the fourth day, Grouard says, Crazy Horse woke him at sunrise and told him he was ready to depart. Not a mouthful of food or drop of water had passed that father's lips during those three awful days and nights of mourning, and he rode back to his people and desolate tepi with a heavy heart but stolid face. None of the tribe knew where he had been, and he never whispered the object of his errand.

More than a month before his tragic end, he told

GRAVE OF CRAZY HORSE'S DAUGHTER.

Grouard he was looking for death, and believed it would soon come to him. He had a dream, and the vision to him was pregnant with promise of eternal quietude. He said he thought he stood upon some lofty height and saw a mighty eagle soaring far above him. He watched it as it floated in the quiet sky, and presently it seemed to fold its wings and fall. The eagle's body anchored at his feet, and when he looked upon it, lo! it was himself. An arrow had pierced its body, and its life was gone. Only a little month, and the mighty chief had found the peace his soul had thirsted for so long. A hasty thrust with a sword or bayonet — it makes no difference, now, which — and Crazy Horse was no more. In the hour when death found him, he lay with his head pillowed upon his father's breast, lost to all thought of fear in his approaching dissolution and happy in the contemplation that the spirits of those he loved were awaiting his coming to the far-off Happy Land.

What, may I ask, is more pathetic or better suited to this closing scene, than the words of Touch-the-Cloud, chief of the Sans Arcs, who, bending over the body of Crazy Horse and laying his hand upon the chieftain's breast as his warrior spirit took its flight, said:

"It is well. He has looked for death and it has come."—AUTHOR]

CHAPTER XLVII.

AFTER HORSE THIEVES AND HOLDUPS.

The fall of 1876 and the three years following were noteworthy on account of the wholesale thieving that was going on in the territories. It just seemed as if all the thieves in the universe had been turned loose in Nebraska, Wyoming, Oregon, Idaho, Montana and Dakota. They had no regard for property or human life, and were, in my opinion, infinitely worse than the Indians ever were. Among the more notorious characters who infested the great west in the years referred to were the James boys — Jesse and Frank — and their gang; Billy the Kid, Cully, Bill Zimmerman, Tom Reece, Phœnix, Odell, Jerry Overholt, Madison, Dutch Henry, Black Hank, Persimmon Bill, Jack Campbell, Herman Leslie, Bill Evans, Teton Jackson, McGloskey and Big Nosed George.

These men were leaders and had a following that was truly surprising. They stole from the settlers, they robbed the passengers on stages, they rifled the mail bags and money chests on overland routes, held up trains on the Union Pacific, looted stores, run off Indian ponies, and, very often, shot or hanged their victims. They kept the entire country in an uproar, and terrorized the settlers

SPOTTED TAIL.

SPOTTED TAIL

to such an extent that one-half the robberies committed by them were never made known. They had their spies and agents at all points, even at the government posts and agencies, and at last the United States authorities were compelled to call into requisition the troops to suppress them.

During the year 1877 my orders kept me swinging like a pendulum between the Red Cloud and Spotted Tail Agencies, and Forts Laramie, Robinson, Fetterman, Reno (McKinney) and Sheridan, now being on the trail of some horse-stealing gang, and then trying to locate a holdup outfit.

On one occasion in 1877 the thieves stole about one hundred ponies from the Indians at Spotted Tail Agency. From the number of horses taken I thought the thieves were in such force that I took a detachment (M troop of the Third Cavalry) from the Spotted Tail Agency and followed them. We struck the tracks of the ponies leading towards the Black Hills. They were very easy to follow, being so many of them. We gained on them very fast, and overtook them the next day on the Cheyenne river, right where Edgemont, S. D., stands at the present time. When I first discovered the thieves they were cooking their dinner. They had turned the ponies out across the creek, with the exception of one or two. These they kept in the vicinity of the fire where they were preparing their meal. Getting as close to them as I could without being seen and riding in between them and the ponies, we captured the herd without any trouble.

But while I was looking after the ponies three of

my men had ridden up to where the horse thieves were. The first thing I heard were three or four shots fired, and two of the soldiers came riding back to me hallooing that one of my men was shot and killed. There were four of the horse thieves, and before I could reach the place where the shooting occurred, two of them had jumped on their ponies and started toward the Hills. The other two, as soon as they saw me riding toward them, commenced to fire at me. That made me so hot that I did not ask them to surrender, but commenced to fire at them, killing one and capturing the other without any trouble. They had got me so angry I did not stop to think. I knew we did not want to be bothered with them ; so I put the captured thief on his horse, tied one end of a rope to the limb of a tree, the other end around his neck, and drove the horse out from under him. Did not even stop to look back, but gathered up the ponies and started for the agency. I heard four or five days afterward of a man hanging to a tree, and suppose he was the man I had swung up ; but he gave me good cause to do what I did. If he had not killed one of the men who were with me I should have turned him loose, and his partner would never have been shot if he had not helped to kill one of my men.

It is hard to tell how many thieves I did capture that year, but there were a great many. When I started after them I most generally got them. It was in 1877 that the road agents began to hold up the Black Hills stage, and I was sent out from Fort Laramie to assist in capturing some "gentlemen of the road." It was near Fort Laramie in the fall of 1876, for the second time in my life, I came in contact with the noted Bill Bevins. He had left Cheyenne and made his way over to Running Water. On his way he had stolen a number of horses some time during the night. I started out after the thieves, overtaking them on Running Water. I took the stolen horses away from them, but while doing so Bevins had recognized me and told me he would drop the horses if I would hold off, which I was willing to do on account of his being so friendly to me in my boyhood when I met him at Helena years before. So, taking the horses, I turned them back to the owners, saying that I could not catch the horse thieves ; that they had dropped the horses when they saw me coming and had made off to the hills.

Two days afterward the stage was held up at the government farm on the Platte river. I was sent out to trace the robbers up, which I did, catching four of them before sun-down. From that on until the latter part of 1877, I was kept very busy after these road agents, and I caught a good many of them, but as I never kept a record I cannot give their names or the number. Some of them were turned loose, and some were sent to the penitentiary. I followed two of these gentlemen on horseback from Bull's Bend, on the Platte, to Green River, a trifle over three hundred miles, catching them just as they were sitting down to breakfast. I was at the breaking up of these gangs, and I did everything in my power to help capture all the horse thieves that were in the northern country. Kept me busy until I was ordered to Fort Reno in December, 1877 ; but I remained at Red Cloud agency until the Indians were moved from there over to the Missouri river. Right after the removal of the Indians I started for Fort Mc-Kinney (old Fort Reno, on the Powder river), reaching there about the first of January, 1878. I had not been there but a short time before I found there was a big gang of horse thieves in that locality. They had a regular trail running through Wyoming, from Oregon to Minnesota. They were stationed at points all along the line, so it made it hard to catch them, as there was always a different party stealing horses along the road.

These parties had stolen some horses from the beef contractor at the Post, and I was informed of it. The next morning in going up to where they had stolen the horses, I found their tracks and followed them up. The tracks led toward the Black Hills. Thinking that I could soon overtake the thieves, I started out without any provisions or preparation. After following them about twenty miles, I saw that I would have to make a long ride to overtake them, which I did, following them some four hundred miles without catching up with the band, but capturing one of their number who had turned the stolen horses over to some confederates. I caught this one big fellow, and, working on his fears, made him believe I was going to hang him. Then he gave everything away, which was the means, later on, of capturing the whole gang, or nearly all of them. Anyway, twenty-eight thieves was about the number we got. We had no difficulty in getting this gang of horse thieves after we had them located. Every one of the party was sent to the penitentiary, their sentences ranging from fourteen to thirty years. They did not give us any trouble after that.

CHAPTER XLVIII.

CAUGHT IN A BLIZZARD.

On my return to McKinney, Captain Edmund (commander at that Post) informed me that he had orders to take his command, composed of three companies of cavalry and four of infantry, down on the Belle Fourche. There was a rumor that some of Lone Deer's band were making their way up from there into the Little Powder river country. We were to march down the Belle Fourche and intercept them, if possible. So taking three companies of cavalry and two of infantry we started for the Belle Fourche. This march was what is known in army circles as "Pollock's Sage Brush Expedition." Reaching the forks of the Belle Fourche and searching the lower country, I failed to find any trace of the Indians, and was perfectly satisfied that there were none in that part of the country, and I reported to Captain Pollock to that effect. The command was then ordered back to the Post. Next morning, just as we were packing up to start, it commenced snowing, but not hard enough to delay our traveling. On the way back to McKinney, I informed Captain Pollock that there was a short cut across the country to the Post if he desired to take it. It would save a great deal of hard travel and get us to McKinney between 3 and 4 o'clock in the afternoon of the same day we started. The Captain decided to take this cut-off trail. He sent the wagon train by the old road, however, and it was two days getting into quarters, it having to travel a considerable number of miles more than was traversed by the command to reach the same destination.

After we got out on the prairie some eight or ten miles, the snowstorm changed into one of the hardest blizzards, or as hard a one, as I ever saw. It made it very severe traveling for us. After we had been traveling for about an hour, a young officer who had just come from West Point (he was the engineer of the expedition) came dashing up to me, telling me we were traveling around in a circle. He spoke so loud that a great many of the officers and men heard him, but I merely told him to go back and attend to his part of the business, which of course, quieted the men down. I suppose he got turned around, as nearly everybody else had. All the old officers had the good sense to keep still. On account of the wind changing, I could hardly see my horse's head in front of me. About half an hour after his first visit, the young engineer came riding up to me again, and by that time the whole company had the same idea he had — that we were traveling around in a circle. After delivering himself of the same speech he had made before about our traveling in a circle, I made the remark to him that if he was taking this command through I would go back and stay in the rear of the

column, and he could lead. He said he was not the
pilot. I told him if he was not to go back and stay
where he belonged, for one of us would have to take the
lead.

I then told Captain Pollock if he did not make that
man go back and stay in his place, I would stop where
I was. All the command had overheard this talk, and I
do not think I exaggerate it a little bit when I say
that half of them were sitting on their horses crying,
thinking they were lost. Captain Pollock was the
only one in the command who did not think so. He had
all the confidence in the world in me, and I had confidence in myself, if I was not bothered. At the same
time I was satisfied that if the command got turned
around and we happened to miss the trail between the
two Pumpkin Buttes every last one of them would be
frozen to death. When I saw the men crying I told
them to have a little more courage and confidence, as I
would take them through all right. I tried to encourage
them as much as I could. I think every man who was
in that command will acknowledge today, if living, that
it was one of the hardest marches they ever made. I
went right on through the blinding storm. Not a word
was spoken further by any one. At least I could not
have heard it if there was, on account of the noise of
the storm. It was just 3 o'clock when I reached the
trail leading through the buttes and went down the pass.
The storm cleared up as soon as we got through the
forest, and I knew we were but a short distance from
the Post. I never saw a lot of men more tickled than

the soldiers in that command were. Some of them pulled
me off my horse, carrying me around on their backs for
a little while. They were almost crazy with thankfulness
that they had got through all right. They all realized
that if we had missed the trail we would surely have
perished in the storm that had overtaken us. I do not
think I went two hundred yards out of the way at any
time during the march; but I knew the country perfectly,
and it was next to impossible for me to have lost my
bearings under any circumstances.

CHAPTER XLIX.

THE NEZ PERCES WAR.

Early in the spring of 1878 I was ordered to join
Gen. Merritt's command. He had been ordered up on
Clear creek, or up in that country. I kept a lookout for
Indians, but there was nothing of note happened from
the fore part of the summer up to the first of September. I had taken some dispatches down to Fort McKinney (Reno), and while there dispatches came in ordering
Gen. Merritt's command to the Wind river country to intercept Chief Joseph and his band, who were said to
have left Idaho and were on their way through the National Park, headed for the Big Horn mountains.

I left the Post about eight o'clock in the evening,
reaching Gen. Merritt's command at three o'clock on
the morning of the third of September. The General
immediately gave orders, after receiving the dispatches,
for the command to move, ordering me to take the scouts
(I had twenty-six of them), with Lieut. Cherry of the
Third Cavalry and a detail of twenty men, and start out
to find the trail of Chief Joseph, or to locate his camp.
Gen. Merritt was to follow up our trail until he reached

OLD CROW.

the Big Horn river; then, if not hearing from us, he would proceed to Fort Washakie.

We left the command about nine o'clock the next morning. As we started out it commenced to rain and snow. The storm kept up until the next day about noon, so that we had a big snowstorm to travel through. It made it a little hard for us to cross the mountain, as the snow fell to the depth of over a foot, and Gen. Merritt was unable to follow up our trail, which the snow cov_ ered. Reaching the Big Horn river on the third day out, and starting to cross at the old bridge crossing, and not finding any signs of the Indians, we struck out in a northerly direction until we reached Clarke's Fork, there finding the place where Chief Joseph and his band of Nez Perces had camped the night previous. The hostiles had left there early in the morning; but as our horses were completely tired out we concluded it was no use to follow them; besides there was too large a party for us to tackle. We therefore started south to overtake the command before it reached Fort Washakie.

[The Nez Perces war was the direct result of double dealing on the part of the government with this tribe of Indians. In 1855 certain lands had been secured to Chief Joseph and his people in the Idaho valleys. The Nez Perces were a very intelligent and industrious people, and their fine farms and prosperity aroused the cupidity of a certain class among the whites, finally leading to the making of a new treaty in 1863, which did not re-

ceive the sanction of one half the tribe. This treaty ex-
cluded from their original reservation the rich valleys of
the Lapwai and Wallowa. The Indians were very loth
to give up this stretch of rich country, and a very bitter
feeling was engendered between them and the whites
who insisted upon settling in the valleys named. This
feeling was greatly augmented in 1875, when one of the
Nez Perces was killed by the whites during a dispute
over stock, and an uprising was averted then only by the
intervention of the military.

The question of the ownership of the lands in the
Lapwai and Wallowa valleys was now agitated anew, and
commissioners were sent out from Washington to
decide the matter. As in every other case of a similar
nature, the Indians were given the worst of it, and in
the spring of 1877 they were forced to give up their
homes in the valleys which the whites demanded. This
led to an open breach in the month of June, when three
white men were killed by the Nez Perces. Gen. Howard
sent troops to the scene of trouble, who found Chief
Joseph and a band of one hundred and fifty warriors
ready for battle at White Bird Canyon, where the first
engagement occurred. Lieut. Theller and thirty soldiers
were killed in this battle, and the success of the Nez
Perces encouraged them to continue the struggle.

Gen. Howard, reinforced, took the field, and then began one of the most remarkable Indian campaigns known
to history. Looking Glass, one of the head men of the
Nez Perces nation, had declared himself and band of one
hundred warriors friendly and neutral, but fears were

entertained that he would not remain so, and orders were given to thoroughly and completely disarm him and his people. In the attempt to do this, the troops killed several of Looking Glass' men (who were totally unprepared for trouble), destroyed the camp and drove off over seven hundred head of ponies. For this atrocity, all the Looking Glass Indians who had been friendly toward the whites, joined Chief Joseph and remained with him until the end at Bear Paw mountain.

From the date of the battle with Looking Glass (June 27th) up to the 11th of July the Nez Perces made matters interesting for the troopers, and on the 11th day of July Gen. Howard, with four hundred men, found Chief Joseph on the Clearwater (where Looking Glass had been camped in June, with some two hundred and fifty warriors, and a pitched battle ensued and lasted for two days, the Nez Perces (having their families with them) finally drawing off and abandoning lodges and other property. The Indian loss amounted to over a score killed and as many wounded. Gen. Howard lost thirteen men and had twice that number wounded to care for.

The Indians were pursued over the Salmon river, through the Lolo valley and into the Bitter Root mountains. Gen. Gibbon, then at Helena, mounted his infantry and with what soldiers he could get from the Second Cavalry at Fort Ellis, started out to meet Chief Joseph. On the 9th of August the two forces met in the valley of the Big Hole and a desperate battle was waged for two days, the soldiers sustaining a loss of twenty-nine and the Indians twenty. From this point the Nez Perces passed on to the National Park, followed the entire way by the troops. The route taken by the Indians led them down the Clarke's Fork plains, and here Gen. Sturgis (with six companies of the Seventh Cavalry) was waiting to intercept them. But receiving information that the Nez Perces were coming down the Stinking-water pass, Sturgis moved his command to that point, and, the day following, Chief Joseph and his people made camp near where the Seventh Cavalry had been in waiting. On the 12th of September the Indians crossed the Yellowstone, the next day passing up Canyon creek and made for Crow Island, on the Missouri, closely pursued by Sturgis.

Gen. Miles had been apprised by Gen. Howard of the coming of Chief Joseph, and Miles lost no time in getting a force together (two troops of the Seventh Cavalry and mounted three companies of the Ffth In-fantry) and going in hot haste toward the British line to head off the fleeing Indians, being reinforced on his way by the Ellis battalion. On the evening of the 29th of September, Miles located the hostiles on a creek bottom at the foot of the Bear Paw mountains, and the next day made an attack upon the camp. The siege which ensued lasted four days, the Indians surrendering at the end of that time. Among their dead was Chief Looking Glass, who had been killed during the first day's en-gagement. The Indian loss amounted to over two score warriors, while the soldiers had Captain Owen Hale, Seventh Cavalry, and Lieutenant Biddle and twenty-two

enlisted men to add to their loss. The Nez Perces prisoners were sent to the Indian territory, where their ranks
were soon thinned by death. Some few of the band
escaped to the British possessions and surrendered in
1881, and were afterward sent to the Indian territory,
but very few ever getting back to their former homes
in Idaho.

E. S. Topping, in his very interesting book entitled
"Chronicles of the Yellowstone," pays this high tribute
to the Nez Perces :

"So closed a remarkable campaign, in which Joseph
figures as the most remarkable of the actors ; in which
he, through an enemy's country, traveled nearly two thousand miles, and in that distance crossed the Rocky mountain range three times. The fight at the Big Hole, where
his people were surprised and driven from camp, and yet
were rallied by him and regained the ground lost and
more ; the attack on Howard at Camp Prairie, which from
the loss of stock crippled and held that General back ;
the five days' fight at Bear Paw, with a force double the
size of his own, shows plainly the work of a master
mind. That all of his people showed courage and endurance, is true ; but any power to be of use must be guided
by intelligence, and every turn or move made by the Nez
Perces was wisely planned and bravely executed. It is
true also, that in their march this people committed many
atrocities. Though no Indian apologist, nor having any
of that sentiment (whose root is ignorance) which poses
all Indians as martyrs, yet, knowing many of these people personally, the writer feels for them a sentiment of

pity. They thoroughly believed that their homes in Wallowa were unjustly taken, and in their desperation commenced a war. The gathered hate of years burst out
against the settlers of that part of Idaho, and none were
spared that could be found. When away from this locality, they expressed their intention of harming no civilians,
but so many of the settlers joined with Gibbon in the
Big Hole fight, and afterwards with Howard, that their
hearts hardened against all whites. With their only partially subdued Indian nature, and with every man's hand
against them, the only wonder is that so many whom
they might have killed were spared.

"During the third day's fight at Bear Paw, Looking
Glass, a chief second only to Joseph, was killed. He was
of magnificent stature, being six feet two inches in height
and well proportioned. He had always been a friend to
the whites, and would probably have continued so but for
the uncalled for attack on his camp at Stillwater, by
Whipple. This unjust act stirred his fiery nature, and
joining Joseph, he fought to the bitter end. There are
many who say that had he lived, the Nez Perces might have
been annihilated but never would have surrendered. It
is true that at his death the tribe weakened, and but for
Joseph would have surrendered then; but that chief held
out till nearly all of the warriors had deserted him, and
he was then forced to succumb. Looking Glass was both
feared and loved by his warriors. He was feared for the
swiftness with which he punished disobedience (he had
killed one man with a pistol shot and had cut another
down with a saber, on the march,) and loved for his valor,
wisdom and perfect sense of justice."—AUTHOR.]

CHAPTER L.

Upon reaching Fort Washakie we found that Gen. Merritt had received dispatches ordering him to start down the Platte river, as the Cheyennes had broken out in the Indian Territory, and were making for the north, killing a great many people as they went along. We only stopped at Washakie one night, long enough to get supplies, and then started across country and down the Sweetwater, following the old California trail. Our first camp after leaving the post was in the vicinity of the Sweetwater river. About ten o'clock that night there was a big thunderstorm, and, for some cause I never could learn, all our cavalry horses stampeded. I had my horse hitched right close to where I was sleeping. As soon as I heard the stampeding I made a grab for the rope, my first thought being that the Indians had got amongst us and driven off our horses; but after I had saddled up my horse and inquired the cause of the excitement, I heard that it was only the stampeding of the horses. They told me that none of the animals had been picketed, but simply hobbled, and it was thought from what could be learned that every one of the horses had gone.

I took what scouts there were and started after the herd, overtaking a great many of them at daylight. Part of them I did not overtake until the second day. After we gathered them all up we started back with them. Toward evening I met the command in motion, some of the men packing their saddles on their backs. We had been very lucky in getting all the horses back. On reaching Fort Fetterman, Gen. Merritt received dispatches stating that the troops had captured the Cheyennes, and the Fifth Cavalry was ordered back to winter quarters. I was ordered back to Fort McKinney, for which Post I left that night. By the time I got back there, they had begun to build their new Post on Clear creek, (new Fort McKinney) three miles west of Buffalo, and about fifty miles north of the site of Fort Reno.

On reaching the Post I found mail waiting for me, telling me that Frank and Jesse James had come up into the northern country, and for me to be on the lookout for them. They also sent descriptions and photographs of the two brothers. While talking with the commanding officer (Capt. Pollock) one day, he said that a great friend of his was camping above the Post, telling me what a jolly man he was. He talked so much about him that I finally asked him what sort of a man he was, getting him to describe him, which he did. His description tallied with that given me of one of the James brothers, so I went and got the photographs and showed them to Capt. Pollock, asking him if his friend looked like either of the pictures, and he admitted that his friend was the very same man whom the picture said was Frank James.

He turned the photographs over to look at the names on the backs, and, when he saw who it was, he tried to deny it was the same man. He was perfectly convinced, however, that it was Frank James, and asked me what I was going to do about it. I showed him the dispatch I had received from Internal Revenue Collector Snow of Cheyenne, and he told me that I should not go after James. In fact, he forbade me to go after him, and finally ordered me to remain at the Post. Commander Pollock went out and informed Frank James that I had papers for his arrest, and told him not to come in contact with me if he could help it. Capt. Pollock was serious in whatever he did. He thought a great deal of me, and he did not want either one of us — James or myself — to get killed. He told him everything, to keep him away from me ; to keep on the watchout, and not to have any trouble with me. I suppose that it is a good thing that he did tell him, as it saved me from getting killed, later on.*

After I had got away from Capt. Pollock's control (the Post having a new commander), I started out and made an effort to arrest James. He and I would certainly have met if it had not been for a lady living in the northern part of the country. Frank James was at this woman's house one day when I came along. She saw me coming over the hill toward her place. Looking through her glass, she recognized me and gave James warning. On reaching the house I asked her who the party was that had just left there, and she told me it was a ranchman who lived on Goose creek. Then I

---

*A circumstance explained at end of chapter.

started to follow him. I had not gone but a few miles after leaving this woman's house before I found that she had put me on the wrong trail, and he escaped me. Try as hard as I would, I never was able to get on the right track of Frank James.

———

[*Some time after Grouard had his first talk with Capt. Pollock about Frank James, the authorities became convinced that a man by the name of Billy Runyon (who lived on Box Elder creek, near Lake De Smet, about a dozen miles north of the Post,) was either one of the holdups' confederates or was (as many claimed) weakminded and being made a tool of by the thieves. It was concluded, finally, to take him into custody. Runyon was also wanted as a witness against the men who had visited T. J. Foster's ranch on Piney, hanged Foster until he was nearly dead and then robbed his house, as it was claimed that Runyon knew all about the matter, as well as being acquainted with the parties to the outrage. Grouard rode up to Runyon's to arrest him, and got to within fifty yards of the door when a gang of thirty-two holdups sprang out of the house and covered the scout with their guns. One of these men, whom Grouard recognized as Frank James, ordered the others not to fire, and Grouard turned his horse and rode rapidly from the locality. Had it not been for the action of Frank James, Grouard would certainly have been riddled with bullets. This is the incident referred to in the foregoing page where the scout says Capt. Pollock's talk with Frank James saved his (Grouard's) life.—AUTHOR.]

THOMAS J. FOSTER, ONE OF THE "OLD-TIMERS."

CHAPTER LI.

CAPTURING A ROAD AGENT.

It was in the spring of '78 that the road agents began operating so boldly in northern Wyoming. Mr. Trabing had a store on Crazy Woman, and one night the highwaymen went in there, held it up, and took what goods and provisions they wanted. There happened to be a big crowd of government teamsters at the store on the night of the robbery, but, of course, they were held up also; made to stand in a row and hold up their hands, giving what money they had to the robbers. The stage was held up that same night on Nine Mile creek out from Buffalo. Mr. Tillotson, who owned a half interest in the store, and Mr. Sneider, of San Francisco, were on the stage when it was held up. Mr. Tillotson had been paid a great deal of money just before leaving the Post, the amount being about twenty-two thousand dollars in currency. But just before starting the paymaster at the Post had given him a check for all the money except three hundred dollars. The road agents must have had a tip that Mr. Tillotson had this big pile of money with him, and they anticipated a nice, fat haul, which they would certainly have obtained if Mr. Tillotson had not

changed the currency for a check.   When holding up the
stage that night, the highwaymen mentioned the amount
of money the merchant was supposed to have, thereby
giving away the fact that some one at the Post stood
in with them; but they only got about three hundred
dollars from Mr. Tillotson, and a valuable watch from Mr.
Sneider that he had received as a present from his wife.
Some three or four months afterwards the watch was returned to him by his nephew, E. U. Sneider, who in some
manner got possession of it.

There were so many robberies occurring in that part
of the country that year, that I could not look after
them myself.   Officers were sent up from Laramie City
to work on the cases; but they would no sooner reach
the Post than they would get a very polite note from the
road agents, embellished with cross-bones and skull, telling
them what would be their fate if they did not return to
the railroad.   The officers always took the hint and returned to Laramie.

About two weeks after the first robbery of the Trabing store, it was held up again.   Upon getting word
of this the next morning, I started for the scene of the
robbery.   Before reaching there I met some of the road
agents coming toward Buffalo, but they recognized me
just before getting up to me and turned off the road.
Of course, I did not know at the time that they were
road agents until they commenced running and shooting
at me.   I followed them some distance, but was unable
to overtake them.   In their haste to get away they left
three horses behind laden with goods stolen from the

Trabing store. I drove these animals back to Crazy Woman, where the particulars of the robbery were given me. Mr. Bowman, who was the head clerk of the store, told me he had considerable money in the store at the time of the robbery, but that he had put it in a bag and covered it up with a lot of potatoes, and the robbers did not find it.

It was impossible for one man to do anything with this big gang of robbers—next to impossible to catch them, single handed; so I wrote to Cheyenne and told the authorities there that they would have to send me assistance if they wanted anything done. They sent up a man by the name of Llewellyn from Omaha to help me catch the thieves or drive them out of the country. When Mr. Llewellyn came up he hired out at the Post as a carpenter, and nobody suspected who he really was. He worked around the Post some two weeks so as to get acquainted with the country and the people who lived around there; and one morning, without saying any-thing, he quit his job and went off and joined the road agents. Of course, nobody knew his whereabouts or object but myself. How he got in with the thieves I do not know; but he got in with them, and afterwards kept me informed of their movements. He left letters at a big rock two miles from the Post, whenever he wanted to communicate with me, or whenever any of the road agents were to be at the Post.

We were perfectly aware of the fact that the road agents had spies and confederates at Fort McKinney, but it was a difficult matter to discover exactly who they were. Llewellyn's scheme was to keep in such close touch with all the thieves by joining them that he could find out who their confederates were, let me know and I was to pounce down on them before they had time to get away. There were a great many gambling dens about the Post, and one in particular that bore a hard name. It was kept by a negro, who also run a barber shop and shaved most of the officers. In this latter capacity he was enabled to converse with the officers and find out nearly everything that was going on, and it transpired in time that he was the resident agent of the holdups. One of the robbers would go to the Post, visit the negro's place of business, get his tips and then return to the headquarters camp of the thieves and put up the robberies.

One day I found a letter at the rock from Llewellyn stating that one of the thieves would visit the Post that evening and giving me a description of him. Going to this colored man's shack that evening, I saw my man as quick as I stepped into the house. He was sitting at the end of the table playing faro, and had his chips in front of him. There were a lot of people at the table, and nobody took particular notice when I sat down. Buying a stack of chips I commenced playing so as to catch this man without any disturbance. The first good opportunity that presented itself, I drew my gun and set it up against his breast, told him very quietly that he was my prisoner, and that if he made any noise I should pull the trigger. I commanded him to hold his hands down between his knees so I could put the handcuffs on his wrists, which he did. This was done below the level of the table, so that I do not think there were many who noticed he wore the irons when I took him out of the house. Hurrying him over to the government guard house, I put him in there for safe keeping.

After securing him, I thought the next best thing I could do was to go down and break up the negro's gambling house. I went to the commanding officer and told him what I was going to do, and he gave me some assistance. We then broke up the gambling den, taking possession of all the colored man's tools, telling him that he was not allowed to gamble at the Post.

On the following morning I came down to the Post, and found the negro setting on the bar-room steps. As I started to go into the place he jumped up and commenced firing at me. He fired five shots at me, and how he missed me I never could make out. I had no arms with me, so I could not do anything, and I thought if I moved he would be more apt to kill me. I stood there until five shots were fired. Just as he fired the fifth shot I jumped into the billiard room.

As soon as I jumped inside the building the negro sprang from the steps and ran around the corner of the house, dropping his six-shooter and a big carving knife as he ran. I followed him as quickly as I could, supposing he had gone clear around the house; but instead of going around the house he went into a side door, and through the back part of the building up into the loft. I made a close search, but failed to find him. I learned afterwards that he had gone up into the loft. There was another negro working in the place who told me he had helped to hide him up there. He made good his escape, however, and I never saw him afterwards.

The road agents had a saloon (called Hold Up Hall) situated nine miles south of the Post, where they hung out. They did not live there, but would stop to get drinks when they wanted to. Two or three days after making the arrest of the road agent I received a letter with cross-bones and skull, and the picture of a tree and a rope hanging from a limb, telling me that hanging would be my fate if I should attempt to take my prisoner down the road ; that the writers would be on a continual watch for me at the Hold Up Hall saloon ; that I never could pass there with the prisoner. I did not like the idea of being dictated to as to what I should or what I should not do, and I resolved to take the prisoner down that very night.

Going to the commanding officer, I showed him the letter I had received, and told him I should start out that night, or rather toward morning. I asked him if he would give the necessary orders to turn the prisoner over to me whenever I should call for him. He said he would. I left the guard house about 4 o'clock the next morning with the prisoner, putting him on the floor of the buggy on his back and warning him that if he made any noise or any kind of a break while I was passing this saloon at Nine Mile I would shoot the top of his head off; that in case of trouble he would be the first one I would shoot. The road ran right past the saloon —within fifty yards of it. This road was built down a sort of hollow. As I came up on the top of the hill I could look down and see lights and hear the people in the saloon laughing and yelling. I supposed they were on a general drunk from the noise they were making, and thought the best thing I could do was to try to drive past the saloon before anyone inside recognized me. I did this, and went on to Crazy Woman, reaching there about half-past six in the morning.

When I arrested the prisoner I had telegraphed to the United States marshal at Cheyenne to come and get him, and I found two deputies waiting at Crazy Woman to receive the robber, and I turned the prisoner over to them. I had my team fed, got my breakfast and waited around about an hour, I should judge, before starting back to the Post. I knew if I tried to pass Hold Up Hall on my return I would have a fight on hand, and I came to the conclusion that the best thing I could do would be to drive right up to the door of the saloon. I thought if I could get up there and into the house before they discovered that I was anywhere in the vicinity, it would be the best thing for me. If I had to have a fight I would have a better chance at close quarters than at a distance.

So I drove up to the saloon and jumped out of the buggy into the door before anyone inside knew who I was. As soon as I jumped in I saw there were only six men in the room, one of them being the bartender. The other five were sitting around the fireplace. As soon as I set eyes on them I recognized the leader of the road agents—a big fellow by the name of Cully.

Another I recognized was Tom Reed ; another Bill Zimmerman. The other two I did not know. I had on my overcoat, the night having been chilly. When I jumped into the house I had both my hands in the breast pockets of my overcoat, where I had two guns.

The five men looked up as I entered. They recognized me at once, but the bartender was the only one who spoke. He remarked that it was very early in the morning for me to be so far away from home, and said it was "pretty chilly." I told him I had found it warm enough, having just taken a prisoner down the road, and was on my way back to the Post. I watched the five thieves (had my eyes on them all the time) to see what effect my words would have on them. I was prepared to go to shooting the first break they made. There sat three men that I wanted very badly ; that I had been after for a long time ; in fact, would have given anything to have made my prisoners. But there were five of them and only one of me. If I should undertake to arrest them I would get killed. I would get two of them, but they would get me. If I had had someone with me to take their arms away from them while I covered them with my gun, I would have had no trouble at all in arresting them. There was a large reward on three of them, and they knew that if they made a move I would not hesitate a second in shooting. As the old saying goes, "I was afraid, and they dasn't ; " that was about the size of it.

I asked the bartender if his friends would take a drink. He asked them. There was not one of them that would look up until he asked them the second time. As they raised up to come to the bar, I stepped up with my back to the wall, so I could see that none of them went behind the bar, as I was a little afraid they would get behind the bar and commence shooting at me, but they did not try it. They all came up to the bar and called for whisky, drank it and went back to their seats without saying a word. After I paid the bartender for the drinks, I backed out of the door and then backed clear around to the opposite side of the buggy, got in and started the horses up. I turned square around and faced them as I drove off, in order that I might watch their movements, if they came to the door. But for some reason they did not see fit to make an attack, and I met with no further adventure on my way to the Post.

CHAPTER LII.

THE KILLING OF M'GLOSKY.

Late one night in the fall of 1878 an Indian from the Crow Reservation came to my house at Fort McKinney and brought me a note from Tom Irving, the Sheriff of Yellowstone county, Montana, informing me that two men hailing from northern Wyoming had stolen a couple of race horses from a party on the Yellowstone river, and wanted me to be on the lookout for the thieves, as they were supposed to have come south with the stolen property. At the time I received this communication Charlie McCleod, afterward shot and killed in the city of Buffalo by a man named Johnson, was rooming with me.

I caught up my horse that same night and started out to head off the thieves, and ran across them at Ed. O'Malley's dance house (some two and a half miles from the Post) at ten o'clock the next morning. I rode up to O'Malley's and got off my horse. There were fully one hundred people standing in front of the house when I got there. As I was shaking hands with one of the party, I saw McGloskey coming around the corner of the stable directly toward the spot where I stood. He was riding one of the stolen horses. His partner followed him around to the corner of the stable, but noticing, I presume, that I was awaiting McGloskey's coming, he put spurs to his horse and started off in the direction of Crazy Woman creek. McGloskey must have recognized me, for he knew me well, and had made threats a hundred times during the year that he would kill me on sight. I held my carbine in my left hand as McGloskey came up. My intention was to grasp the bridle rein of his horse and arrest the thief. As he got up to me I raised my right hand and told him to stop, that I wanted him, at the same time trying to grasp his bridle rein. But he put spurs to his horse and threw down on me with his revolver, shooting as he passed me.

I don't know how he could have missed killing some one in that big crowd, but he did. When he had got off about one hundred yards he turned in his saddle to take another shot, but he was too late. I covered him with my carbine and fired, and McGloskey went several feet into the air and fell off his horse. E. U. Snider ran to where McGloskey lay and I got on my horse, rode out and caught up the stolen animal and started for the other fellow, who had struck out toward the red hills. He had a big start and escaped, although I followed him about fourteen miles.

I stopped long enough by McGloskey's side before following the other thief to see that he was done for, and just then the pack train came along on its way to the Post. I got one of the packers to ride in and have an ambulance sent out, and then continued on after McGloskey's partner. I did not get back to the Post until sun-down. Then I went to see the wounded horse thief. The doctor told me there was no chance for him, so I asked the man if he had any relatives or friends he would like to send a message to. All he would do was to curse me. I could get nothing else out of him. He said he merely wanted to live long enough to have one shot at me. I told him he could have the first shot. There was no chance for him to get well. He died that night at eight o'clock, hurling curses at me with his very last breath.

He was a bad man and had committed many crimes in our section. He was wanted for murder in Fremont county, and the Kansas authorities were also anxious to get him for a similar offense, but I did not know this until after his death. The killing of McGloskey seemed to give the tough class of individuals notice to quit the country, and they quit.

SITTING BULL, AFTER HIS RETURN FROM THE BRITISH POSSESSIONS.

CHAPTER LIII.

SITTING BULL.

The commonly accepted idea that Sitting Bull's diplomacy and cunning made him a laggard in battle, is erroneous, according to Grouard. When the latter met the great chief of the Uncapapas, Sitting Bull was in his prime, being about thirty-six years of age. He was a very cunning Indian. In stature he was not much over five feet, and he weighed close to two hundred pounds. His body tapered from the shoulders down. His nose was the prominent feature of his face. His eyes, which were steel blue in color, looked through and not at you. They were very large, and in his anger became bloodshot, like a mad animal's. His face was massive and was somewhat rounding, with a great width of lower jaw. His mouth was large, but his lips were thin, though firm. He had a low, broad forehead. His head was crowned with a profusion of long, black hair.

His father was a noted Sioux warrior, and met death in battle with the Crows on Grand river several years before Grouard's capture. In 1870, his mother, who was over eighty years of age, lived in the Uncapapa village with her only daughter, White Cow, then a woman of thirty, a widow with two children, one, a daughter, being a deaf mute.

Sitting Bull was a great practical joker, and even in serious council, he found immense delight in telling a joke on some chief or warrior present.   Among his own people he was constantly laughing.   He was quick tempered, but soon recovered his good nature.   He was totally unforgiving and never forgot an injury.   As an Indian, says Grouard, he was a mighty shrewd one, and in all his councils looked to and talked of the future of his tribe and people.   He had a set idea that the Sioux nation was doomed and that there was no salvation for it.   He constantly maintained that the life of the Indian meant war at all times, and boasted that he would be the last of the Sioux chiefs to surrender.   He gloried in his chieftancy and the renown his deeds had brought him.   So firmly was this sentiment implanted in his breast that even his bitterest foes respected him for it. All the young warriors worshiped him.   His life and deeds were the beacon lights that guided them on to victories.   As a general rule, he was a good-natured Indian.

At the time of Grouard's capture Sitting Bull had three children — two boys and a little girl — the latter named Plenty Horses, whose mother had died on Tongue river when the little one was three years old.   This child was a perfect blonde, and Grouard always thought she was a white captive.   Grouard says the chief always treated all the children well, especially this little girl. Sitting Bull seemed to have a penchant for acquiring wives from the ranks of widows. Both his squaws had a son each of their own before they accepted situations as sagebrush burners in the tepi of the Uncapapa. Each of these squaws had borne the chief a son.

Sitting Bull was nothing if not diplomatic. He placed a peculiar value upon the friendship of all the old squaws. He knew their influence amounted to nothing in council or on the warpath, but he was shrewd enough to understand that the women were the school teachers of the children. He never lost an opportunity of playing the gallant toward the squaws, who sang his praises to the exclusion of every one else. What the children learned at the knees of their mothers, they remembered in their youth and manhood, so that the lessons taught yesterday bore fruit on the morrow, and Sitting Bull's fame and prowess as a warrior grew by what it fed on.

He was no laggard in camp. He took a lively interest in the young braves, and organized hunts and distributed prizes ; got up feasts, and gave of his stolen plenty to the poor. The name of Sitting Bull was a " tepi word " for all that was generous and great. The bucks admired him, the squaws respected him highly, and the children loved him and were taught to emulate his example. He would have proved a mighty power among our present day politicians — a great vote getter with the people — had he been a white man with a congressional ambition. He might, then, in truth, have been renowned as a political economist ; but in his savage economy he utterly and persistently refused to celebrate ration day at an agency, or exchange his wild freedom for the bondage of civilization.

He was forced, at last, to bow to the inevitable ; but even the enemies of Sitting Bull must concede that the uncompromising savage was far advanced toward the twilight of life before he accepted the white man's protection or bounty. It was simply a case where he had nothing else to do. The land he had loved and fought to retain had been wrested from his hands ; his people had been gradually driven into agency exile or killed in battle; the game had sought shelter from the encroaching Caucasian in a land·where other powerful tribes lived and flourished ; and the matter resolved itself into a question of suicide by starvation or humble submission to the will of Government. The women and children were ragged and hungry, and the spirit of the chief was broken. Diplomatic, even to the end, he laid away the weapons of the warrior, submissively folded his arms across his crime-hardened breast and accepted the agency—and death.

"Many of the high-minded and most of the vicious among the Indian nations of the northwest found their leader in Sitting Bull, who, though often unpopular with his fellow chiefs, was always potent for evil with the wild and restless spirits who believed that war with the whites was, or ought to be, the chief object of their existence," writes Finerty in 1879, a twelvemonth previous to Sitting Bull's surrender. "This was about the true status of the Indian agitator in those days. He had strong personal magnetism. His judgment was said to be superior to his courage, and his cunning superior to both. He had not, like Crazy Horse, the reputation of being recklessly brave, but neither was he reputed a dastard. Sitting Bull was simply prudent, and would not throw away his life so long as he had any chance of doing injury to the Americans.

"I don't care," observes this same writer during the year above mentioned, "what any one says about Sitting Bull not having been a warrior. If he had not the sword, he had, at least, the magic sway of a Mohammed over the rude war tribes that engirdled him. Everybody talks of Sitting Bull, and whether he be a figure-head or an idea, or an incomprehensible mystery, his old-time influence was undoubted. His very name was potent. He was the Rhoderick Dhu of his wild and warlike race, and, when he fell, the Sioux confederation fell with him, even as dropped the pine of Clan Alpine when its hero sank before the sword of the Knight of Snowdoun."

Captain Bourke speaks of Sitting Bull as a "medicine man and a great talker, and rarely let pass an opportunity for saying something." But Sitting Bull was a warrior, as well. He not only pointed out the way, but led the way. He may not have fought with the apparent fearlessness of Crazy Horse, but his hand-to-hand encounter with a foe in his youth on the Porcupine settled for once and always the question of his personal bravery. Like Cæsar, he would rather tell his people what was *to be* feared than what *he* feared. He was boastful, but he had some reason for his egotism, for did not all the other chiefs and warriors count their coups during religious worship; and why not he?

It took generalship to hold and lead a large village

away from the enticements the government held out to the hostiles. Ammunition had to be secured, and Sitting Bull's camp was always well supplied. He needed no intercessor between himself and the latest improved breech-loaders. He made treaties, but they were with the Santees and northern tribes. He scorned to deal with the whites. There was nothing of the traitor about the man. He did not profess open friendship to hide his enmity. He was not as politic, perhaps, as Spotted Tail or Red Cloud, but the Government never miscalculated on his hatred.

He asked no quarter. In 1875, when he was appealed to for concessions regarding the Black Hills country, he sent the following characteristic answer back to the commission that awaited his coming at the Red Cloud Agency:

"Are you the great God who made me; or was it the great God who made me who sent you? If He asks me to come to see *Him*, I will go; but the Big Chief of the white men must come see *Me*. I will not go to the reservation. I have no land to sell. There is plenty of game for us. We have enough ammunition. We don't want any white men here."

These are the words attributed to Sitting Bull on that memorable occasion by Captain Bourke, and they are too characteristic to be erroneous. Napoleon's message to the Pope was not more exacting; but ruin, exile and death followed in both cases. Little did Sitting Bull realize in 1875 that he would so soon be driven from the lands secured to him and his people by solemn treaty with the

Great Father at Washington. The massacre of 1866 was already bearing its fruit. Ten years from its date found Sitting Bull and the warriors who had participated in that butchery wanderers and asylum seekers. They were no longer hunting, but hunted. Crook's column of daring, dashing soldiers had invaded the country from the south, and swept hill and valley in their northward march. Like the voice that was forever sounding in the ear of the Wandering Jew, an irresistible force commanded Cheyenne and Sioux to "Move on! Move on!" They stopped to give battle when pressed and weary, but they gained only temporary respite. From the Platte river valley to the Powder fled the Indian, and hot in his wake went the blue coats with their death-dealing magazine guns and howitzers. Onward, through the rich valleys of the Tongue, affrighting the antelope and driving the buffalo before them, still fled Sioux and Cheyenne. The pursuers slackened not their pace. From the north, over the very trails the Indians were taking, came a new and un-thought-of danger—Terry and Gibbon, and Custer and Reno and Benteen! The armies of the Great Father were merciless. The natural instincts of the savage were nomadic, but rest was as necessary to him as it was to his civilized brother. In the face of all the threatened dangers he could not pause to rest. The edict said, "Move on! Move on!"

There was no return. Death and Devastation was behind; the Sword and Destruction in front. To the redman the case was desperate. In the words of Macbeth, there was "No flying hence nor tarrying here!"

No wonder, then, that, like the cry of the Scotch Monster, the savage wail went up,

> Blow, wind; come, wrack;
> At least, we'll die with harness on our back!

Six thousand hostiles were in the panting army moving northward toward the less inhospitable possessions of the English queen. Thousands more would join them on the way, and the year 1878 found the hostile bands under the protection of the British flag. The line of boundary between the country where they found asylum and their native land was no longer an imaginary one. The soldiers of the Great Father patrolled it with jealous care. Distasteful as had been the thought of the American agencies to the Indian, it was now conceded to be no worse than perpetual banishment from the haunts and homes they loved. Despair reconciled them to the hard conditions of the Great Father; and, in the end, the ghosts of the legion that once populated the mighty west flitted over the border and stood silent and submissive on the great American reserves. It was not the return of prodigals. It was the incoming of a broken-spirited horde of homeless heathen. The eagle had feasted on the hawk, but there were no wrens for the hawks to prey upon! The words of Cettewayo were indeed prophetic. His estimate of civilization was sound, at least: "First came the missionary—then came the soldiers!"

Many crimes are laid at thy door, oh, Civilization! Perhaps unjustly, but they are laid there, all the same.

CHAPTER LIV.

THE "SWORD BEARER" TROUBLE.

It was, I think, in the fall of 1886, that the trouble occurred on the Crow reservation between the Indians and troops. Sword Bearer, one of the Crow braves, was the victim of the uprising. It was at the time that considerable talk was indulged in about reducing the army and abandoning many western posts, so something had to be done to stir the country up to a realization that the Indian still existed and had not forgotten the tricks of his fathers. I don't think there would have been any trouble at all if it had not been brought about by the whites.

Sword Bearer, who had very little following among the Crows, had spent three nights and as many days at the base of Clouds Peak, in the Big Horn Range, making medicine, and when he got back to the reserva-he told some startling stories of what he could accomplish with the medicine he had made. He got quite a number of the Indians excited and finally the troops were called into requisition. I was dispatched from Fort McKinney to the reservation to find out the cause of the excitement. When I arrived at the Crow reserve

I met Sword Bearer and learned that his influence had not spread to over twenty bucks, and so reported to Gen. Ruger. I informed the general that it would be the easiest matter in the world to arrest those concerned in the trouble and thus end the matter, but he did not seem to want to take that kind of action, and sent word to the Indians that if Sword Bearer and his active allies were not surrendered by twelve o'clock on the following day he would attack the village.

In the meantime Sword Bearer had declared that the bullets of the troops could not injure him, and he made quite a number of the Crows believe that he could decapitate all the soldiers at once, by one swoop through the air with his sword. The troops were drawn up near the village ready for action at noon, when Sword Bearer and his followers jumped their ponies and charged down upon the soldiers. When the attacking party was pretty close to the blue coats one of the Indian police named Medicine Tail shot Sword Bearer in the arm, and the great medicine man started from the field as fast as his pony would carry him, followed by Crazy Head, who overtook the fleeing man by the side of the creek and tried to persuade him to return, telling him he had tried to make the Crows believe he was big medicine, had got them into the trouble and should now face it out, and he grasped the wounded warrior's horse and started to lead it back into camp. But Sword Bearer had got quite enough of war and was crying piteously, and said he wished to be allowed tò go into the hills and die. Just then two Indian police came up, one of

whom berated Sword Bearer severely and told him that he
had claimed that bullets could not enter his flesh, and yet
a bullet had shattered his arm. "If a bullet can't harm
you," said the policeman, "then how is it your arm is broken?" So, to satisfy himself, the policeman put his gun
behind Sword Bearer's head and pulled the trigger. The
result was that Sword Bearer fell to the ground, dead,
without a groan.

I arrived on the scene almost at the moment the shot
was fired, examined the body and reported the affair to
Gen. Ruger. He asked me if there could not be some
mistake about the dead man's identity, and I told him no.
He thought it would be well to have some of the officers
visit the place where the killing occurred and make a
sworn statement regarding the identity of the dead man,
together with all the circumstances surrounding the
tragedy, which was done, and that ended the war on the
Crow reservation, for which there was not the shadow
of an excuse, anyway. The Crows were never unfriendly
toward the whites, but had been our allies during the
campaign of 1876 and at other times. Deaf Bull and
Crazy Horse were sent to Bismark, where they were kept
some little time, and were then permitted to return to the
reservation. The soldiers were returned to their quarters.

CHAPTER LV.

THE SOUTH DAKOTA OUTBREAK.

Some time before the outbreak of the Sioux and Cheyennes at Pine Ridge, S. D., in 1890, Grouard was ordered to proceed to the Rosebud Agency and find out, so far as lay in his power, the cause of the discontent among the Indians. The ghost dances were already in progress at that time. The scout went among the Indians and found they were on the verge of starvation. It was not alone the thought of the coming Indian Messiah that crazed them, but the want of enough to eat. The Cheyennes had killed a man on the Rosebud, and it was reported that depredations were being committed in all quarters of South Dakota. The cattlemen claimed that their range stock was being butchered by the Indians, and matters were assuming a serious aspect. While Grouard was in the vicinity of the excitement a cowboy was killed on the range.

Upon his return to McKinney, the scout made his report to headquarters. He had learned enough to satisfy himself that all the trouble was caused by the government employes, aided and abetted by outside parties who saw a chance of making money through an Indian up-

YANKTON CHARLIE.

YANKTON CHARLIE.

rising. Even the police and friendly Indians were shaking their heads ominously.

"Of course," says Grouard, "as an excuse it was made to appear that the ghost dance was the cause of all the trouble. From what I learned from the Indians no outbreak would have resulted from the ghost dances. If left alone, the craze would have died a natural death. Every ten or twenty years the Indians go wild — some hallucination takes possession of them; but they quiet down again in their own good time if left to themselves. It was known, however, that if some good excuse were provided, the government would spend considerable money in putting troops and provisions in the vicinity of the Pine Ridge Agency, and mercenary motives prevailed."

It is to be supposed, therefore, that Grouard's report to headquarters stated these matters; but before any further inquiry could be instituted the "outbreak" occurred. Grouard was then ordered to report at once to headquarters at Pine Ridge, which he did.

Months before the appearance of any war cloud, Indian Inspector Armstrong sent the following graphic report from Pine Ridge to the Secretary of the Interior, but no particular attention was given the matter:

"In former years this agency was allowed 5,000,000 pounds of beef. This year it has been reduced to 4,000,-000 pounds. These Indians were not prepared for this change. No instructions had been given the agent that 1,000,000 pounds of beef would be cut off from the Indians this year. Consequently, issues were made from the beginning of the fiscal year — July 1st, 1889 — until the date of final delivery of beef, about October 15th, 1889, on the basis of 5,000,000 pounds for the year. This necessitated a large reduction in the beef issue afterward to catch up with the amount, and came just at the worst season of the year. The Indians were kept at the Agency between three and four weeks in the farming season of 1889, when they should have been at home attending to their corn. This enforced absence attending the Sioux Commission caused them to lose all they had planted by the stock breaking in on their farms and destroying everything they had. They have been compelled to kill their private stock during the winter to keep from starving, and in some cases have been depredating on the stock of white people living near the line of reservation.

"A bad feeling is growing among the Indians out of this, and may lead to trouble between the settlers and the Indians. The killing of a hog made the Nez Perces war, with Indians far more advanced than these people. The full allowance of beef should be given them. They complain and with good grounds, that they were told by the Sioux Commissioners that their rations, etc., should not be reduced ; that while this talk was going on, the Department in Washington was fixing to cut off one-fifth of their meat supply, but did not let them know it, until they had signed the Sioux bill. They had a good start in cattle, but have had to kill over three times as many of their own cattle, old and young, as they did the year before ; that they had been deceived in doing what they did by the Government, and that they don't get as much now as they did before.

"I think cutting off this 1,000,000 pounds of beef and thereby forcing them to kill their own young cattle, has put them back two years or more in raising stock, and has created a feeling of distrust, which, unless something is done to repair it, will lead to trouble and bad conduct. They have now killed many of their own cattle and will next commence to kill range cattle. Already hides and other evidences of this are being found on the reservation borders.

"Men will take desperate remedies sooner than suffer from hunger. Not much work can be expected with the present feeling. The Indians who advocated signing are now laughed at and blamed for being fooled. They don't even get their former rations, and ask where are all the promises that were made. The Government must keep faith as well as the Indians.

"The attention of the Department has frequently been called to the condition of the Cheyenne Indians at this agency, their dissatisfaction and determination to do nothing to better their condition. They now openly say they will leave there this spring, and therefore have no intention of putting in crops or doing any work.

"They may be held here by force, but it is questionable if it is a good policy to keep them at Pine Ridge agency any longer. The nine hundred Cheyennes at Tongue river, Montana, and these five hundred Cheyennes of the same band here, should be concentrated at one agency. The Sioux don't want them here, and they don't want to stay. They should not be kept as prisoners only. The Tongue River reservation is, I know, wanted by cat-

tlemen.   They should be a secondary consideration.
These Indians should be concentrated there, and a reservation obtained for them from the Crows, and the Cheyennes should be moved to it.   They will then be satisfied,
settle down, and go to work.   No good can ever come
to the Cheyennes if the course pursued toward them
during the last six years is continued, and much bad
feeling may result.

"Why should Indians be forced to stay where they
never located through choice?   Put them where they
want to live and can make a living, and let them stay
there and do it.   Without some prompt action regarding this beef matter, and also in the Cheyenne matter,
on this reservation, the Department may, this summer
or fall, expect trouble.   I have thought this of sufficient
importance to lay it before the Department, and to go
in person to ask that some action be taken.   I have
seen this Cheyenne matter brewing for two years, and
I see now the Sioux put back in the principal industry
on which they have to depend.   With prompt action in
this matter, and the proper arrangement of districts for
the issuing of rations, a plan for which I will submit,
these people will go ahead.   If not, they will go backward, which to them is the easier road."

While it is not the desire of the author of these
pages to load this volume down with official reports on
any subject, he cannot refrain from giving so much of
the correspondence as passed between "headquarters in
the field" and the authorities at Washington, especially
when the tenor of those reports convey the idea that

hostilities were actually forced on the Indians. Brigadier General Ruger, telegraphing from Pierre, S. D.,
November 16th, 1890, to the Assistant Adjutant General of the Division of the Missouri, said:

"From information had by conference with the Indian Agent at the Cheyenne River Agency, the Commanding Officer at Fort Bennett, and otherwise, the
condition seems as follows: About nine hundred persons, mostly Minneconjou Sioux, are affected by the
excitement concerning the expected Messiah and the ghost
dances—about two hundred males, sixteen years and up-
ward, are involved. The dancing began about September 20th. The Indian police were at first able to
stop the dancing, as ordered by the Agent, and had not
the excitement been fed by Indians coming from other
agencies, Pine Ridge and Rosebud, in particular, the
agent could probably have controlled matters; but he
is not now able to stop the dancing by means of his
police, nor would the police be able to make arrests.
The police, who are armed with pistols only, have done
well. Settlers have reported the killing of a few cattle
in the vicinity of the reservation. The agent states
that Indian owners of cattle have sold some to whites,
contrary to orders.

"The Indians affected by the craze are nearly all
those who did not sign the treaty to cede the lands.
Hump is the principal leader. Big Foot is also concerned in dances. There is not likely to be an outbreak
of these dancing Indians at present nor during the winter.
They are somewhat sullen, but have made no threats

against the agent or employees, and I have directed that a company be sent from Fort Sully to Fort Bennett at the agency. Also shall keep the force from Meade, that is camped on the Cheyenne river near southwest corner of reservation, in the field. No further action seems immediately called for as to the Cheyenne River Reservation.

With respect to the Pine Ridge Reservation, where there has been no military force at hand, I infer from the reports made by the officer in command of the force at Oelrichs and information otherwise, that the proportion of Indians affected by the craze is greater than at Cheyenne River or Standing Rock, and the excitement greater, and that the agent is unable to enforce his orders by aid of Indian police. This reservation is the place where principally the excitement started amongst the Sioux,' and from which it is fed by emissaries to other reservations. The agent, Royer, by telegram this date asks for a military force; that Commissioner of Indian Affairs told him to report state of case to me. I would recommend that a force strong enough to overawe the Pine Ridge Indians be sent, as soon as conveniently may be, to the vicinity of the Pine Ridge Agency; that such force be taken in preference from elsewhere than this department, both to save time and also because the force still at Fort Meade, the most accessible in this Department, should, I think, be kept disposible for the present."

Ten days later Gen. Ruger made a more detailed statement from St. Paul, Minnesota, the substance of which follows:

"I made reports by telegraph November 13th and 16th from Mandan, North Dakota, and from Pierre, South Dakota, of the condition, essentially, of the state of affairs at those dates on the Standing Rock and Cheyenne River Reservations, respectively, of which copies are forwarded herewith. The state of case as to each reservation has not since essentially changed, but the excitement on the Standing Rock Reservation has somewhat abated. The proportion actively affected is about one-fourth, men, women and children, included by families—nearly all of whom belong to the Uncapapa band. There has not, I think, been a time since the excitement began that the agent could not (certainly with a slight show of military force to support his Indian police) have made arrests by the latter for any disregard of his orders or the regulations by individual Indians.

"On the Cheyenne River Reservation there appears, by the latest report, to be somewhat less excitement relative to the ghost dance; the number affected by the excitement remains about the same as at the date of my telegram, November 16th, comprising in all, by families, about one-third of the Indians on the reservation, nearly all of whom belong to the Minneconjou band. The Indian agent would not, I think, by means of his Indian police alone, be able to arrest any of those actively engaged in the dances or in sympathy therewith, provided it was supposed the arrests were attempted for reasons relating to the dances or disregard of the agent's orders to individuals prominent in inducing or keeping up the excitement. The most unfavorable condition on this reservation is the inability of the Agent to enforce his authority and the disregard of his orders relative to the dancing.

"On both reservations, as might be expected, those most affected are the Indians who have been opposed most to the policy of the Government for the settlement of the Indians and to the disposing of any part of the reservation—those, in general, who have always been discontented. There was no evidence, direct, nor fact from which inference might be drawn, that there was an intent, by the Indians concerned in the dances on either reservation, to become "hostile;" but the opinion of the best and most intelligent Indians was, if the matter should be allowed to go on without check, that trouble would come; also that those concerned in originating the excitement should be arrested.

"The view of the better Indians is undoubtedly correct; for, although the excitement would probably die down after a time, no outbreak occurring, the dissatisfied leaders, ambitious to gain following, would revive it from time to time, gain strength, and effect an organization, comprising Indians on all the reservations, that would necessarily lead to hostilities.

"With respect to the action required to suppress the present state and prevent a recurrence, reference is necessary to the ground reasons of the excitement and the facts of its development:

"Within a few years, comparatively, the whole manner of life and surroundings of the Sioux Indians have been changed by a violent wrench of fortune, whereby

the individual has been deprived of his former liberty
of coming and going at will, and subjected to many irk-
some rules of the reservation, and has had at times, it
must be admitted, cause for just complaint; and the
leaders have been deprived, in great degree, of their influence and authority.

"The greater part have accepted, and some in good
spirit and purpose, the change; but a part, those now
most disaffected, have not, further than they felt com
pelled. These were exactly in the condition of discontent
and lack of hope in the future, from their point of view,
although savages, in which, for all time, tribes as well
as people are ready to welcome, if they do not look for,
a Moses or Messiah to bring them to a better state; and
the leaders, without whose impulsion to the excitement
there would have been no strong resistance to the
authority of the Indian agent, took advantage of the
condition to try to regain control and influence. In
the development of the "craze," as it has been called,
there have been modifications to suit the locality, the
temper and surroundings of Indians immediately concerned,
and the objects of the leaders. As originally preached
to the western tribes, the coming of the Indian Messiah — doubtful whether white man or Indian — was to
be the beginning of a time of peace and good will between
the whites and Indians, and all good men were to be
happy; but amongst the Sioux the teaching has been that
the whites are to disappear, and all good things to the
Indians (in accord with old ways and wishes) are to come.

"The proper course to be, in the first instance, taken,

it seems to me, is, after the excitement has somewhat
subsided, or at least during the winter after the weather
becomes severe and there would be less probability of
parties scattering from the reservation, that those Indians
prominent on the different reservations who have been
using their influence in the past to make trouble on the
reservations and who have been active in promoting the
present excitement, shall be arrested and removed to a
distance and kept there, at least until they could no
longer influence others for harm; that a force be kept
as long as may seem necessary at those Sioux agencies
where we have not heretofore had garrisons at hand;
that when necessary the authority of the Indian agents
be supported by the troops; and that all Indians belonging on the Sioux reservation who may be found off their
proper reservations without authority, be arrested by the
military, and if armed, their arms taken and kept.

"I think the course indicated, if followed, would re-
store the authority of the Indian agents, and that the
leaders in creating trouble being removed, there would be
little probability of trouble hereafter from any cause
similar to the present. Any Indians ambitious to gain
following against the authority of the Indian Agents could
be easily arrested by the Indian police, whose power,
under the direction of the agents, would be much strength-
ened by the removal of the present influential disaffected
leaders.

"The question occurs, of course, whether the Sioux
Indians shall be disarmed, which I shall not be able to
consider in the time remaining since receiving the dis-

YELLOW WOOD'S CAMP, NEAR PINE RIDGE.

patch of this date, saying the Division Commander desired my report forwarded by this evening's mail in order that he might receive it before leaving for Washington. Such disarming, if done, could not properly be undertaken for some time, and I will write upon that subject hereafter."

It would not appear from the above that General Ruger viewed the situation with such alarm that he was satisfied of a coming conflict. He did not, in fact, think the ghost dance meant anything worse than a religious craze. In the meantime, General Gibbon, commanding the Department of the Pacific, had sent Mr. A. A. I. Chapman to Nevada to discover and report upon the Indian Messiah who was said to be located at or near the Walker Lake Indian Reservation. Mr. Chapman's report is dated December 6th, 1890, and, as it covers the matter fully, is reproduced here:

SAN FRANCISCO, CAL., December 6th, 1890.
GENERAL JOHN GIBBON,
    Commanding the Division of the Pacific,
        San Francisco, Cal.

Sir :—In accordance with your instructions of the 28th ultimo, to proceed to Walker Lake Indian Reservation, Nevada, and elsewhere in that vicinity, and gather certain and all information regarding the Indian who personated Christ at that place a year ago, I have the honor to report that I left this city at 7 o'clock p. m. on the day of receiving my instructions, and arrived at the Walker Lake Indian Reservation on the 30th following,

at three o'clock p. m.   Here I found quite a number of
Indians, including women and children, in groups here
and there, sitting on the ground playing cards.   I made
myself known to Mr. J. O. Gregory (Indian farmer), who
was in charge of the agency, and inquired of him whether
he knew anything of an Indian in that part of the
country by the name of John Johnson.   His answer was
that he did not, but that there was a very old Indian
living near the agency they called old Johnson, and
another they called Squire Johnson.   I then asked him if
either of these Indians claimed to be a prophet, or
preached to the Indians at any time.   He said they did
not, but that there was an Indian in the country by the
name of Jack Wilson, who claimed to be the new Messiah, and had been preaching for the last two or three
years, and of late these ceremonies were becoming more
frequent, and had a much larger attendance; that there
were a great many strange Indians who attended these
dances, who he had understood had come from a great
way off; that these dances were held at intervals of about
three months, first at one place and then at another; that
this Indian, Jack Wilson, was mostly raised by a white
man who lived at Mason Valley, fifty miles from the
agency, and that he had understood from the white people in that portion of the country that this new Messiah
(Jack Wilson) had a good name for being an honest,
hard-working Indian.   Mr. Gregory remembers very distinctly the big dance which occurred near the agency,
when the Cheyennes, Sioux, Bannocks and other strange
Indians were present, that this meeting took place some

time in last March. At this time the Indians were gathering around in considerable numbers, and Mr. Gregory
introduced the Captain of the Indian police, Josephus,
who said he could tell me more about the new Messiah
(Jack Wilson) than he could.

Captain Joseph, of the Indian police, said : I am a
Piute Indian, and was born at Carson Sink (sinking of the
Carson river). I am now about forty-eight years old.
I am captain of the police, and also interpreter for the
government. I am well acquainted with Jack Wilson,
this man who preaches. He is a Piute ; his Indian
name is Quoitze Ow ; he was born here at this place of
a poor family, and when quite a large boy he went to
live and work for Dave Wilson, a white man who lives
in Mason Valley. When this Jack Wilson grew to be
about twenty years old he got married and still lived
with Mr. Dave Wilson (the white man) and worked on
the farm. About three years ago Jack Wilson took his
family and went into the mountains to cut wood for Mr.
Wilson. One day while at work he heard a great noise
which appeared to be above him, on the mountain. He
laid down his axe and started to go in the direction of
the noise, when he fell down dead, and that God came
and took him to heaven, and showed him everything
there ; that it was the most beautiful country you could
imagine ; that he saw both Indians and whites, who were
all young ; that God told him that when the people died
here on this earth, if they were good they came to
Heaven, and he made them young again, and they never
grew to be old afterwards ; that the people up there were

dancing, gambling, playing ball and having all kinds of sports; that the country was nice and level and green all the time; that there were no rocks or mountains there, but all kinds of game and fish; that God brought him back and laid him down where he had taken him from.

He woke up and went to camp and went to bed. God came to him again that night and told him to tell all the people that they must not fight, there must be peace all over the world; that the people must not steal from one another; but be good to each other, for they were all brothers, and when he had finished his work God would come after him again. God came and took him to Heaven again, and he saw all the Indians and white people who had died heretofore, that they were all young and having a good time, dancing, etc.; that he saw his own mother; that God had given him great power and authority to do many things; that he could cause it to rain or snow at will, and many other things; that they would learn hereafter that God directed him on his return to say to his people that they must meet often and dance five nights in succession, and then stop for three months.

Josephus (Captain of the police) said: At this time I did not believe in the new Messiah, and thought I would try his power over the elements, as the country was very much in need of rain, that unless they got rain they would have no crops of any kind, and it looked as though there was going to be great suffering amongst the people.

So Josephus concluded he would visit the new Messiah and ask him to give them rain, or otherwise they would suffer. He took his horse and rode to the new Messiah's home, arriving there late in the evening, and explained to him the importance of his mission. He said that Jack Wilson sat with his head bowed but never spoke a word during all this time, but he went off to bed and was up early the next morning. When he came in where Josephus was he said to him:

"You can go home, and on the morning of the third day you and all the people will have plenty of water."

Josephus said that he went home and told not only his people but the white people, too, and shortly afterwards it commenced to rain, and on the morning of the third day he got up at daylight to find Walker river out of its banks and all the lowlands overflown.

"Now," said Josephus, "I am a strong believer in the unnatural powers of the new Christ."

Ben Ab-he-gan, of the Indian police, was present during all the time that Josephus was making this statement, and corroborated every word spoken. I will state here that Mr. J. O. Gregory and Mr. Peas, employes of the agency, were both present during this interview with Josephus, and corroborated his statement in regard to the water. In fact, all the white people I talked with about the agency and in Mason and Smith valleys, admitted that the rain did come, but they can not convince the Indians that Jack Wilson had nothing to do with its coming. Some of the Indians of his own tribe, and those of the adjoining tribes, were inclined to look upon the

new Messiah (Jack Wilson) as an imposter, and he sent
them word to come and see him and hear him talk, and
he would convince them. This invitation has been the
cause of many Indians visiting the Piutes and taking
part in their dances.

Among the tribes that have been represented there,
so I was informed by Josephus and Ben Ab-he-gan (both
of the police force at Walker Lake) are as follows:
Cheyennes, Sioux, Arapahoes, Utes, Navajoes, Shoshones,
Bannocks, and a tribe to the south of them that they
call the Umpaws. I was told that the Indians numbered
about sixteen hundred at the big dance near Walker
Lake, and were fed on pine nuts and fish principally
during the meeting. Learning that the new Messiah was
at his home, at the head of Mason Valley, I took the
train and came back on the road as far as Wabuska,
where I took the stage for Mason, arriving there at 5
o'clock in the evening.

I had not been in the place long before I learned
through Ben, the Indian policeman, who had come with
me from Walker Lake, that Jack Wilson had gone two
days before to Desert Creek Valley, distant sixty miles,
and across one range of mountains. I had made arrangements for a team the next morning, and taking Indian
Ben with me, started at 6 o'clock for Desert Creek Valley. After traveling thirty miles on the Desert Creek
road we met some Indians on this road coming up from
Bodie, California. They told us that they had camped
at Desert creek the night before and learned that Jack
Wilson, the Messiah, had gone to Wellington, on the

west fork of Walker river. We changed our course for Wellington, arriving there late in the evening. I sent for Jack Wilson to come down to Mr. Pierce's house, as the weather was not suitable for holding outdoor meetings, it raining and snowing alternately. He put in his appearance and I was introduced to him by Captain Ben, the Indian policeman. We shook hands, Jack Wilson remarking that he was glad to see me. I responded, saying that I surely was glad to meet one of such notoriety, and that I heard a great deal of him through the newspapers, and would like to ask him a few questions, which I hoped he would answer freely.

Question. What is your name?

Answer. Jack Wilson.

Q. What is your Indian name?

A. Quoitze Ow.

Q. What tribe of Indians do you belong to?

A. Piutes.

Q. About how old are you?

A. About thirty years old.

Q. Is your father living?

A. Yes.

Q. How many brothers have you?

A. Three, all younger than myself.

Q. Have you ever been away from your own country?

A. No.

Q. Are you a chief?

A. Yes, I am Chief of all the Indians who sent representatives to me.

Q. What do you mean by chief of all the Indians?
Do you mean that you are Head Chief?

A. No, I mean that I am Council Chief.

Q. How many Indians are there in your tribe?

A. I do not know.

Q. When did you commence to preach to the Indians?

A. About three years ago.

Q. What did you preach to the Indians?

He then stated in substance about the same as
Josephus, captain of the Indian police at Walker Lake,
had told me about going to heaven and seeing all the
people who had died here on this earth, and what a nice
place it was, the dancing and other sports, etc ; that
God had visited him several times since and told him
what to do; that he must send out word to all the
Indians to come and hear him, and he would convince
them that he was preaching the truth; that he must tell
the Indians that they must work all the time and not
lie down in idleness; that they must not fight the white
people or one another; that we are all brothers and
must remain in peace; that God gave him the power to
cause it to snow or rain at his will; that God told him
or gave him the power to destroy this world and all the
people in it, and to have it made over again; and the
people who had been good heretofore were to be made
over again and all remain young; that God told him
that they must have their dances more often, and dance
five nights in succession and then stop. * * * That
their dancing would commence again next Saturday.

Said he: "This country was all dry early last spring there was nothing growing, and the prospects for the future were very discouraging to both the Indians and the whites, and they came to me and asked me for rain to make their crops grow. I caused a small cloud to appear in the heavens, which gave rain for all, and they were satisfied. I think that all white men should pay me for things of this kind, some two dollars, others five, ten, twenty-five and fifty, according to their means. I told all the head men who came to see me (meaning the representatives of other tribes) that when they went home to say to their people that they must keep their peace ; that if they went to fighting that I would help the soldiers to make them stop." That the people (whites) of this country do not treat him and his people right; that they do not give them anything to eat unless they pay for it. If the whites would treat him right he would have it rain in the valley and snow on the mountains, during the winter, so the farmers would have good crops.

Captain Sam and Johnson Sides, two Piute Indians who did not believe in his doctrine, he said, are telling all over the country that the soldiers were coming to take him and put him in a big iron box, and take him out to sea on a big ship and sink him in the ocean; that he wanted them to stop talking to the people in this way, and not be afraid, but come and talk to him; that he hired out to white men all the time; that he liked to work.

Mr. Wilson, I want to ask you one or two more questions, and that will be all.

Q. Did you tell the Indians that if they got into trouble with the whites that they must not be afraid, that you would protect them against being hurt?

A. That was my dream; it has not come to pass yet.

Q. Did you tell them that you were bullet-proof, and to prove it you spread a blanket on the ground and stood upon it, with nothing on you except a calico shirt, and had your brother shoot at you at a distance of ten feet, and the ball struck your breast and dropped to the blanket?

A. That was a joke.

He said: "I heard that soldiers were coming up after me. I do not care about that; I would like to see them. That is all I care to talk now. We are going to have a dance next Saturday."

In conclusion I would say that I saw three of their dance grounds. They had been cleared of sagebrush and grass and made perfectly level, around the outer edge of which the willow sticks were still standing, over which they spread their tenting for shelter during these ceremonies. The cleared ground must have been from two to three hundred feet in diameter, and only about four places left open to enter the grounds. The Piute Indians, men and women, dress like the white people, and equally as good as the average white man of that country. The men part their hair in the middle and have it cut square off even with the lower part of the ear. The women have theirs banged, and are exceedingly well dressed for Indian women.

The white people generally throughout the country
spoke well of the Piutes as an industrious and hard-
working people, but preferred to work for the white
people than for themselves. Only a few of the white
men, Mr. Pierce of Wellington, particularly, was suspicious of Wilson's doctrine, as it was giving him too
much influence, and he feared trouble in the end; that
he could see that the Indians were a little more exacting every day. Only recently did one of them with all
his stock move into a white man's field, and would not
go out when told to do so. When the white man threatened to come down with his wagon and haul him out
if he did not go out himself, the Indian said: "You
had better bring a crowd if you attempt it." The
Piutes are a very numerous and healthy tribe, and are
increasing very rapidly (so the whites tell me who have
been living there for the last thirty or forty years).

After gathering all the information I thought of interest, I started on my return, arriving at Reno on the
4th instant, where I had a short interview with Johnson
Sides, who appeared to be very much opposed to the
doctrine preached by Jack Wilson; that he believed it to
be all lies, and that it was only exciting the Indians and
was liable to lead to trouble in the end.

In regard to the Cheyenne Indian, Porcupine, who
gave an account of his visit to the Piute camp at Walker
Lake, I will say that it is wonderfully correct, as far as
I am able to learn; that on his visit he first met with
the Piutes at Winnemucca, and then at Wadsworth, on
the Central Pacific Railroad, where he fell in with Cap-

tain Dave of the Piutes, who took him and his comrades
in a wagon and hauled them to Pyramid Lake Agency,
where they remained several days, when Captain Dave's
son took them in wagons and hauled them to Wabuska,
where they took the cars for Walker Lake. This was
told me by Captain Ben, one of the Indian police of
Walker Lake, and from other information I believe it to
be true.

Very respectfully,

Your obedient servant,

(Signed)   A. I. CHAPMAN.

By the 20th of November there were at least six
thousand soldiers in the immediate vicinity of the threatened war. Rumors of depredations flew about from camp
to camp, and from agency to agency. At one hour reports came in that the Rosebud Indians had gathered in
force and were about to make an attack; the next, denials
poured in. Everything was uncertainty. Those who
visited the Indians to size up the situation came back
with every conceivable kind of report, but nearly all admitted that the Iudians claimed that they were frightened
by the coming of the troops, and did not know what to
do. Preparations among the Indians were making, but
the authorities could not understand what the intentions
of the redmen were. The authorities at Washington were
slow to act. But it was finally decided that the course to
persue was to arrest Sitting Bull and disarm all the Indians who remained outside the agencies.

Sitting Bull's camp was distanc over forty miles from
Fort Yates on the Grand river. Those who spoke au-

thoritatively said Sitting Bull had signified his intention of leaving his home, and this was construed into a threat to join the hostile bands that were known to be moving into the badlands. The ghost dances were continued with unabated vigor. The half-crazed Indians were reported to be dancing with war-bonnets on their heads and weapons in their hands. Every breeze that blew brought in its wake a breath of war, and the angry clouds that hung over the heads of the unfortunate Indians grew darker and darker. The arrest of Sitting Bull had been fully determined upon, and probably no event of the decade attracted more general attention. The author has been favored with an account of Sitting Bull's arrest and killing, and the subsequent flight of the Uncapapas to Big Foot's camp on Cheyenne river from the pen of Mr. James McLaughlin, Indian Agent at Standing Rock in 1890, given upon request to Mr. Herbert Welsh, corresponding secretary of the Indian Rights Association of Philadelphia, Pa., which is hereby reproduced :

UNITED STATES INDIAN SERVICE,

STANDING ROCK AGENCY, NORTH DAKOTA, Jan. 12th, 1890.

My Dear Mr. Walsh:—Your letter of the 16th ultimo was duly received, and should have been answered earlier, but I have not had a moment to spare since its receipt. The newspaper reports regarding the arrest and death of Sitting Bull have nearly all been ridiculously absurd, and the following is a statement of the facts :

I was advised by a telegram from the Indian Office, dated November 14th, 1890, that the President had directed the Secretary of War to assume a military responsibility for the suppression of any threatened outbreak among the Sioux Indians, and on December 1st, 1890, another telegram instructed me that as to all operations intended to suppress any outbreak by force, to "co-operate with and obey the orders of the military officers commanding on the reservation." This order made me subject to the military authorities, and to whom I regularly reported the nature of the "Messiah Craze" and the temper of the Indians of the reservation.

As stated in my letter to you, dated November 25th last, the Messiah doctrine had taken a firm hold upon Sitting Bull and his followers, and that faction strove in every way to engraft it in the other settlements; but by close watching and activity of the police we prevented it from getting a start in any of the settlements outside of the upper Grand river, which districts were largely composed of Sitting Bull's old followers, over whom he always exerted a baneful influence, and in this craze they fell easy victims to his subtlety, and believed blindly in the absurdities he preached of the Indian millennium. He promised them the return of their dead ancestors and restoration of their old Indian life, together with the removal of the white race; that the white man's gunpowder could not throw a bullet with sufficient force in the future to injure true believers; and even if Indians should be killed while obeying the call of the Messiah, they would only be the sooner united with their dead relatives, who were now all upon the earth (having returned from the clouds), as the living and dead would be reunited in the flesh next spring. You will readily understand what a dangerous doctrine this was to get hold of a superstitious and semi-civilized people, and how the more cunning "medicine men" would impose upon the credulity of the average uncivilized Indian.

This was the status of the Messiah craze here on November 16th, when I made a trip to Sitting Bull's camp, which is forty miles southwest of the agency, to try and get Sitting Bull to see the evils that a continuation of the ghost dance would lead to, and the misery that it would bring to his people. I remained over night in the settlement, and visited him early next morning before they commenced the dance, and had a long and apparently satisfactory talk with him, and made some impression upon a number of his followers who were listeners, but I failed in getting him to come into the agency, where I hoped to convince him by long argument.

Through Chiefs Gall, Flying-By and Gray Eagle, I succeeded in getting a few to quit the dance, but the more we got to leave it the more aggressive Sitting Bull became, so that the peaceable and well-disposed Indians were obliged to leave the settlement, and could not pass through it without being subjected to insult and threats.

The ghost dancers had given up industrial pursuits and abandoned their houses, and all moved into camp in the immediate neighborhood of Sitting Bull's house, where they consumed their whole time in the dance and the purification vapor baths preparing for same, except on every second Saturday, when they came to the agency for their bi-weekly rations. Sitting Bull did not come into the agency for rations after October 25th, but sent members of his family, and kept a body guard when he remained behind while the greater portion of his people were away from the camp; this he did to guard against surprise in case an attempt to arrest him was made. He frequently boasted to Indians, who reported the same to me, that he was not afraid to die and wanted to fight, but I considered this mere idle talk, and always believed that when the time for his arrest came and the police appeared in force in his camp, with men at their head whom he knew to be determined, that he would quietly accept the arrest and accompany them to the agency, but the result of the arrest proved the contrary.

Since the Sioux commission of 1889 (the Foster, Crook and Warner Commission,) Sitting Bull has behaved very badly, growing more aggressive steadily, and the Messiah doctrine, which united so many Indians in common cause, was just what he needed to assert himself as "high priest," and thus regain prestige and former popularity among the Sioux by posing as the leader of disaffection. He being in open rebellion against constituted authority, was defying the Government and encouraging disaffection, made it necessary that he be arrested and removed from the reservation, and arrangements were perfected for his arrest on December 6th, and everything seemed favorable for its accomplishment without trouble or bloodshed at that time; but the question arose as to whether I had authority to make the arrest or not, being subject to the military, to settle which I telegraphed to the Commissioner of Indian Affairs on December 4th, and on the 5th received a reply which directed me to

make no arrests whatever, except under orders of the
military, or upon an order from the Secretary of the
Interior.

My reason for desiring to make the arrest on December 6th, was that it could be done then with the
greater assurance of success, and without alarming the
Indians to any great extent, as the major portion of them
would have been in for rations at the agency, forty miles
distant from where the arrest would have been made, and
I also foresaw, from the movements of the military, that
the order for his arrest would soon be issued, and that
another ration day (two weeks more) would have to elapse
before it could be so easily accomplished.

On December 12th the following telegram was received by the Post Commander of Fort Yates, who furnished me with a copy :

"HEADQUARTERS DEPARTMENT OF DAKOTA,
"ST. PAUL, MINN., December 12th, 1890.

"To COMMANDING OFFICER, Fort Yates, North Dakota :

"The Division Commander has directed that you
make it your especial duty to secure the person of Sitting Bull. Call on Indian Agent to co-operate and render
such assistance as will best promote the purpose in view.
Acknowledge receipt, and if not perfectly clear, report
back.

"By command of General Ruger,
"(Signed)   M. BARBER,
"Assistant Adjutant General."

Upon receipt of the foregoing telegram, the Post
Commander sent for me, and held a consultation as to

the best means to effect the desired arrest. It was contrary to my judgment to attempt the arrest at any time
other than upon one of the bi-weekly ration days, when
there would be but a few Indians in Sitting Bull's neighborhood, thus lessening the chances of opposition or excitement of his followers. The Post Commander saw the
wisdom of my reasoning, and consented to defer the arrest
until Saturday morning, December 20th, with the distinct
understanding, however, that the Indian police keep Sitting
Bull and his followers under strict surveillance, to prevent
their leaving the reservation, and report promptly any
suspicious movements among them.

Everything was arranged for the arrest to be made
on December 20th; but on December 14th, at 4 p. m. a
policeman arrived at the agency from Grand River, who
brought me a letter from Lieutenant of Police Henry
Bull Head, the officer in charge of the force on Grand
River, stating that Sitting Bull was making preparations
to leave the reservation; that he had fitted his horses for
a long and hard ride, and that if he got the start of
them, he being well mounted, the police would be unable
to overtake him, and he therefore wanted permission to
make the arrest at once. I had just finished reading
Lieut. Bull Head's letter, and commenced questioning
the courier who had brought it, when Col. Drum, the
Post Commander, came into my office to ascertain if I
had received any news from Grand River. I handed
him the letter which I had just received, and after reading it, he said that the arrest could not be deferred longer
but must be made without further delay; and imme-

WOMAN'S DRESS.

diate action was then decided upon, the plan being for the police to make the arrest at break of day the following morning, and two troops of the Eighth Cavalry to leave the Post at midnight, with orders to proceed on the road to Grand River until they met the police with their prisoner, whom they were to escort back to the Post; they would thus be within supporting distance of the police, if necessary, and prevent any attempted rescue of Sitting Bull by his followers.

I desired to have the police make the arrest, fully believing that they could do so without bloodshed, while, in the crazed condition of the ghost dancers, the military could not; furthermore, the police accomplishing the arrest would have a salutary effect upon all the Indians, and allay much of the then existing uneasiness among the whites. I, therefore, sent a courier to Lieut. Bull Head, advising him of the disposition to be made of the cavalry command which was to co-operate with him, and directed him to make the arrest at daylight the following morning. Acting under these orders, a force of thirty-nine policemen and four volunteers (one of whom was Sitting Bull's brother-in-law, "Gray Eagle,") entered the camp at daybreak on December 16th, proceeding direct to Sitting Bull's house, which ten of them entered, and Lieut. Bull Head announced to him the object of their mission. Sitting Bull accepted his arrest quietly at first, and commenced dressing for the journey to the agency, during which ceremony (which consumed considerable time) his son, "Crow Foot," who was in the house, commenced berating his father for accepting the arrest and consenting to go with the police; whereupon he (Sitting Bull) got stubborn and refused to accompany them. By this time he was fully dressed, and the policemen took him out of the house; but, upon getting outside, they found themselves completely surrounded by Sitting Bull's followers, all armed and excited. The policemen reasoned with the crowd, gradually forcing them back, thus increasing the open circle considerably; but Sitting Bull kept calling upon his followers to rescue him from the police; that if the two principal men, "Bull Head" and "Shave Head," were killed the others would run away, and he finally called out to them to commence the attack, whereupon "Catch the Bear" and "Strike the Kettle," two of Sitting Bull's men, dashed through the crowd and fired. Lieut. "Bull Head" was standing on one side of Sitting Bull and First Sergt. "Shave Head" on the other, with Second Sergt. "Red Tomahawk" behind, to prevent his escaping; "Catch the Bear's" shot struck Bull Head in the right side, and he instantly wheeled and shot Sitting Bull, hitting him in the left side between the tenth and eleventh ribs, and "Strike the Kettle's" shot having passed through Shave Head's abdomen, all three fell together. "Catch the Bear," who fired the first shot, was immediately shot down by private of police "Lone Man," and the fight then became general—in fact, a hand-to-hand conflict— forty-three policemen and volunteers against about one hundred and fifty crazy ghost dancers. The fight lasted about half an hour, but all the casualties, except that of Special Policeman John Armstrong, occurred in the first few minutes. The police soon drove the Indians from around the adjacent buildings, and then charged and drove them into the adjoining woods, about forty rods distant, and it was in this charge that John Armstrong was killed by an Indian secreted in a clump of brush. During the fight women attacked the police with knives and clubs, but in every instance they simply disarmed them and placed them under guard in the houses near by until the troops arrived, after which they were given their freedom. Had the women and children been brought into the agency there would have been no stampede of the Grand River people; but the men, realizing the enormity of the offense they had committed by attacking the police, as soon as their families joined them, fled up Grand River, and then turned south to the Morian and Cheyenne Rivers.

The following is a list of the killed and wounded casualties of the fight:

Henry Bull Head, First Lieutenant of Police, died eighty-two hours after the fight.

Charles Shave Head, First Sergeant of Police, died twenty-five hours after the fight.

James Little Eagle, Fourth Sergeant of Police, killed in the fight.

Paul Afraid-of-Soldiers, Private of Police, killed in the fight.

John Armstrong, Special Police, killed in the fight.

David Hawkman, Special Police, killed in the fight.

Alexander Middle, Private of Police, wounded, recovering.

Sitting Bull, killed, 56 years of age.

Crow Foot (Sitting Bull's son), killed, 17 years of age.

Black Bird, killed, 43 years of age.

Catch the Bear, killed, 44 years of age.

Spotted Horn Bull, killed, 56 years of age.

Brave Thunder, No. 1, killed, 46 years of age.

Little Assiniboine, killed, 44 years of age. (Sitting Bull's adopted brother.)

Chase Wounded, killed, 44 years of age.

Bull Ghost, wounded, entirely recovered.

Brave Thunder, No. 2, wounded, recovering rapidly.

Strike the Kettle, wounded.

This conflict, which cost so many lives, is much to be regretted, yet the good resulting therefrom can scarcely be overestimated, as it has effectually eradicated all seeds of dissatisfaction sown by the Messiah craze among the Indians of this agency, and has also demonstrated to the people of the country the fidelity and loyalty of the Indian police in maintaining law and order on the reservation.

Everything is now quiet at this agency, and good feeling prevails among the Indians, newspaper reports to the contrary notwithstanding. No Indians have left this agency since the stampede of December 15th, following the conflict with the police, and no others will. There were three hundred and seventy-two men, women and children left at that time, of whom about one hundred and twenty are males over sixteen years of age, and of whom two hundred and twenty-seven are now prisoners at Fort Sully, and seventy-two are reported to have been captured at Pine Ridge Agency some time ago.

With kind regards, I have the honor to be very respectfully, your obedient servant,

JAMES McLAUGHLIN,

Indian Agent.

Capt. E. G. Fechet of the Eighth Cavalry (now Major of the Sixth Cavalry, stationed at Fort McKinney, Wyoming), who commanded the detachment charged with the duty of executing the order of Sitting Bull's arrest, reported under date of December 17, 1890, to the Post Adjutant at Fort Yates as follows concerning the part his command took in carrying out the order of Gen. Miles:

For the information of the commanding officer I have the honor to report the operations of the battalion of the Eighth Cavalry, under my command for the purpose indicated in Orders No. 247* of this Post.

The command consisted of Troop F, Eighth Cavalry, Lieutenants Slocum and Steele, and forty-eight enlisted men; Troop G, Eighth Cavalry, Captain Fechet, Lieutenants E. H. Crowder and C. E. Brooks, and fifty-one enlisted men; Captain A. R. Chaplain, Medical Officer, and Acting Hospital Steward August Nickel, two Indian scouts, Smell the Bear and Iron Dog; Mr. Louis Primeau, Indian Department, Standing Rock Agency, guide and interpreter.

One gattling gun was attached to G Troop and one

*Orders No. 247 will be found at end of Maj. Fechet's Report.

breech-loading steel Hotchkiss gun was attached to Troop F. There was furnished the command one four-horse spring wagon, carrying one day's cooked rations and one day's grain for the whole command, and one red cross ambulance.

The commanding officers were Capt. E. Fechet, commanding° battalion; Lieut. E. H. Crowder, commanding G troop; Lieut. S. L'H. Slocum, commanding F troop; Lieut. E. C. Brooks, commanding field artillery.

The command moved out at midnight, December the 14th, and by rapid marching was by daylight within three miles of Sitting Bull's camp, which is fully from forty-one to forty-two miles from Fort Yates. After daybreak I expected every minute to meet the Indian police with Sitting Bull their prisoner, it having been arranged by Major McLaughlin, Indian Agent, that they would make a decent on Bull's camp about daybreak, arresting Bull and delivering him to me for conduct to this Post. It will be seen by reference to the first paragraph of the order that the command was to proceed only to the crossing of Oak river, which was eighteen miles from Bull's camp.

After receiving this order, on consultation with Col. Drum, commanding the Post, it was decided that I should move as close to Bull's camp as possible without discovery, and there await the police. A short time after dawn a mounted man was discovered approaching rapidly. This proved to be one of the police, who reported that all the other police had been killed. The substance of his report, with the additional statement that I should

move rapidly and endeavor to relieve any of the police
who might be alive, I forwarded to the commanding
officer.

The command was at once put in condition for immediate action. A light but extended line of skirmishers
was thrown in advance ; the main body was disposed in
two columns, in column of fours, about three hundred
yards apart, the artillery between the heads of columns.
A few minutes after making these dispositions another of
the police came in and reported that Bull's people had a
number of the police penned up in his house. The command was moved with all speed to a point on the high
lands overlooking the valley of Grand river, and immediately opposite Sitting Bull's house and the camp of the
ghost dancers, distant some 1,500 yards.

A hasty examination showed a party of Indians,
apparently forty or fifty, at a high point on our right
front, some 900 yards distant, but whether a party of
police and friends or Bull's people could not be determined. While trying to make out the position and
identity of the two parties there were a few shots fired
by the party on the hill, and replied to from Sitting
Bull's house. There was also firing from the woods beyond Bull's house, but on whom directed it was impossible to tell. I caused a white flag to be erected on the
crest where I was located (a prearranged signal between
the soldiers and the police), and directed a few shots to
be fired from the Hotchkiss into the woods mentioned.
In answer a white flag was displayed from Bull's house,
and Indians were seen leaving the woods going in the

direction of the hills to the south, across Grand river. The Hotchkiss gun was then turned upon the party on our right front; this, with some fire from a dismounted line of F troop, caused them to retreat rapidly from their position up the valley of Grand river to the northwest.

Lieutenant Slocum, with his troop dismounted, was ordered to advance immediately upon the house. Lieut. Crowder, with G Troop mounted, moved rapidly to the right along the highlands, covering the right flank of the dismounted line. As the dismounted line approached the house the police came out and joined the command. The line was advanced through the timber, dislodging a few hostiles, who disappeared rapidly up the river through the willows. This line, after advancing through the willows some six hundred yards, fell back to the immediate vicinity of Sitting Bull's house, leaving pickets at the farthest points gained by the advance.

Lieutenant Crowder, in the meantime, observing the Indians gathering at houses up the river about two miles from Sitting Bull's camp, moved in pursuit of them. The Indians fell back from every point upon the approach of the troops, not showing any desire to engage in hostile actions against the soldiers. All the houses for a distance of about two miles were examined, and all were found deserted, but showed signs of recent occupation. Failing to come up with the Indians in this direction, G Troop fell back and joined the main command at Sitting Bull's lodge.

Upon arriving at this place I found evidence of a most desperate encounter between the agency police and

Sitting Bull's followers. In the vicinity of the house, within a radius of fifty yards, there were found the dead bodies of eight hostiles, including Sitting Bull. Two horses were also killed. Within the house were found four dead and three wounded policeman. It was learned through the interpreter that the hostile Indians had carried away with them one of their dead and five or six wounded, making an approximate total of fifteen casualties in Sitting Bull's band. A list of casualties, by name, on both sides are hereto attached.

From the best evidence obtainable I am led to believe that the police, under the command of Bull Head and Shave Head, about forty strong, entered Sitting Bull's camp about 5:50 a. m. on the 15th instant, for the purpose of making the arrest of Sitting Bull. Sitting Bull was taken from his house, and while the police were parleying with him, endeavoring to induce him to submit peacefully, Bull Head was shot by Catch the Bear in the leg. Bull Head immediately shot and killed Sitting Bull, when the melee became general, with the results heretofore given. The fight lasted but a few moments, when the police secured the house and stable adjoining, driving Sitting Bull's men from the village to cover in the adjoining woods and hills. From these positions the fight was kept up until about 7:30 a. m., when the troops came up. I learn that soon after the occupation of the house and stable by the police, volunteers were called for to carry a report of the situation back to the approaching troops. Hawk Man offered to perform this perilous service, and at the imminent risk of his life. Assisted by

Red Tomahawk, he effected his escape, being shot through his coat and gloves while engaged in the attempt. This was the first scout met by the command.

My orders were explicit as to the arrest of Sitting Bull, but contemplated no pursuit of his band. I therefore did not feel authorized to follow the Indians up the valley, especially as I felt satisfied, from the report of Lieutenant Crowder, that it would only result, unnecessarily, in frightening peaceful Indians away from their homes, and that the withdrawal of the troops, together with the message I communicated to the Indians to the effect that only the capture of Sitting Bull was desired, would tend to re-assure those who were loyally disposed toward their agent.

Accordingly I gave orders for the command to withdraw to Oak creek, of which the commanding officer was informed by courier, with the request that he communicate his further orders to me at that point. Previous to leaving, word was sent up and down the valley to the friendly Indians of this movement, in order that they might avail themselves of the protection of the troops in their withdrawal to the agency, which they did in considerable numbers. All the dead Indian police, together with their wounded, and the body of Sitting Bull, were brought in by me.

Upon reaching Oak creek, at 6 p. m., I was met by a courier, who informed me that the commanding officer of Fort Yates, with two companies of infantry and ten days' supplies, would reach Oak creek some time in the night. Upon their arrival at 12 o'clock I turned over the command.

The attention of the commanding officer is invited to the celerity of this movement. In brief, the command marched from here to Sitting Bull's camp and back to Oak creek in seventeen hours. This, with the ground covered in getting into position, and the demonstration to the right by Lieut. Crowder, made a total distance of at least seventy miles. It must be taken into consideration that the movement back to Oak creek, eighteen miles, was made very slowly. Thus, it will be seen that the march out, including the movements into position, were made at a rate of over six miles an hour. During the whole march the column moved steadily, without stretching out or closing up — a most satisfactory commentary upon the drill and discipline of the two troops composing my command. To say less would be a want of appreciation on my part of the command under my orders.

E. G. FECHET,
Captain Eighth Cavalry, Commanding.

---

*ORDERS No. 247.

FORT YATES, N. D., December 14, 1890.

2. Captain E. G. Fechet, Eighth Cavalry, will proceed with troops F and G, Eighth Cavalry, the Hotchkiss gun and one gattling gun, to the crossing of Oak creek by the Sitting Bull road, for the purpose of preventing the escape or rescue of Sitting Bull, should the Indian police succeed in arresting him.

The command will move out at 12 o'clock midnight, in light marching order, and will be supplied with fifty rounds of carbine and twelve rounds of revolver ammunition per man, 4,000 rounds of ammunition for Gattling gun, 25 rounds for Hotchkiss gun, cooked rations and one day's forage.

After receiving the prisoner Captain Fechet will return with his command to this Post, reporting to the commanding officer on arrival.

If, on arrival at Oak creek, Captain Fechet learns that the police are fighting or need assistance, he will push on, and if necessary, follow Sitting Bull as long as possible with his supplies, keeping the post commander informed by courier of his movements.

The march will be so regulated as to reach Oak creek by 6:30 o'clock a. m., to-morrow, the 15th instant. Should arrest be made, every precaution will be taken to prevent escape or rescue.

Two Indian scouts will accompany the command. Assistant Surgeon A. R. Chapin, Medical Department, will report to Captain Fechet for duty with the expedition.

First Lieutenant S. L'H. Slocum, with Troop F, will report to Captain Fechet for orders.

Second Lieutenant E. C. Brooks, Eighth Cavalry, will also report to Captain Fechet for duty with the expedition.

One hospital ambulance, with necessary supplies, will accompany the expedition, the Quartermaster's Department furnishing the necessary team.

By order of Lieutenant Colonel W. F. Drum:

E. C. BROOKS,

Second Lieutenant, Eighth Cavalry, Post Adjutant.

The killing of Sitting Bull was hailed with delight by people generally, but not by the Indians. The fears entertained by the redmen when the soldiers first put in an appearance about the agencies did not seem to be groundless, now that a once mighty man of their nation had been, as they were led to believe, ruthlessly slain. Wild with excitement and filled with religious zeal over the announced appearance of their promised Messiah, and haunted by the fear that they were to be first disarmed and afterward butchered, it is hardly to be wondered at that they should combine to protect themselves.

Chief Big Foot, whom the government seems to have marked out from the first as a disturber, was related, both by birth and marriage, to many of the Indians who had escaped from the scene of the Sitting Bull killing, and when they came to his camp, clad in rags and literally starving, the old chief took them in and fed them, and his people gave them shelter. Deny, if you will, that the Indian nature is wanting of all the attributes of humanity, but do not try to reconcile it with this act of poor old Chief Big Foot, who, when asked by Colonel Sumner why he had permitted the Standing Rock refugees to enter his camp, replied:

" What else could I do ? They came to me almost naked, were hungry, footsore and weary, many of them my brothers and relatives ! "

The humanity of this savage stirred the better impulses of Colonel Sumner's heart. He had met, where he had expected to find hostility, a living exemplification

438 THE SOUTH DAKOTA OUTBREAK

of the Divine command. The weary had been rested;
the hungry fed. No wonder, then, that Colonel Sumner was convinced that Chief Big Foot did not mean to
join the hostiles in the badlands, and permitted him and
his people to remain in their homes. But because he
did this, he brought upon himself the censure of his
superiors. Let the military man tell his own story.
In his report, under date of February 3d, 1891, to the
Assistant Adjutant General, Department of Dakota,
Colonel Sumner says:

I have the honor to acknowledge receipt of your
communication directing me to submit a report of the
flight of Big Foot's band from Cheyenne river and all
circumstances connected therewith. In compliance therewith I respectfully submit the following statement :

On my arrival on Cheyenne river, December 3d, rein-
forcing the command there under Captain Hennissee,
Eighth Cavalry, with D Troop, Eighth Cavalry, I took
command of troops in the field. This command, then,
was C, D and I Troops, Eighth Cavalry, and F Company,
Third Infantry (later C Company, Third Infantry), and
two Hotchkiss guns. My instructions were set forth in
Post Orders No. 254, dated Fort Meade, S. D., November
29th, and telegraphic instructions from Headquarters Department of Dakota, attached copy herewith presented.
In compliance with these instructions I moved the camp
up the Cheyenne river nearer to Smithville, and opened
a trail directly east over the hills and established an outpost at Davidson's ranch, twenty miles east of my camp
at head of Deep creek, and on the trail between Big

Foot's village and Pine Ridge. This trail was not practicable for wagons, but could have been used by cavalry,
and the outpost was established to give information of
any Indians passing north or south.

My orders specified protection to settlers on Belle
Fourche and vicinity, as well as a watch on Big Foot's
camp. A few days after my arrival most of the chiefs
and head men called to see me, including Big Foot.
They remained two days about my camp, and, without
exception, seemed not only willing but anxious to obey
my orders to remain quietly at home, and particularly
wished me to inform my superiors that they were all on
the side of the Government in the trouble then going on.
This information was furnished December 8th, by letter
dated Camp Cheyenne, December 8th ; also in letter from
same camp, dated December 12th ; also in letter from
same camp, dated December 16th. Frequent communication, and always friendly, was kept up with all these
leaders until about December 15, when Big Foot came
to my camp to say good-by, as he and all his men,
women and children were going to Bennett for their annuities, again assuring me that none of the Cheyenne
River Indians had any intentions or thoughts of joining
the hostiles at Pine Ridge.

Notwithstanding this assurance, however, I was at
that time impressed with the idea that Big Foot was
making an extraordinary effort to keep his followers
quiet, and seemed much relieved at having succeeded in
getting them to go to Bennett. With this impression on
my mind it appeared to me that he required at that time

all the support I could give him, and I never failed, in the presence of his own men and others, to show good feeling and the utmost confidence. About this date came the telegram from department headquarters, dated December 16th. Under the circumstances, and owing to the delicate situation of affairs at that moment, as described above, viz., my belief that Big Foot could alone control the young men, and was doing so under my advice and support, I thought it best to allow him to go to Bennett a free man, and so informed Division Commander by telegraph December 18; also telegram to department headquarters same date ; also telegram to Division Commander at Rapid City dated December 19th. I invite special attention to this dispatch, as showing that every effort was being made to keep informed, to inform my superiors, and to make the most of my command, and in this connection see copy of dispatch to General Carr, Sixth Cavalry, dated December 19th ; also letter to Mr. Dunn same date, on Belle Fourche. On this day, December 19th, later in the day, intelligence reached me from a detachment sent down the river to look after Standing Rock Indians, that the Cheyenne River Indians had stopped on their way down to Bennett, and had assembled at Hump's camp to meet Sitting Bull.

On receiving this information from the officer in advance, Lieutenant Duff, Eighth Cavalry, I marched at once down the river with two troops of cavalry and one company of infantry, reinforced to fifty men and two Hotchkiss guns, and was soon in support of the troop, Goodwin's Eighth Cavalry, near Big Foot's camp. On Decem-

PRETTY EAGLE AND SHOSHONE FRIEND.

ber 20th reached Narseilles ranch and went into camp, and there received a letter from Big Foot stating that he was my friend and wished to talk. December 21st, made an early start to join Goodwin's command, and to either fight or capture Big Foot if any resistance was offered. While on the march, and four miles east of Narseilles, Big Foot came to me, bringing with him two Standing Rock Indians. He expressed a desire to comply with any orders I had to give, and said all his men would do the same. I asked at once how many Indians were in his camp. He replied one hundred of his own and thirty-eight Standing Rock Indians. I asked why he had received the latter, knowing them to be off their reservation and refugees. His reply was certainly humane, if not a sufficient excuse, and was to the effect that they were brothers and relations; that they had come to him and his people almost naked, were hungry, footsore and weary; that he had taken them in, had fed them, and no one with any heart could do any less. The Standing Rock Indians with Big Foot, that is, those whom I saw, answered his description perfectly, and were, in fact, so pitiable a sight that I at once dropped all thought of their being hostile or even worthy of capture. Still my instructions were to take them, and I intended doing so. Since the flight of Big Foot and the fight at Wounded Knee, I believe I was to some extent imposed upon in regard to Standing Rock Indians, and I now think there were perhaps some warriors with them who were kept out of sight, but near enough to get food and to act in support should a fight take place.

However, everything went on quietly and I was not aware of it if any other Indians than those in sight were near us. I directed Capt. Hennissee, Eighth Cavalry, to go to the Indian camp with Big Foot, get all the Indians and return to my camp at Narseilles ranch, where I encamped on the night of the 21st. Goodwin's troop was called and at 3 p. m. Hennissee marched in with three hundred and thirty-three Indians; the increase in numbers as given by Big Foot to me on the road being something of a surprise. I arranged my camp accordingly, and was fully prepared for anything that might occur. The Indians went into camp as I directed, turned out their ponies and made themselves comfortable while preparing for the feast I had promised. The night passed quietly, and on the morning of the 22d we all made an early start for my home camp, Big Foot, at the time, seeming willing to go there. On the march some of the young bucks undertook to pass the advance guard, and Lieut. Duff, the officer in charge, drove them back, and in so doing deployed a line faced to the rear. This action seemed to frighten some of the Indians and the squaws in the wagons whipped up, threw out some of their loads and screamed, and this excitement was soon communicated down the column. I rode at once to the head, found Big Foot, who was driving his wagon, and asked him what this excitement meant. He laughed, and in reply said: "Nothing the matter; some old woman screamed." I told him to have it stopped, and he at once got on his pony, rode about and allayed all confusion, and the march continued to the village.

[Col. Sumner here introduces copies of his dispatches sent to division and department commanders on the 19th, 21st and 22d December.] In that of the 19th, I state Indians were reported to me as defiant. That report was false, and I did not find them to be so. In another dispatch I used the term surrender more in anticipation of what might have taken place.

When the meeting took place there seemed to be no occasion for surrender, and in all later dispatches I relate the fact that the Indians "come in," and all statements in those dispatches are based on the supposition that I had only to deal with one hundred and thirty-eight Indians, whereas the number coming in was three hundred and thirty-three. Still, as will be observed in dispatch of December 21st, I hoped to carry out my designs with even that number, but on arrival at the village I saw that Big Foot himself could not control or overcome the desire they all had to go to their homes, and he came frankly to me and said:

"I will go with you to your camp, but there will be trouble in trying to force these women and children, cold and hungry as they are, away from their homes." And further said: "This is their home, where the Government has ordered them to stay, and none of my people have committed a single act requiring their removal by force."

I concluded that one of two things must happen — I must either consent to their going into their village or bring on a fight; and, if the latter, must be the aggressor, and, if the aggressor, what possible reason could I pro-

duce for making an attack on peaceable, quiet Indians
on their reservation and at their homes, killing, perhaps,
many of them, and sacrificing, without any justification,
the lives of many officers and enlisted men. I confess
that my ambition was very great, but it was not sufficient
to justify me in making an unprovoked attack on those
Indians at that time, and even if an attack had been
made to enforce my wishes, the result would have only
been to have driven the Indians out of the country sooner
than they did go. I was prepared to fight at any moment should provocation be afforded, but with my small
force I could not have surrounded the Indians, nor could
I have prevented their fleeing from me and going to the
badlands, or even to the hostile camp, with a reasonable
demand for protection, which, in going as they did, they
did not have.

Dispatch (December 21) indicates the fear I had
of a sudden departure of the young men in a stealthy
manner. I considered that Big Foot's presence and influence with them would be more powerful to prevent
that than anything I could do; he was, as it were,
working with me to accomplish my ends, and I had every
confidence that he would be able to hold his people on
the reservation, and also to deliver the Standing Rock
Indians to me, as he promised to do, and as I still believed he desired to do. It was not practicable at that
time to select the thirty-eight Standing Rock Indians out
of the crowd, as no one but the Indians themselves
knew who they were. I therefore, for the reasons stated,
left Big Foot with his people, and in connection with

such action I believe I was acting in accordance with many precedents of early timers of later years, and with those established at Pine Ridge in the present campaign, where, even in the presence of a much larger force proportionately than I had, Indians were allowed to be friendly one day and hostile the next, and then to return to a friendly status. It is fair to presume that those Indians who surrounded and fired upon the Seventh Cavalry December 30th came from the hostile camp and returned to it again.

Leaving Big Foot, then, with his people in his village, but taking his promise to see me the next day and bring with him the Standing Rock Indians, I returned to my camp, and purposely all the way there, to establish confidence, after the excitement on the march, which might have been continued, or perhaps increased, had I encamped and taken up an offensive position near the village, but which was no doubt allayed by my apparent reliance on the chief, whom I was bound at that time either to support or fight. Up to that time I had no reason to doubt the integrity of the chief ; on the other hand, had every reason to believe in the sincerity of his motives. I decided to trust him, and in doing so was wholly unmindful of orders received, and desirous only of accomplishing what I understood to be the wishes of my superiors, especially those of the Division Commander, believing that his plans were to settle matters, if possible, without bloodshed.

I have already stated what in my opinion would have occurred if I had taken the other course. While in my camp on the night of 22d and 23d, I received the dispatch from General Miles. I had no thought of the escape of the Indians as a body, but was only anxious lest a few warriors should run away, and I supposed I had taken the best precaution against that, and was therefore obeying orders. The information relative to Indians from the north made me hesitate to leave my camp at all, but I hoped to accomplish matters with Big Foot on the 23d — get him started for Bennett and hurry back to camp, although I marched towards the village with every soldier I could take, and fully intended to enforce my orders for Bennett and make any refusal sufficient provocation to fight, and in that extremity take the chances on the call to Meade. My anxiety at this time to meet all the calls made upon me is apparent in dispatches to General Miles dated 22d and 23d.

At noon on 23d December, not hearing anything from Big Foot or from any of my scouts who had been sent to the village, I had ordered the march of my command, and was about moving when Mr. Dunn, a citizen living on Belle Fourche and friend of Big Foot's, appeared at my camp. I obtained Mr. Dunn's service to go to the village and see what was going on, and instructed him to take my order to Big Foot to go with his people to Bennett, and also to say to Big Foot that I would enforce the order. What Mr. Dunn said or did is a question. I was at one time inclined to believe that Mr. Dunn had played me false, but he is a man of good reputation, and from his statement and statements of officers who have seen and interviewed him since, I am now sure that I did him an injustice, and I do not believe or claim that Mr. Dunn was in any way responsible for events which afterwards occurred.

Mr. Dunn after seeing Big Foot, met me on the march and informed me that Big Foot and all his people had consented to go to Bennett—that there was a good deal of feeling among them—no desire to fight or in any way to oppose my orders, and that they would move next morning. Big Foot intended to visit my camp that evening. I had no suspicion, nor had anyone else in my command, that anything else would happen. This record shows what confidence I already had in Big Foot, and certainly Mr. Dunn's report was not calculated to weaken it; besides this I had still later reports from my interpeter, Benoit, who left the village after Dunn, that everything was all right and everybody going to Bennett.

About 7 p. m. two scouts came in, one stating that he thought the Indians were going south, and the other expressed a belief that although they were going up Deep creek, he thought they would turn towards Bennett after reaching the divide, and that they did this to escape the soldiers coming up the Cheyenne River from Bennett. On the possibility that they had gone south I sent the dispatch to Col. Carr, Sixth Cavalry, dated 23d, and also dispatch to Gens. Miles and Ruger. On the morning of December 24th, I received dispatch from Gen. Miles dated 23d. It will be observed that in this dispatch Big Foot is considered both hostile and defiant by the Division Commander, and that positive orders were sent me for action against him, but those orders came too late and could not be carried out.

The opinion of the Division Commander was quite the reverse of my own experience with these Indians and I may therefore be reasonably excused for not anticipating such orders, and with the exception of the dispatch from Gen. Ruger indicating the desirability of arresting Big Foot, it will be difficult to find in any of my orders or instructions any intimation of hostility on the part of those Indians. On the other hand, all anxiety seemed to point to my preventing their becoming hostile. I believe that duty was best performed in the course pursued up to the time they left their reservation; an event I did not look for, could not anticipate, and could not have prevented.

Any move on my part to the south of Big Foot's village would have left the settlements unguarded, the citizens unprotected, who were by orders under my protection, and my supply camp on the river at the disposal of the Indians on their way south by that route, instead of the one they took. If Big Foot had been hostile and defiant in attitude, I was not aware of it until receiving the orders making him so and authorizing his arrest and the arrest of others. My course would have been very plain if I could have received these orders in time, or could have known the wishes of the Division Commander. The result, however, would probably have been the same, as any display of hostile intent on my part would have caused the Indians to flee, and I could not have interposed any force to prevent.

The fact that even in the opinion of my superiors I did not have sufficient force to do that, is, I believe, made apparent in several dispatches from Department Headquarters stating that I would be reinforced first by Wells' command, then by Adams' First Cavalry and Cheyenne scouts, then by Colonel Merriam, Seventh Infantry—none of whom ever reached me in time; also in several of my dispatches are reports that I did not have force enough to guard the trails leading south. I did not ask for more troops or for any reinforcements.

I never for a moment considered that my command was not strong enough to meet any force likely to be brought against it, but that is quite a different matter from surrounding and capturing an enemy, especially of the character of the Indian, who considers a surrender merely a halt in the fight to be fed, but had no idea of being disarmed. In the case of big Foot's band now under consideration no surrender was made—no arms were demanded. The march to the vicinity of Big Foot's camp, situated down the Cheyenne river twenty-two miles below his village, was for the purpose of arresting any warriors from the Standing Rock Agency who were supposed to have been concerned in the Sitting Bull fight, and who, it was feared, might go further south; to have a check on Big Foot's band and other Cheyenne river Indians.

As I already stated, the mere appearance of the few Standing Rock Indians in sight as reported, precluded anything like the use of military force against them. The Big Foot band and other Indians belonging to Cheyenne river were on their reservation and willing to go to their village in compliance with my wishes. This was a complete surrender as far as I was authorized to act—any further demand on my part would have provoked hostilities and would have placed me clearly outside of my orders, and even beyond any excuse for such action. Nor could it be presumed that an attack by my force on Big Foot would have resulted in any other way than that experienced by every commander in our service who has made such an attack. The Modocs were attacked and fled to the Lava Beds, killing every citizen within reach; the Bannocks were attacked and scattered over the country, killing innocent people and committing depredations; the Nez Perces were attacked by General Howard and led his command and others for thousands of miles, and when finally surrounded and attacked by fresh troops a number succeeded in escaping to Canada. In the '76 campaign on one occasion the Indians were met in hostile array and the troops were withdrawn, and it is supposed the commanders, having discretion, did a wise thing. In the campaign of this year, at Pine Ridge, it is the common rumor, and generally supposed to be true, that Two Strike's band and other bands of Indians were allowed to pass back and forth between the agency and the hostile camp, always armed, and alternately friendly and hostile, at their own will.

I do not presume to question the management of these affairs or the wisdom of the policy pursued, but in connection with the management and policy I would like to have my action considered. My orders were positive to prevent the escape of the Indians I had in charge; to prevent any Indians from coming from the south and joining those on the Cheyenne river; to protect the settlements in my rear and on the Belle Fourche; and to watch for Indians coming from the northwest (that was in my rear), and to be prepared to march rapidly to Fort Meade. In the face of these several duties, all to be preformed by my small command, I could only hope to succeed by using a peaceful policy rather than force.

I hoped to hold Big Foot and that he would be able to control his men and take them to Bennett, and up to 7 p. m. on the night of the 23d, I felt reasonably assured that I would not only succeed in that measure but I would also be prepared for any other demands. So that, instead of being in disobedience of orders as reported by the division commander, I was, I know, doing my utmost to carry out his orders, and even to fullfil what I thought were his wishes.

The flight of Big Foot's band, no doubt, interfered with the plans of the campaign; I was prepared to hear that, and further, perhaps, that I had not met with the expectations of the Major General commanding in permitting the Indians to go. I should have regretted even that censure; but to see that I am accused of disobedience of orders is a surprise to me, and, in my opinion, is as unjust as it is unwarranted either by facts, circumstances, or a possibility of intention. My orders from General Miles after the flight of the Indians for Pine Ridge, were to return to my camp and remain in that vicinity.

Since the departure of the Indians I have learned through other Indians that Big Foot was forced to go with his people; that there was probably no intention of hostilities, but rather a desire on the part of all to seek the crowd at Pine Ridge Agency, and being there to get better terms than at Bennett. My opinion is that the advance of Colonel Merriam up Cheyenne river and the report that the Standing Rock Indians at Bennett had been disarmed, caused a sudden change of plan in Big Foot's village, and that the young men, on account of the situation, were able to overcome all objections to going south. They certainly passed through the country without committing any depredations or harming anyone.

They passed near a detachment from my command at Davidson's ranch, on head of Deep creek, passed within sight of citizens at Pinaugh's ranch, at Howard's went through his pasture filled with horses and cattle, and, it is reported, disturbed nothing. They had passed all roads, as I understood it, to the hostile camp, and were met by Maj. Whitside twelve miles from the agency and going in that direction, were willing to surrender to him and did march with him to his camp and remain quietly with him all night. This command having, as was reported, captured Big Foot's band, was as large, if not greater than mine, and was in supporting distance of other troops.

Still, Maj. Whitside asked for reinforcements, and they were promptly sent, as he reported he did not consider it safe to make the attempt to disarm them with his command. Reinforcements having arrived, this band

of Indians was then in the presence of regimental headquarters, eight troops cavalry and three or four guns with
artillery detachments; a fight occurred, the details of
which have been published, and have no place here except to show that any attack by my command, although
without provocation, would, if successful, have driven the
Indians out of the country, but could not have held or
disarmed them.

It will be observed from the evidence accompanying
this report that òn the day on which the Major General
commanding was writing his dispatch, December 23, pro-
claiming Big Foot to be hostile and defiant, and ordering
his arrest, he, Big Foot, was in reality quietly occupying
his village with his people amenable to orders, having
given no provocation whatever, to my knowledge, for
attack, and no more deserving punishment than peaceable
Indians at any time on their reservation. I was not
aware that Big Foot or his people were considered hostile, and am now at loss to understand why they were so
considered, every act of theirs being within my experience directly to the contrary, and reports made by me
were to the effect that the Indians were friendly and
quiet.

As will be seen from the report submitted by Col.
Sumner, Big Foot's people had shown no hostility toward
the whites, nor had they given any indication that they
intended to act contrary to the orders promulgated by
the Government. On the contrary, the old chief had
declared himself in every way friendly, and his contem-

plated trip from his village to Fort Bennett for annuities
was made no secret of by him in his talk with Col.
Sumner. That he had changed his original plans and
started for Pine Ridge instead of Bennett, must be admitted ; but this is officially explained in the statement
that Big Foot's people, having heard of the disarming of
all the Indians at Bennett, thought they would be treated
better by the Pine Ridge Agency authorities. But their
trip toward Pine Ridge was construed as an endeavor to
join the hostile Indians in the badlands, and orders were
at once given to intercept Big Foot and his people, disarm them and send them as prisoners to Omaha.

"If Big Foot had been hostile and defiant in attitude, I was not aware of it," says Col. Sumner, "until
receiving the orders making him so, and authorizing his
arrest and the arrest of others."

When on December 28th, within twenty miles of the
Pine Ridge Agency, Big Foot and his people were met
by Major Whitside and command, they, without offering
any resistance, accompanied the troops to the military
camp on Wounded Knee creek. Word of the capture of
the band was immediately sent to headquarters, and Gen.
Brooke at once dispatched Col. Forsyth with the troops
of the Seventh Cavalry to reinforce Major Whitside and
disarm the members of Big Foot's band, numbering, all
told, three hundred and thirty-three people. The Indian
camp had been surrounded by Major Whitside's command before the arrival of Col. Forsyth, and the Indians
were apprehensive when they saw preparations going on
for the accomplishment of some object they could not

comprehend. The killing of Sitting Bull a short while previous, and rumors of the disarming of all Indians who had surrendered at Bennett, were promoting causes of fear and distrust, and every act on both sides was made subject to misapprehension.

Grouard says he was ordered out from Pine Ridge with Col. Forsyth's command on the night of December 28th, but was recalled by courier before he had traveled half the distance between the agency and Wounded Knee, where Big Foot was camped. He is positive that the trouble which occurred the following morning arose through a misunderstanding on both sides, and that the awful catastrophe might, as well as not, have been averted.

When Col. Forsyth arrived at Wounded Knee on the morning of December 29th, Big Foot was in his lodge suffering from pneumonia. The trip from the Cheyenne river through the biting cold had incapacitated the old chief, and from all accounts his condition was desperate. Of course the soldiers knew nothing of this. They were about to carry out orders given by superior authority, and they had learned the first duty of soldiers too well to disobey, no matter what their knowledge or inclination might be.

When the final order to disarm the Indians was given by Col. Forsyth, at eight o'clock in the morning, December 29, the male members of Big Foot's band were brought forward and closely surrounded by the troops— Custer's old regiment, the Seventh. The Indians at this juncture knew the intention was to disarm them, but they did not understand what was to follow when they were rendered helpless by obeying the order to give up their arms. Big Foot did not come out of his lodge, but his nephew—a young, scatter-brain fellow—was in the crowd, dressed in all the paraphernalia of the ghost dancers. The tents of the soldiers and the tepis of the hostiles were very close together; in fact, it might be said that the two camps were one. When the order was given to produce their arms, the members of the band came forward and sat in a semi-circle on the ground. The weather was very cold, and the bucks were wrapped in their blankets, many of them having their guns concealed beneath these coverings.

Instead, however, of giving up all their weapons at once, as demanded, the Indians handed in so few that the officers conducting the disarming became suspicious and ordered tepis and Indians both searched. Authority is conflicting at this point as to whether any searching of the persons of the Indians was or was not done; but there was great suppressed excitement, in the midst of which Good-for-Nothing, the nephew of Big Foot, jumped to his feet and began to harangue the camp. He is said to have exclaimed that the soldiers could not injure him, as he had his ghost shirt on, and that now was as good a time to test its efficacy as he would ever have. He took a handful of dirt from the ground and tossed it in the air over his head, and then discharged his gun, the soldiers claim at them, the Indians say in the air.

By this time all the Indians were in a high state of excitement, and the soldiers, believing the action of Good-for-Nothing to be a prearranged signal for an attack,

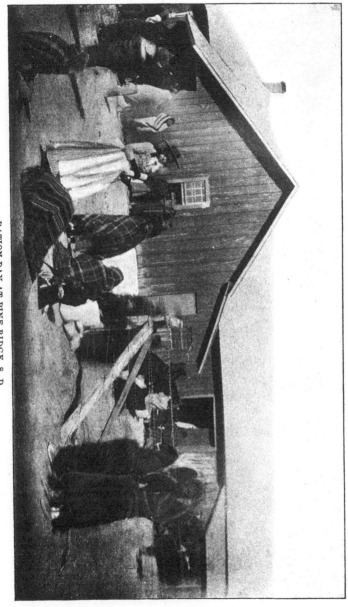

RATION DAY AT PINE RIDGE, S. D.

poured a volley of lead into the Indians, and instantly
the fight became general. The soldiers, being on all
sides of the Indians and within twenty feet of them,
could not help but cross-fire, and no doubt killed many
of their own number, though it has never been denied
that the members of Big Foot's band fought desperately,
and to kill.

The battle lasted perhaps an hour, but not at the
spot where the trouble begun, as a great many were
killed at the first volley, and those among the band who
could get out of the camp through the cordon of troops,
started for the adjacent bluffs, the soldiers pursuing and
shooting them down as fast as they could overtake them.
The number killed has never been definitely ascertained,
though it is estimated at about one hundred and fifty, a
large number of the slain being women and children.
Many have strongly condemned the action of Col. Forsyth's command in shooting down the squaws and children, and refer to it as a wanton slaughter; but it must
be remembered that when the first gun was fired the Indians became mixed up indiscriminately, and no distinction could be made between the men and the women.
There certainly is no good reason for attaching blame to
the command for the killing of women and children
under these circumstances; nor does the fact that dead
bodies of slain females and babes were found on the
frozen ground at distances from the camp varying from
one hundred yards to an eighth of a mile disprove the
claim made by the troops that these unfortunate beings
were mowed down by the rain of bullets and shot which

was poured upon the fleeing bucks after the fight in the
camp was over and the Indians were endeavoring to find
shelter in the neighboring hills.

After the battle the body of Big Foot was found
outside his tepi. The body of the old chief, rigid in
death, had been pierced by a score of bullets. Death
must have been instantaneous. He had apparently risen
from his bed when the firing first begun, and rushed out
of his lodge at the moment when the awful storm of
bullets broke from the soldiers' rifles. His squaw was
found dead inside the tepi, her nerveless fingers still
clutching a loaded Winchester. The chief's lodge stood
but a few feet back from where the Indians had squatted
on the ground previous to the commencement of disarming, and the fusilade from the troops fairly riddled the
tepi's sides. The squaw, being inside and standing upright, was struck and killed by the bullets which tore
through the thin canvas of which the walls of the lodge
were composed.

When the battle ground at Wounded Knee was
gone over the troops found twenty-seven of their comrades cold in death, and more than thirty seriously
wounded. Capt. George D. Wallace of K troop was
among the slain. The dead were given burial with military honors and the wounded were removed at once to
the agency and given the best of care.

A large number of wounded Indians were taken to
the agency and placed in the hands of doctors and skilled
nurses, but many of them succumbed to their injuries.

Some little time after the battle Col. Forsyth was

relieved of his command pending an investigation of the charge that women and children were killed wantonly by the soldiers of Col. Forsyth's command at the Wounded Knee battle, but Col. Forsyth was honorably acquitted and promoted shortly afterward.

Among other commands that had been sent out to keep an eye on the hostiles and intercept Big Foot's band was Col. Guy V. Henry's (Ninth Cavalry,) whose camp was distant about thirty-five miles from the Pine Ridge Agency. On the day of the Wounded Knee battle word had been sent to Col. Henry to report with his command at headquarters, which he accordingly did. But he had no sooner arrived in camp than word came that his wagon train, which was moving into the agency at leisure, had been attacked by the hostiles, and he immediately went to its relief, driving off the attacking party and bringing in the train.

In the meantime a fire at the Mission, five miles from the agency (supposed to be, from reports brought into Pine Ridge, the Mission building itself undergoing destruction at the hands of the hostiles), caused an order to be issued for Col. Forsyth and a detachment of the Seventh Cavalry to repair at once to the scene of the fire and drive off the Indians. Upon arriving there Col. Forsyth was entirely surrounded by the hostiles, and a request for reinforcements was at once dispatched to headquarters. Col. Henry's tired troopers had just arrived at the agency when this request arrived from Forsyth. In fact, the cavalrymen had barely dismounted when "boots and saddles" was sounded, and away flew Henry and his men to rescue the threatened Seventh. And they did it, too !

No officer in the army is held in higher esteem by his men than Colonel Henry. His regiment, then, the Ninth, composed entirely of colored troops, would charge any position or follow any forlorn hope where he led. Brave as a lion and gentle as a woman, he has rare qualities for leadership, and his knowledge of Indian warfare has been acquired by years of campaigning on the border with such heroes as Crook and Custer. Grouard places him in the foremost rank as an Indian fighter, and says his judgment in such matters is today superior to that of any officer in the United States army. His services during the '76 campaign were heroic, and his scarred face (the result of a rifle shot received at the battle of the Rosebud, when Chief Crazy Horse with six thousand warriors attacked Crook's command,) appeals more eloquently for deserved recognition than can words of commendation.

The hostile camp, which, up to the 11th of January, 1891, was located fifteen miles from the Pine Ridge Agency, contained no less than 3,500 souls, about six hundred being fighting warriors. Chief Red Cloud had been forced into the hostile camp and could not get away. On the 7th of January Lieutenant Casey of the Twenty-second Infantry, commanding a company of Cheyenne scouts, left the camp of Colonel G. B. Sanford, on the bank of White River, opposite the mouth of White Clay creek, to reconnoiter the hostile village located at No Waters, on White Clay creek, about eight miles from its mouth. He had employed his scouts up to the day of his death in locating and watching the Sioux camp. The day preceding the murder of Lieutenant Casey, says Lieutenant Robert Getty, he had invited a number of Sioux warriors to his camp, where he entertained and had a friendly talk with them.

On the day following, about nine o'clock in the morning, he left camp with two scouts, telling Lieut. Getty that he was going out to get a view of the hostile village. About one o'clock the two scouts returned with Lieut. Casey's horse and reported that he had been killed by the Sioux. By permission of Gen. Brooke, who had established his headquarters with Col. Sanford on January 5th, Lieut. Getty took a troop of scouts and proceeded up White Clay Creek, where he found Lieut. Casey's body on the right bank of the creek within a mile and a half of the Sioux camp. Part of the clothing had been taken, but the body was not mutilated. He had been shot through the head, the ball entering at the back and coming out under the right eye, killing him instantly. The Sioux offered no resistance to the recovery of his body.

White Moon, one of the scouts with Lieut. Casey, says the officer proceeded up White Clay creek, and a short distance from the hostile camp met a Sioux woman, with whom he talked in English. He then proceeded on, and within a short distance of the Siorx camp came to a party of Indians butchering cattle, with whom he shook hands. While White Moon was conversing with these Indians Lieut. Casey rode on. The other scout, Rock Road, turned back, but White Moon followed the Lieutenant.

When he caught up with him the Lieutenant was talking with Pete Richard, a half-breed. On Richard's right stood a Sioux, and on his left a little in rear of the Lieutenant was Plenty Horses, the Indian who did the killing. While the conversation was in progress Plenty Horses shot the young officer from behind. White Moon says he rode toward the Lieutenant, hoping to catch him before he fell from his horse, but did not succeed. He caught the horse, however, and, accompanied by Richard, took it back to Gen. Sanford's camp and reported the matter to General Brooke. Plenty Horses was afterwards surrendered and brought to trial, but escaped conviction on the technical ground that the killing occurred during open hostilities, and under the rule of "war" he could not be held for murder.

After the murder of Lieut. Casey old Red Cloud knew matters were coming to a crisis, and, in company with his daughter, set out from the hostile camp for the agency and nearly froze to death in making the journey. The hostiles were desirous of keeping the old warrior in their midst, and he had to steal away in order to accomplish his purpose. While plodding agencyward through the deep snow and bitter cold, some of the hostiles, who had either followed him or were out in the hills scouting, fired on the old chief and his daughter several times; but they threw themselves in the snow drifts and escaped the bullets, finally arriving in safety,

though nearly frozen, at Pine Ridge Agency. There seems
to be no reason to doubt the statement of Red Cloud
that he was forced to leave his home and go to the hostile camp in the badlands, as he certainly sent word from
the latter place to Lieut. Casey (when he saw that officer
coming toward the hostile village on the morning of the
7th) not to approach nearer for fear of being killed, and
he also sent a request to Pine Ridge for the authorities
to rescue him from the hostile village.

On the 11th day of January Gen. Miles decided to
send a courier to the hostile camp and ask the Indians
to come in peaceably and surrender. From the date of
the battle on Wounded Knee the troops had been gradually drawing a tighter cordon about the Indian camp,
and by the 11th they were completely and effectually
surrounded. Gen. Miles' policy was a humane one. He
had not gone to Pine Ridge to make war, but to enforce
order and secure peace. He had shown the utmost
patience and forbearance under most trying and exasperating circumstances, and, in the eleventh hour, did not propose to be diverted from his mapped out course by the
clamor of those who demanded immediate surrender of
the hostiles, regardless of consequences.

Gen. Miles entrusted his message to the hostiles to
Grouard, who, accompanied by Yankton Charlie (a Sioux
scout who was one of Grouard's warmest friends), started
out on his dangerous mission after dark, his object being
to get into the hostile camp unobserved as near one
o'clock as possible. He arrived there an hour later than
he had calculated upon, and went direct to the lodge of

Yankton Charlie's brother, informing that hostile gentle-man that he was the bearer of a message from Gen. Miles, and asking him to call into the tepi the head men of the village and also some Indian who could read and interpret the General's letter.

It was but a few minutes before the lodge was filled with the leading spirits among the hostiles, who were surly enough when they saw Grouard, but listened atten-tively to the General's kind and friendly communication. They did not want to act hastily in the matter, however, and consumed the time from 2 a. m. until sun-up deliber-ating on the proposition submitted, at the end of which time they informed Grouard that they had decided to break camp at once and move closer to the agency, from which point some of the head men would go in and con-fer with Gen. Miles, and, if everything were satisfactory, would surrender and give up their arms.

Grouard and Yankton Charlie waited about until the Indian police (Dog Soldiers) surrounded the camp and the tepis were taken down and packed, when they moved off some hundred yards and awaited the moving of the cav-alcade, made up of as fantastic and ragged a horde as ever painted for the warpath or started for the poorhouse. Some had guns and others were armed with clubs. Dur-ing the time that Grouard waited the moving of the camp, the Dog Soldiers fired a number of volleys in the direction where he was stationed, but high enough in the air not to do him injury, thereby intimating that they had it in their power to prevent his return to the agency, but forebore exercising it.

When the Indians were at last on the move toward the agency, that is.when the last of the hostile band had "folded their tents" and joined the famished, ragged caravan which moved through the extended lines of infantry, cavalry and artillery, Grouard and Yankton Charlie rode leisurely along toward the head of the procession, some of the Indians being on horseback, some in dilapidated wagons, while the majority were afoot. The Dog Soldiers were at the head of the line, and Grouard rode in amongst them. One of the police, who was armed with a big club, nodded his head up the road and pointed to the scout, remarking that the latter had better go, when Yankton Charlie spoke up and told his hostileship that they would go when they got ready. Charlie could not have been induced to visit the camp if it were not for the fact that Grouard had been ordered to go, and the scout says that while he and Charlie were on their way to the hostile village from the agency, the Sioux told him that they were the biggest fools on earth to make the trip, as the Indians had it in for both of them and would kill them on sight. "But," said Grouard's fearless friend, "if you go, I shall accompany you; I don't believe either of us will ever come back, though."

Grouard and Charlie soon drew away from the hostiles and returned to the agency, reporting to Gen. Miles that the Indians were moving toward army headquarters. In answer to his message the hostiles sent word that they would hold a conference with Gen. Miles on the following day. They did not desire Mr. Cody (who had sent them word that he intended to visit their camp) to come among them, so Mr. Cody did not go.

On the following day some of the head men came to the agency and held a council. Gen. Miles told them he wanted them to come in and give up their arms, promising to pay for every gun taken from them, and the Indians finally concluded the best thing for them to do was to act upon the General's advice, which they did on the 15th. A place near the agency was designated as the spot where the disarming should take place (an immense flat visible from headquarters). Grouard says anyone who witnessed the parade of the hostiles on that day will never forget it. The line was fully five miles long, and the Indians rode and marched in twos with all the proud bearing and precision of soldiers, the mounted men representing Indian cavalry and the footmen (walk-a-heaps) infantry. Some were armed and others carried clubs, but all had something in their hands or on their shoulders representing weapons. They marchd in review of the officers and troops, deporting themselves as proudly as if returning from a conquest. Their garments were the odd ends of every conceivable kind of male attire, with here and there a bright colored blanket and a stovepipe hat.

Grouard says he preceded the column to the flat where the Indians gave up their weapons and saw them surrender all the firearms they then possessed; but he was satisfied that not over one gun out of ten which the bucks really had were given up, as they had taken the precaution to bury them before coming in to the agency the day previous. They did not fail, however, to turn in all the old useless weapons they had in their camp. When taken from them each gun was properly marked for identification, and afterward each Indian received remuneration for what he had given up. A feast was provided for the surrendering host. Afterwards the Indians were returned to their respective reservations, and peace once more spread its wings over the Dakota hills and valleys.

While this memorable campaign was productive of one result that was inevitable, it should have also taught the Government that humane treatment of the Indians can accomplish greater ends than may be attained through conquest. It must be conceded by all that no one is more interested in the management of the Indians on reservations than the Indian himself. Having been forced to yield to the force of a supreme power, he has the right to expect just consideration and honest dealing. And the government can do no better than adopt many of the suggestions which come from its savage wards, when it cannot but realize that such action would preclude the possibility of Indian outbreaks, and save life and the expenditure of millions of dollars.

There is no use in theorizing. There is a practical side to the problem, "What shall we do with the Indian?" Why, treat him like a human being. Properly clothe and sufficiently feed and shelter him. He cannot be expected to learn our ways if he is neglected and furnished no teachers. Make his surroundings so pleasantly comfortable that he will be attracted instead of repelled, and his condition will change so rapidly that he will be self-supporting in a decade. His superiors should be those in whom he has confidence. No human being, nor any wild animal, either, can be won by cruelty.

Submission *may* follow starvation, but the spirit cannot be conquered so. "Kills every man the thing he does not love?" We proudly boast that the Indian is American! Then in the name of reason, treat him as an American, and make a man of him. The author of these pages has witnessed scenes on Indian reservations that would scarcely be credited were they recited here. I have seen — not once, but many, many times — an Indian woman and her children emptying the offal barrels and boxes at the rear of kitchens at the Posts and on the reservations, and eating the filthy food to satisfy the pangs of hunger — hunger that was apparent in their gaunt faces and wasted forms ; hunger that shone in the startled look within their eyes. Ah, says someone, they have no preference when it comes to food — " He that is filthy, let him be filthy still."

Let me state right here, that no class of people on earth ate better or more nutritious food than the savage before the government drove him to the starvation pen on the reservation. It may not be the fault of the government that he is half clad and worse than not fed at all ; but I think it is. The policy that has permitted and still permits favored persons to control Government reserves and grow fat in bank accounts on what they filch from the poor Indian, is a Government policy, and one the Government cannot discountenance and discontinue any too soon. It is a shame and disgrace, in light of the fact that this matter has been aired so often, that such conditions still maintain. What is the remedy? Why, listen to the prayer of the Indian himself, and save him from civilian rule and robbery by vesting the reservation government in the War Department, for, when truth is told, the military man is the only practical friend the half-clad, half-starved, outraged, pilfered Indian has, and, knowing this, and asking that the agents be appointed from among the soldiery, the Indian is taking the first step he has ever taken on the highway of civilization.

The author claims no originality for these observations. Their source is to be found in the masterly arraignment of the Government by no less a personage than Chief Red Cloud, who, appealed to in 1890 by that Christian martyr, Father Jule, for an expression of opinion on the causes leading up to the last Indian outbreak, said:

"When first we made treaties with the Government, this was our position : Our old life and our customs were about to end ; the game upon which we lived was disappearing ; the whites were closing around us, and nothing remained for us but to adopt their ways and have the same rights with them if we wished to save ourselves. The Government promised us all the means necessary to make our living out of the land, and to instruct us how to do it, and abundant food to support us until we could take care of ourselves. We looked forward with hope to the time when we could be as independent as the whites and have a voice in the Government.

"The officers of the army could have helped us better than any others, but we were not left to them. An Indian Department was made, with a large number of agents and other officials drawing large salaries, and these men were supposed to teach us the way of the whites. Then came the beginning of trouble. These men took care of themselves, but not of us. It was made very hard for us to deal with the Goverment except through them. It seems to me that they thought they could make more by keeping us back than by helping us forward. We did not get the means to work our land. The few things given were given in such a way as to do us little or no good. Our rations began to be reduced. Some said that we were lazy and wanted to live on rations, and not to work. That is false. How does any man of sense suppose that so great a number of people could get to work at once, unless they were at once supplied with means to work, and instructors enough to teach them how to use them?

"Remember that even our little ponies were taken away under the promise that they would be replaced by oxen and large horses, and that it was long before we saw any, and then we got very few. We tried, even with the means we had, but by one pretext or another we were shifted from place to place or told that such a transfer was coming. Great efforts were made to break up our customs, but nothing was done to introduce the customs of the whites. Everything was done to break the power of the real chiefs, who really wished their people to improve, and little men, so-called chiefs, were made to act as disturbers and agitators. Spotted Tail wanted the ways of the whites, and a cowardly assassin was found to remove him. This was charged upon the Indians, because an Indian did it, but who set on the Indian?

"I was abused and slandered, to weaken my influence for good and make me seem like one who did not want to advance. This was done by the men paid by the Government to teach us the ways of the whites. I have visited many other tribes, and find that the same things were done among them. All was done to discourage and nothing to encourage. I saw the men paid by the Government to help us, all very busy making money for themselves, but doing nothing for us.

"Now, don't you suppose we saw all this? Of course we did, but what could we do? We were prisoners, not in the hands of the army, but in the hands of robbers. Where was the army? Set by the Government to watch us, but having no voice in setting things right, so that they would not need to watch us. They could not speak for us, though we ·wished it very much. Those who held us pretended to be very anxious about our welfare, and said our condition was a great mystery. We tried to speak and clear up this mystery, but were laughed at and treated as children. So things went on from year to year. Other treaties were made, and it was all the same. Rations were further reduced, and we were starving. Sufficient food was not given us, and no means to get food from the land were provided. Rations were further reduced. A family got for two weeks what was not enough for one week.

"What did we eat when that was gone? The people were desperate from starvation — they had no hope. They did not think of fighting; what good would it do? They might die like men, but what would the women and children do? Some say they saw the Son of God; others did not see Him. I did not see Him. If He had come He would do some great things as He had done before. We doubted it, because we had saw neither Him nor His works. Then Gen. Crook came. His words sounded well; but how could we know that a new treaty would be kept any better than the old one? For that reason we did not care to sign. He promised to see that his promise would be kept. He, at least, had never lied to us. His words gave the people hope. They signed. They hoped. He died. Their hope died with him. Despair came again. The people were counted, and wrongly counted. Our rations were again reduced. The white men seized on the land we sold them through Gen. Crook, but our pay was as distant as ever. The man who counted us. said we were feasting and wasting food. Where did he see this?

"How can we eat or waste what we have not? We felt that we were mocked in our misery. We had no newspapers, and no one to speak for us. We had no redress. Our rations were again reduced. You, who eat three times a day and see your children well and happy around you, can't understand what starving Indians feel. We were faint with hunger and maddened by despair. We held our dying children and felt their little bodies tremble as their souls went out and left only a dead weight in our hands. They were not very heavy, but we ourselves were very faint, and the dead weighed us down. There was no hope on earth, and God seemed to have forgotten us. Some one had again been talking of the

Son of God, and said He had come. The people did
not know; they did not care. They snatched at the
hope. They screamed like crazy men to Him for mercy.
They caught at the promise they heard He had made.

"The white men were frightened, and called for soldiers. We had begged for life, and the white men thought
we wanted theirs. We heard that soldiers were coming.
We did not fear. We hoped that we could tell them
our troubles and get help. A white man said the soldiers meant to kill us. We did not believe it, but some
were frightened and ran away to the badlands. The soldiers came. They said: 'Don't be afraid; we come to
make peace, and not war.' It was true. They brought
us food, and did not threaten us. If the Messiah has
really come, it must be in this way. The people prayed
for life, and the army brought it. The Black Robe
(Father Jule) went into the badlands and brought in some
Indians to talk to Gen. Brooke. The General was very
kind to them, and quieted their fears, and was a real
friend. He sent out Indians to call in the other Indians
from the badlands. I sent all my horses and all my
young men to help Gen. Brooke save the Indians. Am
I not right when I say that he will know how to settle
this trouble? He has settled it.

"The Indian Department called for soldiers to shoot
down the Indians whom it had starved into despair.
Gen. Brooke said: 'No. What have they done? They
are dying. They must live.' He brought us food. He
gave us hope. I trust to him now to see that we will
be well treated. I hope that the despair that he has

driven away will never return again. If the army had
been with us from the first there never would have been
any trouble. The army will, I hope, keep us safe and
help us become as independent as the whites."

Red Cloud did not have a very high opinion of Sitting Bull. "He was nothing," said the old chief, "but
what the white men made him. He was a conceited
man who never did anything great, but wanted to get
into notice, and white men who had something to make
by it, encouraged and used him. When they had made
him as great as they could, they killed him to get a name
by it. The fight at his arrest would have been made (by
the Indians) for any one arrested in the same way. If
he was a little man, he was a man, and should not have
been murdered uselessly. What is worse, many good men
were killed, also. The soldiers came in time to prevent
more murders, but too late to save all. If the army had
wanted to arrest him they knew how to do it, and never
would have done it in that way. You see how they are
doing here. The agent does not interfere with the army,
and the army saves lives and does not do anything cruel.
No Indian wants to fight; they want to eat, and work
and live ; and as the soldiers are peace-makers, there will
be no trouble here. The Indian Department has almost
destroyed us. Save us from it. Let the army take charge
of us. We know it can help us. If this can be done,
I will think that all this late trouble has been only a
storm that broke the clouds. Let the sun shine on us
again."

"Nature," says Jean Ingelow, "before it has been touched by man, is almost always beautiful, strong and cheerful in man's eyes; but Nature, when he has once given it his culture and then forsakes it, has usually an air of sorrow and helplessness. He has made it live the more by laying his hand upon it and touching it with his life. It has come to relish of his humanity, and it is so flavored with his thoughts, and ordered and permeated by his spirit, that if the stimulus of his presence is withdrawn, it cannot for a long while do without him, and live for itself as fully and as well as it did before."

———

Conspicuous among those whose services during the uprising were of incalcuable value to the Government were the Sioux and Cheyenne Indian scouts, more particularly Yankton Charlie, Woman's Dress (who acted as body guard to Gen. Brooke), and No Neck, who gave complete proof of their regeneration. The author has been enabled to secure the photographs of these courageous men, copies of which will be found in these pages.

CHAPTER LVI.

GROUARD'S LIFE UP TO DATE.

Before the opening of the spring campaign of 1876 the Government purchased a large number of horses — some of the animals having been bred and raised on the Laramie plains, and, like many of the Wyoming-raised horses, had a strain of cayuse or broncho in their blood. One of these horses fell to Grouard. Its original cost was only sixty-three dollars, but its real worth could not be computed in greenbacks or gold. This animal was used by the scout on very many of his most hazardous undertakings, and never failed to respond when called upon for duty.

During the summer of 1880 the telegraph line between Fort McKinney and the Powder river (a distance of fifty-three miles) was kept in such wretched repair and became so unreliable that Grouard was compelled at least once every week for several months to make the trip on horseback to deliver and receive official messages at both ends of the line. It was his custom to leave the Post in the morning at sun-rise, take dinner at the Powder river telegraph station, and, returning, reach Fort McKinney in time to witness dress parade (sun-down). Here was a distance covered of one hundred and six miles in twelve hours, with time enough taken out to feed and rest the animal and its rider.

There was nothing about the horse to indicate its great fleetness or powers of endurance. It stood about sixteen hands high, weighed ten hundred and fifty pounds, was rangy in build and light bay in color. It was a very affectionate animal, and seemed to understand everything its master said to it. Grouard had obtained possession of the horse when it was three years old, broke it himself and never permitted anyone else to ride it. If it were out on the prairie, all that was necessary for its master to do to get it in the corral was to call or whistle. It would follow Grouard like a dog, and became a general favorite about the Post, and among the officers' and soldiers' wives and children. It was the only animal permitted to stray or remain upon the parade ground. Everybody in the country knew the animal, and was familiar with the qualities which made it of such value to the scout. Mr. Trabing, who kept the store at the head of Six Mile Lane, south of the Post, once counted out five hundred dollars in gold and offered it to Grouard for the animal, but the offer was promptly refused, Grouard remarking that the money could do him no good if he were in a tight place where he needed a horse which he could rely upon, while the possession of the animal was better than an insurance policy against accident.

On one of his long journeys from the Post, Grouard became so thoroughly worn out from fatigue and loss of

sleep that he fell from the back of the animal to the
ground while unconscious, where he must have lain for
several hours. Upon awaking, however, he found his
faithful horse standing quietly by his side, it not having
moved twenty feet from the spot where the scout's resting place had been. Grouard offered many times to
wager five hundred dollars that he could ride the animal
from Fort McKinney to Custer, a distance of one hundred and thirty-nine miles, on any fair day, between sun
and sun, but nobody was ever found rash enough to
accept the wager.

The animal was feeding on the parade ground one
day in 1887, and was noticed by the Post veterinary
surgeon to go over to one of the irrigating ditches and
bend down its head as if to get a drink. A moment
later it fell to the ground, and when those who witnessed its
fall arrived at its side, the animal was dead. Grouard,
whose love of animals is as great as his knowledge concerning them, gave evidence of genuine grief over his
loss, and he had the carcass buried with as much care as is
bestowed upon the bodies of many mortals.

The author might cite many instances of the scout's
love of animals and the care he always bestowed upon
them. Nothing so exasperated him as to see some brute
in the shape of a man abusing a dumb creature. I remember once of riding with Grouard and a man who had
indulged a little too freely in the ardent. The man insisted upon driving, but the scout quietly took the reins
in his own hands and refused to give them up. His
action somewhat nettled the would-be driver who, mak-

ing the remark that he would. like to run the animal
into a gulch and break its neck, grasped the whip and
attempted to strike the horse. Grouard snatched the
whip in a twinkling, with these words, spoken so low
and yet so deliberately that they were terribly distinct:
"I am one of those kind of men who think a great
deal of a horse, and never permit one to be abused in
my presence!" With that he put the whip in the bottom of the carriage, placed his foot on it and drove
along as if nothing had happened to disturb his usually
quiet nature, while the would-be driver ruminated on the
proposition that it was a "h—l of a notion that a man
couldn't do what he pleased with his own property."

After his return to McKinney from Pine Ridge at
the close of the Indian uprising, Grouard was sent to
Fort Washakie, Wyoming, and into Idaho to investigate
and report upon the ghost dance excitement which had
prevailed in the vicinity of the former Post and Fort
Hall. His trip and labor occupied his time for some
months, and his report was satisfactory to those who
commissioned him. Since that time he has been doing
duty about Fort McKinney, where he lives in a home
of his own, surrounded by all the comforts necessary
to make the average mortal contented and happy. He
keeps several fine horses, and is prepared at a moment's notice to depart the Post on any mission intrusted
to him by his superior officer. His dairy stock is
high grade, and are, like all animals that come under
the scout's influence, gentle and thoroughly domesti-
cated. Up to a year ago his kennel comprised old Flo

(the dog saved from Grouard's house at the time the
Sioux records were destroyed) and a beautiful thorough-
bred water spaniel named Bird. Twelve months since,
poor, old, faithful Flo stretched her aged body on the
porch with her eyes turned toward her master's win-
dow, and ceased to be. Grouard buried her with his
own hands, but never spoke about her death. When
the author asked him what had become of her, he
answered with a sign that was more eloquent than words,
and there the matter ended.

During the spring of 1893 great efforts were made
by the people of Sheridan County, Wyoming, and those
living in the eastern portion of the Big Horn Basin, to
establish a mail route from Sheridan to Hyattville, over
the Big Horn mountains. This matter was agitated during the entire summer, and the postal authorities, convinced at last that northern Wyoming was settling up so
rapidly that increased mail facilities was a necessity, decided to establish the route prayed for if a practicable
pass across the snowy range could be secured. By the
time this decision was reached, the year 1893 had become a lean and slippered Pantaloon, and the great
storms that visit the Big Horn were in progress. February and March are the two worst months of the year
in the mountains of northern Wyoming, and it was in
the latter month of the present year that Grouard received orders to cross the range and find a practicable
mail route—one that could be traveled at all seasons
of the year. The intrepid scout, accompanied by a
Wyoming character called "Shorty"—one of that class

of men, who, if they ever had a surname, have lost
sight of it during their progress through and knocks
against the rough edges of the world—at once started
on his errand.

Those acquainted with the character of the mountains through which the scout was forced to pass, shook
their heads and expressed themselves as certain that
Grouard and his companion would perish on top of the
range, if they ever got that far. The two men abandoned their horses at Big Horn, and, putting on snow
shoes, started up the Little Goose creek canyon for the
divide. They carried, besides their firearms, one blanket
apiece and rations sufficient for five days. They passed
from the Little Goose to the Big Goose creek and
Tongue river, thence to a point six miles northeast from
Clouds Peak (the highest point in the range), thirteen
thousand feet above the level of the sea. They were
on top of the range for eight days, three of which were
spent in huge snowdrifts without fire or food. They
finally found their way down the Paint Rock canyon to
Hyattville, but they were sorry looking mortals upon arriving at the latter place. One of Grouard's eyes was
completely closed from snow blindness, and the other
was nearly useless. His face was swollen to such an
extent and frozen so badly that he was unable to leave
the house for two weeks, at the end of which time he
started across the range for Fort McKinney. "Shorty"
had fared no better than the scout, and he suffered terribly from frozen face, hands and feet.

The object of the trip had been attained, however,

GROUARD'S LIFE UP TO DATE

and Grouard's report was acted upon by the postal authorities. The mail route was established as he had laid it out.

The result of this journey, so far as Grouard is concerned, has proved very unfortunate, as the scout's eyesight was permanently impaired, and eminent oculists have so far failed to give him any but temporary relief from his sufferings. His service in the army covers a period of nearly nineteen years, and this service has continued uninterruptedly until the month of August last, when he departed for St. Joseph, Mo., to consult eminent specialists concerning his eyesight.

Grouard has made a trip to St. Louis, which point is the farthest east he has ever been, and that city is the largest one he has ever seen. From his nineteenth to his twenty-sixth year he was a captive among the Sioux, and he has been with the army from shortly after the time of his escape from the hostile Indians to the present day. He passed his forty-fourth milestone in life's journey on the 20th day of last September. Physically he is a superb specimen of manhood, and, with ordinary care, should live for many years to come. Men, however, who have faced the hardships, dangers and privations such as have fallen to the lot of Grouard, are not proof against sudden decline by reason of natural physical ability to resist disease. In fact, it is the rule that army campaigners, such as the scout has been, have no certainty on a lease of life beyond To-day. The Grim Reaper is forever busy, and humbles young valor and gray service without distinction.

GEN. GEORGE CROOK, IN "CAMPAIGN UNIFORM."

PART SECOND.

CHAPTER I.

GENERAL GEORGE CROOK.

Gen. George Crook was born at Dayton, Ohio, in 1829. He was nineteen years of age when he received his appointment to the West Point Military Academy. In 1852 he graduated and was assigned to duty, as Second Lieutenant, with the Fourth Infantry. Two years later, after campaigning with his regiment in Oregon and California against the Indians, he received his appointment as First Lieutenant. Until the breaking out of the civil war he was in active service in the west, and in 1859 was dangerously wounded by an Indian spear head, a portion of the missile remaining in his side to the day of his death. His record during the civil war is a glorious one. Rising to a Captaincy in the Fourth Infantry in 1861, he became colonel of the Thirty-sixth regiment Ohio volunteers four months later. In August, 1862, he was appointed Commander of the Third Provisional Brigade, and in the fall of the same year, for gallant

services at the battle of Lewisburg, Va., was breveted
Major in the regular army. Not long afterwards he was
promoted to the rank of Brigadier-General of volunteers.
He took command in July, 1863, of the Second Cavalry
division. In 1864 he was breveted Major-General of
volunteers for gallant conduct in the Virginia campaign,
joining Sheridan in the Shenandoah valley the same year,
and commanding the cavalry branch of the army of
the Potomac in 1865, his brevet Brigadier-General
rank in the regular army dating from the same year.
He was present at the surrender of Lee at Appomatox
Court House. After commanding the District of Will-
mington, North Carolina, in 1866, he was made Commander of the Boise, Idaho, district, and turned his
attention to the hostile Snake Indians, and after subduing
them went to the Department of the Columbia and quieted
the Umatilla and Nez Perces. His next field of operations was in the Department of Arizona, where he assumed
command in June, 1871. Here he made such a brilliant record in his campaign against the Apaches that
President Grant made him a Brigadier-General, his commission dating in 1873. In 1875 he was transferred to
the Department of the Platte. Serving in the latter Department until 1882, he again took charge of the Department of Arizona, where he succeeded in subduing the
Apaches in 1883. Again he was made Commander of
the Department of the Platte. In 1888 he assumed con
trol of the Military Division of the Missouri with the
rank of Major-General. His death, which was sudden
and unlooked for, occurred in Chicago on the 21st of

March, 1890, and his body was interred during the fall of the same year in Arlington Cemetery, Virginia, opposite Washington.

No man can place a proper estimate upon the military services of General Crook. He was a plain, blunt man, hating and avoiding ostentation, was beloved by his intimates and associates and respected and feared by his foes. There was not a spark of rashness in his makeup. Doggedly courageous, with a superb judgment, all his enterprises were eminently successful, and he rose to position and honor upon his deserts. Grouard, like all men who knew him and were with him in his campaigns, says he was the master of every emergency where coolness and courage were essential. His chastisement of the hostile Indians was tempered with mercy, and the name of "Lone Star" was both feared and revered among the redmen.

Crook's career was an honorable and active one, and reflects great glory on the military achievements of the American army. His insight and knowledge of the Indian character made him master of the situation which presented itself on the frontier in 1876. His theory was that the savage would remain in his primitive condition just so long as he was permitted to hold sway over those great stretches of public domain where game was ample to furnish food. In the summer season the Indian's nomadic nature kept him on the move; in the winter he pitched his tepi with a view to enjoying the greatest shelter and security. Crook was the first army officer to intrude upon the redman's winter security. His campaign

in the spring of '76, when he fell upon and destroyed
the village of Crazy Horse, with the thermometer regis-
tering sixty below zero, was a revelation to the country
and carried consternation to the heart of the savage.   All
seasons were Crook's, and the redmen awoke to a full
realization of this' fact before the snows of 1876 covered
the plains of the great midwest.   He drove them from
"pillar to post;" from the Platte valley to the Yellowstone; from plain and mountain to exile and the agency.
He made war against their customs and traditions, destroyed their villages, subdued their spirits and broke
their hearts.   On this line of campaigning he pursued
them in season and out of season, until the Indian feared
an ambuscade in every draw or suspected the presence of
"Lone Star" behind each sagebush.   Crook was undeni-
ably the greatest Indian fighter of the century, and he
did his work so thoroughly and well that little or nothing
of like nature is left for his successors to do.   He determined the status of the Indian — solved the question —
and his memory will ever have a high niche in the
temple of fame.   Humanity is so deeply obligated to his
warrior spirit and generous nature that it will always remain his debtor !

> His life was gentle, and the elements
> So mixed in him, that Nature might stand up
> And say to all the world, "This was a man."

CHAPTER II.

GENERAL GEORGE A. CUSTER.

General George Armstrong Custer was born at New Ramley, Ohio, on the 5th of December, 1839. He entered West Point Military Academy in 1857 and was graduated in 1861, being assigned to the Second Cavalry, with rank of Second Lieutenant. He participated in the first battle of the rebellion (Bull Run) and served with great bravery and distinction throughout the civil war. General McClellan was the first to discover the right kind of metal in the young man, and made him an aide-de-camp. Custer never forgot his first promotion nor the donor of it, and McClellan, throughout the years of his vicissitudinous career, always found, a warm champion in the man he had marked for distinction. He led a grand charge under Hancock on the 3d of May, 1862, and won golden opinions and a Brigadier-Generalship under Kilpatrick when that General confronted the Confederate forces under Stuart in 1864, being promoted from a Captaincy. He was then but twenty-three years of age. His courage was the theme of every camp fire, and his brilliant achievements under Sheridan in the Shenandoah Valley are remembered as vividly today as in the '60's.

He is said, as a General of Cavalry, to have led sixty successful charges. After the close of the war he served for a short season in Texas as Major General of volunteers, and in '66 was assigned to the Seventh Cavalry, with the rank of Lieutenant Colonel. Upon joining his new regiment in Kansas he found plenty of work to do in subduing the Indians, and in 1868 fought the famous battle against the allied forces of the Arapahoe, Cheyenne and Kiowa tribes in the Indian Territory, known as the Battle of the Washita, in which he captured the pony herd of the savages, destroyed their village with its entire contents and killed over one hundred of the hostiles, including their two principal chiefs. The Yellowstone (Montana) campaign followed. Then came the Battle of the Little Big Horn and — the end of Custer's remarkable career.

Custer and fear never were introduced to each other. He inspired his men by his rare courage. There was not a soldier in his regiment but would have followed him into the mouth of perdition had he but led the way. A story characteristic of him is told by Captain Whittaker in his "Life of Custer," which will illustrate the man's inspiring spirit :

At Brandy Station, Va., during Meade's fall back, Custer and cavalry brought up the rear, and all soldiers know it is the worst place on God's footstool to cover a retreat. To allow the infantry ample time to cross the Rappahannock the cavalry kept fooling around, with an avarage of 10,000 rebs on all sides of them. Once when a lull had seemed to come with ominous stillness, some one remarked: "Hello, look ahead!" and sure enough, about 5,000 rebs were suddenly seen to be massed in our front, and right in the path we must travel if we ever saw "the girls we left behind us." Custer was sitting on his horse at the head of the regiment, the Fifth Cavalry. He took one look of about ten seconds, then snatched off his hat, raised up in his stirrups, and yelled, "Boys of Michigan, there are some people between *us* and home; I'm going home; who else goes?" Suffice it to say, we all went. Gen. Alger, then Colonel of our regiment, can vouch for our flying movements as we followed Custer, with his bare head and golden locks, and long, straight saber, putting the very devil into the old Fifth Cavalry, until a clear track was before us. When out of the woods, up came Kilpatrick and sung out: "Custer, what ails you?" His reply was: "Oh, nothing, only we want to cook some coffee on the Yank side of the Rappahannock."

CHAPTER III.

JOHN F. FINERTY.

The subject of this sketch, Hon. John F. Finerty, was born in the city of Galway, Ireland, on the tenth day of September, in the year 1846. For many years his father followed the profession of journalism and was for a long time editor of one of the leading papers in Ireland. The boy gave early indication of a bright and inquiring mind, and was afforded every opportunity of acquiring a splendid education at the hands of private tutors. He left his native land when twenty years of age and served in the Union army during the close of the war. He also became interested and active in the cause of Ireland, being one of the organizers of the American Fenian movement. For some time he acted as correspondent for the Irish Press, connecting himself, in 1869, with the Chicago Republican. Three years later he was promoted to the city editorship of that paper, which position he left, just previous to the great Chicago fire, to accept a remunerative one on the evening Post, and shortly afterward went to the Tribune, remaining on that journal until the year 1875. In the latter year he became the candidate on the People's ticket for clerk of the .super-

HON. JOHN F. FINERTY, "THE FIGHTING CORRESPONDENT."

ior court, but was defeated at the election. During the
winter of '75 he became identified with the local staff of
the Chicago Times, and the following spring was detailed
by Editor Story to accompany Gen. Crook's expedition
against the Sioux and Cheyenne Indians. His assign-
ment to the important work is best told in his own words.
He says:

In the beginning of May, 1876, I was attached to
the city department of the Chicago Times. One day
Mr. Clinton Snowden, the city editor, said to me, "Mr.
Story wants a man to go out with the Big Horn and Yel-
lowstone expedition, which is organizing under Generals
Crook and Terry, in the departments of the Platte and
Dakota. There is apt to be warm work out there with
the Indians, so if you don't care to go, you needn't see
Mr. Story. "

"I care to go, and I'll see Mr. Story," was my
answer.

The famous editor of the Chicago Times did not, at
that period, show any significant indication of that "withering at the top" which subsequently obscured his wonderful faculties. He was a tall, well-built, white-haired,
white-bearded, gray-eyed, exceedingly handsome man of
sixty, or thereabout, with a courteous, but somewhat
cynical manner.

"You are the young man Mr. Snowden mentioned
for the plains?" he asked, as soon as I had made my
presence known by the usual half-shy demonstrations, because everybody who did not know him well, and who
had heard his reputation on the outside, approached the
formidable Vermonter in somewhat gingerly fashion.

I replied in the affirmative. "Well, how soon can you be ready?" he inquired.

"At any time it may please you to name," was my prompt reply.

"You should have your outfit first. Better get some of it here—perhaps all. You are going with Crook's column," said Mr. Storey, with his customary decisiveness and rapidity.

"I understood I was to go with Custer," I rejoined. "I know General Custer, but am not acquainted with General Crook."

"That will make no difference, whatever," said he. "Terry commands over Custer, and Crook, who knows more about the Indians, is likely to do the hard work. Custer is a brave soldier—none braver—but he has been out there some years already, and has not succeeded in bringing the Sioux to a decisive engagement. Crook did well in Arizona. However, it is settled that you go with Crook. Go to Mr. Patterson (the manager) and get what funds you may need for your outfit and other expenses. Report to me when you are ready."

It will be seen from the above that Mr. Finerty came within an ace of accompanying the ill-fated Custer command. In fact, had it been left to his own choice, he would probably have followed the fortunes of the gallant leader of the Seventh, and the fate which overtook poor Mark Kellogg, of the St. Paul Press, would have been his also. He endeared himself alike to the officers and men of Crook's command, and shared all their dangers and deprivations. In the famous Sibley

Scout he played no unimportant part, and the journalistic profession has just cause for pride over the conspicuous bravery that characterized this "fighting correspondent," as Frank Grouard calls him. The Scout says Finerty importuned him to be permitted to accompany him on every scouting expedition that was organized, but not until the starting of the Sibley party did the correspondent have his wishes gratified ; and while he bore himself with soldierly decorum on that occasion, he made no further request (so says the scout) to be one of any future scouting parties.

Mr. Finerty's labors on the Chicago Times were continuous until the year 1881, the interim having been filled in reporting the Nichols-Packard trouble in Louisiana and the Pittsburg riots in 18u7, and in visiting and writing up Texas and old Mexico during the years 1878–9. He was with Gen. Miles in the latter's campaign against the Sioux, and with Gen. Merritt during the Ute outbreak in '79. The next year found him doing the southern states for the Times, and acting, in the year following, as editorial correspondent for his paper in Washington, D. C. He also, during 1881, made a tour of the Canadian and Northern Pacific railroads, and in the fall was assigned as war correspondent with Gen. Carr in that officer's expedition against the Apaches. He withdrew from the Times in November, 1881, and organized the first Irish National Land League convention, which was held in the city of Chicago during that winter. On the 14th of January, 1882, he established The Citizen, a publication devoted to Irish-American interests, and the venture has proven a successful and profitable one. In 1882 Mr. Finerty was an independent candidate for Congress from the Second district of Illinois, and was elected. "In 1884 he supported James G. Blaine in the Ohio campaign," says John C. Flinn's Handbook of Chicago Biography, "and was himself again a candidate for Congress, running as a Blaine Independent. In this contest he was nominally defeated by disreputable means. In April, 1885, he was Republican candidate for City Treasurer, but was defeated, having been counted out with Sidney Smith, candidate for Mayor, and was afterward appointed City Oil Inspector, in which office he served during Mr. Roche's administration."

Mr. Finerty has been twice married. He is a member of the Chicago Press Club, has twice been elected President of the Irish-American Societies of Chicago and Cook county, and is widely known as a political writer and lecturer, being a protectionist and Republican. In 1890 he gave to the world a volume of personal experiences and adventures in the Big Horn and Yellowstone expedition of 1876, entitled "Warpath and Bivouac; or, the Conquest of the Sioux." This book has reached its second edition, and is one of the most interesting and best written stories of its kind published.

WASHAKIE, CHIEF OF THE SHOSHONES.

WASHAKIE, CHIEF OF THE SHOSHONES.

CHAPTER IV.

WYOMING INDIANS OF TODAY.

There are no Indians in Wyoming today except the Shoshones and Arapahoes, who together occupy an area covering 1,520,000 acres. This reservation, being a portion of Fremont and Johnson counties, is called the Wind River Reservation, and is one of the finest agricultural sections in the state. The Big Wind river cuts the reservation almost in two from the northwest to the southeast, while the Little Wind river flows eastward to its junction with the parent stream in the southeastern corner of the reserve. Besides these two great rivers, there are several large streams that water the holdings of the fortunate redmen, among the principal ones being the Owl creek, which forms the northern border of the reservation, the North Fork, the Big and Little Popo-Agie, Beaver Creek, Muddy, Mill Creek and Dry Creek, the latter being one of the innumerable feeders of the Big Wind river.

Statistics from the Interior department place the total number of Indians on the Shoshone or Wind River reservation at 1,819. Of these 978 are Arapahoes and 841 are Shoshones. Of the former, there are 215 male adults and 269 women, .233 male children and 261 female children; while of the Shoshones there are 212 men, 252 women, 203 male children and 174 female children. From these figures it is easy to see that the fear of an Indian outbreak in Wyoming is very slight if the question be considered from the Wyoming Indian standpoint. Such a contingency could only arise through the joining of the turbulent Sioux on the east and the Crow on the north with the Arapahoes on the Wind River reservation, and even such a move would be hard of consummation by reason of the watchfulness over the Arapahoes on the part of their ancient foes, the Shoshones.

Washakie, chief of the Shoshones, is reputed to be over ninety years of age, and delights in the boast that he has always been the firm friend of the white man; that he has never lifted his hand against his pale-faced brother or allowed his blood to be spilled.

This grand old man is probably the best preserved Indian on the Wind River reservation. His footstep is as light and every movement of his body as graceful as that of a young girl. There is nothing awkward about him. Washakie is over six feet in height and weighs nearly 250 pounds. His head sits proudly on a short, full neck, and his shoulders are broad and slightly tapering. He stands as erect as a giant oak. His forehead is broad and high and but slightly wrinkled with age, while his steel gray eyes are as bright and full of fire as those of the mountain eagle. His hair, which hangs in profusion over his shoulders, is white as the spotless snow.

Altogether this remarkable savage furnishes an ideal object for the student of Indian character. His word is law, and no man of his tribe dare rebel against it. His bravery is beyond question, and his hospitality is as large as the glowing heart which beats within his bosom.

Sharp Nose, the head chief of the Arapahoes, hates this mighty man with all the venom of his treacherous nature. Years ago, in battle, these two warriors met in single combat. It was breast bared to breast against that terrible weapon, the hunting knife. The contest was witnessed by the warriors of both the chiefs. It was long, terrific and bloody, and Sharp Nose has never forgotten or forgiven the magnanimous foe who overcame but spared him. From that hour to the present day the head chief of the Arapahoo nation has exerted an influence over those alone who were his immediate followers in his former conflict with the Shoshones and the sharers in his hatred of Chief Washakie.

Some years ago, when what is now the city of Lander was a hamlet, Washakie's oldest son, in company with half a dozen other young Indians, left the Shoshone reservation for Lander, and finding the mother of Isaac Axe (a woman over sixty years of age) alone in the home of her son, attempted to commit a brutal outrage upon her. The house was a log affair consisting of one room, the single apartment being divided in the center by curtains. The rear portion was used as the living room. The screams of the old woman attracted the attention of her nine-year-old grandson, Allie Axe, who, unknown to the Indians, was amusing himself in the back yard. The boy hurriedly entered the house by the rear door, and peeping through the curtains, saw his aged grandmother struggling with half a dozen young Shoshone fiends. Taking his father's repeating rifle from its place against the wall, the boy began pumping leaden objectors into the body of the old lady's assailants. The first shot gave young Washakie a mortal wound, and his companions hurriedly carried him from the house, placed him on his horse and started for their home on the reservation in hot haste, young Washakie dying before he could be carried to the lodge of his father.

The tragic death of this young buck, a general favorite with his tribe and in direct line as his father's successor to the chieftaincy of the Shoshone nation, created the wildest excitement on the reservation, and it was but a short time before a large war party was organized to go to Lander and wreak vengeance upon the people for the death of the Shoshone favorite.

When old Chief Washakie heard of this, he sent for the leaders of the movement, and said:

"If tibo (white man) come to Indian tepi and outrage Indian squaw, kill him; if Indian go to tibo's tepi and outrage white squaw, kill him!"

SHARP NOSE, CHIEF OF THE ARAPAHOES.

LEFT HAND, CHIEF OF THE ARAPAHOES.

Deep and bitter as was his grief over the loss of his boy, his savage sense of justice shone out even brighter than his parental affection, and his people, unused to disobeying the commands of their revered chief, laid away this grand old chieftain's son and buried their hatred and cry for vengeance in the boy's sepulchre.

Strange as it may seem, the eastern "Lo, the poor Indian" societies, tried in every way imaginable to hound young Allie Axe into state prison for life for his heroic defense of his aged grandparent, but they met with very poor success.

At the time of the massacre of Custer's command on the Little Big Horn, Sharp Nose and a dozen other Arapahoe cutthroats were participants in that butchery, and sneaked back to the reservation in the same manner they had stolen away from it.

Sharp Nose, the head chief of the 'Raps, has one of the most villainous countenances imaginable. His eyes are black and piercing, and his lips are thin and indicate the utmost cruelty. His gait is very peculiar. Although lamed from a wound received in battle, this fact does not at all interfere with the serpentine glide that characterizes his movements. He is an expert horseman, and a man of remarkable powers of endurance. He has not a single trait to redeem his naturally low and groveling nature, and in the summer season travels over the reservation roads with several degraded squaws, disposing of their wares to a class of whites as degraded as themselves.

When the first white men went into the Popo-Agie valley to find homes the country was wild and full of danger. Half a dozen immigrants camped on the spot where Lander was afterwards built. It is one of the most beautiful and picturesque locations for a city in the world, the center, too, of a rich agricultural section. Two young and handsome women — wives of two of the immigrants — were in the party of newcomers, and one day they were left alone in camp while the men folks prospected the valley. No pen can draw a picture of the horror that presented itself to the men of the party when they returned to the camp in the evening. One of the women was a corpse; the other was suspended in mid-air at the end of a sharp-pointed tepi pole, one end of which had been thrust into the unfortunate woman's abdomen, the other into a badger hole. Life enough still remained in the young woman's body to permit her to tell the horrible story of outrage and murder. Sharp Nose and some twenty-five of his followers had been at the camp in the absence of the white men, satisfied their lustful desires and added murder as a finale. Yet this same Sharp Nose was permitted to live, and to-day is head chief of the Arapahoe tribe!

In the winter of 1888, a man named William E. Jewell went on the Shoshone reservation and secured permission from the agent (Col. Thomas Jones, of Georgia, a fine southern gentleman and a very humane man,) to trade for horses with the Indians. Early in the spring of '89 his body was discovered in a bayou,

under the floating ice. A bullet through the head told
the cause of death. A coroner's jury sat upon the case,
and returned a verdict that deceased came to his death
at the hands of some person or persons unknown. This
was eminently satisfactory, so far as the jury was concerned, but not to the author of these pages, who was
at that time editing the Lander Mountaineer. For three
months the newspaper man devoted his time to the
discovery of the perpetrators of the Jewell murder,
and was at last rewarded by finding nearly all the dead
man's possessions in the tepis of Sharp Nose and Gar-
field Wolf (the latter a graduate of the Carlisle, Penn-
sylvania, Indian school). Warrants were sworn out, the
suspects were arrested and remained in jail awaiting
trial for nearly a year. There was evidence enough
against these two cold-blooded assassins to have hanged
them a dozen times over; but, as in the case of Allie
Axe, the eastern sentimentalists became "interested" in
the matter, plenty of money was furnished, clever law-
yers were retained, and when the case was called — the
Indians were turned loose. They returned to the reservation to feast on dog and mock at the white man's
"legal formulæ"

The last congress, however, went so far as to make
the case of Sharp Nose an exceptional one, and granted
him a pension of twelve dollars a month; but why this
was done, unless to reward him for the part he played
in the Custer massacre or to set this sum aside as a
premium on crime, would be hard to tell. There are
hundreds of deserving soldiers whose demands for pen-

sions have been persistently and cruelly ignored by the Government — men who have sacrificed health and limb in the service of the nation. To the man who keeps in touch with national legislation, the giving of a good-sized pension to Sharp Nose, in whose crime-steeped bosom there burns nothing but the fires of the most bitter hatred against the whites, and whose whole life has been a never-ending chapter of savage cruelty, presents a curious commentary on the boasted justice of our Government to the men who sacrificed everything upon the altar of country. It is hardly compatible with sound reason and good policy to pension the criminal savage and ignore the deserving patriot, and the author desires to enter his most emphatic protest against such unseemly and un-American procedure.

There is a broad distinction between the women of these two tribes — the Shoshones being susceptible of rapid advancement, while the Arapahoe is lazy, lecherous and repelling. Virtue is maintained to a remarkable degree by the former, and is almost totally lacking in in the latter. Intelligence among them is on about the same plane as that upon which their estimates of virtue stand. Plurality of wives is not sanctioned or practiced among the Shoshones, while the Arapahoes disregard all marital laws and every parental obligation.

Black Coal, who for many years was the war chief of the Arapahoes, and in later years the head chief of the tribe, died in 1893. He was known among the whites as a very good and kind-hearted man, though his early life had been given up to cruelty and the warpath.

BLACK COAL, WAR CHIEF OF THE ARAPAHOES.

BLACK COAL, WAR CHIEF OF THE ARAPAHOES.

He had no voice in the naming of his successor, otherwise Sharp Nose, whom Black Coal thoroughly detested and abhorred, would never have risen to the head chieftancy.

As has been before remarked in this chapter, the Arapahoe is not a progressive nation, and little, if any, heed is paid to the selection of head men, especially now when the tribal relation has been so broken by life on reservations that it is but a memory. For these reasons it was easy for Sharp Nose, cunning in all things, to secure his election as the successor of Black Coal. The Arapahoes thought a great deal of the latter chief, and manifested sincere grief at his death. The influence of Sharp Nose does not amount to much, at best; but he is, of all the men of his tribe, the least to be trusted with authority.

CHAPTER V.

MULTUM IN PARVO.

In answer to a letter requesting dates and facts regarding his life as a government scout, "Ben" Clark, one of the most modest and brave plainsmen in the country, writes Grouard as follows:

FORT RENO, O. T., June 20, 1894.

DEAR FRANK : — Your letter came all right and I was glad to hear from you. I have no more pictures on hand except one which was copied from an old one taken in April, 1869, at Camp Supply, when I was on the point of starting to take a company of the Tenth Cavalry 'cross country to Fort Larned. It was taken by a clerk in the Post Trader store, who was taking pictures for fun.

I left Fort Leavenworth on the 2d of June, 1857, and drove team to Fort Bridger, enlisted in battalion of U. S. volunteers at Bridger on December 3d, 1857, was mustered out at Camp Floyd on 13th of August, 1858. Camp Floyd was in Cedar Valley about sixty-five miles south of Salt Lake City. I served three years and six months in the war in the Sixth Kansas Cavalry. Was guide for Gen. Sully in summer and early fall of 1868 in the Indian campaign. Was chief guide and scout for

BEN CLARKE, A BRAVE MAN AND CLEVER SCOUT.

Custer from October, 1868, until Gen. Sheridan took the field in person. After that was Sheridan's chief guide until the close of the war in spring of 1869. I was assigned to Camp Supply by Gen. Schofield in May, 1869, as post guide and interpreter. Was transferred to Fort Reno in October, 1876, by order of Gen. Pope; have belonged here ever since, though I have been away a good deal on detached service under special orders. I was chief guide for Gen. Miles in the summer, autumn and winter of 1874. You remember of my being attached to Gen. Crook's command in 1876 on the Crazy Horse trip.

The above is a brief record of my service, and I may add that I have plenty of proof in the way of discharges and so on to satisfy anyone as to the truth of it. You know there are lots of Commanche Bill's and Buffalo Joe's, and such, with long handles to their names, whose records are manufactured principally out of lies.

Well, Frank, wishing you success and good luck, I remain,   Yours very truly,

B. M. CLARK.

CHAPTER VI.

AN OLD TIMER'S STORY.

O. P. Hanna, the subject of this sketch, was born in Metamora, Illinois, May 10th, 1851. At eighteen years of age he packed his "grip," and started west on the 11th day of August, 1869. He landed on the headwaters of the Yellowstone river, Montana, where Livingston now stands. It was then a wild, unsettled country, inhabited only by Indians (the Crow tribe). He had an anxiety for a wild, frontier life, and he soon found a party of hunters who made their living hunting, bear trapping and poisoning wolves.

His history is quite interesting, and is given below in his own words:

In a short while I could handle a gun with any of them, and at the end of our hunting and trapping expedition I could show as fine a lot of furs as any of them. I could write pages describing my adventures during the six years I spent on the headwaters of the Yellowstone; but be it enough to say that I was with Professor Hayden (Geographical Surveyor), who explored and surveyed the National Park to see if it was a suitable place for a national reserve, and it was on his report that Congress

O. P. HANNA, FIRST SETTLER IN SHERIDAN COUNTY.

passed the bill to reserve that portion of Wyoming as a National Park. That was in 1870. In 1872 I was scout for Col. Baker's expedition down the Yellowstone, and was with him when he had the fight with the Sioux at Baker's battle-ground, near where Billings now stands. I was with Gen. Custer on one of his expeditions in the Yellowstone country. I was also with the noted Bodeman expedition, which consisted of one hundred and forty-five old hunters, trappers and prospectors, that stood off from eight hundred to two thousand Sioux Indians, and fought their way to civilization for a distance of two hundred and fifty miles.

In the spring of 1875, six of us hunters and trappers built flat boats near Fort Benton on the Missouri river, loaded them with furs and buffalo robes, and started down the river for St. Louis, a distance of three thousand five hundred miles. We arrived safely in Omaha in about seventy days, and there disposed of our robes. We had many adventures on the way down the river, and were attacked by the Indians several times ; but the piles of robes on our boat offered good protection.

After spending the winters of '75 and '76 at my old home in Illinois, the spring found me in Denver, Colorado, dead broke, and longing to be with my old comrades on the headwaters of the Yellowstone, but having no way to get there unless I walked. I found a party of Englishmen that wanted a hunter and guide. After giving sufficient proof that I was an old hand at the business, I made a deal with them, and I was soon in the mountains again, and happy. I put in the summer of '76 in the mountains of Colorado. In the spring of 1877 I started from Denver with pack animals for the Black Hills. When I arrived in Cheyenne an expedition was organizing to take one hundred and twelve wagons with four hundred and fifty work oxen (wagons all loaded with Indian supplies) to Pine Ridge Agency on White river. There were eighty-five men in the expedition, and I soon got a situation as hunter, there being plenty of game in the country which we had to travel through. We got as far as Red Cloud Agency (where Crawford now stands), and there we learned that the Indians at Pine Ridge were on the warpath, and we were ordered by the Interior Department to lay up at Red Cloud until we had received further orders. We stayed there for eight months. Finally the Indian trouble was settled, and we pulled down White river and turned the outfit over to old Chief Red Cloud.

Out of a job again, with a rigging, horse and pack horses, myself and a little fellow by the name of Ferguson started early in 1878 for my old camping ground, Bozeman, or the headwaters of the Yellowstone. It was only seven hundred miles across an uninhabitable country, but that little distance to travel on horseback was nothing in those days. In about three weeks from the time we started we camped on Clear creek, northern Wyoming, where Fort McKinney now stands.

There were several companies of soldiers camped there. They were laying out the grounds for the new fort. As we had traveled over three hundred miles, without seeing anyone or hearing any news, it was a treat to talk with some one besides ourselves. We laid over there for two days. Met Frank Grouard, the scout, there; and when he found that I was with the noted Bodeman and other expeditions on the Yellowstone when he was with the Indians, we had quite an interesting time talking the matter over.

On the morning of August 10th we packed up and started on our journey for Bozeman. When pulling down onto the Piney, where old Fort Phil Kearney used to stand, Ferguson says, " By thunder! Hanna, I believe there is a woman." Looking ahead, sure enough, there was a woman. On arriving at the cabin we found Mr. and Mrs. T. J. Foster. As we hadn't seen a woman in two months, you can imagine what a treat it was to sit down to a nice clean meal, cooked by a woman, and enjoy her company while eating it.

Mr. and Mrs. Foster had a nice garden, and they insisted on us helping ourselves to all the green groceries we wanted. After laying over there a day we went on our journey. As we pulled across Massacre Hill and along the head of the Prairie Dog, I thought it was the prettiest country I ever set my eyes on. The grass was knee high, and nothing to eat it but wild game. When coming down into Little Goose Creek valley, where Big Horn City now stands, it was a grand sight, and I said to Ferguson:

" Charlie, there is a future for this country. This land, in a few years, will be valuable. I am going to drive my stake. "

He looked around and said:

"My God, man, are you crazy? What will you do here?"

"Take up a ranch and quit running around,"

"Yes, take up a ranch and get killed by the Indians," was his response. Although he did not approve of the idea, he finally consented to stop with me for a while, anyway.

The next two days we looked the country over, and found there was but one cabin partly finished in what is now Sheridan County. We learned later that it was built by road agents and horse thieves. Quite a number of suspicious characters called at our camp. In the course of ten days I had located my ranch just above Big Horn, and had constructed a neat little cabin about ten feet square—large enough for me, though.

The next question was, how were we going to make a living? But I soon solved that question. I went over to Fort McKinney (forty miles south) and found that the soldiers had to depend on getting wild meat or go without, as there were no cattle nearer than two hundred miles of the fort. I soon closed a contract with the commanding officer to furnish three thousand pounds of elk, deer and other wild meat every week. I got a hunter by the name of White, as he had two mule teams and wagons, to go with me. We got two men to drive the teams and deliver the meat to the fort, and while he and I did the hunting. Game was so plentiful that we would often load down both wagons in half a day. Bear was plentiful. I killed eight the first two months I was hunting. Fishing was fine; could catch forty or fifty pounds daily.

In the fore part of the winter there was a mail route established from Rock Station on the Union Pacific railroad, by way of Fort McKinney and Fort Custer, to Junction Station on the Yellowstone, a distance of five hundred miles. It was a weekly, and Ferguson and I took the sub-contract to carry it from Fort McHenry to Fort Custer. As mail pouches were scarce, he generally put the letters in his pocket. The weekly gathering of mail consisted of three or four letters. We carried it on horseback. Ferguson did most of the riding, and when he would reach the ranch he would lay what he called the United States mail on the mantelshelf for a day or two and go with me and have a hunt. A man by the name of Fisher had the contract; had taken it very cheap; went broke and Ferguson never got anything for his services. He was held up several times by the road agents. They would examine the contents of the letters to see if there was anything of value. If there wasn't anything to pay them for their trouble they would warn him that the next time they caught him on the road with the mail without something of value they would "shoot his light out."

The spring of '79 Patrick brothers secured the contract and got it increased to a daily; put on buckboards and went flying through the country, although I could have carried all the mail at the time in my coat pocket. They got, so I understood, about ninety thousand dollars a year. It was one of the great Star Route swindles. But it was a good thing for the country. It helped to develop it.

In the fall of '78 a merchant by the name of A. Trabing, from Laramie City, put up some log buildings on Crazy Woman, and laid in a stock of general merchandise. Trabing had gone back to Laramie and left a man by the name of Bowman as manager. One evening there were four or five men in there talking, when they heard the command at the door, "Hands up." Looking toward the door, they found double-barreled shot guns staring them in the face. They were being held up by the road agents. The men in the store were all ordered to stand facing a big pile of flour, and one fellow guarded them while the leader of the gang (said to be Jesse James) took over one hundred dollars' worth of goods, bade the manager good night, told him he had a very nice stock of goods, and that he could count on him as one of his regular customers.

Two days after the robbery of Trabing I was hunting up Little Goose creek. I had wounded a deer and was trailing it through the brush, when I ran into a camp in the thick brush. It belonged to this same gang that had gone through Trabing's store. The thieves were looking the goods over. I tried to step back without them seeing me; but they saw me and were up with gun in hand ready for defense in a moment. As soon as I found they had seen me, I walked towards camp, looking as innocent as I could, with a

"Halloo, boys, you have a nice camp. Did you see anything of a deer go through? I wounded one and trailed it into the brush here."

I was very careful to keep my back on the pile of

new clothes and groceries. It was a tough gang. They had ditched a train on the Union Pacific railroad in the fall for the purpose of robbing it, and a posse of men followed them and laid for them in Red Canyon, when the holdups killed two deputy sheriffs. The Union Pacific railroad offered a big reward for their capture. They were known to be in the Big Horn country. I had written down to the authorities on the Union Pacific road and got a description of all the gang, and was also getting paid for reporting anything in regard to them. If they had examined my pockets they would have found a description of the whole party, consisting of seven. I would not have lasted long if they had done so. But I played it so well that I got out all right without their suspecting me, though they warned me not to tell anyone where they were camped.

That night I went to Fort McKinney and sent a dispatch to Laramie that I had found the camp of the whole gang. I then went back to my ranch, and that night Big Nosed George, one of the gang, rode up and wanted to know if I had any liniment, as his horse had fallen on him and hurt his knee. I gave him some liniment. He stayed all night. There was a three thousand dollar reward for him and I knew it, and could have arrested him easily, but had no place to take him. There were about twenty men left Laramie shortly after I notified them where this gang was. They rode night and day, but the gang got wind of it, and when they got into the country the gang had flown to the Yellowstone. Before they left they held up the Trabing store the second time, notwithstanding the fact that the manager kept guards around the store night and day.

The Union Pacific Railroad authorities wanted me to follow the gang to the Yellowstone, but I did not want any more of it; wouldn't have lasted long if they had caught me on their trail in that country.

Mr. and Mrs. T. J. Foster were held up during the winter. The gang hung Mr. Foster up by the neck until he was almost dead, to make him tell where his money was, as they thought he had quite a boodle. They also held up old Tony Yetzer's ranch on Big Goose creek, and took what they wanted. The stage was held up regularly at what is now known as "Hold-up Hollow," north of Fort Fetterman. They went through the mails. I had written a letter to the detectives on the Union Pacific. The robbers got the letter. Shortly after this I got a picture of a man hanging by the neck and a notice giving me twenty-four hours to leave the country. I sent them word that I was not going, and if I caught any of them around my cabin they would get a "darn warm reception." That night I dug a hole under the hill in front of my cabin and moved my bed there. For the next month I never sat down to a meal without my gun across my lap.

I learned later that a gang of them met one night for the purpose of stringing me up if I didn't leave the country; but, as I was known to be one of the best shots in the country, the wise heads in the gang concluded it was a rather dangerous undertaking, and so decided to leave me alone.

In the spring of '79 I desired to put in a small crop on my ranch. I had no seed nor plow, and Cheyenne was the nearest point where I could procure them. I got me a light wagon, hitched up a couple of ponies, and, the last of February, started for Cheyenne. I was gone about six weeks; traveled altogether about seven hundred miles; camped out all the time, but arrived safely at my ranch in April, with the first plow that ever broke sod in Sheridan County. I also bought six hundred pounds of oats and some garden seeds. Charley Farwell was in Big Horn then. He had a large team and helped me do the plowing. I got in about seven acres of oats and garden during the summer. Cattle and cattlemen poured into the country from all sections, and the horse thieves and road agents had to take a back seat. I raised a fine garden and had a ready market at my own price. In the fall I flailed out about three hundred bushels of oats and sold them at ten cents per pound, or a seamless sack full for ten dollars.

In December, 1879, I received a letter from my old friend, Jim White, the buffalo hunter, saying he had found a good place to hunt buffalo. It was on the head of Sundy creek, on the Yellowstone, in Montana. Although it was two hundred and twenty-five miles away, snow deep and very cold, I decided to go to him. I packed a pony, and, with a good riding horse, set out. I was ten days making the journey. The weather was very cold, and I never saw a soul for the first two hundred miles. When I got to White's camp I found

him with three men building a "shack" out of buffalo
hides to live in. He was expecting me, as we had an
understanding before he left Goose creek that if he
found a good camp I was to come. Buffaloes were very
plentiful. We hired six skinners and went to work. In
two months we had twenty-five hundred hides, and were
killing from forty to sixty animals per day, and clearing
at least fifty dollars. Notwithstanding we made money
so fast, it was not our luck for good fortune to last.
Although it was in a hostile country, we had thus far
seen no signs of Indians.

On the 10th we had killed about sixty buffaloes, and
about sundown White said if I would go in and get supper he would help the skinners, as they were behind with
their work. We had eleven head of horses and mules,
and they were grazing just above camp. I went into
the "dugout" and started a fire. After starting the
fire I went out and looked in the direction of the horses
and saw about twenty Indians after them. I fired several
shots after them, but to no purpose. They got away
with every hoof of stock. Well, we had a "red hot" time
from then on to protect our hides. The snow was so deep
we couldn't get them to Miles City to market, so we had
to stay there and guard them for six weeks. We finally
got them to Miles City and sold them, and after paying all
expenses we were losers; but later we got our mules back.

In May, White and I came back to the Big Horn
mountains. I rented my ranch to a man by the name of
Benefield. White was killed in the mountains that season
by a man named Miller who was hunting with him. They

had some whiskey and got into a drunken row. There is
no doubt but that White had killed more buffaloes than
any man in the world. Killed sixteen thousand in seven
years in Texas alone.

In July '80 I got a letter from Richard Frewen of
Powder river wanting me to guide a party of English
lords from London on a bear hunt in the mountains. I
went down there and made a bargain with them at eight
dollars per day. I went out with several parties during
the summer. We had killed thirteen large bear during
the season, and the last one gave me a terrible shaking
up. I was out hunting with a lord by the name of Wise.
We had wounded a large grizzly and had trailed it to a
brushy swamp. The Englishman wanted to trail it into
the brush, but I wouldn't go, as I knew we would be
taking desperate chances, and I was satisfied the bear
would be on the fight. I told the Englishman to go
around the brush one way and I would go the other, and
we would try and get a shot at bruin. The Englishman
did not go far until he saw the brute. He gave it a
shot and the bear made for him. The Englishman beat
a hasty retreat with the bear at his heels. I was standing about fifty yards away. I got in a shot just in time
to save the Englishman. The bear would have had him
in another jump. The bear fell when I shot, and the
Englishman had time to get behind a bunch of brush,
out of its sight, but I was in plain view. With one roar
that made the mountains ring, it made for me. I got
another cartridge in my gun, and when the bear was
within about fifteen feet of me I let him have it. I

then wheeled and ran and tried to reload my gun, but caught it in a sage brush, and it flew out of my hands. I reached to get it, and here the bear came again. I did not have time to get my gun, but I had a good six-shooter which I pulled out, and just then I fell over a sagebrush, and in an instant the bear was on me. I fired six shots into him with my six-shooter, and he rolled off of me dead. The Englishman was shooting at him all the time. Just as liable to hit me as the bear, though. I had a very heavy buckskin shirt on, and it protected me some, but I was bleeding from head to foot when I got on my feet. I finally got to camp and laid there for twenty days, not able to get up without assistance. The Englishman gave me the best care he could; stayed with me night and day; said that I saved his life, and he couldn't do too much for me. I have not hunted bear much since; came to the conclusion that a man was foolish to take the chances.

During the summer of '80 the country settled up rapidly. Over fifteen thousand head of cattle were driven in during the summer. In the spring of '81 a few others and myself organized a town and called it Big Horn City. It was the first town laid out in Northern Wyoming. We also took steps toward organizing Johnson County. I was foreman of the first grand jury in Johnson County, and we were in session six days.

————

[Mr. Hanna is one of Sheridan's (Wyo.) most prosperous business men, and is the present postmaster. He is identified with the growth of Sheridan, and holds a

warm place in the affection of her people. The picture
of this gentleman found in these pages is an excellent
reproduction from a photograph taken quite recently.
Not being old (except in adventure) he has settled down
to enjoy the fruits of his early labors, and fortune having favored him, he leads a life of contentment within
easy distance of his old haunts — "The headwaters of
the Yellowstone."

CHAPTER VII.

A SAMPLE " ONE-HORSE HOLDUP."

To show what exasperating conditions confronted the early settlers of Northern Wyoming, the following letter is published. Mr. Foster, the writer, is Register of the United States Land Office at Buffalo, and still " holds down" the ranch he took up on the advice and with the assistance of Frank James :

BUFFALO, WYO., August 24, 1894.

FRIEND DE BARTHE:—Your favor of the 18th instant received today, and in compliance with your request, in regard to our (my and wife's) Wyoming history, will say as follows :

We came from Idaho in the summer of 1876 to Laramie, Wyoming, where shortly afterwards I began the occupation of a freighter, on a small scale, which I continued until the spring of 1878, when we took up our line of travel for a location in the Big Horn country, leaving a point about thirty-five miles northwest of Cheyenne on the 10th of April of that year. We arrived on Clear creek, in what is now Johnson county, and near the present site of Buffalo, on May 6th, when we were met by a man with whom we had been acquainted during the previous spring, and who insisted upon our going to the site of the abandoned Post of Phil Kearney, instead of looking for a location in the Clear Creek valley, as we had about concluded to do. As there was not yet an actual settler between Powder river and Fort Custer, we had the selection of a location in our own hands, with the whole northern Wyoming to choose from; and it was considered advisable, in view of the fact that the Post of Fort McKinney, then on Powder river, was on the point of removal to its present location on Clear creek, and the probability of a reservation of uncertain dimensions being declared, to act upon the advice of our former acquaintance, and at least see some of the fine country to the north.

Accordingly, on the 8th of May we passed to the site of the old Post of Phil Kearney, and, concluding it was good enough to camp on, we did so, inspecting the surrounding country the next day, and fully deciding to remain.

Our life for the initial year was uneventful, although prosperous; and, by the way, our prosperity seemed in a fair way to become our ruin. For, although during our first year's residence on the Piney we did fairly well, enjoying the benefit of a monopoly of the truck trade of the new fort (McKinney), raising the first garden between Colorado and the Yellowstone, selling everything at a little more than the Irishman's "one per cent profit," we readily acquired a reputation as capitalists, arousing the cupidity of certain gentlemen of the road, who, to the number of three the following spring — April 17, 1879 — made a descent upon our little log mansion (built for a hen house) while no one but myself, wife and little boy, the latter but four years of age, was about, presented their little guns (forty-five Colts) with the injunction "Throw up your hands," which order was promptly obeyed.

They then, after securely tying my hands behind me and facing us all to the wall, proceeded to ransack the house for any surplus cash which might be lying around loose. In this they were only partially successful, obtaining but fifteen dollars, including what was in the little boy's safe (a cigar box), it containing money to the amount of seven or eight dollars.

Not being satisfied with the extent of the enterprise, and feeling certain that we were the possessors of "untold wealth," they then marched me, bound and blindfolded, to the barn, a log structure, and proceeded to administer what, in their minds, would be an antidote for my reticence in regard to the location of my supposed "cache," which, they maintained, must exist in the immediate neighborhood. Placing a rope they found in the barn around my neck, they pulled me up and allowed me to remain long enough to pass over the "big divide," which I did to all intents and purposes.

Upon regaining consciousness, after what seemed but a few minutes, they again demanded to know the whereabouts of my hidden wealth, and emphasized their demands by a series of kicks and blows upon my person, which I was helpless to avoid or mitigate in the least. Upon being told, as soon as I was able to speak, that they had already secured all that was available, and finding that threats were productive of no results, they again pulled on their little rope, but through their fear of carrying the matter too far, as I heard expressed by them in the first instance before my complete recovery, they did not allow me to remain suspended long enough for complete loss of consciousness, but instead, employed all their "eloquence," and not a little muscle, finally cocking a revolver with the threat to "croak" me "anyway," in order to persuade me to "give away the cache."

Finally, with the remark that I was "a good one," we, "the jolly four," returned to the house, where the chief, not being satisfied with the former search, conducted by the other two, began a systematic hunt on his own account. Failing to unearth anything further in the form of lucre, we were informed that if we would kindly prepare supper for them they would quit us, to which proposition we very readily agreed, and in due time a very elaborate frontier spread was being enjoyed by the worthies, which, being completed, they proceeded to possess themselves of our horses, three in number, with saddle and accouterments, the principal part of my best clothing, all the provisions they could take (of which we had a good supply), with all the firearms in the house—three or four pieces—when, about midnight, they bid us a fond adieu.

By the way, I must not omit to mention that the "former acquaintance" who piloted us from Clear creek to the old fort, was no other than Frank James, the

notorious Missouri bandit, of which fact I had no suspicion until informed by the man himself, after two or
three months of the most pleasant acquaintance. For a
time we entertained some doubt as to his being the veritable Frank James, but from our minds all doubt has
since been removed. He has passed from our personal
knowledge since the following fall, but we hold him in
kindly remembrance for the kindnesses shown us during
our short acquaintanceship. He never advised any one
to follow in his footsteps, and was never known to engage in any one-horse holdups. He was after bigger
game—feared not to take the chances, and would have
been an invincible ally in our case of robbery, had he
been present.

I cheerfully enclose photos of myself and Mrs. Foster,
taken nine or ten years ago, and, if I thought it necessary, would make the use of her picture a condition of
the use of mine. She is the pioneer woman settler of
northern Wyoming.

I probably may have been more successful in the
matter of length than interest in this account, and will
say, if the former, it is easily abbreviated, while if less
complete you could not readily add to it. Abbreviate
and season to taste. No fiction in it.

With the wish for the greatest success in your enterprise, I remain,   Yours very truly,

                                        T. J. FOSTER.

CAPT. JOHN SMITH, ONE OF THE "HORSESHOE FIGHT" HEROES.

CHAPTER VIII.

THE BATTLE OF HORSE SHOE CREEK.

TRABING, WYOMING, December 20, 1893.

FRIEND DE BARTHE:—I herewith enclose (as per your request) a true statement of the "Horse Shoe" fight, which occurred in this immediate vicinity in 1868. I have written it out in my own way, explaining details as well as I can remember them. A quarter of a century is a long while, and old people's memories fail, you know.

Yours respectfully,

(Capt.) JOHN R. SMITH.

The attack was made on the morning of March 19th, 1868, the fight lasting three days.

At about 8 o'clock on the morning of the date given, Chief Crazy Horse, with his band of Ogallala and Minneconjou Indians, numbering sixty-seven, came to our ranch, where Marion Thornburg, Bill Worrell, Bill Hill and myself were living. Our place was known as the Horse Shoe road ranch, formerly kept by the notorious overland stage agent, Slade, who was afterwards hanged in Montana. The Indians secreted themselves behind a butte some four hundred yards from the house. The first warning we had that anything was up was given by the dogs,

who scented the Indians, there being a stiff breeze blowing at the time. Thornburg and myself volunteered to go
to the top of the butte to see what was up. Worrell
and Hill were to stay at the house and watch while we
were gone. The dogs went along with us, and at once
scampered up the butte. The Indians, anxious to see
what effect the barking of the dogs would have on those
at the house, stuck up their heads so the boys in the
house could see them; but we were far enough under
the butte to miss the signals our companions were trying
to give us to return.

Seeing a coup stick, I told Thornburg, and he gazed
at it with the remark, "Yes, and it did not grow there."
Just then the dogs raised the top of the butte, and the
Indians jumped to their feet and came rushing toward
us, yelling and shooting as they ran. Thornburg and I
retreated toward the house until we got down to the flat,
stopping there and returning the Indians' fire. They split
up into two parties, then, one going around the house in
one direction, the other in another. We made a run for
the house, and made it, opened· the port holes, barred the
door and got ready for a siege. The fight was pretty
warm for the rest of the day, the Indians losing two men
and having two wounded. We had plenty to eat, but
nothing to drink except Red Jacket bitters, and we took
a good many drinks to the ill-health of old Red Cloud,
whom we thought at that time was leading the attack.

We finally had to have water. The Indians had set
the stockade afire, and the well was inside this enclosure. So we drew lots to see which one would go for

the water. It was settled in this way, that Worrell and Hill should draw the water, while Thornburg and myself were making a rush at the Indians, most of whom were in hiding behind a pile of telegraph poles across the road. But when we made the charge, we discovered that the Indians had left their place of hiding and concentrated behind the stockade, so that when Worrell and Hill made the attempt to draw the water, they opened fire on them, and we had to retreat to the house in quick time. Then the red devils set fire to the stables and killed two of our horses and one mule, badly wounding a third animal. When night came the Indians drew off to Twin Springs, three miles from our ranch, where they secured food from old man Muso, Bill Harper and George Harris, who were keeping a road ranch at the Springs.

They did not come back to us until after dark, but did not show themselves in the light of the fires, which were still burning, but got off some little distance and barked like coyotes and hooted like owls to draw us out. Their cunning tricks did not work, however. We put in a long and tiresome night. When daylight came it showed in sight, now and then, black heads peeping from hiding places. We soon opened up the fight again. About 10 o'clock Lieutenant Norton of the Second United States Cavalry, came up, accompanied by "Doc" Mathews, Crow Indian agent, with annuities. The Indians left while they stopped, which was only a short time, and when they passed on out of sight the redskins returned and engaged us for the balance of the evening to the queen's taste. They felt on all sides and ends of the house and got all the port-holes located after dark came on.

Along about 10 o'clock at night they crept up to the house and commenced building a fire between the port-holes, which began to put us to thinking and planning. Knowing the house would be in flames in a short time we made up our minds to crawl down into our little fort, which was dug in the ground; a sod wall was built up around it on top of the ground about three feet high, making it high enough to stand up in and room enough for four men. The walls being eighteen inches thick, a ball would not penetrate it. We had some four or five port-holes in it. We had a dug way to it which led from the floor of the kitchen, some ten or twelve feet from the walls of the house. After entering the tunnel we took a shovel and filled the entrance with dirt.

After we all got into the fort the house was well under headway burning. The house was built of pitch pine, and it was not long until the roof was tumbling in. The roof was dirt covered, and, being very heavy, smothered the fire to a considerable extent, so that it did not make much light. Our plans were soon laid. When it got dark, we took our shovel and commenced cutting the sod wall down sufficiently to get out, which we quietly did, while the red devils were dancing and howling with glee to think we were burning up. In slipping out, we got hold of the horse which had been wounded, and put what extra clothing we had on the animal, under the shadow of a bluff near the east side of the ranch.

The Indians, all being on a bluff west of the house, could not see us.

Then we started for Twin Springs to join George Harris and Bill Harper. I forgot to state that Muso, after the Indians had visited him, took his half-breed family and went to Fort Fetterman the previous day with Lieut. Norton's train, so we were six strong when Harper and Harris joined us. We then commenced, all hands 'round, to talk over our situation. We thought it was quite dangerous to stay there and fight, as we felt that we might have to fight until our ammunition was exhausted before a train would come along so that we could get away. However, we came to the conclusion to dig a hole down under the middle of the house and cache all the ranch property, or goods, such as flour, sugar, coffee, tea, canned goods and some wet goods (in the shape of a ten gallon keg of whiskey.) We worked like beavers and when daylight came we had our cache completed.

We reconnoitered to see if the Indians were near about, but could not see any. We had decided that night to burn the ranch house down, and when the dirt roof fell in it would hide all traces of our cache. This was the third morning since the attack, and a beautiful morning it was. We lit a fire in the house and closed every crevice and opening so the flames would be confined. This action, we calculated, would give us time to get quite a ways off before the Indians discovered the fire. We decided to go to Fort Laramie, thirty-six miles to the east, and started. On the road we would come to the one intervening ranch kept by Bill Wilson and Jim Bellamy, which was situated on the Big Cottonwood, eleven miles away. We had put all our clothing on the two horses and one mule we still possessed. One of the horses belonged to George Harris and the mule was the property of Bill Harper. Harris and Harper, not having been in the previous two days' fight, had plenty of ammunition, but the rest of us had but little. About eleven o'clock we met a man on the road named David Dampier (a Frenchman who had been in the employ of the Hudson Bay Fur Company), to whom we related our experience. He informed us that he was on his way to Twin Springs to hunt his horse, which was running on the Platte river at a point called Bull's Bend, some three miles (as we informed Dampier) from where Crazy Horse and his renegades were camped. When the Frenchman heard this he remarked that he didn't want any horse, and started back with us. We trudged along until we struck the foothills on the west side of Little Bitter Cottonwood.

Looking back from this point over a level plain, we discovered a band of sixty-three Indians coming from the direction of Bull's Bend. They were about three-quarters of a mile away, and were coming for us as fast as their ponies would carry them. Our party of seven looked rather small beside this big crowd. The Indians were well armed with guns and bows and arrows, and had plenty of ammunition. We made for the foothills, but were soon entirely surrounded. When the Indians made their charge, their yelling and shouting stampeded our horses, and the animals departed with all our worldly effects. What money had been in the possession of the crowd had been given to me, some five hundred dollars, and I had placed this money in the pocket of a pair of pants which had been put in the pack on one of the horses. Later on I saw these pants (with the unmentionable part of them cut out) on one of the Indians, so I suppose he fell heir to the money.

By 12 o'clock things had become pretty warm. I had stopped among some rocks and pine to get a shot at Chief Crazy Horse, the rest of the party going to the top of a knoll, sparsely covered with small pines. One of the Indians crept up the hill and took a shot at me, the ball passing through my clothing, grazing the skin over my heart, and flattening itself against the rock behind me. As I could not get a chance to shoot the savage, I moved my position with considerable haste, joining my companions on the knoll. As I reached this spot Bill Harper turned and faced me, with the spear of an arrow almost buried in his right eye. He pulled the spear out with his own hand, and the contents of the eye followed it; and, with the blood running down his cheek, he remarked, "I will fight that much harder."

During this time we were being surrounded, with the exception of a small space to our southwest, and the Indians, getting well located in the rocks and pine timber, had a great deal the best of it. I made the remark to Bill Worrell that we had better get out of that onto lower ground, so we started southwest—the weakest portion of the Indian lines—and cut our way through to get up to some high cedar badlands, or brakes, on the top of which was a large level plain. The Indians, being afoot, it gave us quite a little start while they were getting their horses to follow us up; but we were trapped in the cedar brakes, the Indians beating us to the top of the hills and cutting us off from the level plain. Our chances were bad, then, for getting on any kind of ground to give them a fight, so we had to take shelter in a deep washout, a waterfall, rather, where they completely surrounded us.

We had done but little execution up to this time. As far as we could discover we had disabled but few of the savages. We made a fight in this position for about two hours, during which time they got a chance to locate us and shoot arrows into us. Many gunshots were fired by the Indians, but piles of arrows were fired into this washout and rocks were thrown in on us. We kept up a hot fire most of the time the rocking melee lasted. Bill Harper got hit over the left eye, the flesh being shaved down, and covering the eye completely, which disabled him. We were getting badly used up. I was watching to get a shot at an Indian about twenty feet from where we stood, who had thrown a stone and hit the side plate on my Winchester and almost disabled it. The gun worked, but hard. While watching, I saw him throw, or saw his hand come in sight, and a rock larger than my two fists came over and hit me in the forehead, cutting a terrible gash and scruffing the skull up and knocking me half senseless.

During this time all of us were getting pounded more or less over the body, and while George Harris and

myself were lying close together at the lower end of
the washout, an arrow was shot, passing through Harris's
coat sleeve, also going into my coat sleeve at the elbow,
scraping the hide off my arm for about six inches, and
pinning Harris and myself together. Things were now
getting "hand to hand." The Indians set the cedar
timber on fire, and the smoke was nearly suffocating us.
I suggested the idea of cutting our way back to the hollow a few hundred yards, and then quitting the hollow
and going west a couple of miles, which would put us
on level ground near what is known as the Cheyenne
Cut-off road. The suggestion was agreed to, and I, being
at the lower end of the hole, was to make the break,
which I did; and when I raised up to run, I went to
shooting as fast as I could, as there was plenty of red
game to shoot at. I made it through the line of Indians, with the balance of the boys following. Bill Harper came last, with one hand holding the mangled flesh
up out of his left eye, so he could see. As I stated
before, he had his right eyeball shot out by an arrow,
and he could not see how to get along very fast. While
we were running and fighting and driving the Indians
off of Harper, I think we did more execution than we
had all the rest of the day, for they crowded on us
close.

The first to fall was poor Bill Harper, and a part
of the red devils stopped to finish and mutilate him.
Worrell and I stopped and fired a few shots as the Indians had bunched up around Harper, and we got our
work in in good shape, getting some of them. I turned

to run and catch up with the boys, and got shot through the right arm with an arrow. I pulled the arrow out of my arm and caught up with Harris, Thornburg, Dampier, and Bill Hill, when Worrell came up behind with an arrow through his left foot, severing all the tendons on the top, side and back of his toes, crippling him badly. Just as we got together the Indians were leaving Harper, having finished him. They then made another rush on us with bows and arrows, one arrow hitting Bill Hill in the back of the head. At this time we were leaving the hollow to the west for level ground, and Dave Dampier yelled:

"I am be-damned if I go any further!"

At that instant a ball struck him in the back, and he never spoke again, but started and ran to a blown down pine tree distant about twenty steps, and fell under it. Our party was then reduced to five, with three of us wounded. Marion Thornburg and myself took Hill between us and started to reach the level plain a mile away. While the Indians were running back to get their horses and some had stopped to scalp Dampier, we got off from under fire as much as a half a mile, where we had to leave Bill Hill. He had bled so much from his wound that he was about gone, being too weak to walk any further. He begged us to shoot him, but we couldn't do it. After we had gone perhaps forty yards, I looked back to see if the Indians were coming, and I saw the smoke from a small Colt's five-shooter which Hill had on him. The poor fellow had ended his misery by blowing the whole top of his head off. The Indians soon got to him, where they all stopped to scalp him.

That gave us sufficient time to get out on the flat, where we waited for them to come. They came up to a dry sand creek where we had crossed, and stopped in the bed of this gulch, about four hundred yards from us. We could see when they came up out of the gulch that they were not all there, and could see some of them packing their dead and wounded off down to Bull's Bend on the Platte river. After they saw our position and knew there were but four of us left, they (over forty in number) formed in line and charged us. We repulsed and split them, but they circled around us with a great deal of whooping and yelling. This move was repeated three times before they gave it up. We stood our ground without a quiver. We felt that the position we held was the one we had been trying to get all day, and as we had it we would hold it to the last. So, with seven of their number killed and one almost dead, making eight in all, the Indians · concluded to give the fight up, satisfied, seemingly, in making a treaty with us, which was done right then and there.

We maneuverd with them until we got to talk with one of them, he going back and forwards three times. Chief Crazy Horse finally came up and we told him what we would give him out of what we had cached back four or five miles at the Twin Springs ranch. We were all feeling pretty well played out. The excitement dying out, we began to realize that our ammunition was about exhausted. I had then nineteen rounds left (out of three hundred and seventy-five in the three days' fight), and the rest of the party were in about the same boat. We were glad to talk treaty. The Indians were sometime considering our proposition, but finally the chief came up and said it was "Washta."

"You four brave men. We kill three of you. We don't want to fight you any more," remarked Crazy Horse. This Indian could talk fair English. He further said their last supper was no good, and they would go back with us. We told Crazy Horse to fetch three men with him and keep the rest back; we would go back to the Twin Springs ranch with them and give them the grub. The sun was then getting low, perhaps two hours high, when we started. We walked as fast as we could. We were very thirsty, having been without water all day. At last we came to the great springs, and all the Indians came up also. I remember one Indian carrying an old black coffee pot. He put it down while he bent over to drink. I picked the coffee pot up to dip up a drink. I looked in it, it being heavier than it should be, and discovered the three scalps from Hill, Dampier and Harper. I quietly laid it aside, and lay down beside the Indian that claimed the coffee pot and its contents and drank.

Business then began. First in order was for one man to get behind the sod wall of an out building as picket; next was for the Indians to unstring their bows and stack guns, bows and arrows up at the old hitching rack; next was to put the Indians in a half circle with the chief in the center, with one of us to watch them while the other two of us were digging the dirt off the cached goods. After awhile we got everything in order

and handed the stuff out to them. They divided it out
to the rest of the warriors. When I came down to the
ten-gallon keg of whiskey (it was in behind a blacksmith's
bellows), I turned the faucet and let the greater part
of it run out in the bottom of the pit, and the Indians
knew nothing about it; but when the savages who were
helping us lift out the grub saw the keg, they told the
Indians who were sitting in the half circle, and they
all made a rush with cups and old cans — anything they
could get to hold the fire-water. But we fooled them
and would not let them drink it there, and gave it to
their chief to take to their camp on the Platte river.

The Indians then left us, four or five of them taking
a parting shot at us before going away. We had what
we called a fort at the ranch — a hole dug in the ground
about four feet deep, protected by a stone wall, full of
port holes. Into this fort we went, after securing a keg
of water and dressed our wounds. We managed to save
some crackers and cheese from the cache, and so we were
not entirely supperless. I was almost sure the red devils
would come back again and it wasn't long before I heard
them signaling to each other with eagle-bone whistles.

After we had made sure they were coming back
again, we went to planning how to get away. My
proposition was to light a candle for each port hole and
set it up in the hole, so as to make them think we were
in the fort; then slip out into a deep draw and start for
Fort Laramie, as our supply of ammunition was not sufficient to carry us through another battle. So we left
the fort after lighting the candles, myself and Thorn-

burg helping Bill Worrell along, as his foot was about played out and swelled so we had to cut his boot off and wrap the foot with bandages made from wagon sheets. We made eleven miles straight in that way (or about fifteen miles the way we had to go to get around the country where the dead men lay, as the Indians had set fire to the cedars). We got to Bill Wilson's and Bellamy's ranch about half past two o'clock that night. They took us in and provided us some coffee and supper, which we certainly relished.

Jim Bellamy started at once for Fort Laramie, made the ride before daylight, and reported to General Slimper (who was in command of the Post at that time). He sent E Troop of the Second United States Cavalry, commanded by Captain Dueese, who came to Cottonwood by noon the next day. He gave Thornburg, Harris and myself a horse apiece, and instructed us to proceed with the troop to the field of battle, bury the dead, and bring back what signs of Indians could be picked up, to prove to the Post Commander (General Slimper) that it was Indians whom we had been fighting. On our arrival on the battlefield, two or three hours by sun, we found the dead men.

The first body recovered was that of poor Dampier. It was lying under the old tree where he had fallen when shot. The fiends had scalped him after firing six bullets and many arrows into his body. We buried him where he fell and went in search of the others. Bill Harper had fourteen bullet holes in him, and fourteen arrows were sticking in his body. His scalp had also been taken. His ears had been cut off and there were five long gashes in his nose. We. laid him to rest where we found him. Bill Hill's body had not been mutilated, except being scalped. It was about the cleanest bit of scalp work I ever saw, as there actually was not a single hair left on the dead man's head. A grave was made for him on the spot where his body was discovered.

The soldiers gathered many trophies of the fight, such as bullet pouches, powder horns, bloody blankets and arm-loads of arrows. That night we camped on the Big Cottonwood creek, and the next day the troops returned to Fort Laramie. We four were in such a desperate condition that they had to haul us in the ambulance. It was ten days before I got out of the hospital, as I had one wound in my head and another in my arm, the latter wound having been made with .a poisoned arrow, and it proved a bad one. The other boys were in bad shape, too, each one of them being wounded in several places.

In counting up our loss we found we were out about sixteen thousand dollars in ranch property, goods, hay, stock, horses, mules and work cattle, thirty-six head of the latter having been taken, not to say anything of the five hundred dollars in cash that had fallen into the hands of the Indians. I served four years and seven months in the civil war and was in some hard battles, and I have been in several fights with the Indians, but I never had as hard a time as I experienced in the three days' engagement with Crazy Horse on Horse Shoe creek. I cannot begin to tell half the incidents of this fight. It took place twenty-five years ago, but I remember the main features of it very distinctly. It pauperized us all, and we had nothing to do but " begin life over," as the saying goes.

———

[The author might add that Captain John R. Smith was one of the first settlers of northern Wyoming, and that he is at present a prosperous ranchman. He has passed through many vicissitudes and has a fund of anecdotes probably as great as any man in the west. His account of the battle of Horse Shoe creek is correct in every particular, and the marvel of it is that any of the men who stood off Crazy Horse and his warriors for the three days referred to ever lived to reach Fort Laramie, much less tell the story of the fight. The photograph published in these pages of Captain Smith is an excellent likeness of the original.]

CHAPTER IX.

"THE BATTLE OF BY CRIPES."

When the future historian writes of Fremont county, Wyoming, his story will not be complete if he omits the famous "Battle of By Cripes." The participants in that conflict are among the first settlers of Lander (formerly Camp Brown), and have stayed with the country and become some of the best known and most highly respected citizens. The following account of the "Battle of By Cripes" was furnished by one of the participants, and was written out by Mr. Winfield S. Collins, U. S. Court Commissioner, of Bonanza (Big Horn Basin). Wyoming:

On the night of the 23d of April, 1875, some Sioux and Cheyenne Indians from the Red Cloud Agency, stole ten head of horses from Lander and vicinity. A. A. Conant, nicknamed "Pap," Joe Coenett, Frank E. Coffee, "Doc." Curry, Herman, Harry Burke, Tom O'Neal, Pete Anderson, Charlie Baldwin and John Mc-Collum started from Lander on the morning of the 24th after them. They followed them all day and all night. The trail led down the Popo-Agie river, ten miles below Lander, then struck across Beaver, to about four miles above its mouth.   At daybreak, they found the Indians on Muskrat creek, about sixty miles from Lander.

There were fifteen Indians in the party.   They had with the ten stolen head about fifty head of other horses. Charlie Baldwin and Harry Burke, whose horses had played out, were behind some four hundred yards.   In the charge that followed, Joe Coenett, Frank E. Coffee, "Doc" Curry and Herman cut all the horses out but one, and ran them off about half a mile from the scene of the battle.   Pap Conant, Tom O'Neal, Pete Anderson and John McCollum stayed behind to keep off the Indians. One Indian put on his war bonnet, mounted the one horse left them, rode out and took the bunch away from the four men.   In the meantime the four men who were holding back the Indians had three of their horses shot, and were being hotly pursued ; and had not Charlie Baldwin, who had fallen behind in the charge, came up from a gulch behind the fighting crowd and held the Indians at bay, the four men would all have been killed.

As it was, they were compelled to fall back.   Mr. Conant, who had his horse killed at the first fire, was shot through the body in the beginning of the battle, but kept on fighting until the battle was over.   Three Indians were killed.   It was an evenly-contested battle, both sides mutually withdrawing from the fight.

The party of whites, with Mr. Conant almost helpless from a supposed mortal wound through the bowels, and three horses killed (leaving the Indians in possession of the stolen horses), started back toward their homes.

When guyed about his bravery, "Doc." Curry, whose

pet expression on the occasion of the fight was "By Cripes," said about the lone Indian brave in the war bonnet who, on the Indian pony, took the whole bunch of horses away from the four guards, "And did you see his horns? By cripes! and what signifies a poor cayuse to a man's life?"

From Curry's expression the skirmish took the name of "The Battle of By Cripes."

It was a slow, toilsome journey of two days back to Lander, part of the men being on foot. Mr. Conant suffered much, his only relief being in a constant change of horses, the different gaits of the animals furnishing change, if not relief from pain.

One of the Lander men, who was mounted on a magnificent, grain-fed stallion, hurried ahead into town, secured assistance and met the party out fifteen miles with a light spring wagon, to which Mr. Conant was immediately transferred. Mr. Conant finally recovered from his wound, and remained in the Lander valley, since which time he has acquired quite a competence. "Doc." Curry has held many positions of honor and trust in Fremont County, and is one of the most popular men in northwestern Wyoming. He never mentions the battle above referred to, nor does he ever lose a chance to get in his favorite expression of "By cripes." The other members of the party are still alive, and reside at or near Lander.

CHAPTER X.

Grouard has never had any but the most kindly feeling for the many scouts he met and served with while campaigning with Crook and other generals. Among them all he especially esteemed Ben Clarke, Big Bat (Baptiste Pourier), Little Bat (Baptiste Gaunier) and Yankton Charlie (the Sioux). He had always been a great admirer of Charlie Reynolds (one of the scouts who perished with the Custer column), although the two men had never met. As he tells, all through the pages of this volume, stories of the scouts, it is not the author's purpose to enlarge upon the facts he has already stated, but to recall a few incidents that have escaped the body of the narrative.

Grouard says that Little Bat was the greatest hunter he ever met, and that he could outrun the fleetest horse in a long distance contest. He has known him to start out after a band of elk, shoot them as he ran, and follow them until he had killed the very last one in the band. He was an excellent shot, and never wasted ammunition. Cool and brave, he made a dangerous enemy, but a royal good friend. Little Bat is still a Government scout, and is stationed at Fort Robinson. He has a family, who reside midway between the Post and Crawford, Nebraska.

Of Charlie White (Buffalo Chips) Grouard has already spoken, and also of California Joe. He was very proud of Ben Clarke, because he did not pose as the slayer of all "good Indians," nor did he wear his hair streaming over his shoulders for effect. Clarke is still in the Government employ.

Baptiste Pourier (Big Bat) was with Grouard a great deal, and the two men were fast friends from their first meeting; but Bat has already received attention in preceding pages. He lives on Wounded Knee creek, not far from the Pine Ridge Agency, where he has a fine farm and quite a large herd of cattle. He is not at the present time in the employ of the Government. He is an elegant sign-talker, and has had a great deal of experience with the Indians. He accompanied the Sibley Scout to the Big Horn range, and was the man that Grouard sent ahead with the troop when the retreat from the battlefield begun, a move which required nerve and caution, and one which, had it been perceived by the enemy, would have led to the massacre of the entire command under Lieutenant Sibley.